Pension Security in the 21st Century

Pension Security in the 21st Century

Redrawing the Public–Private Debate

Edited by

GORDON L. CLARK AND NOEL WHITESIDE

OXFORD UNIVERSITY PRESS

OXFORD
UNIVERSITY PRESS
Great Clarendon Street, Oxford OX2 6DP

Oxford University Press is a department of the University of Oxford.
It furthers the University's objective of excellence in research, scholarship,
and education by publishing worldwide in

Oxford New York

Auckland Cape Town Dar es Salaam Hong Kong Karachi
Kuala Lumpur Madrid Melbourne Mexico City Nairobi
New Delhi Shanghai Taipei Toronto

With offices in

Argentina Austria Brazil Chile Czech Republic France Greece
Guatemala Hungary Italy Japan Poland Portugal Singapore
South Korea Switzerland Thailand Turkey Ukraine Vietnam

Published in the United States
by Oxford University Press Inc., New York

First published 2003
First published in paperback 2005

British Library Cataloguing in Publication Data

Data available

Library of Congress Cataloging in Publication Data

Data available

Typeset by Newgen Imaging Systems (P) Ltd., Chennai, India
Printed in Great Britain
on acid-free paper by
Biddles Ltd., King's Lynn, Norfolk

ISBN 0-19-926176-8 978-0-19-926176-5
ISBN 0-19-928557-8 (Pbk.) 978-0-19-928557-0 (Pbk.)

1 3 5 7 9 10 8 6 4 2

ABOUT THE EDITORS

Gordon L. Clark is the Halford Mackinder Professor of Geography, Fellow of the Said Business School, and Faculty Associate of the Institute of Ageing at the University of Oxford. Noel Whiteside is Professor of Comparative Public Policy and Senior Fellow at the Institute of Governance and Public Management at Warwick University and Zurich Financial Services Fellow.

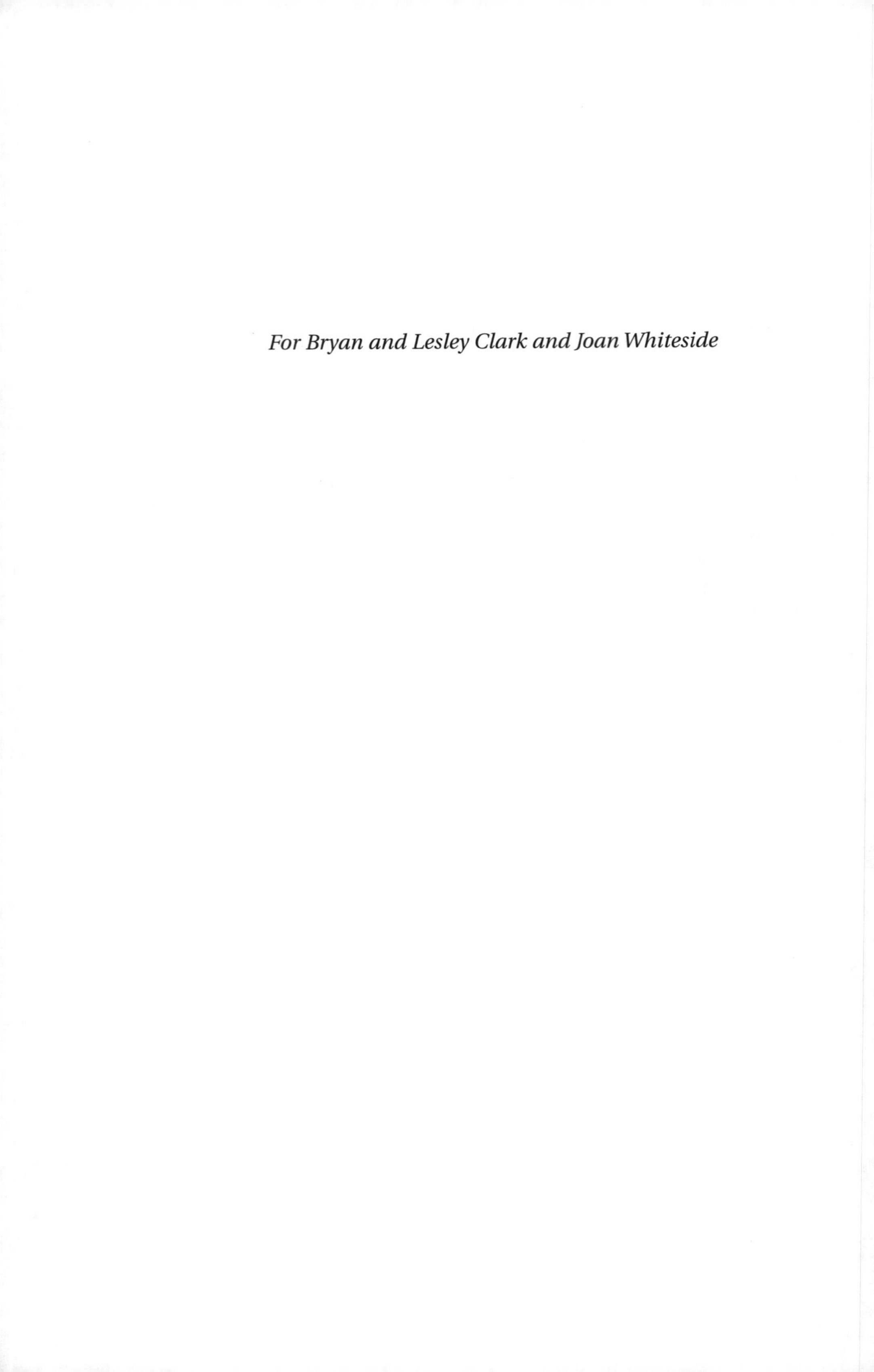

For Bryan and Lesley Clark and Joan Whiteside

CONTENTS

PREFACE

In the years immediately after 1945, pensions and social security formed a relatively stable component of social policy and political economy. This stability fostered the academic classification of welfare states into categories that reflected degrees of social redistribution and types of protection characterised by national systems. Over the 1990s, however, this analytical logic was thrown into question. Repeated concerns were raised about the capacity of state pension schemes to accommodate the retirement of the baby-boom generation from 2010. Issues of demography and finance have ruptured the previously isolated sphere of social welfare. Pension security is more fragile than hitherto believed, even though many academics in social policy and across the social sciences remain convinced that national welfare states are sacrosanct and deeply embedded in the collective consciousness of nation-states.

In Europe, doubts about the capacity of nation-states to fund the retirement of the baby boom generation have brought these issues to a head. Following Maastricht and European Monetary Union, EU member states have sought to restructure welfare, to contain future public obligations, focusing specifically on state pensions—thereby provoking alarm within the EU about the future provision of sustainable retirement income. Pay-As-You-Go (PAYG) state-sponsored social security appears unable to meet public expectations and future burdens, when compared to pension systems that rely upon a mix of partially funded public and fully funded private provision. This brings into focus distinctions between (for example) continental European traditions and the institutions and principles underpinning Anglo-American social security and funded supplementary systems.

Such gross distinctions conceal much variability between countries within categories and commonalities between countries from different categories. There are, for example, significant differences between the Netherlands, Germany, and France—countries frequently included under Esping-Andersen's European continental-corporatist banner. Likewise, there are significant differences between the United Kingdom and the United States, particularly as the Labour government has sought to augment pension benefits and to introduce a state-sponsored 'stakeholder pension' for the many low-income uncovered working people while the Bush administration has contemplated the partial privatisation of social security. As 'reform' accelerates in many countries, settled expectations about system-specific public and private responsibilities are changing. There is as much to be learnt from the Dutch and Swedes as from the Anglo-Americans.

As we know, PAYG systems of pension security are very vulnerable to demographic trends. Most obviously, lower birth rates combined with longer life expectancy makes a considerable difference to any country's population/age distribution. Where each generation is smaller than the next (as in continental Europe over the next fifty years), there are concerns about economically overburdening successive generations. Given the economic risks in overburdening successive generations, there seem to be at least four options: (1) the discounting of promised pension benefits; (2) the allocation of more responsibility for pension security to the private sector (e.g. employer-sponsored pensions); (3) the promotion of personal retirement accounts; and (4) altering the age of retirement. In some cases all four 'reforms' have been introduced; other countries have tried a mix of these options. For much of the twentieth century, the state was the assumed guarantor of pension security. In a world of global finance, massive financial flows between markets, and the development of financial products that price and discount sovereign risk, the state is a smaller economic agent. The nation-state is no longer capable of guaranteeing pension security notwithstanding the claimed desirability of such a role by many on the left.

Clearly, demography, finance, and public accountability are crucial to current political debate. But there are other important issues. The problem of paying for the retirement of the baby-boom generation has exposed profound differences between western developed economies in terms of their financial institutions and infrastructure. The EU and some academic commentators in France and Germany have argued that funded pension systems are a vital component in any programme designed to promote the economic growth of continental Europe. Pension security has been reconceptualised, in part, as an issue of global finance and international comparative advantage bringing with it a redefinition of risk and pension security. Equally, the changing nature of work and the concomitant decentralisation of career opportunities and career choices to individuals as opposed to whole social classes indicate that social security pension schemes may be inconsistent with the new economy of the twenty-first century, with its emphasis on networks, not hierarchies. As work changes, should not pension institutions themselves become more flexible? If so, in what way?

For these reasons, the prospects for pension security are widely debated. Established welfare systems are challenged by demographic, financial, and political considerations to bring larger economies into line with changing global economic developments that are rarely accommodated within a social policy perspective. This brings us to the goals of our book. They can be expressed in the three simple (but enormously complicated) questions posed to our contributors:

1. How are major continental European and Anglo-American countries dealing with the demographic, financial, and political pressures on pension and retirement income?
2. To what extent are responses to these pressures redrawing the boundaries between public and private responsibility for (and provision of) pension security?
3. What are the implications of these new public–private partnerships for the financial organisation and infrastructure of European and global financial markets—and the future of nation-based welfare states?

We selected expert contributors from a variety of countries and academic disciplines to discuss developments in the changing division between public and private pensions and social security institutions. Our objective is less to revisit old ground than to expose the interrelationship between two spheres commonly considered separately in the literature: old age security and global finance. The sources of Europe's pension problem (demographic crisis, public expenditure constraint, industrial restructuring, etc.) are well documented as are the policy reforms considered and implemented by EU member governments. Less attention has been paid to the influence of Anglo-American global pension funds and even less to the various regulatory frameworks that seek to reconcile private provision with public purposes. On the one hand, the global economic influence wielded by the financial services sector appears to make regulation of their activities by national or EU governance redundant: attractive retirement packages available privately to the better-off threaten the solidarity that previously sustained universal state welfare. On the other, wholesale privatisation of pensions is not politically sustainable in any EU state, or in the western world as a whole. Various publicly approved private options are emerging as solutions to the dilemmas noted above.

Our book has a deliberate comparative perspective juxtaposing continental European traditions with Anglo-American initiatives and institutions. The selection of countries, as exemplifying or exploring specific typologies of public–private mix, is a means of establishing how and why circumstances are changing. Contributors to the book come from a variety of fields: political economy, economics and social policy, social history, political science, economic geography, and finance. We would argue that an interdisciplinary approach offers a valuable perspective on such a significant and highly topical subject. We recognise that pensions and finance is a relatively small and specialised market. At the same time, we believe that the logic and structure of the book invites a broader audience across the social sciences, financial services, and in policy-making circles.

To sustain coherence of the book project, while enabling an overarching perspective, we ran a one-day conference at the Rothermere American Institute, University of Oxford, sponsored by our partners the UK Economic and Social Research Council and Zurich Financial Services, with the support of the Oxford Institute of Ageing. We acknowledge their help and sponsorship in the next section. The conference was an opportunity to 'manage' the book and to provide a public forum for the contributors and for the project as a whole. Having established the three questions for each contributor to address, having put in place a mechanism for consultation and peer review via the conference format, we nevertheless recognise that edited books can lose coherence over time. We provide an introductory chapter and a certain order of contributions and arguments designed to drive through the relevant issues culminating in a chapter designed to set the issues in a global context.

Ultimately, pension security is one of the most important issues facing our societies over the twenty-first century. It carries with it the potential to divide nations, to engender enormous conflict over the division of social resources, and to introduce a level of inequality that was antithetical to western democracies in the second half of the twentieth century. We are currently living through a period of profound change: one that promises to introduce a different prism through which pensions will be viewed and that will necessarily revise current assumptions about the responsibilities of the state for ensuring old age security. We remain convinced, however, that the boundaries between public and private responsibility for pension security will continue to be central to public debates and for this reason our book is focused on reconstruction and reappraisal of this public–private divide.

ACKNOWLEDGEMENTS

This book was made possible by the support of the UK Economic and Social Research Council (ESRC) and Zurich Financial Services. We would also like to thank the Institute of Ageing and the Rothermere American Institute at Oxford University for their support of the conference. In particular, we wish to acknowledge the help and support of Professor Ed Page (Director of the ESRC Future Governance Programme) and Mr Karl Snowden (Zurich Financial Services), as well as Dr Sarah Harper (Oxford Institute of Ageing), Mr David Musson (Oxford University Press), Ms Madeline Mitchell, Ms Andrea Beighton, and Ms Jan Burke. Assistance at the related conference was willingly provided by Ms Tessa Hebb and Dr Dariusz Wojcik, and editorial assistance was provided by Isobel Lawrence and Merridy Wilson. We are very grateful for all their contributions. We also acknowledge the permission of Pion Ltd to republish portions of Chapter 10 which previously appeared as Gordon L Clark "Pension security in the global economy: markets and national institutions in the 21st century" Environment and Planning A (2003) 35, 1339–1356.

In preparing the book, we were very fortunate to enlist the expertise and hard work of Kate Williams, Emiko Wakasugi, and Jane Battersby. They brought a clear-sighted view of the entire book, adding a great deal to its final shape and structure. Similarly, Dr Chloe Flutter and Kate Williams made significant contributions to the final manuscript by translating two of the chapters.

Of course, the editors are responsible for the final manuscript and any views or opinions expressed rest either with the editors or the contributors.

LIST OF FIGURES

LIST OF TABLES

LIST OF ACRONYMS AND ABBREVIATIONS

ABP	Algemeen Burgelijk Pensioenfonds (Pension fund for government and education authorities) (Netherlands)
ADR	Age Dependency Ratio
AGIRC	L'Association Générale des Institutions de Retraite des Cadres (Association of pension schemes for managerial, technical and white-collar workers) (France)
AGRR	Association Générale des Retraites par Répartition (Association of contributory (PAYG) pension schemes) (France)
AMF	Major occupational pensions company (Sweden)
ANEP	Association Nationale d'Entraide et de la Prévoyance (National Association of mutual aid and providence societies) (France)
AOW	Algemene Ouderdom Wet (General Old Age Pension Act) (Netherlands)
AP	Allmän Pension (National pensions fund) (Sweden)
AREPPER	Association de Recherche et d'Études pour l'Épargne et la Retraite (Association for research into savings and retirement) (France)
ARRCO	Association des Régimes de Retraite Complémentaire (Association for complementary retirement schemes) (France)
ASF	Association pour la gestion de la Structure Financière (Financial structure management association) (France)
ATP	Allmän Tilläggspension (General supplementary pension scheme) (Sweden)
AWG	Ageing Working Group

BEPG	Broad Economic Policy Guidelines (EU)
CDU/CSU	Christlich Demokratischen Union/Christlich-Soziale Union (Christian Democratic Union/Christian Social Union) (Germany)
CEA	European Committee of Assurance
CEC	Commission of the European Community
CEEP	Centre Européen des Entreprises à Participation Publique (European association of public sector employers)
CFDT	Confédération Française Démocratique du Travail (French democratic federation of workers—French trade union) (France)
CFTC	Confédération Française des Travailleurs Chrétiens (French Christian workers' confederation) (France)
CGC	(Usually CFE-CGC) Confédération Française de l'Encadrement—Confédération Générale des Cadres (Management confederation-general confederation of white-collar workers) (France)
CGT	Confédération Générale du Travail (General confederation of labour—trade union confederation) (France)
CNAV	Caisse Nationale d'Assurance Vieillesse (National agency for old-age insurance) (France)
CNPF	Confédération Nationale du Patronat Français (National employers' confederation) (France) (renamed MEDEF in 1998)
COR	Conseil d'Orientation des Retraites (Pension advisory council) (France)
COREVA	Contrats de Complément de Retraite Volontaire Agricole (Pension scheme for agricultural workers) (France)
CPB	Centraal Planbureau (Central bureau for economic policy analysis) (Netherlands)
CPP	Canada Pension Plan
CPPIB	Canada Pension Plan Investment Board
DB	Defined Benefit
DC	Defined Contribution
DG	Director General
EC	European Commission
ECHP	European Community Household Panel
ECOFIN	The European Union ministers of economics and finance
EFC	Economic and Financial Committee (EU)
EFRP	European Federation for Retirement Pensions
EMS	European Monetary System

EMU	Economic and Monetary Union
EPC	Economic Policy Committee (EU)
ERT	European Round Table of Industrialists
ETUC	European Trade Union Confederation
EU	European Union
EUR	Euro
FDC	Financial Defined Contribution system (Fully funded individual accounts)
FDP	Freie Demokratische Partei (Free Democratic Party) (Germany)
FEFSI	European federation of fund managers
FEN	Fédération de l'éducation nationale (Federation of National Education—Trade Union) (France)
FFSA	Fédération française des sociétés d'assurance (French federation of insurance companies) (France)
FO	Force Ouvrière (Another term for CGT-FO, a branch of CGT—trade union confederation) (France)
FONPEL	Fonds de pension des élus locaux (Pension fund for elected local government officers) (France)
FP	Flexiblare pensioneringssystem (Flat rate benefit pension) (Sweden)
FRS	Financial Reporting Standards (UK)
FSV	Fonds de solidarité vieillesse (Retirement solidarity fund) (France)
GDP	Gross Domestic Product
GEMA	Groupement des Entreprises Mutuelles d'Assurances (Grouping of mutual insurance companies) (France)
HM	Her Majesty's (UK)
INSEE	Institut nationale de la statistique et des études économiques (National institute for statistics and economic studies) (France)
IORP	Institutions for Occupational Retirement Provision (EU)
IP	Income Protection (Pension scheme)
IRA	Individual Retirement Account (US)
ISA	Individual Savings Account (UK)
ITP plan	Industrins och handelns tilläggspension (Supplementary pension for industry and commerce) (Sweden)
ITP-K	Kompletterande industrins och handelns tilläggspension—(Complementary ITP pension plan) (Sweden)
KBT	Kommunalt Bostadstillägg (Municipal housing supplement) (Sweden)

KLM	Koninklijke Luchtvaart Maatschappij (Royal Dutch Airlines) (Netherlands)
KPA	Major occupational pensions company (Sweden)
LEL	Lower Earnings Limit (UK)
MEDEF	Mouvement des entreprises de France (French business confederation) (France)
MIG	Minimum Income Guarantee (UK)
NASDAQ	National Association of Securities Dealers Automated Quotations System (a computerized system that provides quotations for over-the-counter and some stock-exchange securities) (US)
NDC	Notional Defined Contribution system
NHS	National Health Service (UK)
NI	National Insurance (UK)
NIC	National Insurance Contributions (UK)
NJAC	National Joint Advisory Council (UK)
OECD	Organisation for Economic Co-operation and Development (Paris)
P/E	price/earnings
PAYG	Pay as you go
PBGC	Pension Benefit Guaranty Corporation (US)
PET	Primary Earnings Threshold (UK)
PGGM	Pension fund for the healthcare and social welfare sector (Netherlands)
PPM	Premiepensionsmyndigheten (Premium pension authority) (Sweden)
PREFON	Caisse nationale de prévoyance de la fonction publique (Pension scheme for state employees) (France)
PRO	Public Records Office (UK)
PSW	Pensioen- en Spaarfondsenwet (Pension and savings act) (Netherlands)
PT	Pensionstillskott (A supplement paid by the state to people with low pensions) (Sweden)
RATP	Régie Autonome des Transports Parisiens (Paris Public Transport System) (France)
RFV	Riksförsäkringsverket (National social insurance board) (Sweden)
RSV	Riksskatteverket (National tax board) (Sweden)
S&P	Standard & Poors (US)
SEK	Svensk Krone (Swedish Krone—currency)

SER	Sociaal-Economische Raad (Social and economic council) (Netherlands)
SERPS	State Earnings Related Pension Scheme (UK)
SNCF	Société Nationale des Chemins de Fer Français (French Railways)
SOU	Statens Offentliga Utredningar (State public inquiry [State Commission]—Sweden)
SPC	Social Protection Committee (EU)
SPD	Sozialdemokratische Partei Deutschlands (Social Democratic Party) (Germany)
SPP	SPP Livförsäkring AB (Major occupation pensions company) (Sweden)
SPV	Statens pensionsverk (State pension authority) (Sweden)
STP	Särskild Tilläggspension (Collectively bargained pension scheme) (Sweden)
STAR	Stichting van de Arbeid (Dutch labour foundation) (Netherlands)
TEE	Tax contributions, Exempt investment income, Exempt pensions from tax (pension system)
TMT	Technology, Media, and Telecommunication
TSP	The federal Thrift Savings Plan (US)
TUC	Trades Union Congress (UK)
UDF-RPR	Union pour la démocratie française—Rassemblement pour la République (Union for French Democracy-Rally for the Republic—Political coalition) (France)
UNICE	Union of Industrial and Employers' Confederations of Europe
UNIRS	Union des Insititutions des retraites des salariés (federation of employees' retirement pension schemes) (France)
VAT	Value Added Tax (UK)
WKA	Wet Koppeling met Afwijkingsmogelijkheid (Conditional indexation act) (Netherlands)
WRR	Wetenschappelijke Raad voor het Regeringsbeleid (Scientific council for government policy) (Netherlands)

EDITORS AND CONTRIBUTORS

Gordon L. Clark (co-editor) is the Halford Mackinder Professor at the University of Oxford, Fellow of the Saïd Business School, and Research Associate of the Institute of Ageing. Prior to his appointment at Oxford he taught at Harvard University, the University of Chicago, Carnegie Mellon University, and Monash University. The author of many papers and books, his most recent book is *European Pensions & Global Finance* (Oxford University Press, 2003). Other books include *Pension Fund Capitalism* (Oxford University Press, 2000), the *Oxford Handbook of Economic Geography* (co-editor; Oxford University Press, 2000), and *Pensions and Corporate Restructuring in American Industry* (Johns Hopkins University Press, 1993). Professor Clark serves on the Panel of Academic Experts for the UK National Association of Pension Funds (NAPF).

Noel Whiteside (co-editor) was appointed Professor of Comparative Public Policy at Warwick University in 2000. Previously, she held appointments at Bristol University and has held visiting appointments at the University of Wisconsin-Madison and at the Ecole Normale Supérieure (Cachan, Paris). The author of numerous articles, her books include *Governance, Industry and Labour Markets in Britain and France* (Routledge, 1998), co-edited with Robert Salais, and *Casual Labour* (Oxford University Press, 1985), co-authored with Gordon Phillips. Professor Whiteside is a member of the Scientific Council of the Maison des Sciences de l'Homme (Ange Guepin). She was appointed Zurich Financial Services Fellow in November 2000.

Carl Emmerson is Programme Coordinator on Pensions, Saving, and Public Finances at the Institute for Fiscal Studies in London. He is an editor of the IFS Green Budget and his research has included analysis of the effect of UK pension reform on inequality, labour market mobility, and individuals' incentives to save. Recent publications include 'Public and private pension spending: principles, practice and the need for reform', *Fiscal Studies*, 21 (2000), 1–63 (with James Banks), and 'Pension reform and economic performance in Britain in the 1980s and 1990s' (with Richard Disney and Sarah Smith) in Richard Blundell, David Card, and Richard B. Freeman (eds.), *Creating a Premier League Economy* (University of Chicago Press, 2002).

Anton Hemerijck is Deputy Director of the Netherlands Council for Government Policy (WRR) and Senior Lecturer in the Department of Public Administration, Leiden University. Between 1997 and 2000 he was a Research Affiliate of the Max Planck Institute for the Study of Societies, working on *Welfare and Work in the Open Economy*, which was published by Oxford University Press in 2000 (edited by Fritz W. Scharpf and Vivien A. Schmidt). Publications include (with Jelle Visser) *A Dutch Miracle: Job Growth, Welfare Reform and Corporatism in the Netherlands* (1997); (with Maurizio Ferrera and Martin Rhodes) *The Future of Social Europe: Recasting Work and Welfare in the New Economy* (Report for the Portuguese Presidency of the EU, 2000). More recently he participated, together with Gosta Esping-Andersen, Duncan Gallie, and John Myles in *Why We Need a New Welfare State* (Oxford University Press, 2002).

Alicia H. Munnell is the Peter F. Drucker Professor in Management Sciences at Boston College's Carroll School of Management, and Director of the Center for Retirement Research at Boston College. Prior to this appointment, she was a Member of the President's Council of Economic Advisers (1995–97) and served as Assistant Secretary of the U.S. Treasury for Economic Policy (1993–95). Her most recent book (co-edited) is *Framing the Social Security Debate: Values, Politics and Economics* (Brookings, 1998). Professor Munnell is a member of the American Academy of Arts and Sciences, the Institute of Medicine, the National Academy of Public Administration, the Pension Research Council at Wharton, and the National Academy of Social Insurance. She also serves on the boards of National Bureau of Economic Research and the Pension Rights Center.

Bruno Palier is chargé de recherche (CNRS) at the Centre d'Études de la Vie Politique Française (CEVIPOF) in Paris. His research interest is in welfare state reforms, both from a French and a comparative perspective. He co-edited (with Christine Daniel) *La Protection Sociale en Europe, Le Temps des Réformes* (La Documentation Française, 2001), and recently published 'Defrosting the French welfare state', *West European Politics*, 23 (2000), 113–36; (with Giuliano Bonoli) 'From the cradle to where?

Current pension policy trends in Western Europe', *Yearbook of European Administrative History* (2001); and 'Changing the politics of social programmes: innovative change in British and French welfare reforms', *Journal of European Social Policy*, 8/4 (1998), 317–30. He is currently writing and co-editing (with Rob S. Sykes and P. Prior) *Globalization and European Welfare States: Challenges and Changes* (Palgrave, 2003).

Joakim Palme is Senior Researcher at the Swedish Institute for Social Research at Stockholm University. He has published several studies on the public–private mix in the Scandinavian pension systems including (with Olli Kangas) 'The development of occupational pensions in Finland and Sweden', in (ed.) Michael Shalev, *The Privatization of Social Policy* (Macmillan, 1996). Other publications include studies on the distributional consequences of differences in institutional design of social policy—see especially 'The paradox of redistribution and strategies of equality', *American Sociological Review*, 63 (1993), 661–87 (with Walter Korpi). More recently, he is the author of 'Will Social Europe work?' in Martin Kohli and Mojca Novak (eds.), *Will Europe Work?* (Routledge, 2002).

Philippe Pochet is Director of the Observatoire Social Européen (Brussels), an Affiliate at the Centre of European Studies (Free University of Brussels), and also a visiting lecturer at the Catholic University of Louvain-la-Neuve, where he co-chairs the study group on Active Welfare State (with P. Vielle). He is the Digest Editor of the *Journal of European Social Policy* and his main research fields are: the social impacts of the European Monetary Union, the social dimension of the European Union, and the challenges of globalisation. He recently edited *Monetary Union and Collective Bargaining in Europe* (P. I. E.-Peter Lang, 1999), *Social Pacts in Europe—New Dynamics*, with G. Fajertag (ETUI-OSE, 2000), *Building Social Europe through the Open Method of Coordination*, with C. de la Porte (P. I. E.-Peter Lang, 2002), and *Wage Policy in the Eurozone* (P. I. E.-Peter Lang 2002).

Bart van Riel is Senior Policy Officer at the Netherlands' Social-Economic Council (SER). He was involved in preparing the SER-advisory reports on *Ageing in the EU* (2002) and *Labour Mobility in the EU* (2001). This report deals with the question of pension portability in Europe. From 1995 to 2002 he worked for the European Parliament, focusing on economic and monetary integration. Together with Alman Metten, he published *The Choices of Maastricht* (Van Gorcum, 2000, in Dutch), which deals with the road to EMU. He wrote his dissertation, *Unemployment Divergence in Coordinated Systems of Industrial Relations* (Peter Lang Verlag, 1995), while working at the Technical University of Darmstadt, Germany. His most recent published articles are 'Ageing and public pensions: the perspective from the 1950s' (in Dutch); 'The advocacy coalition for European employment policy' (with Marc van der Meer); and 'Harmonisation and competition as means to economic integration' (in German).

Winfried Schmähl teaches economics at Bremen University (Germany) and is Director of the Economic Department of the Centre for Social Policy Research of the university. He was member of the Federal Government's Commission for Pension Reform (1996–97), Chairman of the (permanent) Social Advisory Board on Pension Policy to the German Federal Government (1986–2000), and is on the Enquête–Commission of the Federal Parliament on demographic changes (1992–94, 1995–98, and since Dec. 1999). His most recent books (co-edited) are *Alterssicherung von Frauen* (Westdeutscher Verlag, 2000), *Transformation of Pension Systems in Central and Eastern Europe* (Elgar, 2001), *Soziale Sicherungssysteme und demographische Herausforderungen* (Mohr, 2001).

Jelle Visser is Professor of Empirical Sociology and holds the Chair of Sociology of Work and Organisation at the University of Amsterdam, where he is Scientific Director of the Amsterdam Institute of Advanced Labour Studies. He is also associated with the Max Planck Institute for the Study of Societies in Cologne, Germany, and has acted as consultant to the OECD and the ILO on industrial relations, social dialogue, and social statistics. Recent publications include *The Future of Collective Bargaining in Europe* (with Tito Boeri, Lars Calmfors, and others) (Oxford University Press, 2002), *Trade Unions in Western Europe Since 1945* (with Bernhard Ebbinghaus) (Macmillan, 2000), and *A Dutch 'Miracle': Job Growth, Welfare Reform and Corporatism in the Netherlands* (with Anton Hemerijck).

Introduction

Gordon L. Clark and Noel Whiteside

The future provision of old age security is a major political issue in all developed countries. As is widely acknowledged, increased longevity and the imminent retirement of the post-war baby-boom generation have undermined the financial viability of state pensions based on Pay-As-You-Go (PAYG) principles. Funding pensions from the public finances is increasingly problematic, believed by many policy analysts to be economically unsustainable (if pension benefits are kept as promised). Yet as electorates age, so they also become increasingly defensive of their established pension rights, resisting attempts by national governments to reduce state provision. These tensions and dilemmas are at the core of current political debate about nation-state capacity and are the basis of the structure and contents of this book.

How are Europe, the United Kingdom, and the United States dealing with the demographic, financial, and political pressures on pension security? To what extent are responses to these pressures prompting the redrawing of the boundaries between public and private responsibility for, and the provision of, pension security? And what are the implications of these new kinds of public–private partnerships for the financial organisation and infrastructure of European and global financial markets? As noted in the Preface, these are the questions our contributors address: large questions hardly amenable to simple answers and very much conditioned by the experience of different countries with different historical trajectories. Sensitivity to the historical record is one attribute of our country-specific contributions; recognition of changing circumstances and the gathering demographic and economic forces is another attribute of the book. In fact, the questions addressed here incorporate broader issues concerning the current status and likely future of the nation-state as the proper locus for collective social welfare. These questions are also at the very heart of recent debates over the nature of identity, the borders of just communities, and the corrosive forces of globalisation.[1]

Integration, monetary union, and the stresses and strains occasioned by industrial restructuring have brought enormous pressures to bear on national governments to reconsider their pension systems. On the one hand, the structural decline of traditional industries from the late 1970s allowed workers who would otherwise have been declared redundant the dignity of early retirement. If humane and politically motivated, this policy has exacerbated the PAYG pension crisis of many countries (Clark 2003). On the other hand, preparation for (and preservation of) the Euro has forced a reappraisal of state welfare obligations in major European economies. Here, pensions formed (and still form) a focal point for the debate over the costs and benefits of the Stability and Growth Pact (see Pochet's contribution in this book). Considerable interest has developed in the private funded provision of pensions supplementing, even replacing, state schemes. Booming equity markets over the mid-1990s seemingly offered a larger and more viable alternative source of pension funding than state-based PAYG pensions. However, the downturn in financial markets at the new millennium, revelations of incompetence and corruption in corporate governance, and increased uncertainty in international relations have together provided European Union (EU) member states with a profound dilemma.

On the one hand, fiscal probity demands retrenchment: pensions form a major component of social security budgets that are rising inexorably. Official reports from the European Commission (EC), policy reviews by the Organisation for Economic Co-operation and Development (OECD), and commentaries by the World Bank and other similar organisations have all sought to emphasise the limits of nation-state fiscal capacity and the inevitable added burdens accompanying the ageing of national' populations over the coming 30 years or so. On the other hand, the volatility of global finance exposes pension savings, both individual and corporate, to much higher levels of risk and uncertain rates of return (see Clark, this volume). If income security in old age is essential for economic prosperity (encouraging risk-taking and innovation amongst younger generations of working people), greater uncertainty about future welfare may create acute tensions between the generations and stifle the development of new systems of economic accumulation. For many European nations, concerned about their individual and collective place in the world over the coming century, the pensions crisis is not only a threat to fiscal probity, but also a threat to long-term economic growth.

In this Introduction, our goal is to simply set the scene. Given the questions posed to our contributors and the economic and political sensitivity of the issues concerning pension policy and reform, we aim to establish some initial connections between the individual chapters. In doing so, we are mindful of the very deep links between nation-state social welfare and pensions systems, and of the role that these institutions have played over the past half century in managing and mediating social and political conflict. At the same time, we also believe the past is not necessarily a reliable predictor of the future. Each contributor shows that, as nation-states grapple with the likely burdens of inherited pension systems, they do so in ways that seek an accommodation with the imperatives of economic union, of economic development, and of globalisation. These threads continue through the book to the concluding chapter. In total, the book is designed to make the connections we believe to be essential in understanding current dilemmas and future prospects.

BACK TO THE FUTURE?

The first major debates about pensions occurred in the final decades of the nineteenth century. Then as now, rising longevity and new production technologies had marginalised growing numbers of older workers, many being forced back on communal systems of poor relief. Solutions to the consequent financial problems this posed varied. In the 1880s, Germany introduced earnings-related social insurance, offering a small pension as a household income supplement to workers whose failing capacities had forced their earnings to below one-third of previous income. The German paradigm was imitated and adapted elsewhere. But it also provoked criticism: for its compulsory nature, its sole focus on industrial workers, and its failure to redistribute resources from rich to poor. Early schemes in New Zealand, Denmark, and (following much debate) the United Kingdom, rejected worker contributions in favour of tax-funded pensions. The Swedish scheme, introduced in 1913, was largely tax-funded, but incorporated an earnings-related element for urban workers, whose cost of living was higher than their rural counterparts (Baldwin 1990: ch. 1). In France, the 1910 introduction of compulsory contributory pensions for workers and peasants faced widespread non-compliance, forcing extensive state subsidies that transferred pension costs from contributor to taxpayer (Renard 1994). How pensions should be funded, whether it was feasible for personal savings to protect against old age destitution, and whether such saving should be compulsory or voluntary, were the focal points of debate in the years before the First World War.

In Britain, then as now, advocates of state pensions confronted both a parsimonious Treasury and neoliberal ideologies that insisted that, as earnings were rising at this time, workers should save for themselves (Macnicol 1998; Thane 2000: chs 10–11). Detailed social investigations in East London by Charles Booth in the late 1880s had shown that poor marginal workers (particularly women) could not accumulate sufficient savings for old age in the course of a working life. Women's greater longevity and domestic obligations were translated into intermittent work in low-paid jobs, making regular saving problematic. Evidence from poor-law administrators, charitable organisations, and others reinforced Booth's analysis: the problem of old age poverty was predominantly female. It was not due to idleness or lack of foresight, and therefore, was not responsive to potential solutions reliant on individual or collective thrift. Yet, personal savings were widely assumed to offer a solution. Joseph Chamberlain advocated state subsidies for voluntary Post Office annuity accounts, an initiative similar to the current British stakeholder pension scheme, to help the poor save for their old age:

> In dealing with the poor some economists expect from them a virtue that we certainly do not find in ourselves . . . it is a little too much to expect of them . . . the extremely penurious lives which would be necessary if they were to make by their own efforts, a sufficient provision for old age . . . If you told a rich man that he was to give up every chief enjoyment of his life, every recreation, in order to make provision of this kind, I do not think he would make it.
>
> (Joseph Chamberlain (1894), cited in Thane 2000: 186)

Such an observation carries a certain resonance today. However, social investigation demonstrated that this solution would not get to the roots of the problem.

Charles Booth's enquiries in East London had convinced him that the elusive search for a private solution based on personal savings was pointless. The elderly poor could no longer work. Their poverty was the consequence of an unanticipated longevity, not personal failing. Booth argued for universal, tax-funded old age endowment available to all at a specified age. This would cost £20 million p.a., or about one-sixth of annual government revenue. Highly redistributive in principle, in contrast to the German precedent, it offered equitable treatment irrespective of gender or work record and established a single pension age, an ideal at the heart of much of the debate today.

Thanks to the support of organised labour, this scheme formed the foundations of the Old Age Pensions Act (1908). It marked a complete break with the past. It acknowledged that old age poverty was not the consequence of personal fecklessness or poor character; the pension was based on citizenship, not employment. Elderly women received support as of right, not as dependants of contributing husbands. Its receipt did not require retirement; the small sum served to supplement household income reduced in consequence of lower earning capacity. But thanks to its cost, it was immensely unpopular with the Treasury, whose officials succeeded in removing its universal coverage (it became means-tested). The Treasury aimed from the start to replace tax funding with social insurance; this was partly realised in the Widows, Orphans, and Old Age Pensions Act (1925) and finally assured by the Beveridge Plan of 1942. In consequence, the state pension in Britain ceased to be based on citizenship but derived from labour market participation (making a non-working married female pensioner's rights dependent on her husband's contributory record). But this recipe for retirement income was not particularly generous. Beveridge's pensions always required personal savings (or a means-tested supplement) to raise income to subsistence level. British state pensions were (and remain) among the lowest in the world.

Current discussions of pension futures have resuscitated some of the features that characterised the early debates. Then as now, widespread faith in private individual saving as the bedrock of old age security complemented official desire to minimise taxpayer obligations to the elderly. The merits of commercial insurance and personal saving were advocated alongside different types of public–private partnership (such as Chamberlain's state-subsidised Post Office annuity scheme). Then, as now, British politicians tried to distinguish those who could save for a pension from those who could not, to target public support (to use current terminology) on the poor. Then as now, it proved impossible to leave the aged poor to poverty and deprivation; in one way or another, rate payers or taxpayers came to foot the bill. Finally, then as now, the focus on private saving failed to acknowledge the gendered nature of the pension problem. Past, present, and future majorities of pensioners were, are, and will be female, many will be living alone, and most with previous earning (and saving) capacity reduced by uneven employment histories—the consequence of their efforts to combine domestic duties with waged work (Ginn 2001).

It would, however, be wrong to claim that the situation has not changed. First, the demographic dimension of the problem is much larger today. Between 1901 and 2001, the number of elderly (retirement age) people in Britain has more than quadrupled (Thane 2000: 478). Second, the early pensions were never supposed to offer a subsistence income, while today the common expectation is that they should do precisely that. Finally, Booth and Bismarck developed their schemes at a time when the merits of state support were gaining ground within British and European political systems. Recent discussions have occurred against a backdrop of dwindling faith in state-funded welfare. In the early 1900s, the political left could argue that state provision offered better and more equitable security than either the inefficient and patchy coverage supplied by mutual aid or charity, or the profit motive driving commercial concerns. In more recent years, resurgent liberalism combined with public choice theory has countered such views: individuals hold the best information about their needs and markets offer the best way of meeting them. Such theories also support the merits of private markets and saving products.

During the 1990s, a booming American economy stood in marked contrast to its stultified European counterparts that were beset by persistently high unemployment and low rates of growth. The solution to European woes was assumed to lie in the adoption of American labour market practices and the acceptance of neoliberal orthodoxies, requiring labour market deregulation and workfare policy strategies (OECD 1994). A more flexible labour market and an alignment to Anglo-American systems of capital formation would, it was hoped, promote a successful adaptation to the new economy. Pension fund capitalism allowed old age security to be married to investment finance for restructuring, economic innovation, and development. This happy union could also be extended to finance social resources and projects including urban regeneration, transport projects, and so on, thereby obviating the need for heavy taxation that would undermine enterprise and foster the burden of state bureaucracy. The American paradigm, in short, demonstrated how funded pensions could offer a solution to Europe's economic problems. The sheer size of Anglo-American pension funds dominated transactions on global financial markets. Such growing influence has provoked a mixture of hostility and admiration. The promise of high returns on global investments has excited considerable political interest in the viability of funded schemes as a solution to the pension crisis.

On the other hand, the adaptation of US employment practices has threatened job security: labour market deregulation risks raising the number of 'working poor' while cutting them off from the benefit systems associated with job tenure. Extensive industrial restructuring is recasting previously monolithic corporations into networked franchises of small businesses. The so-called 'a-typical' jobs—part-time work, short-term contracts, and self-employment—proliferate, particularly among female workers, and facilitated by new IT applications. Inevitably, contingent and less secure employment makes it harder for unskilled workers to save for a funded pension. Current pension reforms that raise the significance of private personal saving run the risk of exacerbating an already visible gender gap in the future income security of elderly men and women. This gap is at its widest in countries—like the United States and the United Kingdom—where private funded pensions are most developed (Ginn et al. 2001). Labour market inequalities and current policies to encourage private pension savings through tax breaks benefit high earning male workers over low earning females. As our Swedish and German contributors show, some countries have taken steps to protect female pension rights, to prevent gender-based income discrepancies among future pensioners. Otherwise, very large numbers of elderly women may be condemned to residual state support—in contravention not only to principles of social justice, but also to the economic arguments that supported the promotion of a private solution to the pension problem in the first place.

While greater labour market flexibility and mobility are desired by many employees and employers, all the evidence suggests that pension saving through defined contribution plans results in lower contribution rates and, in many cases, lower long-term benefits. Retirement no longer implies total withdrawal from the waged work. One implication from these patterns and trends is that the ostensibly pensioned-off are to be contracted back into employment to supplement existing resources. The EC's commitment to active ageing reflects the tendency for many European states to revise (upwards) the number of contributory years required to receive a full pension. This corrosion of a fixed retirement age again recalls earlier periods, when any pension (private or public) supplemented earned income rather than replaced it.[2]

MARKET IDEALISM AND PENSION PROVISION

Emphasis on reform and the challenges facing national pension systems offer a different approach to welfare policy analysis to that based on models of welfare as established by Esping-Andersen (1990). The focus on welfare regime continuities has deflected attention from the ways in which nation-states have constantly adapted and borrowed from each other in welfare policy (see Zeitlin 2003; Salais 2003 for criticism of Esping-Andersen's analysis). Approaches that stress the significance of historical trajectories in pension policy and the importance of institutional factors that shape the nature of current debates offer productive starting points (e.g. Myles and Pierson 2001). However, while institutional longevity is important, welfare reform initiatives are rarely shaped by inherited institutions on their own. There has, for example, been a shift towards the OECD's and World Bank's recommended multi-pillar pension system within Europe. This has been encouraged by the EC's goals of fostering greater cross-national labour mobility while developing Eurozone-wide pension funds as key elements in the integration of EU financial markets (Bonoli and Palier 2001; Pochet, this volume). One way or another, EU member states now acknowledge the need for partially funded pensions and have encouraged private supplements to bolster shrinking state provision. Academic attention has also begun to focus on the contrasting strategies pursued by states with mature earnings-related pension schemes and those of 'latecomer' states, where statutory earnings-related supplements are a relatively recent invention (Hinrichs 2000). This approach begins with different geographies, but allows for external factors to influence change and innovation.

We prefer a framework that begins with difference while providing points of common reference in understanding change. The welfare state 'models' so common in the comparative welfare literature are largely based on the years of economic growth and stability following the Second World War. This historical horizon ignores the instabilities that have preceded and followed this period. Further, this kind of analytical logic has kept attention focused on the features held in common by members of the welfare regime families while concealing both points of difference within categories and commonalities between countries in different categories. As our contributors show, there are major differences between the Netherlands, France, and Germany on matters related to the public–private divide—countries frequently subsumed beneath the European continental-corporatist banner—just as similarities exist between the Swedish reforms and those under discussion in continental Europe. The 'models of welfare' approach also tends to treat other spheres of economic and social life as irrelevant or unrelated to the imperatives driving model formation and stability. As our contributors show, there are important connections between global finance on the one hand and pension reform on the other hand (for related arguments see Deacon 1995; Schwartz 2001; Clark 2003). The prospect of global capital markets offering a solution to the current pension crisis requires more attention than it commonly receives.

In fact, as is observed in each and every contribution to the book, the relationship between financial markets and pensions is firmly on the reform agenda of all countries represented here. At the heart of arguments over the proper public–private divide are arguments over the virtues and vices of markets. For many analysts, drawing upon recent events and trends in employment, old age protection would be most effectively secured by returning to the individual the freedom to choose the saving scheme best suited to his/her future. The assumption that action based on individual interest offers the best way forward rests on neoliberal tenets of political economy; these argue that markets, untrammelled by state intervention, can secure the most efficient distribution of goods and services. Such arguments, in turn, rest on the logic of rational choice. Here, it is contended that rational individuals, if left to their own devices, seek out and utilise pertinent information for the purpose of optimising their personal interests. Therefore, by implication public sector interventions should be minimal and confined to residual provision for those unable to assume responsibility for their own security. At best, market provision offers choice, and market competition ensures that choice is available at efficient prices. This summary of how rational choice can and should shape decision-making, is a model that offers a unification of private interests with the public good.

The theory of rational choice is not the subject of this book. Each and every contribution has a strong empirical thread recognising that we urgently need better knowledge of the changing public–private divide if we are to say anything sensible about pension security. In any event, given the broad scope of the book and the various disciplines represented herein, it is doubtful that we would agree on any single social or economic theory to sustain a collective analysis. Even so, none of the contributors is sanguine about the virtues of markets, and none of the contributors suggest that markets can or will 'trump' state provision. So, in this section we wish to raise a number of critical issues about market idealism—a sentiment which, if taken to its logical conclusion, would have state sponsored social security consigned to history in the face of an uncritical belief in the future of global capital markets.

The vision of pension security based on rational individuals using market information to secure their long-term retirement income assumes an unlikely degree of systematic and focused action.[3] To secure specified outcomes, individuals presumably make decisions based on their expectations concerning the consequences of their actions and the relationship of those actions to the actions of others in relation to their desired goals. This implies the pre-existence of a collective understanding about right and proper behaviour within specific environments. In market relations, the conventions underpinning the design and fulfillment of contracts—the very identity of what a contract means and what contractual obligations imply—must be mutually understood and respected if there is to be continuity of transactions and exchanges. Inevitably, frameworks of common understanding (or common knowledge) take time to establish and sustain, and are often culturally specific. These frameworks structure the rules, norms and conventions governing economic and social coordination (across many economic issues including pensions). The state, solely sovereign in such matters, may act as an economic coordinator of last resort: guaranteeing collective social justice by establishing the rules of the game, by identifying and punishing fraudulent behaviours, and by protecting the polity from external threat or the sudden alien imposition of new rules.

Market relations can take a multiplicity of forms and the rules of competition and contract, of agency and its just remuneration, have developed in different ways in different countries (as noted by our contributors). As market relations vary over space, product, and time, so too, do governance structures. But importantly, there are commonly recognised functional requirements. For instance, regulation is needed in all market societies: should markets wobble or threaten to fail, the public will turn to government for more legislative protection, not greater deregulation. When seen from this angle, division between 'state' and 'market' (and hence between 'public' and 'private') is less clear than many would have us believe. In the countries surveyed here, implicitly or explicitly, the state is ultimately charged with the responsibility of underwriting a socially just market performance, even if there are grave doubts about the state's capacity to deliver on a guaranteed *amount* of pension security. Uncertainty as to market performance or the willingness of the state to underwrite it may, however, provoke inaction and non-participation, leading to the breakdown of whole pension regimes. If we hand over money on the promise of future income, can we be assured of its receipt? If we trust an intermediary to act on our behalf, should we offer a gratuity, or is this a bribe for special privilege? In the absence of system-wide institutional integrity, in the absence of adequate conventions that govern economic coordination (reinforced by law), we will not trust those charged with pension security. Who can say with confidence that this is *not* the emerging reality facing many citizens in continental Europe and the UK?

Uncertainty should be distinguished from risk or hazard, the concept that underpins the insurance world. Here, possible adverse outcomes are identifiable and, with the aid of expert diagnosis, actuarial evaluation helps to shape the calculation of premiums with the offer of compensation in the event of action or accident producing a recognised but undesired result. As we know, risk or hazard may be insured individually or collectively. Classical mechanisms of collective social insurance allow premiums to be averaged or shared: where low risk cases or categories compensate for the high risk cases. These kinds of institutions have long protected working people against conventionally defined 'risks' that threaten their livelihood: illness, unemployment, invalidity, and old age. In different countries, protection against some or all of such risks is assumed to be a collective responsibility—nevertheless, current pension debates demonstrate how this balance can change. Further, close examination of how such risks are defined (who are the 'unemployed' as opposed to the economically inactive and what degree of physical impairment constitutes invalidity) reveals variation both between different national frameworks and over time. As indicated above, protection against collectively acknowledged risk forms a necessary part of establishing the confidence necessary for the performance of many kinds of pension institutions. However, as a number of our contributors show, there is evidence that reforms have undercut collective institutions of risk insurance in favour of transferring risk to individuals.

Emphasis on how socio-political influences continually modify networks of trust and confidence, vital to the operation of any market system, has important implications. First, it explains why markets in similar products operate in different ways in different countries. Institutional frameworks differ in accordance with collective expectation about what conventions should be respected and how security is to be guaranteed. To do the same business in different places requires an appreciation of both a written and unwritten understanding of how business is done. It does not suffice to assume a competitive process based on economic 'best value' alone. Hence, socio-political factors cannot be dismissed as marginal to economic activity, but form the foundations of its operation. Second, it follows that official institutional arrangements that underpin pension systems do not translate easily between different countries. Even when frameworks of action appear similar, such institutions incorporate different historical trajectories concerning the role of state agencies mutual associations and commercial corporations in the operation of economic and social transactions. They embody the conventions consequent on past collective norms and decisions concerning socio-economic coordination. Hence, the preference of governments and other institutions for dealing with agencies they know—and who understand the 'rules of the game'. To deal with an outsider invites at best misunderstanding, at worst inefficiency, the collapse of trust, and thereby the failure to achieve specified objectives.

This much has become apparent in the UK in recent decades. British governments have been less concerned with the creation of new markets than with the adaptation of established ones to serve the policy objective of containing public liability in this area. This has translated into the multiplication of regulatory agencies and the extension of new rules and requirements designed to clarify procedures for customers and to promote collective confidence. State subsidies (tax incentives) are to reshape public behaviour. To encourage the purchase of personal savings and pension products, government has extended official controls over marketing, sales, and customer relations, raising the administrative costs of an increasingly complex system and stimulating legal debates over whom (if anyone) should compensate for market failure. More significantly, this new 'partnership' has blurred previously assumed distinctions between public and private while simultaneously obfuscating both market signals (through increased regulation) and public accountability. The failure to clarify who is precisely responsible for what—the complete confusion of pension finance and pension governance—distinguishes the British system from others documented in our book. Constant change and modification has undermined collective confidence and trust; uncertainty is raised, the public fails to act, and the policy fails.

As many analysts have noted (Storper and Salais 1997; Dore 2000), contractual relations, the institutions that enforce them, and their underlying conventions vary widely over space and time. Most importantly, it is clear that market systems vary in terms of their 'background' definitions of the common good. We currently inhabit different 'possible worlds' of economic coordination, each reflecting context-specific sets of expectations concerning the principles of justice applicable to citizens' situations (Storper and Salais 1997). Far from being external or absent from market activities, therefore, the state is bound up in their daily operation: as guarantor of a collective good that is not realised *a priori*, but is continually modified and developed in the course of economic and social activity (Salais 1998). If entirely obvious (to us at least) as a matter of fact, it is also obvious that the presumption in favour of *a* state, of *a* national system of pension institutions and conventions, and of *a* pension promise is precisely the issue currently contested.

Demography, European integration, and globalisation have conspired to question the integrity of national continuity.

PENSION FUTURES

In the opening contribution, Whiteside examines the historical foundations of supplementary, earnings-related pensions after the Second World War. European post-war growth prompted policies to provide the elderly with a share of rising national prosperity. This was realised in various ways. While major European states extended public schemes or made occupational pension provision compulsory, British governments made unprecedented efforts to encourage firms to take their employees out of new state schemes. This drove a wedge between public and private provision and created powerful institutions of pension fund capitalism alongside the lowest state-provided pensions in Europe. Elsewhere in Europe, the split between public and private never fully emerged. In Germany and Sweden, the extension of earnings-related provision was primarily vested with the state, albeit along different lines. In Germany in particular, employer-sponsored supplementary pensions remained with large firms in manufacturing sectors. In the Netherlands and in France, the state extended existing occupational schemes (using rather different mechanisms) to all workers. In all cases, pension policy was renegotiated and developed during a period of institutional continuity; different systems of accountability generated complex relationships between public and private provision, operating within clear legal frameworks. Making comparison across the EU, the gap between public and private provision is most profound in the United Kingdom—the product of deliberate public policy (the subject of Whiteside's chapter).

Currently, the EC is promoting pension reform. While pension provision as a component of social security remains the responsibility of national governments, EC initiatives focus on specific reforms that invoke a recalibration of public (collective) and private (individual) protection. As Philippe Pochet shows, EC interventions are driven by multiple agendas: to guarantee the Stability and Growth Pact following monetary union, to create a single market in European financial services, to foster labour mobility, and to protect future pensioners from the risk of poverty. Recent trends indicate a growing 'Europeanisation' of pension debates, as policy networks develop, as member states' interest in each other's budgetary deficits increases, and as EU institutions have become central in setting the agenda. The impact of EU initiatives at the grass root level remains weak, but Europe is emerging as a forum for determining the nature and direction of change. Pochet's chapter allows us to see these connections, providing an invaluable reference point for subsequent chapters that concentrate on nation-states.

The following four chapters demonstrate how different member states are responding to the need for reform. In the Netherlands, traditions of corporate governance and collective bargaining are mirrored in privately run, joint-managed, defined benefit, funded supplementary occupational schemes, underpinned by a generous basic state pension. For many, the Dutch model of 'flexi-security' has an enviable reputation as a solution to prevailing continental labour market hysterisis and pension funding problems (Levy 1999). However, as Visser et al. argue in this book, the appearance of stability may be deceptive. As the global recession gathers momentum, it appears that Dutch public finances are not in a healthy state. The generous basic state pension threatens intergenerational equity and the private supplementary pension funds are increasingly vulnerable to the downturn in global stock markets. Sustaining the balance between public and private provision may require adjustments in the tax treatment of wealthy contributors and pensioners. Government's formidable influence on and regulation of the private funds is increasing, pointing to a recalibration of the public–private divide.

As Palme shows, recent Swedish pension reforms are more radical, embracing new forms of public–private partnership. The universal, flat-rate state pension is means-tested, the earnings-related element has been raised, and a compulsory, personal, funded component has been introduced—all signalling an apparent transformation in old age retirement income security with entitlements switched from defined benefit to defined contribution. This model is widely admired by policy analysts, being often invoked as a means of social security reform that goes closest to the Anglo-American model based upon notional individual retirement accounts (see Feldstein and Siebert 2002). How far the end-product of reform represents a profound shift from public to private responsibility is debatable; the role of the state remains central even if radically reconceptualised in terms of who carries the burden of long-term pension liabilities. It is arguable that the main change has been in the ethos governing the investment of pension assets: a shift pitching advocates of internal investment against those seeking the higher returns available from global markets (see also Clark's final chapter).

In Germany, the reform process has been, as Schmähl shows, even more contentious. In fact, the political consensus is favour of reform and restructuring the public–private divide has been shown to be fragile and very vulnerable to party politics. Time and time again, elections have been fought, won, and lost on the issue of pension reform. During the 1990s, the discounting of earnings-related PAYG state pensions and the conversion of many German corporations, politicians, and economists to the merits of global finance, focused attention on the role of private and occupational pension savings in developing German capital markets. And yet, reform has been modest and incremental in effect. Furthermore, as Schmähl shows, new market-based pensions systems are proving complex and confusing. The take-up rate has been disappointing, and it is widely acknowledged that these schemes may do little for the welfare of those groups most in need of supplementary assistance. As German economic performance has faltered over the past decade, and as federal budgets have gone beyond the terms set by the Stability and Growth Pact, long-term pension liabilities assume greater and greater significance. In many respects, the German predicament epitomises the European dilemma—how to resolve intergenerational conflicts between long-established social policy provision and the promise of global financial futures. The German experience has long-term implications for the whole of Europe.

In France, as Palier demonstrates, there is widespread unease with pension reforms that would rely upon or allow the invasion of Anglo-American financial institutions. And yet, Palier believes funded schemes are urgently required to supplement the dwindling value of state-sponsored pensions. Furthermore, many analysts believe that funded pensions offer the chance to build new types of financial institutions consistent with the imperatives of the 'new' economy. To date, opposition from the left and from public sector trade unions has blocked change. Disparities between levels of public and private sector pensions are marked and, if anything, appear to be widening. How to generate reform along agreed lines to collective satisfaction while avoiding further intrusions of Anglo-American institutions into European (specifically French) economic affairs remains the central political issue. Currently, any attempt by government to introduce reform provokes demonstrations and protest in major city centres in the name of social solidarity, invoked as central to French republican ideals.

As others have noted (e.g. Bonoli and Palier 2000*b*; Hinrichs 2001), pension schemes in European states are progressing along a similar trajectory. Basic state provision is increasingly contained; its funding is more than ever reliant upon national taxation than on social security contributions. As a consequence, greater interest in funded schemes has emerged, varying in accordance with political circumstance and economic objective. Where funded pension provision is established, the state and its associated official agencies retain a central regulatory role: drawing up new rules, participating as market agents, regulating sales, investments and fund management, and determining forms of pension governance. The terms 'private' and 'public' are blurred in these circumstances—private schemes are developed to serve public goals. More importantly, the terms public and private are used to identify other desirable features of the pension regime. Therefore, 'private' may denote individual (as opposed to collective and redistributive), funded (as opposed to PAYG), or defined contribution (as opposed to defined or salary-based benefit). Within the Anglo-Saxon world, the language of public and private takes on other dimensions: the distinctions between the separate realms of public provision and private responsibility have deeper resonance in liberal political economy. Here, the economic ideology of individual responsibility and rational choice (rather than mundane budgetary imperative) has helped to promote pension reform.

As Emmerson shows for the United Kingdom, the Labour government's agenda has been to extend private (personal or occupational) cover and to target state pensions on the poor. At the same time, of course, that which was assumed fixed and secure (employer-sponsored defined benefit plans) has been turned upside down by new accounting standards, the downturn in the global financial system, and declining contribution rates amongst those now increasingly covered by defined contribution plans. Recurrent rounds of pension reform, designed to foster personal saving outside of employer-sponsored schemes, have produced a complex range of public and private pension entitlements. But state policies designed to encourage market mechanisms to foster private personal responsibility have not been as nearly successful as once hoped. The 'stakeholder' initiative has not made coverage for low wage-earners any easier or more likely. In fact, notwithstanding the relatively secure UK fiscal position (compared to its nearest continental neighbours), the UK system seems increasingly problematic. Unlike their continental counterparts, British pension policies are threatened less by financial than by political non-sustainability, as constant legislative modifications to an already complex system reduce transparency, discourage participation, and store up future electoral pressure for more state support.

Arguments against the conversion of public pensions into private personal provision are also found in Munnell's chapter on the United States.

There, Social Security offers PAYG pensions considerably more generous than their British counterparts. With the stock market boom of the 1990s, the idea of transforming collective provision into funded, personal accounts received much attention and comment. Advocates in favour of converting a portion of social security into individual investment accounts (analogous to defined contribution funds) claim that this would benefit financial markets and contributors by opening up the gains available from equity-based investments to all. Munnell argues that this approach is based on a serious misassumption; the conversion of a collective scheme into multiple personal accounts cannot, of itself, enhance social security funding, or improve returns to individuals, or help financial markets. If this strategy were adopted, she believes that state trust fund management would probably offer better returns than the collective consequences of individual choice. This issue is widely debated; there are increasing studies done about the comparative investment performance of public versus private pension funds. At its core, though, is the idea that pension security can be found in the performance of markets as well as nation-states. This is why some argue that pension security ought to be an individual rather than a collective responsibility.

In a final chapter, Clark explores the most general of all issues: the prospects for pension security over the coming decades. He exposes the dilemmas facing policy-makers and the public when choosing between public and private systems of old age protection. Here, political risk (that future nation-state pensions will be reduced) confronts economic risk (that market returns or the pension provider will fail to deliver as promised). Our continental European contributors demonstrate how governments have circumscribed market-based pension provision in order to guarantee pension security; but, of course, they also show that these guarantees are unsustainable in the face of the likely burdens associated with the retirement of the baby-boom generation. At the same time, employer-sponsored schemes are buckling under the weight of recent economic events. Market uncertainties show that the earlier reputation of funded schemes rested on assumptions regarding market performance that were themselves the product of historically contingent circumstances. Market-dependent income cannot be taken for granted. So neither European nor Anglo-American pension provision offers a secure retirement for the baby-boom generation. If the public–private divide is redrawn in favour of private provision, it will be done on the basis of apparent nation-state fiscal incapacity and guesses made about the long-term path of global integration, development, and investment performance (Clark 2003).

In summary, we offer a collective response to the three main questions we set our contributors at the outset of this project. First, Anglo-American and European governments alike have been seduced by the spectacular returns available on global financial markets in recent years. Hence, political leaders have sought to deal with financial and demographic pressures on pension security by raising the age of retirement and by limiting tax-based provision to make space for funded schemes. In so doing, political pressures have invoked greater state regulation of market operations: all the more so as uneven market performance in the new millenium has exposed the insecurities involved in such strategies. The consequence of growing faith in market mechanisms, moving to our second question, has been a shift away from the state as provider towards the state as guarantor, thereby reshaping old boundaries between public and private responsibility. Previous distinctions have become increasingly blurred, as many governments have sought to clarify market operations in order to facilitate the transition from collective and public to personal and private pensions.

As recent events surrounding reforms in both Germany and Britain indicate, the problem is not simply one of getting the finances right, but also of building collective trust and confidence in new systems—the necessary foundations for collective participation. In the light of the multiple agendas that must be served in the process of reconciling old age security with the exigencies of global finance, this is no easy task. However, while a common trajectory of pension reform is clearly visible, countries have embarked from very different starting points. Established systems, of pension provision already in place have heavily influenced the nature of the pension debate, degrees of public acceptance of new schemes, and the extent of change. The introduction of a new policy strategy on diverse established settlements has generated further different geographies of pension provision, but no convergence towards a single model.

At present, the future of pension security currently hangs in the balance. The rules of the game are being redefined. In response to the third question, we have witnessed how global finance has threatened the future fiscal feasibility of nation-based welfare states. As is widely acknowledged, sovereign states are comparatively powerless in contrast to the capacity of financial institutions to instigate massive transfers between markets in response to changing economic circumstances. Consequent fiscal retrenchment has required cuts in public welfare; pensions, as the main budget burden, have been a major target for politicians seeking to restore financial probity. Yet the much-vaunted 'drive to the bottom' (with nation-states competitively cutting public welfare in frantic attempts to attract international investment) has not occurred. Further, the tendency to endow global financial markets with a greater role in the provision of pension security has stimulated political demands for greater transparency and accountability from market agents.

Public interest has been drawn to market operations: to identify (and punish) fraudulent behaviours and to clarify distributions of responsibility and risk. Early examples have included the imposition of international accountancy standards and the prolonged negotiations surrounding the creation of a single financial market in the EU. Hence, the growing influence of global financial transactions has revived dialogue between states and markets: the former needing the latter to fund internal investment and future pension security, the latter seeking the endorsement of the former to extend the legitimacy (and thus, the credibility) of its operations. At international as well as national levels, therefore, the need to establish new conventions of common practice to reduce uncertainty and to guarantee collective acceptance of (and participation in) new systems remains paramount.

Hence, as analysts of pension policy, we rediscover the debates surrounding old age security that characterised discussions before the First World War—reflecting the varied merits of different typologies of funding, of regulation, and of public accountability. Underpinning prevailing notions of private pension provision lie a myriad of different systems encompassing individual and collective provision and public and private administration and management. Such variations on the theme of public–private partnership demonstrate the panoply of arrangements that are possible—and the ways that the state, through regulation and the law, constantly shapes and reshapes their operation. Distinctions between public and private form a curtain of convenience behind which new conventions are being established, and a reconstruction of governance and responsibility is taking place around the world and in Europe, the United Kingdom, and the United States.

NOTES

1. Compare, for example, David Miller's (2000) manifesto proclaiming the virtues of the nation-state with Martin Feldstein's (2002) assessment of long-term pension funding within and across Europe's many borders.

2. A fixed retirement age of was first introduced in the United Kingdom and other major EU member states after the Second World War. This required recipients of a state pension to leave the labour market altogether. Before this date, schemes following the Bismarckean precedent awarded an old age pension once the recipients' earning power had fallen below a specified level. In Britain, a state pension was offered at a fixed age, but the pensioner could still continue working.
3. Empirical research derived from a variety of academic disciplines (geography, history, anthropology, sociology, and cultural studies) demonstrates that apparently irrational behaviour and decision-making is widespread. Social identity and social or family commitments help set parameters on individual choice. Fashion, the 'desire to belong', means that personal choice is also expected to reflect and reinforce more transitional loyalties; this also plays havoc with assumed rationality in individual behaviour (Clark and Marshall 2002). Observation of long-term behaviour in competitive quasi-markets demonstrates how personal contacts and experience play a major role in establishing the confidence and trust that determine the selection of market products; this is much more significant than simple evidence of 'best value' (Whiteside 1997).

CHAPTER

1

Historical Perspectives and the Politics of Pension Reform

Noel Whiteside

1.1. INTRODUCTION

Over the last two decades, pension reforms in Britain have focused on the recalibration of the division between public and private responsibility for old age security, to contain future state liability in this area. This process has exposed a range of different implications hidden behind the vocabularies of public and private. Transfers from public to private may signify more reliance on funded pension provision, a switch from collective to individual protection, and/or a change from a defined benefit pension to a defined contribution scheme. These reforms have aimed to transfer risk from state budgets to other agencies. However, as recent reforms in Britain, Germany, and Sweden have demonstrated, the recalibration of a public–private divide in pension provision has not signified a simple revival of a free market in pensions, nor the return of control to the company, the professional association, or the mutual aid society. On the contrary, new initiatives have been accompanied by a further extension of state regulation of pension systems rather than its removal. Such regulation offers security and is designed to raise public confidence, to win support for new schemes. The process of reform has, thus, generated a multiplicity of new partnerships (or mixes) of public and private responsibility for pensions that is making old distinctions increasingly hard to sustain. However, as this paper will argue, such arrangements are hardly new. The rhetoric of a public–private divide in this area, which resonates through the Anglo-Saxon literature, does not bear close inspection.

This chapter will unpack the historical complexities underpinning the public–private divide with specific reference to the development of occupational, professional, or firm-based pensions in the decades immediately following the Second World War and the ways in which these became accommodated within state schemes. The principle focus will be on Britain, comparing developments there with some key European countries during the years of economic recovery, when systems of old age provision put in place immediately after the war were reappraised. In the 1950s, higher wages and rising living standards were not shared by pensioners: as economic prosperity returned, so European governments of varied political complexions sought to adapt earnings-related pension systems to relieve the exigencies of old age poverty. In some instances, notably in Britain, the Netherlands, and France, this involved the adaptation of established occupational pension schemes to serve policy purposes, albeit in very different ways. Careful inspection of the historical record from this angle, thereby throws into question the existence of families (or worlds) of welfare states that have traditionally considered these three countries to be rooted in very different traditions.

The role politics has played in developing multifaceted systems of pension provision will be our specific concern. Public–private distinctions became blurred because all governments wanted to promote earnings-related old age protection, but adopted very different means to achieve this end. The first section of this paper traces the debate surrounding British pension reform during the 1960s, in the period preceding the introduction of the State Earnings Related Pension Scheme (SERPS). This demonstrates how British governments of all political complexions carefully protected a public–private divide in pension provision at enormous administrative cost: a problem that SERPS did nothing to correct. The second section briefly describes the history of other European pension developments in the same period, demonstrating how pension improvement was secured within varied political trajectories. The third section offers a comparative overview of these developments and concludes that, taken all forms of political and governmental intervention together, the distinction between public and private in this area has been (and continues to be) arbitrary and eclectic.

The object here is twofold. First, it is to draw attention to the difficulties that have emerged when the way pensions are funded is given more political attention than how they are governed. Public accountability is central to public trust; in its absence, market-based systems will fail. Second, the paper will question current assumptions about divisions between public and private sectors: less to argue that one side or the other should be the proper providers of old age security than to contest common distinctions between state and market. For, by establishing how the two are interrelated, the plausibility of mixed solutions becomes more readily apparent and more positively feasible.

1.2. PROMOTING PARTNERSHIP: BRITISH PENSION REFORM IN THE 1960S

> The growth of private pension schemes is to be encouraged; it produces social stability. In the long run, moreover, it should reduce the individual's dependence on the Government scheme and perhaps even enable the Government to get away from the expensive doctrine of 'universality'—and perhaps lead to the adoption of benefit payments according to need.[1]
>
> (Treasury memo 1960)

In Britain, the post-war settlement initiated a universal state pension scheme, extending contributory state pensions initially introduced for blue-collar workers in 1925. Unlike the 1925 pensions, there was to be no contracting out by public sector workers who had their own schemes; post-war state pensions covered everyone. The principles of universalism and of flat-rate contributions in return for a flat-rate benefit, central to the 1942 Beveridge Report, were embodied in the post-war Labour government's (1946) National Insurance Act. However, post-war pension rates remained below commonly accepted levels of subsistence; in consequence, old age pensioners without other resources were forced to top up state benefits with means-tested National Assistance. As means tests were associated with the pre-war poor laws, many old people proved reluctant to do this, leading to a rediscovery of old age poverty in the early 1960s (Able-Smith and Townsend 1961). Post-war state pensions were always designed to act merely as a safety net, to be augmented by personal savings and private provision. 'The State, in organising security should not stifle incentive, opportunity, responsibility,' Beveridge wrote in 1942, and '. . . in establishing a national minimum, it should leave room and encouragement for voluntary action by each individual to provide more than that minimum for himself and his family' (Beveridge 1942: 6–7). In the event, even that minimum was not forthcoming. In exchange for the immediate introduction of full post-war state pensions (as opposed to their phasing in over time, as happened, for example, in France), this national minimum was redefined downwards (Macnicol 1994), thereby reinforcing the need for supplementation from other resources.

The first pension panic in the United Kingdom occurred, not in the 1980s, but in the late 1950s. Official forecasts concluded that, thanks to demographic change and the impact of inflation, state expenditure on pensions would double between 1960 and 1970, as Exchequer contributions to National Insurance (NI) were being cut from 33 to 14 per cent. Inflation had corroded state pension values: conservative governments in the 1950s claimed that high NI benefits were a waste of public money and preferred to target welfare on the very poor. In 1957 Germany introduced pensions graduated according to earnings on a universal and compulsory basis. Such developments provoked criticisms of the Conservative government on the grounds that the British welfare state was falling behind. A scheme developed by Professor Richard Titmuss (London School of Economics) advocated the introduction of inflation-proofed, universal, state-run, earnings-related, funded pensions that would guarantee old age income at 50 per cent of previous earnings. This was adopted as official Labour party policy in 1957. One of Labour's objectives was to raise national savings and the powers of the state (as opposed to private pension funds) to direct investment to capital projects in the national interest (Thane 2000: 373–6). This implied, its critics argued, an extension of nationalisation, both by undermining the attraction of existing occupational pension schemes and by extending state control, as principle investor, over private business. It was opposed by the pensions industry because of its effects on private provision (Hannah 1986: 56) and by Beveridge himself for its cost, its potentially inflationary effects, and for undermining private incentives to save (Harris 1977: 464; Thane 2000: 376). In response, the Conservatives proposed non-indexed, earnings-related state pensions with incentives for firms offering occupational pensions to contract out of the state scheme. [2]

Following the Conservative election victory of 1959 this alternative was put in place. The new scheme represented a reversal of post-war pension policy strategy, returning to the principles embodied in the 1925 legislation: the object was not to extend public obligation, but to contain it by financially penalising all employers who did not opt for private provision. Whereas in the late 1940s the private pension provider had had to accommodate the introduction of the state scheme, now the positions were reversed as the state earnings-related scheme, offering merely residual protection, was designed around the private sector. The object for those on the political right was the eventual abolition of NI. 'A pension is part of remuneration, one of the fringe benefits of a good job that should be negotiated between employer and employee', as an

Institute of Economic Affairs report put it. 'The State has no business here' (Seldon 1960: 34). The new scheme raised graduated NI contributions well above the sums justified by the introduction of a meagre graduated state pension: this was deliberately designed to make surplus contributions underwrite the rising cost of the Beveridge flat-rate scheme. Further, the 1959 Act allowed contributions to be raised every 5 years, without any concomitant rise in pension benefits: the first such hike in National Insurance Contributions (UK) (NICs) was introduced in 1963. NICs were, however, substantially reduced for those electing to contract out. An additional financial incentive thus supplemented the extended tax concessions for occupational or company pensions already offered to employers under the 1956 Finance Act. Moreover, public funded schemes (local government funds and the pensions supplied by the nationalised industries) were enabled, under the 1961 Trustee Investments Act, to place up to 50 per cent of their investments in equities. Thus, stimulated by tax concessions and general government sponsorship, pension funds came to represent over one-third of private savings in the British economy by the mid-1970s—a proportion substantially above that found in the United States (Hannah 1986: 48–51).

The object of Conservative policy was to extend private occupational provision: in this regard, the 1959 legislation was a success. Numbers covered by private schemes rose, from 7.5 million workers (1956) to 9 million (1960) to 11 million (1963) to 12 million (1966) (including 4 million in the public sector, nearly all contracted out of the 1959 Act). This peaked in 1967 at 49 per cent of the employed population (Hannah 1986: 67). By the mid-1960s, contributions to private schemes were running at £1 billion p.a., with employers funding two-thirds of this sum.[3] This trend, bolstered by high returns on equities in the 1950s and 1960s, generated official optimism. Actuarial predictions forecasted continuous further growth, and private scheme cover would reach 13–14 million employees by 1980.[4] Such rates of expansion raised hopes that occupational schemes might replace, not merely supplement, universal state provision. However, not all company schemes contracted out of the 1959 Act. Of the 8 million covered by occupational or private schemes in 1966, only 4.5 million (in 24,000 schemes) were formally exempted;[5] the rest simply topped up to offer a pension package commonly calculated on a defined benefit basis. Treasury fears that extensive state regulation of private superannuation would drive out occupational schemes kept official intervention to a minimum.[6] The Inland Revenue's requirements aside, non-contracted-out schemes were subject to no additional regulation (even though employee scheme membership might be a condition of employment). The Revenue itself was more interested in Exchequer receipts (imposing a ceiling on pension contribution tax relief) than in actuarial verification of funded pensions (Hannah 1986: 52–6). Schemes that did contract out had to guarantee retirement pensions at equivalent age and level to the state scheme and to protect the rights of workers of 5 years' standing who transferred employment—hardly onerous requirements taken the low level of state benefits introduced by the 1959 Act.[7]

This light touch regulation might have been popular with employers and the pensions industry, but the 1959 settlement was not problem-free. First, inflation quickly eroded the value of the state's graduated pensions, forcing more pensioners without additional cover onto means-tested national assistance. This lack of index-linking had been deliberate, in part designed to encourage employers, who were quite unable to guarantee rising values of post-award pensions under the equivalent pension rule, to contract out. However, this meant that the Conservative scheme was widely criticised as a swindle, stimulating popular interest in Labour's alternative proposals. Second, graduated pensions covered very few women (2 million out of 12 million by 1966) and contracted-out schemes were not obliged to offer cover for widows. Hence, reform did nothing for those who lived longest and who were most likely to suffer old age poverty. Third, efforts to protect the pension rights of transferees (from contracted-out to non-contracted-out firms, between public sector and private sector employment) proved inadequate and confusing. Only 8 per cent of employees who recovered previous contributions on leaving a job reinvested the money for pension purposes; the obligations of transferring firms to secure future pension rights of departing employees remained haphazard and uneven, particularly between contracted-out and non-contracted-out schemes.[8]

In the public sector, transfer of pension rights between different employers (local authorities and nationalised industries as well as civil service employees) was in place. However, shifts between public and private sectors remained problematic. Public sector pensions involved 500 different administrations that covered 1,500 employing authorities and schemes, all embodying different retirement ages, varying contributory obligations and pension rights that varied according to job status, gender, and years of service.[9] All had encountered administrative complications in ensuring equity between pre- and post-1948 pension rights for retirees. The 1959 legislation added to these difficulties, as most (but not all) public sector workers were contracted out (Rhodes 1965: ch. 6). Administrative complexity, transference problems, and varying pension obligations and rights all combined to handicap the public sector worker seeking to understand his or her future pension (Rhodes 1965: ch. 8). As employees of nationalised industries had been in private sector employment before the war, the combinations of pension rights were further complicated and were impenetrable to the inexperienced, untrained mind.

Finally, the solvency of some private schemes was distinctly dubious. Although the Inland Revenue required employers to demonstrate that a retirement fund existed and was viable, this did not guarantee its solvency. A 1960 report by the Government Actuary showed that only 50 per cent of non-contracted-out schemes were insured and only 50 per cent of the non-insured were actuarially certified. Many were extremely small; 75 per cent of 40,000 private schemes had less than 50 members.[10] This provoked demands, within Whitehall and outside, for more extensive state regulation. 'If the State allows compulsory deductions to be made from employees' pay packets for occupational pension purposes', a Ministry of Social Security official minuted the Treasury, 'then arguably the state has a duty to see that the employee gets "value for money" for what he pays'.[11] At this point, such demands fell on deaf ears. Arguing that privately provided pensions represented deferred salary, Treasury officials claimed that collective bargaining—not state regulation—was responsible for securing improvements to private schemes. Occupational pensions could not make adjustments for variable rates of inflation in advance; withdrawal of state approval for occupational schemes would hurt workers covered by them more than employers who ran them.[12] However, such arguments concealed the fundamental reasons for unquestioning Treasury support for private pension provision. Occupational schemes contained demands on the public purse while funding private sector investment. By the mid-1960s, annual contributions under private schemes offered significant sums both for internal investment in UK equities and for the growing London market in financial services and products.[13] Hence, governments of both parties sustained and promoted retirement security in the private sphere.

Even so, with Labour's return to office in 1964, official policy was set to change tack. Labour's own plans had been modified since Titmuss' original proposals: the 1964 manifesto promised to introduce wage-related pensions at 50 per cent of average lifetime earnings for all, on a partially funded basis, but contracting out of approved occupational schemes would continue.[14] To prevent earnings-related NI contributions being used to subsidise the basic flat-rate state pension (by 1966 *c.*£1 million p.a. was converted in this fashion[15]). Labour would abolish the flat-rate element and weight earnings-related pensions to help the low paid to rise above means-tested levels.[16] The pension element of NI contributions was to be separated, creating a National Superannuation Fund, to be managed by Trustees charged with its investment in equities, not government stocks:

> Trustees . . . will have the same opportunities to carry out profitable investment of their funds as the trustees of private pension schemes and insurance companies. Thus they will . . . ensure that the national savings piling up in the Pension Fund will be used to help our national capital investment programme.
>
> (Labour Party 1963)

The new scheme also offered quick maturity (full earnings-related pensions would be available within 10 years), cover for widows and dependants, pre- and post-award index-linking. While retaining contracting out, it aimed to extend cover to the 7 million workers still excluded from occupational schemes.[17]

Such changes carried implications for established pension schemes as well as for UK investment finance; from the start, it stimulated opposition from insurance companies, inside Whitehall and within the Labour movement. Treasury officials found no merit in a scheme, which, in the words of one official, was 'piecemeal nationalisation by the back door'.[18] The main objections addressed inflation, private investment, and the public finances. First, although higher contributions (estimated in 1964 at 15 per cent of earnings) would initially be deflationary, the likely effects on wage demands, production costs, and higher consumption among the elderly would stimulate inflation, thereby endangering exports, the balance of payments, and confidence in sterling. Second, in the context of the Labour government's other welfare spending (higher family allowances and basic state pensions), should such extensive resources should be devoted to a scheme whose benefits favoured the better off? Third, there were unanswered questions associated with the National Superannuation Fund's investment. If placed in equities, as Labour originally intended, market prices would be inflated and interest rates on gilt-edged would be forced up, raising the cost of government borrowing for future expenditure on new universities, road building, and general industrial modernisation. Further, state investment in equities set a precedent for other departments, who would demand similar privileges: '. . . if government is going to join in the rush to get out of gilt-edged', one Treasury official noted 'it is difficult to see who can be expected to stay in'.[19] This was a disingenuous argument in the light of the 1961 legislation freeing public sector pension funds to do precisely that.

Conversely, if vested in government securities (as required by Labour's capital building programme), the Fund's obligations would eventually become another additional burden on the public accounts. Finally, the scheme posed a threat to established occupational pension funds: by displacing private investment, it might undermine London's capital markets as well as internal investment for industry. In an era of public expenditure restraint, and with the Fund's obligations due to increase over time, all this appeared infinitely resistible.

As might be expected, the insurance industry and its clients argued that Labour's proposals would initiate a decline in private pension provision. As the government promised widows' pensions, index-linking, early maturity, and superior transferability for mobile workers, the life industry feared that higher NICs would squeeze contributions to private schemes as contracting out would become less viable and both sides of industry would resist contributing to two schemes.[20] It could also point out that the state proposals did not offer such good value to the individual contributor as established occupational schemes and commercial alternatives (because the government diverted more help to dependants and transferees). In view of the expanding number of defined benefit occupational pensions and taking note of the higher contributions required by Labour's scheme, objections to a state takeover were also found in wage-earning circles. Trade unions in the nationalised industries in particular already possessed occupational cover. In some major firms, other unions had won occupational pensions through collective bargaining from employers in lieu of higher wages, periodically held down by official policies of wage restraint. Not surprisingly, therefore, the Trade Union Congress (UK) (TUC) itself opposed any interference with occupational or company pensions, while supporting a rise in the basic state pension.[21] Both sides of industry were thus united in favour of contracting out. Finally, the Cooperative movement, whose multiple schemes covered 2.25 million members, opposed any reform that allowed the state Superannuation Fund to invest in its commercial competitors.

The only support for a comprehensive, universal, state-run scheme of earnings-related superannuation along the lines proposed by Titmuss, was found in the Ministry of Social Security. Here, the division of NICs to create a national superannuation fund invested in equities found its fullest endorsement.[22] A single state-run national fund, based on earnings-related contributions and concomitant benefits in old age, would reinforce collective belief in the need to save: this would probably help (rather than harm) private savings for the same purpose.

Further, this department had extensive experience of the complexities, confusion, and expense involved in administering the existing contracting out system, which, it argued, should be abolished. However, this lone voice emanated from the lowliest of Whitehall's spending departments and its views were easily ignored. Richard Crossman, appointed as Secretary of State to the newly created Department of Health and Social Security in 1968 and charged with introducing much-delayed legislation on pension reform, found political opposition to a Titmuss approach altogether too formidable to be contemplated:

> it was obvious that if we introduced our scheme without any provision for contracting out, all the good private schemes would have to be cancelled and there would be a terrible row . . . They [the insurance industry] would tell their members that the wicked Labour government was depriving them of their pensions. This was politically very dangerous indeed . . . So I announced we wanted a genuine partnership between public and private pensioneering . . . in months of negotiation we did work out an enormously complicated way of fitting some 60,000 private schemes alongside our new earnings-related state pension. No other country has tried to do it.
>
> (Crossman 1972: 20–1)

Two White Papers, published in January and November 1969,[23] laid down the new partnership's terms; partial contracting-out would prevent private schemes cutting back to accommodate the new state scheme. Every effort was made to preserve, even to extend, occupational provision.[24] Interestingly, the option of securing personal earnings-related old-age security through commercial insurance agencies was rejected. 'It would be impracticable . . . the control of a universal network of private schemes, even if one could be set up, would create formidable administrative problems both for the government and for the schemes themselves.'[25] This judgement, pertinent to more recent discussion on UK pension reform, guaranteed that policy would continue to consolidate provision along previously established lines.

Although private pension schemes varied widely in terms of their security, few new regulations were imposed on companies wishing to contract out. State officials bent over backwards to avoid any interference with the private sector: there was to be no central registry of occupational schemes, no state inspectorate, no central fund to guarantee solvency. 'The danger is' a Department of Employment memorandum proclaimed 'that the establishment by the State of a central fund or agency might be regarded as inconsistent with the general desire that, to the greatest possible extent, occupational pension schemes should be left to manage their own affairs.'[26] Old Labour he may have been, but

Richard Crossman could not have tried harder to shore up the private sector.

The new scheme did not completely abandon Labour's original intentions. National Superannuation Fund balances were still to be invested, to create a partially and temporarily funded scheme. However, basic state pension rates had risen in 1966 and other benefits for long-term claimants (the disabled and the long-term unemployed) had to be upgraded accordingly; this, together with income lost by contracting out, ate into future balances available for investment. In the White Paper of January 1969, the Government Actuary calculated that the surplus of income over expenditure would last until 1987–88, when the balance would shift the other way and a review of contributory rates would be required.[27] The White Paper contained little information on how, in the interim, balances were to be invested, or about who should be charged with their investment.[28] In the event, the issue was academic: the National Superannuation and Social Insurance Bill emerged from its committee stage in May 1970, only to fall when Prime Minister Wilson brought the General Election forward from October to June, when Labour lost to the Conservatives.

Sir Keith Joseph picked up the idea of funded state-sponsored superannuation in legislation passed in 1973. This also established the Occupational Pensions Board (less a regulatory agency than a source of information to inform future policy). When the Conservative government fell in 1974 (and following Labour's rejection of Joseph's pension legislation), Crossman's old bill was revised by Barbara Castle. In 1975, the SERPS was introduced. This was both more extensive (and more generous) than Crossman's earlier proposals. The state not only permitted contracting out, but underwrote the viability of established schemes that chose to do so—a move that extended public liability in an unprecedented fashion (thanks to the fact that SERPS pensions were index-linked), which governments have been trying to reduce ever since. Such extensive public commitments effectively founded a new public–private partnership that, in its turn, was superseded by the social security legislation of 1986 that introduced fiscal incentives for individuals to take out a private Personal Pension Plan. The following debacle of mis-selling, compensation, and the emergence of New Labour's alternative proposals have already attracted extensive academic attention (e.g. Bonoli 2000: also Emmerson, this volume). Without rehearsing this subsequent history, we should note how so-called private pensions have become subject to ever-growing amounts of official regulation under a multiplicity of new regulatory authorities, in an effort to iron out problems. In the process, distinctions between public and private became increasingly blurred. During the 1990s, under the Major administration and subsequently under New Labour, the state moved to reconstruct market behaviours of firms and their agents across the whole range of financial service products, with the object of securing individualised social protection for all. In so doing, public officials have been attempting to rewrite established conventions governing pension provision in the hitherto private sector. What has emerged is a public–private hybrid as officials attempt to adapt the market to secure political objectives with astoundingly restricted success.

The preceding section outlines how the retention of a public–private divide became a principal political objective in Britain during the 1960s and beyond. While earnings-related pensions were desirable, the primacy of the private sector in their provision offered the means to reconcile old age security with the need for industrial investment and the development of financial services at minimal public cost. In keeping with the principles of liberal political economy, both political parties implicitly or explicitly endorsed this strategy, aiming to keep state provision in a residual role. As Crossman noted, no other country tried to weave a state earnings-related pension scheme around 60,000 private, more or less autonomous alternatives, creating in the process an administrative nightmare for government, employers, and the financial services industry whose repercussions survive to this day. This complex system is quite impenetrable to the non-expert. It is, thus, virtually unaccountable, politically speaking. It creates costly administrative problems for both private and public sectors. It discourages labour mobility, particularly among those who have established a partial right to a company or public pension. It offers nothing (or, at least, very little) to the most vulnerable future pensioners, largely women whose broken records of employment are due to their domestic responsibilities. For four decades, governments have tried to shift the burden of pension finance onto the private sector. In 2002, numbers without any—or at least inadequate—private or occupational cover were roughly the same as in the late 1960s (around 7 million). One might conclude that it is high time to stop flogging this distinctly dead horse.

1.3. COMPARATIVE TRAJECTORIES: THE EUROPEAN DIMENSION

Britain was not the only European state to reappraise welfare provision for the elderly in the immediate post-war decades. As economic recovery assured rising prosperity, so pressure grew to raise pensions accordingly. Elsewhere in Europe, however, earnings-related provision became located within more rationalised public–private partnerships, operating largely under government auspices and covered by the overarching umbrella of labour law.

The fundamental difference between European and Scandinavian welfare and pension policies in the post-war era and their UK counterparts is reflected in traditions of joint or tripartite decision making and the role of labour law (and government) in underwriting (and extending) employment contracts and collective agreements (Gamet 2000). The foundations of much continental labour law rest on principles of public order: these determine norms governing employment, laying down the rights and obligations of employers and employed (including compliance with social security legislation). Formal collective agreements can set minimum standards. Some states may rationalise these agreements by extending their terms and coverage in a range of predefined ways. Hence, both pension agreements created by collective industrial bargaining as well as those set up under social security legislation are offered the protection of the law. As a result, the depth of the divide between public and private pensions is nowhere near as profound as it is in Britain: established avenues exist through which governments can influence the nature and extent of occupational pension provision outside the direct remit of social security legislation. Furthermore, employers' organisations and trade unions play a central role in administering national social security schemes as well as occupational or enterprise-based systems, reflecting long-established conventions of codetermination in corporate governance in specific cases (strong in, for example, Germany, the Netherlands, and Sweden, but less so in France). The roots of such differences can be traced back to Bismarckean systems of social insurance governance that were revived and re-established in the aftermath of the Second World War. For, although widely acclaimed as providing the foundation for a new social order, the Beveridge system of administering insurance-based pensions through a central, impersonal bureaucracy found no imitators in Western Europe after 1945.

Historically, occupational or firm-based pension schemes were as widespread in continental Europe as in Britain. They had developed for broadly similar reasons: to guarantee the loyalty of key employees, to offset the attractions of state pensions available to workers in the public sector, and to provide employers with another means to facilitate internal labour management. Fiscal concessions to promote the spread of such schemes were common, but variance in state social security meant that occupational and professional provision was integrated into the wider sphere of economic and social politics in diverse ways. In some respects, after the war, each government was faced with a fait accompli. Well-established, legally endowed pension rights of various types were deep rooted; they formed part of a cultural, legal, and institutional heritage that was highly resistant to the prospect of radical change. Hence, post-war processes of extending (and raising) pension rights became one of modifying pre-existent arrangements. With the possible exception of France, the equilibrium between public and private responsibility swung towards greater state-based provision in continental Europe during the immediate post-war decades. Sweden and the Netherlands, for instance, came to provide a basic citizenship pension independent from either contributory record or means test. This protected women (who had difficulty in establishing sufficient contributions), and avoided the problem of means-tests which were widely understood to discourage thrift while raising administrative costs. Adherence to defined benefit pensions was widespread within occupational or professional sectors. However, funded schemes, with the notable exceptions of the Netherlands and Switzerland, were more rare, reflecting how wartime monetary disruption and post-war inflation had damaged faith in the security offered by collective savings. Finally, the governance of occupational and professional pensions was vested from the start with the social partners: a feature partly reflecting widespread joint legal ownership of schemes and their financial reserves, partly the orthodoxy of social solidarity which they embodied. The structure, scope, and boundaries of such solidarity were as contested in the private sector as they were in public schemes (Baldwin 1990). However, the principle that the interests of the insured should be guaranteed through representation on governing councils has a much longer history in continental Europe than it has in Britain.

In Germany as in Britain, fiscal incentives encouraging company pension schemes originated in the 1920s, so that state policy focused not on the creation of separate pension funds, but on guaranteeing the adequacy of company balances to meet these liabilities. Large companies adopted the book reserve model that allowed pension savings to be internally invested, while others preferred group insurance or the creation of pension funds. In the course of the interwar years, these schemes expanded. The association of company welfare with modern scientific management fed into the sophisticated systems surrounding the DAF and Nazi labour policies, structuring rewards around work performance and tying the worker's present and future income to the firm (Fiedler 1996). As statutory social insurance funds were raided to pay for rearmament and the war, so company pensions retained their importance for old age security. In the aftermath of 1945 and the monetary reforms of 1948, German pension funds lost value as they were converted from Reichsmark into Deutschmark on a ratio of ten to one (pensioners under the state insurance scheme benefited from a conversion based on parity). Contributors to book reserve schemes were less penalised, as their future pensions relied not on monetary reserves, but on current contributions and future company profits. Companies continued to offer such pension guarantees, not least because workers' contributions met urgent post-war requirements for internal investment. This underpinned the widespread consensus, shared by employers and trade unions and reinforced by returns on growth in the 1950s and 1960s, in support of the book reserve system. By the 1990s, two out of three salaried workers were covered by these complementary pensions, and invested balances were valued at 250 thousand million Deutschmarks (Reynaud and Tamburi 1994: ch. 4). Not all companies operated a book reserve system. Many smaller ones preferred to vest pension obligations with an insurance company that, in contrast to its Anglo-American counterparts, tended to invest in long-term assets, thereby constraining the development of a market in equities.

In Germany, codetermination in industrial affairs extended to collective management of earnings-related state social insurance funds, which also operate on a PAYG basis. And the legacy of worker representation on works councils, dating back to the First World War and substantially reinforced by the Weimar republic in the 1920s, translated into joint representation in the management of company pension schemes as well. Hence, the principles of social democracy and the social market were equally embedded in company pensions and national pensions policies. Such principles also underpinned long-term investments that, in collaboration with the Landesbanken, aimed to secure viable local economic development (Clark 2000). The public pension initiative of 1957 was a strategy to reconcile the need for wage restraint in a key period of economic recovery (deferring wage rises into old age), with recognition that a liberal market economy was failing to redistribute newly created wealth in an equitable fashion. Following this legislation, state pensions rose by 60 per cent (Abelshauser 1996: 138). Deferred salary was to secure the industrial future: through the Land (under the state pension scheme), or through the company (under the book reserve system)—there was no question of allowing the latter to somehow contract out of obligations under the former. Fiscal policy and state contributions thus combined to secure the same objective. As the pension was deferred salary, and thus wage earners' property, workers' interests were represented in the management of both types of pension provision.

As in Germany, unions and employers combined to realise social security in the Netherlands within the remit of legislation passed by the state. Here, in the post-war years, universal welfare cover replaced state-subsidised voluntary schemes that had dominated welfare provision before 1939. Through the medium of national bargaining under new joint bodies such as the Foundation for Labour (1944) and the Socio-Economic Council (1950), state, employers, and trade unionists negotiated coordinated national strategies for post-war recovery. Agreement on low wages was secured in return for price controls, low rents, and new extensions in state welfare, notably the 1947 Emergency Act that gave a universal tax-funded pension for all aged citizens, pending the creation of social insurance in 1958. The basic state pension, however, was never conditional on contributions. Instead, an earnings-related quasi-private system emerged to complement it. State-sponsored collective negotiations in the early 1950s allowed the consolidation of occupational pensions: sectoral funds emerged that encompassed all small and medium-sized firms operating in predefined spheres of economic activity. This pooling of assets and liabilities raised levels of worker security (as financial decline of one firm would not result in the loss of occupational pension for its workers) while encouraging labour mobility. Thanks to legislation underpinning the initial agreement, employers became compelled to offer an earnings-related pension; those insufficiently large to offer total security against risk were not permitted to contract out of the sectoral collective pension fund. While employees were not compelled to contribute to their occupational scheme, coverage grew steadily, reaching 60 per cent in 1960 and well over 90 per cent in 1990. These privately invested pension funds have recently emerged as a something of a paradigm for future pension provision within the EU (Clark and Bennett 2001). Ostensibly neither public nor private, they represent an achievement of consensus politics pursued in the Netherlands in the post-war years.

Like the Netherlands, Sweden also introduced an extended tax-funded citizenship pension immediately after the war (1946), although in this case, the decision was strongly influenced by national precedent and pressure from an influential agrarian sector that opposed contributions (Baldwin 1990). From 1951, the tide in pension discussion turned increasingly in favour of comprehensive, income-related social insurance. The earlier people's pension had never been designed to offer more than subsistence and, with the public sector and white-collar workers in receipt of earnings-related supplements in old age, social justice required the extension of similar benefits to the less well off. A debate ensued during the 1950s over whether earnings-related supplements should be left to private sector initiative, or be run by the state: whether such supplements should be fully or partially funded or operate solely on a PAYG basis. In the event, the Titmuss-style solution prevailed and, by the margin of one vote, state earnings-related pension supplements Allmän Tilläggspension (ATP) passed the legislature in 1960 (Eriksen and Palmer 1994). As with all earlier state pensions, there was no question of private sector contracting out. While farmers and the self-employed participated on a voluntary basis, the rest of the employed population was obliged to insure under the new state scheme. It also developed measures to redistribute both from rich to poor and to those whose contributory record was incomplete. To accommodate the interrupted working life of women, concessions were made to permit the receipt of partial pensions for those whose contributory record fell between 15 and 30 years. Although ostensibly run on a PAYG basis, contributory income (funded by employers and the taxpayer) was designed to outstrip benefit expenditure. From the start, the scheme accumulated substantial buffer funds; returns on these were sufficient to meet pension payments well into the 1980s. As the combination of supplementary scheme and basic state pension was so generous, little space was left initially for the development of extra 'private' occupational pensions. This issue only re-emerged in recent years in consequence of rising living standards raising a growing proportion of wage earners above the income ceiling set for ATP (see Palme, this volume).

While Swedish governments opted for state-run supplementary pensions, raising old age income in France developed within a very different trajectory. As in other major European economies, both public sector and some company pensions dated back to the nineteenth century. The (comparatively late) advent of contributory state pensions for elderly workers, introduced in 1930, had excluded white-collar workers, technicians, and managers in private industry (cadres). Following mass strikes in Paris in 1936, the Popular Front government endowed collective agreements with legal status (Accord de Matignon). The following year the trade union representing the cadres in engineering negotiated an agreement that created a professional funded pension for their members. Inflation and the impact of war destroyed this scheme's reserves. Following the war, however, the cadres sought to restore their established privileges and negotiated a new interprofessional agreement that extended compulsory earnings-related pensions funded on a PAYG basis (L'Association Générale des Institutions de Retraite des Cadres,

AGIRC), thereby bypassing the new general regime of social security introduced in 1946 (Lion 1962). This established precedent encouraged other sectors to negotiate complementary pension regimes in the early 1950s, some covered by collective agreement, some not,[29] which operated alongside the régime générale. Many firms committed to introduce such systems were very small; their workforces were highly mobile, and, in a period of intense modernisation, many disappeared or merged with other companies. Larger umbrella associations of interprofessional regimes emerged to manage these varied professional schemes. Early examples included the Association Generale des Retraites par Repartition (AGRR), created by collective agreement in 1951; by 1971 this covered 99,800 firms with 780,000 members in sugar, textiles, wood, and furniture. The Association Nationale d'Entraide et de la Prévoyance (ANEP), founded in 1950, covered 7,800 firms in engineering and electricity with 125,000 members in a mixed funded/PAYG scheme by 1970. By far the largest was the Union des Insititutions des Retraites des Salariés (UNIRS), founded in 1957 to coordinate provision between firm-based, regional, and professional sector-based associations of varying size. By 1971, UNIRS covered 298,000 firms with 1.9 million complementary pensioners and 4.2 million subscribing members.[30]

Beveridge's scheme of consolidated, centralised social security was discussed by French experts after the Second World War, but it was rejected (Palier 2002: ch. 2). Both public sector workers and the cadres insisted on retaining acquired social rights; the official general regime remained confined to salaried workers in the private sector. Implemented by local caisses that were administered by trade union-dominated councils and deprived of any state contribution, the state scheme offered very low pensions to very restricted numbers. At the start of the 1960s, the position of state pensions in France bore some resemblance to those in Britain. The rediscovery of poverty among the British elderly was paralleled in France by the Rapport Laroque (1962), which laid bare chronic problems faced by the old. As in Britain, the Gaullist government resisted raising state subsidies, promoting instead the extension of occupational schemes. In 1961, the Ministere de Travail ratified a collective agreement between the main French employers' organisation Confédération Nationale du Patronat Français (CNPF) and the French trade union federations to create The Association des Régimes de Rétraite Complémentaire (France) (ARRCO), an umbrella association of complementary pension associations. Compulsory cover was extended to all firms affiliated to the CNPF. Each member association pooled a proportion of income; funds in surplus subsidised those in deficit. Employers and associations remained free to run additional supplementary schemes if they so wished. ARRCO was charged with safeguarding collective financial viability and with protecting the pension rights of who changed jobs or whose employer ceased business (Veillon 1962). Compulsion enabled complementary pensions to be extended to lower income groups and reduced the previous discrepancies in old age income between modernised and traditional economic sectors (Lyon-Caen 1962). Coordination loosened the ties between employee and firm, fostering labour mobility. In the 1960s, collective negotiations extended the system's cover, to incorporate domestic workers, gardeners, bakers, and patissiers, and the multiplicity of small artisanal trades characteristic of French small town life. Under two ministerial arrêtes (15 March 1973 and 6 April 1976), compulsory cover was extended to all workers in France and its overseas territories.

Thus, although public pension provision arguably remained more fractured in France than in Britain (see Palier contribution, this volume), the reverse was true of supplementary earnings-related pension coverage. While ARRCO and AGIRC, between them, universalised and coordinated at least a basic earnings-related pension for all workers, the British system that emerged from the 1960s remained fractured, unstable, and partial. In French eyes, the British scheme was flawed. The existence of public subsidies for pension funds offering resources for economic investment was highly regarded. However, the small size of many British schemes (and their vulnerability), the omission of most blue-collar workers outside the public sector and the penalties suffered by workers who changed jobs were widely viewed as major weaknesses (Doublet 1962). British voluntarism failed to separate the risk from the firm: affiliating a pension regime to an association of similar schemes transferred the responsibility for paying the pension to that association, whose size rendered the risk negligible. Finally, the general French preference for repartition (PAYG) over funded schemes is partly explained by an ingrained culture of intergenerational solidarity, but also reflected post-war inflationary experience. Pensions supplied by ARRCO and AGIRC remained index-linked, pre- and post-award.

The purpose of these limited historical narratives is to demonstrate how a broadly similar strategy (the promotion of earnings-related complementary pensions) was introduced to tackle common problems (pensioner poverty, funding for inward investment, and wage restraint) in widely differing combinations of private responsibility and public regulation. This is a history of divergent, not convergent trajectories, as political contingency combined with social necessity to generate multiple forms of public–private partnership in the production of old age security. Varied pathways have been taken to secure a common goal. How far such developments should be interpreted as a shift from private to public is highly debatable, and to this issue we now turn.

1.4. CONCLUSIONS: MOVING BEYOND THE PUBLIC–PRIVATE DIVIDE

In each of the nation-states discussed in this chapter, distinctive political agendas influenced how earnings-related pensions were put in place. In each, state provision was endowed with a different role and in none was it totally absent. Features commonly used to identify differences between public and private pensions (their funding, their investment, their ownership, the relationship between final pension and individual contributions, and so on) offer a restricted and unhelpful perspective in developing an analysis. It is, for example, comparatively easy to distinguish totally or partially funded schemes in the 1960s (the Netherlands, Britain, and Sweden) from the apparently unfunded (France). This tells us nothing about ownership, however, where the state-run (Sweden) can be distinguished from clustered provision held in private hands (France and the Netherlands) and from German and British mixed systems. British and Dutch occupational funded pensions used (and use) private fund managers to invest their reserves, but then similar strategies were employed for German company pensions as well as for ARRCO and AGIRC's reserves. Whichever combination of variables is used to approach the issue, the same picture of cross-cutting categories emerges, throwing into question the feasibility of viewing pension policies in terms of regimes. What we witness in the 1960s is a variety of public–private arrangements, some springing from, while modifying, established occupational, professional, and company schemes.

Moreover, closer inspection reveals that the difference between funded and ostensibly unfunded systems remained more apparent than real. By the late 1960s, British pension fund assets largely outstripped their European counterparts. Even so, the funded pension was so called because pension payments were paid from established assets: this did not guarantee such assets were sufficient to meet future liabilities. In the economic downturn of the early 1970s, numerous British employers were forced to shore up their pension funds from other resources; when put to the test, the funding of many company schemes proved less than complete. Equally, when British funds in the mid-1990s appeared to outstrip future pension obligations, firms were encouraged to take pension holidays and cut back on their contributions, with disastrous consequences a few years later. In Germany, companies utilising the book reserve system were (and are) required by law to reinsure against company closure or bankruptcy, to guarantee the social policy objectives of private schemes. Even in France, where the virtues of PAYG finance were (and are) most strongly defended, both ARRCO and AGIRC held one year's national contributions as reserves, these funds being invested by private asset managers operating on contract with their member associations. In Germany, France, and the Netherlands, official legislation and subsequent regulation have guaranteed the viability of occupation-based systems through combinations of reinsurance and systems of pooled assets that permit cross-subsidy to reduce risk. In the last two, these pooling systems mean that labour mobility between employers is no longer discouraged by the risk of the individual transferee losing pension rights in the process. Such schemes allow collective liability to meet the consequences of economic downturn.

Hence, in continental Europe, public policy has been less concerned to distinguish public from private than to guarantee that earnings-related provision meets social objectives and that systems of public accountability are put in place. In countries extending state-run earnings-related pensions (Sweden and Germany), there was (and is) no question of allowing companies to contract out of social security legislation. Nor, in states adapting company or occupational provision to complement state pensions (the Netherlands and France), was there any reluctance to introduce compulsion, enforcing (in the first case) adherence of smaller firms to sectional funds and (in the second) cover for all French workers under the ARRCO scheme. In the latter cases, the European Court of Justice might view complementary pension cover as public, as part of the Dutch or French welfare state; however, the social partners in both countries understand the schemes as private—as the property of the members themselves. The object of these varied partnerships, as with the state-run alternatives, is to reconcile previously private provision with public policy objectives: to minimise risk, to extend cover, to promote mobility, and to encourage transparency through the inclusion of worker representatives on administrative agencies. In this respect, the United Kingdom has stood apart from its European neighbours. In the other cases outlined here, the combinations of public and publicly managed occupational and professional private pension systems are underwritten by official measures designed to guarantee solvency and to promote collective protection, in anticipation of possible disaster. In Britain, since the mid-1980s, regulation has followed in the wake of events that provoked public outcry. State surveillance and the corresponding regulations have developed hand to mouth, burdening employers and the pensions industry with constantly changing quantities of legal requirement that have increased costs and reduced opacity while provoking massive mistrust on all sides.

The reluctance of British governments of all political persuasions to enforce compliance with officially determined standards has reflected an innate faith that something called a market mechanism can promote the collective interest. The trick lies in making market actors behave in a manner that liberal theory suggests that they should. Historical scholarship has already exposed the fallacies that underpin notions of personal freedom in market behaviour, that encourage the liberal state to belie its own principles by forcing specific behaviours on the non-compliant (e.g. King 1998; see also Storper and Salais 1997). In Britain in recent years, we can witness the institutional counterpart: as attempts are made to transform occupational and personal pensions from private business institutions into the means to secure the general public good. In the process, both market mechanism and political accountability have suffered; transparency has disappeared under the regulatory burden. In the process, public disillusion has grown and faith in state-sponsored market-based pensions has all but disappeared. Further, the division between state and market, between public and private spheres of responsibility has become impossible to discern as Treasury conventions, determining what must (and what need not) be entered on the public accounts, dictate policy development. At the time of writing, the UK government is seeking to repair the damage done to collective confidence by establishing systems of compensation for those who lose pension rights through corporate malpractice or company collapse or an insurer's incompetence. This implies a shift back towards pooling risk. Here, continental Europe offers interesting and useful possibilities illustrating how this objective might be achieved, thereby allowing collective faith in public pension policy to be restored.

NOTES

1. Collier to Robertson, 13 Oct. 1960: on file T 227/1426, Public Record Office (PRO).
2. MPNI circular to Official Committee on Occupational Pensions, 14 July 1965: T 227/1425 PRO.

3. National Joint Advisory Council (NJAC) 'Report of the Committee on the Preservation of Pension Rights', Dec. 1965, p. 3: EW 25/219, PRO.
4. Government Actuary to Menner (Social Security) 22 Aug. 1966: ACT 1/1554, PRO.
5. NJAC, 'Report on Occupational Pensions in the UK', (Feb. 1966, p. 9): EW 25/219, PRO.
6. Collier (Treasury) memo. Oct. 1960: T 227/1426, PRO.
7. NJAC, 'Report . . . of Pension Rights', Dec. 1965, p. 3. (see note 3).
8. Under defined benefit schemes, sums transferred by Company A were insufficient at payout time at Company B, particularly when a lump sum on retirement was involved. Questions of tax relief for this sum were also problematic. Inland Revenue Superannuation Office memo to the Government Actuary (20 Feb. 1968): ACT 1/1639, PRO.
9. Ministry of Housing and Local Government to Government Actuary, Apr. 1966, ACT 1/1554, PRO.
10. Collier memo, Oct. 1960, T 227/1426, PRO.
11. On file ACT 1/1555, PRO.
12. Response by Government Actuary, June 1967, ACT 1/1555, PRO.
13. NJAC, 'Report . . . Occupational Pensions', Feb. 1966, pp. 3–5. (see note 5).
14. Summarised in Imp. Inst. Report, pp. 19–20: EW 25/219, PRO.
15. TUC: 'Note for meeting with Ministry of Social Security', 10 Nov. 1967, p. 4: MSS 292B/166.51/1, Modern Records Centre (MRC) University of Warwick.
16. Retaining a flat-rate element required higher existing pension levels: an expensive option that undercut the possibility of funding the whole. Ministry of Social Security, 29 July 1968, 'Question whether the new scheme pensions should contain a flat-rate element . . . ' MSS 292B/166.51/1, MRC.
17. 'The new Earnings-Related Pension Scheme', Ministry of Pensions confidential memo, 14 June 1966: T 227/2223.
18. Papers and memoranda of the Treasury Economic Section, on files T 227/2223–2224, PRO.
19. Baird, Treasury memo: National Insurance Review Committee, 'National Pensions Fund' (14 Feb. 1966): EW 25/219.
20. Life Offices Association: 'National Pensions: occupational schemes as a major factor in the national economy', Jan. 1968: MSS 154/3/SP/2/3, MRC.
21. TUC: Social Insurance and Industrial Welfare Committee: Minutes, 1 July 1968, p. 2: MSS 292B/166.51/1, MRC.
22. Ministry of Social Security 'N.I. contributions: indivisible or divided?', July 1968: MSS 292B/166.51/1, MRC.
23. *National Superannuation and Social Insurance*, Cmnd 3883; *Terms for Partial Contracting out of the National Superannuation Scheme*, Cmnd 4195.
24. DHSS Press Service, 28 Jan. 1969, p. 4: 'The White Paper emphasises that occupational pension schemes have an important part to play in partnership with the state scheme . . . the new scheme is designed to assist in the long-term development of occupational schemes.' MSS 292B/166.51/2, MRC.
25. *National Superannuation and Social Insurance*, Cmnd 3883 1969, p. 35, para. 116.
26. Department of Employment and Productivity memo: 'Preserving Occupational Pension Rights', 31 Mar. 1969, p. 36, T 277/2250–11. PRO.
27. *National Superannuation and Social Insurance*, Cmnd 3883 1969, appendix 2.
28. The Actuary's calculations assumed interest of 3 per cent from 1972–87, ibid.
29. ARRCO, Tenth Anniversary Report, 1972, pp. 11–12.
30. ARRCO, Tenth Anniversary Report, 1972, pp. 27–44.

CHAPTER

2

Pensions: The European Debate

Philippe Pochet
Translation by Kate Williams

2.1. INTRODUCTION

Pensions are not a European Union (EU) responsibility, and a chapter on this topic as such may seem out of place.[1] Recent analyses of national pension reforms (Bonoli 2000; Pierson 2001; Anderson 2002) only touch on the European influence on choices made at the national level. Nevertheless, few would claim that the EU plays no role in the national processes of reform in pension systems. It is on this apparent contradiction that we will try to shed some light in this chapter, which serves to introduce the varied trajectories of pension reform discussed recently within EU institutions.

By 'pension systems' we refer to the totality of public and private resources drawn on to ensure a replacement income at the moment of retirement. So we will be referring to the three pillar structure of pensions: first pillar—public Pay-As-You-Go (PAYG) pensions; second pillar—private occupational pensions schemes; third pillar—private individual pensions;—developed by the World Bank. Many criticisms have been levelled at this division into three pillars, and the misinterpretations they can lead to. However, the division acts as a point of reference in the European debate, as much in the documentation of the Commission as in that of the principal economic and social players in the field.

The question of pensions has been approached at the European level in three phases. The first is linked to creating the internal market (Objective 92). This centres on promoting labour mobility, and on the creation of an integrated financial market. The question of pensions is seen, from this point of view, as a factor limiting effective freedom of movement. From a normative point of view, privatisation is a key issue.

The second wave stems from the adoption of monetary union; here, two strands can be distinguished. First, the limit of 3 per cent of Gross Domestic Product (GDP) imposed on public deficits, and the objectives of the Stability and Growth Pact, to maintain the balance or even a slight surplus in public finances. Since pensions are the costliest item of social expenditure, the pressure to stabilise or even reduce such costs will be reinforced. Elsewhere, fears have been expressed about the capacity to finance pensions in the medium term, and the risks involved for the sustainability of the European Monetary Union (EMU). Here, sustainability is central.

Finally, since 1999 social protection has become the object of more sustained attention from the European Commission (EC) (CEC 1999*a*) and from ministers for Social Affairs. Since the Lisbon summit in March 2000, the open method of coordination[2] had been applied first to poverty and social exclusion, then to pensions (Pochet 2002). This approach focuses on social perspectives such as redistribution and the reduction of poverty among old people.

In variance with other contributions to this book, this chapter will elaborate on how pension policy is currently formulated within the EU: on the policy contexts within which it is located and on the identity of the main actors concerned with its development. As such, it complements the descriptions of national pension reforms in the selected European member states that follow in subsequent chapters. At the European level, the key questions under discussion take on a more normative air as the EU seeks to coordinate reforms under discussion at national level. The questions addressed at European level are:

1. How should EU member states deal with the demographic, financial, and political pressures on current pension security?
2. To what extent should public and private responsibility for pension security be redrawn as a result?
3. What are the implications of new public–private partnerships for the financial organisation and infrastructure of European (and global) financial markets?

The object here is to analyse policy trajectories being developed within EU institutions. As we are examining an organisation without direct sovereign powers in this area, the main focus must remain on developing an understanding of the different factors shaping policy recommendations—prescriptions that are not necessarily acceptable to member states. In taking a European standpoint, we will approach these questions in three stages.

First of all, we need to reconstruct European debates, pointing out where they are consistent, but also identifying their dynamics and interactions. One of the key issues at European level is to define the nature of the problems linked to pensions. We will approach this question from a global perspective. In effect, there is a strong link between public pensions (their level and coverage) and the space, thus, made available for, or left for, other systems. In other words, a reduction in public pensions is one condition for opening up wider possibilities for individual and private schemes (Palier and Bonoli 2000).

It is not only this aspect though, which leads us to favour a more integrated approach. In effect, agreement on the part of ministers for Social Affairs to deal with the question of pensions at the European level has removed one of the main obstacles to a European approach. Insofar as European debates were driven by economic and financial players, by the Directorates General (DGs) for the Internal Market and Economic and Finance Council (ecofin), their impact at national level was de facto relatively limited. Those primarily concerned, the ministers in charge of pensions, could argue at national level that Europe had no jurisdiction in these matters (subsidiarity). National political systems being less fragmented than the European system, European discussions that only tackled one aspect of the multidimensional problem of pensions, had, finally, very little impact on national politics (for a discussion of fragmentation/fusion of European politics, see Wessels 1997).

At this point, we need to understand the different ways in which the EU could intervene in national reforms. This forms the second phase of the analysis. Academic literature on the Europeanisation of national policy is now the dominant theme of European studies (Radaelli 2000). In order to be more specific about the area of analysis that concerns us, we will draw on the work of Dudek and Omtzigt (2001). They distinguish five means by which the EU influences the options available for pension reform.

First, through the forums for discussion created by the EU, ideas are spread, awareness raised, and policy networks created. It is in the realm of ideas, their circulation, and their legitimacy that influence makes itself felt. At the European level, different documents mobilise these policy networks. Reform of capital markets are subject to the Cardiff process; matters concerning Economic and Monetary Union (EMU), are shaped by the Broad Economic Policy Guidelines (BEPG) and matters of employment, by the Luxembourg process. (For a description of these, see CEC 2002*a*).

Second, economic integration and monetary union is making all member states more conscious of the policies pursued by their neighbours. In this context, it becomes more legitimate to hold each of them to account. This has led, for example, to the Dutch employers seeking reforms to the French and Italian pension systems, because they ran the risk, according to the Dutch, of skewing capital markets and the returns obtained via the Dutch pension funds.

Third, the EU has become an agenda setter for member states. The Commission has the power to impose issues that are not necessarily on national agendas, or not on the agenda at a given moment. The fact that the Commission has taken up the issue, and might have received several explicit but different mandates from the European Councils, gives it the capacity, if not the obligation, to maintain the issue as a priority on national agendas.

Fourth, some political leaders use the EU as a pretext. As a recent study by the Commission stated: '. . . besides economic arguments, coordination can also play a useful role from a political-economy viewpoint by helping to implement unpopular but necessary policy actions at national level' (CEC 2002*b*: 4). European-level agreements offer a resource for those who are in tune with the European line of argument, at least in those countries where European integration is considered to be of positive value.

Fifth, the configuration of groups mobilised at the European level is different to that within member states. Lobbying practices or organisational forecasts at the European level do not cover national plans.

Besides these different mechanisms which, collectively, have their impact primarily in the realm of ideas, the impact of the Court of Justice must also be mentioned, particularly in its role as guardian of competition law.[3] In defining what is the responsibility of national collective provision and what is legitimately a function of the market, the Court has had a decisive influence.

Basic public pensions, like other social security mechanisms, are not subject to competition policy. Third pillar provision, however, is bound by competition rules. For other schemes of supplementary retirement income (the second pillar), the situation is less clear. The Court of Justice is increasingly inclined to pronounce on this subject, and in the absence of clear-cut norms exempting complementary forms of social protection from European competition law, it tends to override the liberal economic logic which stems from the texts of the Rome Treaty. Since the Albany judgement (C-67/96 *Albany International BV* v. *Stichting Bedrijfspensioenfonds Textielindustrie*) it seems that the Court may have struck a balance in how it interprets what is and what is not a collective 'second pillar' pension scheme, excluded from competition law (Bosco 2000). It should also be noted that the reform of the treaties adopted at Nice (2000) had added a phrase to article 137 which reads: '. . . shall not affect the right of Member States to define the fundamental principles of their social security systems and must not significantly affect the financial equilibrium thereof'. This implies that the Court could not overturn the fundamental balance within each national system, nor the financial aspects which are evidently central to pensions. Finally, the Charter of Fundamental Rights adopted at the European Council at Nice (2000) changed the balance between the economic mission of the EU and other, more general—notably social—objectives. Its inclusion in the agreements issued by the Convention on the Future of Europe, and the intergovernmental conference it anticipated, should reinforce the attitude of the Court of Justice in its concern not to destabilise the social equilibrium of member states. Nevertheless, some uncertainty remains.

Having outlined the development of European discussion on how pension reform should be shaped, and considered various mechanisms at work between the national and European levels, the effects at national level need to be considered. This is the key concern. We do not anticipate the outcome by underlining the absence of direct effects, or of simple causal mechanisms of on the public–private divide which lies at the heart of this chapter. The argument we propose is that the more complex the discussions at European level are, the more weight they carry, and the more options they offer for dealing with the challenges of ageing. This being the case, radical proposals become marginal. However, the incremental impact of Europe on the redefinitions of the division between private and public needs to be reinforced.

For purposes of clarity, we have chosen a chronological, thematic presentation. Section 2.2 underlines the issues linked to labour mobility, and the creation of an integrated financial space. Section 2.3 shows how this debate has become linked with that of monetary union, and the sustainability of non-prefunded public pensions. Finally, Section 2.4 shows how social issues have moved centre stage in this debate since 2000. This has promoted a new set of interconnections between areas of debate, which had previously tended to remain compartmentalised.

2.2. TOWARDS A SINGLE MARKET

European action in the area of complementary pensions is based on two aspects of the EU treaty. First, free movement of people, goods, services, and capital, and second, competition policy. In both these areas, authority to act at the European level is powerful, and has been validated by innumerable rulings by the European Court of Justice. There are two strands to this debate: on the one hand, showing the ways in which freedom of movement is hindered where (second and third pillar)[4] pensions are concerned; and on the other, how free competition between economic agents is unduly constrained. As Math (2001*b*) noted, various economic actors are pushing for complementary social protection systems—that are currently very much embedded at national level, are often compulsory and monopolistic, benefiting from protective fiscal arrangements—to be subject to European competition policy, and to competition from other sectors (insurance companies, and pension funds). It is clearly no coincidence that European discussion developed under the auspices of liberal European Commissioners.

This has happened in several stages, during which argument has become more focused. The first attempts failed miserably. In the context of creating the single market (Objective 92), a new directive on institutions for occupational retirement provision had to be withdrawn under pressure from several member states. In 1996, the European Federation for Retirement Pensions (EFRP) regretted this failure to accomplish the three objectives it had identified as priorities (De Ryck 1996): freedom of cross-border investment management, of cross-border investment, of cross-border membership.

The Green Paper on complementary pensions (CEC 1997) revived this initiative. This aimed to establish a community framework of 'prudential regulation', and fiscal regulation and to reduce the obstacles to labour mobility. This Green Paper is to play a crucial role. Mindful of previous failure, the tone adopted on institutional questions is very cautious. It specifies that each state is free to choose how it divides its pension system between the three pillars—the first pillar is and will remain dominant, subsidiarity will apply in this area, and so on. The objective is evidently modest—to encourage diversification within a framework dominated by state pensions: 'State pensions (pillar 1) account for the bulk of pension payments (88 per cent), but the need to maintain levels of income in retirement is likely to result in greater reliance being placed on the other main sources of supplementary retirement income.' The different lines of argument developed in the Green Paper will provide the backbone for future action and proposals. The problems of an ageing population, and the demographic trends which form the point of departure for these documents are not dealt with here (see particularly CEC 2000*a*) and are well documented elsewhere.

One of the arguments in the Green Paper is that wage overheads would be less burdensome if the rate of return obtained on financial markets was higher. It gives the following example, subsequently used in various documents: 'Assume that the target is a fixed supplementary pension of 35 per cent of salary on the basis of a 40 year working life. If the real rate of return on assets is 6 per cent, the cost is 5 per cent of salary: all other things being equal, if the real rate of return is 4 per cent, the cost is 10 per cent of salary, and if the real state of return is only 2 per cent, the cost is 19 per cent of salary.' The market needs to be as integrated as possible, so that returns will rise. However, behind this argument lies another argument, that is not explicit but nevertheless evident: as the rate of return from a PAYG system is fairly weak, a partial switch to a private system would be as beneficial for employers as it would be for workers.

Hard on the heels of the Green Paper, in May 1998 the Commission deposited a Financial Services Action Plan, which was endorsed at the Cologne European Council in June 1999. One of the strategic objectives of this Plan is to establish a genuine single market for wholesale financial transactions. The adoption of legislative provisions on investments by the Institutions for Occupational Retirement Provision (IORPs) is presented in the Plan as a prerequisite for attaining this objective. Later, the Lisbon European Council placed strong emphasis on the need to integrate financial services and markets within the EU. A single financial market is seen as a key factor in promoting the competitiveness of the European economy, the development of the new economy, and social cohesion. In its conclusions, the Presidency stresses that priority must be given to removing the remaining barriers to investment in the field of pension funds and has called for the Plan to be implemented by 2005. The Lamfallussy report of 15 February 2001 on the regulation of the European security market goes back to the usual arguments favouring the development of private pensions and pension funds.

A second line of argument is that of mobility. Even though interstate labour mobility is still very weak, supporters of pension policy development will reverse the argument. Movement of workers is weak because a number of obstacles prevent workers from exercising their right to freedom of movement in full. This will lead the Commission to present a Communication on a new labour market, open to all, with access for all. This is followed by a plan of action to promote mobility. Following the recommendations of the Veil report on freedom of movement, the Commission set up a Pension Forum (formally established by the JOCE L196 decision, 20 July 2001) which met for the first time in 2000. Its role is to help the Commission resolve problems linked with cross-border movement. It has indicated that the Commission is willing to increase the number of participants. It represents states and social partners, as well as retirement funds, insurance companies and investment societies. The aim is to depoliticise the discussion and neutralise the ideology surrounding the issue, to turn it into a technical matter. This led to a consultation in June 2002 of the social partners (European Trade Union Confederation, ETUC; Union of Industrial and Employer's Confederations of Europe, UNICE; and Centre Européen des Entreprises à Participation Publique, CEEP) on the portability of private pension rights. The trade unions have responded comparatively positively to this consultation.

Two other aspects are also addressed in the Green Paper. Tax systems: 'Taxation plays an important role in pension provision and scheme design, providing privileged treatment at the level of contributions, fund income and capital gains, and benefit payments. There are regulations in place to control how these fiscal privileges are used.' (ch. V). Following from this, on 19 April 2001, the Commission adopted a Communication on the elimination of tax obstacles to the cross-border provision of occupational pensions. (Difficulties arising from differences in taxation systems are subject to other EU initiatives and are not dealt with in any detail here. For a recent analysis, see Radaelli 2002.) 'Prudential regulations' (ch. III) are also discussed. The strategy of issuing the Green Paper has proved to be a smart move, as in this way the Commission has managed to keep the upper hand, and use the responses to the Green Paper as a basis for setting out new proposals.

These different elements allowed the Commission to set out a proposal in October 2000 for a Directive on institutions for occupational retirement provision (pension funds, superannuation schemes, etc.). The aim is to create a prudential framework at the EU level strong enough to protect the rights of future pensioners and to increase the affordability of occupational pensions. The draft Directive also seeks to enable an institution in one member state to manage company pension schemes in other member states. Once again, this proposal gave rise to numerous debates, but finally the ECOFIN Council agreed to it in June

2002, opening the way for this Directive to be adopted (although the European Parliament has still to give it a second reading). One aspect remains uncovered—tax systems.

Having outlined the main documents and their underlying logic, we now turn to the agencies and institutions who contribute to this section of EU discussion. Amongst these, the European Parliament,[5] the Economic and Social Committee, and the financial services sector have been pressing for several years for the establishment of a European framework for IORPs. If some member states have been (very) reticent, others have, however, shown their support for the Commission's initiatives.

There are numerous private actors in the field. They act as a classic lobby (the European Federation of Fund Managers, FEFSI, the European Committee of Assurance, CEA and the EFRP) to obtain amendments and advance their interests—which are not always identical, as can be seen by the tension between the CEA and the EFRP (see Math 2001*c*) over the Commission's proposal on the activities of occupational retirement funds.

One of the strategies is to legitimise their demands by producing, or referring to, academic studies in the field. In this context, the role of the European Round Table of Industrialists (ERT), a group of about forty senior industrialists,[6] is significant. The ERT set up a working party chaired by De Benedetti which produced a document entitled: '*European pensions, an appeal for reform—Pensions schemes that Europe can really afford*', published by the De Benedetti Foundation (ERT 2001) and widely publicised in the media. As Math (2001*b*) describes it:

> The Foundation has links with leading edge researchers and university personnel, in which one party may not know, or may not seek to know, the close working links between this research centre and the ERT. Its work is presented as independent research, brings a scientific legitimacy to political recommendations, and is widely disseminated notably within a sympathetic financial press.

This stance adopted by one sector of European employers is in strong contrast to UNICE, which brings together national employers' federations, and has kept a very low profile on this issue. It was only in November 2001 that UNICE adopted a 'Strategy Paper on Sustainability of Pensions'. UNICE points out clearly that 'there is no single European model of pension system. A 'one size fits all' solution is neither desirable, nor appropriate or feasible across the EU'. The EU should, therefore, play a fairly modest role, and the only justification for the EU to pursue national pension reforms is to maintain the stability of the Eurozone (Arcq and Pochet 2002).

In the field of private pensions, Europe has a particular role to play in bringing together an asymmetrical group of interested parties. The

Commission, through two commissioners with strong personalities, Brittan in the late 1980s/early 1990s, and Bolkenstein in the early 2000s, has been an important catalyst for putting this subject onto the EU's agenda. The demand for a radical change has been vocal: 'Defusing Europe's pensions timebomb' was the title of a speech by Bolkenstein (2001). For all that, it is hard to make the interests they defend a priority for the Commission as a whole, or to win them support from the wider group of member states. For the time being, various elements have been brought together to develop a more sustained approach. Beyond the general issue of an ageing population, that of the mobility of workers has become more central. Faced with a failure to force the issue, the argument has become more neutral—a pragmatic resolution must be found to the practical problems of labour mobility. Networks favourable to pension funds, and a greater role for private pensions are using the 'Annual Report on Structural Reforms', published in the framework of the Cardiff process (which focused on the market reforms for goods and capital) to support their ideas. Nevertheless, this process is subordinate to the Broad Economic Policy Guidelines (BEPG) which are controlled by the Ministers of Finance (see later) (CEC 2001*a*).

2.3. THE ECONOMIC AND MONETARY STABILITY OF THE EUROPEAN UNION

The second line of discussion developing at European level, stems from the Ecofin Council and their advisory committees, particularly the Economic Policy Committee (EPC), and the Economic and Financial Committee (EFC). The issue is less freedom of movement and competition policy, than the stability of the monetary union. Public, non-prefunded pensions are the focus here. This issue will come to a head in the medium to long term, 2020–40. The declarations of the ECOFIN Councils, and the various statements from the European Councils are not addressed here (for a detailed description, see de la Porte 2002*b*; de la Porte and Pochet 2002*a*). Here, the focus is on the normative descriptions presented in the various documents, and their progressive consolidation.

The battle between the Ministers of Finance and Social Affairs, over who should have the last word, has acted as a dynamic in this area. The first initiative to address the issue of pension reform came in 1997 from the EPC, without having a specific mandate to deal with this issue. Its guiding philosophy was that pension reform needed to be adapted to the circumstances of an ageing population, while ensuring durable fiscal consolidation and improving the condition of European labour markets. The arguments put forward to reform the pension scheme—the demographic argument, the fiscal burden argument, and the labour market efficiency argument—have become permanent features in the architecture of European pension debates. The principal recommendation was containing benefits, as the main instrument for guaranteeing the solvency of PAYG pension systems. The principal means prescribed to achieve this aim was by delaying the age of retirement. A second recommendation was to move away from a solidarity-based system to a pension system based on individual contributions. A third recommendation was gradually to increase the role of funded schemes.

Following this first exercise, a work schedule for validating these propositions by means of various reports will be produced (de la Porte and Pochet 2002*b*). In 2000 the EPC submitted a new, more substantial report which tried, on the basis of shared national assumptions (in particular about demographic projections), to evaluate the burden of public pensions in terms of percentage of Gross Domestic Product (GDP) up to 2050 (for a critical view of these baseline hypotheses see Math 2001*a*, Math and Pochet 2001; for quite different projections, see Fitoussi and Le Cacheux 2002). According to conclusions based on two different future scenarios, one that could be described as normal, the other based on the Lisbon objectives (i.e. raising the employment rate progressively to 70 per cent), pension expenditures as a percentage of GDP are on the rise. The effects on public debt, in particular, were emphasised. The EPC put forward four recommendations:

1. Reforms should primarily aim at delaying retirement.
2. Fiscal policy should be rendered more sound and public debt should progressively be reduced.
3. The link between social contributions and benefits at the individual level should be strengthened, in accordance with the equity principle.
4. The role of funded schemes should be progressively increased.

These recommendations will be quickly taken up in economic and financial circles (see Mantel 2001). A second report was presented on the question of long-term financing, and consideration of the effects of ageing was to be to the costs linked to healthcare (EPC 2001). A working group was set up (Ageing Working Group, AWG) which analysed the effects of parametric reforms (EPC 2002). Three aspects were measured: indexation, postponing the age of retirement, and a retirement more closely linked to life expectancy. The report concluded that, with variations between countries and systems, these three variables should be applied. It mounts an energetic plea for postponing retirement age, because, according to its calculations, this measure not only has a positive effect in terms of global cost, but—most importantly—does not cause a reduction in the relative level of pensions (as would any change in the rules of indexation). Note that this conforms to the central objective of the European Employment Strategy, to raise the employment rate to 70 per cent, and the employment rate for people over 55 to 50 per cent.

One related aspect should be stressed. The Lisbon Council (2000) mandated the Commission to prepare a study on 'the contribution of public finances to growth and employment: improving quality and sustainability' (CEC 2000*a*, *b*). This study also deals with the question of retirement pensions. This question of the quality of public expenditure is important because it is directly related to the stability of the monetary union. The argument runs as follows: 'good' public expenditure has to be distinguished from other public expenditure. For example, investment, education, active measures to stimulate employment are all 'good' areas of expenditure. In this context, and assuming budgets need to be reduced, pensions are in the front line of the category of 'bad' expenditure. This is a strategy for the medium term. Rather than a direct intervention in the pension debate, what we see here is an attempt to reach a common definition about what is or is not acceptable in terms of public expenditure.

The European Central Bank (ECB) is one of the most important players in this debate. It has, in various documents, shown its concern for the budgetary stability of public (non-prefinanced) pensions, and recommends lowering the ratios of public debt, the establishment of financial reserves, and pursuing with 'even greater determination' social security reform. More specifically, the ECB is interested in the effects of ageing on decisions to consume or save, and, through this, on interest rates and the state of public finances.

The BEPG is the key document structuring the networks surrounding the ministers of Finance. In 2001 The European Union Ministers of Economics and Finance (ECOFIN) Council proposed that in future one part of the BEPG should be devoted to ageing and its financial implications. Member states should develop strategies for addressing the longer-term demographic challenge and present them in conjunction with their Stability and Convergence Programmes. The strategies should be examined in the context of multilateral surveillance. This proposal was accepted by the European Council.[7]

The emergence of the EMU as central to the economic debate on pensions has brought about an important change. Here, we find ourselves at the heart of the European project, and current debates on governance: how to make monetary union work when economic controls are, essentially, decentralised. The national actors who carry forward these discussions—including the sustainability of pensions—are central to the architecture of Europe (the ECOFIN Council). ECOFIN is supported by committees which benefit equally from the strength of their members' national institutions (numerous econometric studies are similarly coordinated). Contrary to the debates linked to the internal market, which are very ideological, the EPC studies do not support, as an *a priori* position, a greater role for private pensions. In numerous documents, the risks linked to second and third pillar pensions are underlined.[8] Nevertheless, if the analyses are more subtle, the political conclusions are the same (and sometimes seem disconnected from the analysis). The central argument employed by the EPC to justify a greater role for private initiatives is, classically, that of the diversification of risk. One might note here that the EPC studies move away from econometric calculations as such, to engage more substantially, and in a more normative way, with the performance of the various national systems.

2.4. PENSIONS: A SOCIAL QUESTION?

If free movement and the impact of EMU have contributed to the shaping of the community discussions, this has happened without the national ministers in charge of pensions pronouncing on the subject. On the one hand, there is no clear legal responsibility in the Treaty, and on the other, there is such a wide diversity of national systems, and of reforms already implemented or under way. The issues in terms of medium term financing play a greater or lesser role from country to country. However, in the end, a negative reason has forced them, with reluctance, to address the question: The risk that the problematic nature of pension reform could be shaped by actors other than themselves. As Chassard (2001: 317) notes, 'It is important that the "social experts" should make their voices heard in this concert, so as not to leave the field open to those who view social protection from an exclusively financial angle.' It is worth noting here, an immediate reaction on the part of the Council of ministers of Social Affairs: a Social Protection Committee (SPC) was created. This was immediately given the task of producing a report setting out the evidence on the social aspects of pensions.

In the draft report, the SPC views the inter-linkage of different areas (social protection, employment, and public finance) as crucial. The main message is 'it will be important to bear in mind that financial sustainability cannot be achieved at the expense of the ability of pension systems to meet their social goals'. Only one paragraph is devoted to the reasons for dealing with the issue at European level. This is the weak point of the social approach: If a purely financial definition of the problem is to be resisted, a positive definition of common social objectives is required and this is always problematic.[9] This partly because some Social Affairs ministers share the objective of reforming their national pension system with their Finance ministers (see de la Porte and Pochet 2002*a*).

The creation of a new network around the SPC is designed to analyse pension reform from a more social angle. From the outset, this group is more heterogeneous than its economic counterpart (the EPC), and needs to establish its own legitimacy as much from the analyses it produces as from its political and ideological dealings with the EPC. Nevertheless, the institutional development gives an indication of the dynamic nature of the issue being studied. In this context, the Belgian Minister of Social Affairs and Pensions, Frank Vandenbroucke, played a key role particularly during the Belgian Presidency in convincing his colleagues to adopt common objectives, and then in developing indicators to enable the open method of coordination to be applied. He also commissioned a report during the Belgian Presidency, edited by Esping-Anderson (2001) that set out the reasons for a common social approach to pensions. Following this, and the EPC report (see previous section), the European Council approved three major overall objectives as well as the application of the open method of coordination. These are to:

(1) maintain social cohesion and social solidarity, notably reducing the risk of poverty;
(2) safeguard the financial sustainability of pension systems, in particular by improving employment performance, by adapting the structure and the parameters of pensions systems, and by increasing the budgetary room for manoeuvre; and
(3) adapt pension systems to a changing society and labour markets.

To make these very general principles more concrete, the EPC and the SPC were given the task of producing a joint paper. They finally agreed on eleven objectives (SPC and EPC 2001). Over and above the specific content of these objectives, discussion centred on two wider elements: control over the decision-making process and the role of the BEPGs as a key document. The eleven objectives eventually endorsed (each one the subject of detailed negotiation by the two committees) are presented in detail in the annex to this chapter. Nevertheless, even if the wording is hazy and ambiguous, some considerations merit attention: first, the hierarchy of objectives that places social considerations to the fore; second, the minimum priority accorded to questions of the internal market and labour mobility (only Objective 8 refers to this); third, the priority given to macroeconomic issues—five objectives mention these. These eleven objectives offer a structure for future EU work in this area and discussions will be shaped by this matrix. That said, the tensions between the different approaches have not disappeared, but have gained a framework from the document.

The working agenda for pensions has been defined. In September 2002 member states presented their first national strategy reports for pensions (available on the Commission's website) following the eleven principles defined at European level. These reports are explicit about the need to negotiate changes to pension systems, particularly with the trades unions, and several were drafted jointly by different ministers, which will strengthen their legitimacy. The Commission will analyse the national strategy reports and identify good practice and innovative approaches of common interest to the member states. By spring 2003, the Council and the Commission provided a joint report to assess national pension strategies and identify good practice. For 2004, they will assess the objectives and working methods established and will decide upon the objectives, methods, and timetable for the future of the pension strategy (SPC and EPC 2001).

At the same time the EPC and the SPC were asked to 'develop common approaches and comparability with regard to indicators in order to underpin the open method of coordination relating to the future of pensions. This cooperation should cover the preparation of simulations and projections relating to the medium and long-term prospects and implications of pension policies'. An interim report of the Indicators Sub-group of the SPC notes: 'difficulty arises from the need to define common indicators that are comparable with the wide diversity of pension systems found across the Member States. The common objectives agreed in Laeken can be achieved by very different pension systems and different combinations of public and private provision. Common indicators will have to be neutral to the architecture of a country's pension system' (SPC 2002).

2.5. CONCLUSIONS

The question of pensions emerged as an issue to address at European level with the decision to complete the single market. At this point, in the absence of any legal alternative, the DG responsible for the internal market took up the issue, not the DG responsible for social affairs. This strategy did not meet with success. Nevertheless, during the 1990s various actors, especially economic and financial players, have become increasingly involved. The issue was revived by the Green Paper on supplementary pensions, and also as a consequence of the single currency. This last required more integrated financial markets. National reforms undertaken under the auspices of qualifying for monetary union (France and Italy are examples of this) have stimulated debate on more significant and radical reforms (see Boeri, Siebert, etc.). Even though calls for reform have been strident and relayed by one pressure group or another (see the De Benedetti Foundation), their impact on the ongoing development of European discussion has been marginal. At the same time, the ministers of Social Affairs have succeeded in placing other aspects, going beyond the financial, on the agenda. They have also managed, thanks to the support of the SPC, to develop the common understanding necessary for further discussion. One other aspect has also emerged: the sustainability of public finances. Here, the main focus is on unfunded schemes. However, the outline of the problem developed within this framework does not entirely marry up with the concerns of those inclined to favour private pensions.

Rather than radical reform, the discussions taking place at European level propose incremental change, touching on a range of issues, where efforts are made to reconcile apparently contradictory objectives (collective solidarity and market forces). This, in turn, touches on the close link between the problem of pensions and employment strategies (raising the employment rate and the age of retirement). Radical proposals have had little effect, as the less publicised second, rather disillusioned report by De Benedetti notes, with reference to the impact of the first report (2002).

The weakness of the radical approach can be illustrated by a recent publication by one of its better known and more subtle advocates, Martin Feldstein (2002). As a transitional measure towards a fully investment based system, he proposes the establishment of a 'notional defined contribution system within the broader framework of a PAYG system' (p. 6) following the Swedish model. The advantage of this is that 'they provide an individual account framework within which an investment-based system could later be introduced or expanded' (p. 7). There are several points to consider. The first is a matter of conjecture: it is far from certain that Swedish workers who have lost 30 per cent of the market value of their savings since the new system came on stream are fully convinced by these arguments. But more fundamentally, what Feldstein overlooks is the part played by institutions, particularly in Bismarkian countries. His proposal is addressed to an individual entrepreneur, dealing directly with a worker, each party wanting to gain maximum profit. It is very likely, as Barr (2002) suggests, that workers will prove to be risk averse, but most importantly, as all the reforms adopted indicate, the agreement of the unions (and at least some employers) is essential. To date, trade unions have only accepted reforms that are broadly in line with existing systems, and not those that are designed to achieve radical transformation. To resolve the question of collective solidarity, it is not enough to ask 'What does national solidarity for employees mean in a single Europe-wide labor market?' (p. 4), because the single labour market is so far from being a reality. Even when disguised beneath proposals that are apparently purely pragmatic, Feldstein's arguments highlight the tension between the market and social solidarity. What the short history of European discussion demonstrates is that proposals based solely on the economic arguments of market forces do not offer a constructive way forward.

If we refer back to the five sources of influence outlined in the introduction, a range of developments can be identified. First of all, there are now at least three policy networks. The first, centred around the internal market directorate, consists of numerous lobbying groups sustained—willingly or not—by academic networks that are influential in their field. The second, much more fragmented, surrounds the SPC, which aims to place greater emphasis on the social purpose of pensions. The third consists of the macroeconomists around the EPC. Here, the groups involved are always asymmetrical, and the unions are always poorly represented. Although the member states control the agenda with precise mandates determined by the Heads of State and national governments, the Commission now has the mission of keeping this agenda, and its associated reforms, open at national level. Discussion has had to take on board different interests, and become less fragmented than previously. Given the scenario that the interests represented are wider, and documents show greater agreement, Europe can become a resource for those who want to initiate or pursue reforms drawing on a range of approaches: parametric reforms, public prefinanced reforms (thanks to budgetary surpluses), or recipes for privatisation, under the auspices of the second pillar. What is clear is that the way forward will be based more on continuity than change at national level.

ACKNOWLEDGEMENTS

My thanks to Henri Lourdelle and Jonathan Zeitlin for their careful readings of the text and helpful comments. Usual caveats apply.

ANNEX: 11 OBJECTIVES AGREED

Adequacy of Pensions

- Member States should safeguard the capacity of pension systems to meet their social objectives [. . .]
  1. Ensure that older people are not placed at risk of poverty and can enjoy a decent standard of living; that they share in the economic well-being of their country and can accordingly participate actively in public, social and cultural life;[10]
  2. Provide access for all individuals to appropriate pension arrangements, public and/or private, which allow them to earn pension entitlements enabling them to maintain, to a reasonable degree, their living standard after retirement; and
  3. Promote solidarity within and between generations.
- Financial sustainability of pension systems [. . .]
  4. Achieve a high level of employment through, where necessary, comprehensive labour market reforms,[. . .];
  5. Ensure that, alongside labour market and economic policies, all relevant branches of social protection, in particular pension systems, offer effective incentives for the participation of older workers; [. . .]
  6. [. . .] tak(e) into account the overall objective of maintaining the sustainability of public finances. At the same time sustainability of pension systems needs to be accompanied by sound fiscal policies, including, where necessary, a reduction of debt.[11] Strategies adopted to meet this objective may also include setting up dedicated pension reserve funds;
  7. Ensure that pension provisions and reforms maintain a fair balance between the active and the retired by not overburdening

the former and by maintaining adequate pensions for the latter; and

8. Ensure, through appropriate regulatory frameworks and through sound management, that private and public funded pension schemes can provide pensions with the required efficiency, affordability, portability and security.

- Modernisation of pension systems in response to changing needs of the economy, society and individuals
  9. Ensure that pension systems are compatible with the requirements of flexibility and security on the labour market; that, without prejudice to the coherence of Member States' tax systems, labour market mobility within Member States and across borders and non-standard employment forms do not penalise people's pension entitlements and that self-employment is not discouraged by pension systems;
  10. [. . .] ensur(e) the principle of equal treatment between women and men, [. . .],
  11. Make pension systems more transparent and adaptable to changing circumstances, so that citizens can continue to have confidence in them. [. . .] Promote the broadest possible consensus regarding pension policies and reforms. Improve the methodological basis for efficient monitoring of pension reforms and policies.

NOTES

1. Note Article 44 and Article 137. The first aims at the coordination of public pensions, and the second requires unanimity.
2. Open method of coordination consists of:

   (1) fixing guidelines for the Union combined with specific timetables for achieving the goals that they set in the short, medium, and long terms;

   (2) establishing, where appropriate, quantitative and qualitative indicators and benchmarks against the best in the world and tailored to the needs of different Member States and sectors as a means of comparing best practice;

   (3) translating these European guidelines into national and regional policies by setting specific targets and adopting measures, taking into account national and regional differences;

   (4) periodic monitoring, evaluation, and peer review, organised as mutual learning processes.

3. The EU has also had a significant impact on pensions through its policy of equality between men and women—not dealt with in this chapter.
4. Public pensions are regulated by Rule 1408/71.
5. On 13 April 2000, the European Parliament adopted a Resolution which welcomes the Commission's intention to propose a Directive on supplementary pensions.
6. The ERT played an important role in the dynamic of the internal market and the White Paper of 1985, as well as later in the trans-European networks outlined in Delors' 1993 White Paper. This is one of the most influential groups in Brussels.
7. On the subject of the market for goods (Cardiff), the Annual Report on Structural Reforms is prepared each year by the Economic Policy Committee. It includes a section which covers aspects of 'Ageing, pensions and fiscal sustainability'. This process is later integrated into the Broad Economic Policy Guidelines (see EPC 2002).
8. The report on structural reforms published by the EPC (see note 7) notes on p. 30 'These efforts (additional fiscal incentives) will promote the accumulation of private pension assets, but could also imply deadweight costs and, through the diversion of assets into tax-favoured or subsidised forms, lead to negative long-run influence on the government budget balance. The overall consequences of such incentive schemes for fiscal sustainability are therefore uncertain'.
9. For example, how to draw on the notion of solidarity when the majority of national reforms are designed to link what an individual pays with what they receive in the future.
10. In this respect, benefits and tax advantages other than pensions should also be taken into account where appropriate.
11. Member states' strategies to ensure sound and sustainable public finances are reported and assessed in the framework of the BEPGs and the Stability and Growth Pact and should be in accordance with these.

CHAPTER

3

Is there a Dutch Way to Pension Reform?

Bart van Riel, Anton Hemerijck, and Jelle Visser

3.1. INTRODUCTION

Demographic ageing constitutes one of the most pressing policy problems for the advanced welfare states of the European Union (EU). The real challenge lies in how to allocate the additional expenditure that inevitably accompanies population ageing (Esping-Andersen et al. 2002). Demographic pressures are often compounded by design characteristics in pension systems. The Dutch pension system, with its integrated public and private mandatory provision of retirement income, is often seen as a benchmark for other continental welfare states to emulate. Practically all continental welfare states of Western Europe are based exclusively on public mandatory Pay-As-You-Go (PAYG) systems, financed through wage-based social contributions. PAYG financing invokes high non-wage labour costs with serious negative consequences for employment opportunities at the lower end of the earnings scale (Schludi 2001). Low levels of prefunding, high dependency ratios, together with low levels of employment of elderly workers, it is argued, put significant pressure on public finances. By contrast, the Dutch pension system, with its integrated public and private mandatory pension provision, arguably faces far less fiscal strain as a result of population ageing. It is, indeed, true that the Dutch pension, combining a general revenue financed, basic pension guarantee with funded extensions of earnings-related (mandatory) occupational pensions, is more effective in terms risk-balancing and burden-sharing between the generations than the traditional PAYG system. In addition, it is also the case that a multi-tiered pension system allows for more flexible adjustment to changing economic and demographic conditions.

Beyond the significant advantages of a fully fledged multi-tiered pension system with a strong funded component, it is arguable that the relative vulnerability or robustness of pension systems to economic and demographic change cannot be judged solely in terms of the balance of the mix of public (PAYG) and private (funded) financing (World Bank 1994; Haverland 2001). In addition, levels of maturation of the various tiers, risk exposure of supplementary pensions, and, most importantly, the overall generosity of the pension system, have to be taken in consideration. From a comparative perspective, the Dutch pension system is fairly generous. This is related to a number of features: Flat-rate first pillar pension benefits are higher than welfare benefits and are indexed to contract wages not prices; second pillar benefits are almost all of the defined-benefit (DB) type (mostly based on final pay schemes) and also second pillar pensions are, in normal times, indexed to wages.

In two out of three commonly agreed goals for the open coordination of pensions in the EU—adequacy and modernisation—the Dutch pension system scores quite high. It is, however, not without weaknesses. This chapter argues that, with respect to the third EU goal of financial sustainability, the Dutch system is more vulnerable to the predicament of demographic ageing than is generally assumed on the basis of its seemingly effective mix of PAYG and funded tiers. This is largely due to a conscious political choice not to tamper with the generosity of the Dutch pension. In many other EU countries, pension reform has been directed towards neutralising the cost of public pensions by lowering future benefits in relation to welfare. Obviously, retaining the relative generosity of Dutch pensions in face of demographic ageing population has a price.

In this chapter we will try to answer three related questions. First, what explains the lack of (parametric) pension reform in the Netherlands in recent years? Second, in the absence of significant pension reforms, what other avenues have Dutch policy-makers explored so as to maintain the robustness of the Dutch pension system in the face of an ageing population? Third, does the overall Dutch policy response really suffice in view of important labour market and demographic changes in the twenty-first century? While there may no evident need to recast the design of the Dutch pension system, there is the fear that Dutch pensions, because of their high aspiration levels, may come under increasing financial strain in the not too distant future.

In the next section, there is a short overview of the Dutch pension system, centred on the basic mix of public and private provision of retirement income. Section 3.3 focuses on the changing asset allocation in Dutch pension funds. Section 3.4 examines the long-term challenges facing the Dutch pension system: changes in the labour market (more specifically the growth of part-time and temporary employment) and the ageing of the population. Section 3.5 studies the policy responses to these challenges. In particular, it hopes explain why policy-makers have shied away from major reform endeavours. The final section summarises the argument.

3.2. AN OVERVIEW OF THE DUTCH PENSION SYSTEM

The old age pension system rests on three pillars (see also, Bovenberg and Meijdam 2001; Carey 2002): the public old age pension (providing compulsory PAYG pensions), funded occupational pensions, and private provisions.

3.2.1. First Pillar Pensions

All residents are entitled to a public pension in the first pillar. The means test, which was part of the original old age pension decree of 1947, was dropped in the 1956 General Old Age Act (Algemene Ouderdom Wet, AOW) because of the implied disincentive for private savings. Accordingly, with the public pension as an effective minimum pension biased in favour of low-wage workers, the elderly do not draw on welfare, and thus, do not burden social assistance. The AOW pension provides a flat rate benefit from the age of 65. Entitlement accumulates at a rate of 2 per cent for each year of residence between the ages of 15 and 65. For individuals meeting this requirement in full, the benefit for two persons living together is equal to the net minimum wage (€1214 per month in July 2002) while a pensioner living alone receives 70 per cent of this amount. The statutory minimum wage equals, in net terms, 55 per cent of the average wage and is adjusted in line with average growth of contractual wages (set by collective agreement) twice each year. However, the Conditional Indexing Adjustment Act (WKA 1992) allows indexation to be suspended under conditions of a rapid rise in the number of benefit recipients as a percentage of the employed population, as happened between 1992 and 1995 (Visser and Hemerijck 1997). Indexation has been fully restored since 1996. AOW pensions are financed through contributions depending on taxable income, with premiums levied as part of the personal income tax.[1]

3.2.2. Second Pillar Pensions

The second pillar is based on fully funded occupational pensions, managed by employers and unions (see Clark and Bennett 2001 and Sociaal-Economische Raad, SER 2000 for details). These plans play a major role, with more than 90 per cent of all employees participating and around 50 per cent of all pensioners receiving an occupational pension. Although there is no statutory obligation for employers to make pension commitments to workers, 99 per cent of employers with more than 50 employees do. An important contributory factor is that most workers are covered by sectoral plans, the integrity of which is upheld by mandatory extension of industry-wide agreements between trade unions and employers associations. Admission rules, provisions, and benefits are determined in collective bargaining by employers' associations and trade unions. But self-regulation is enveloped within a tight legal framework of supervision. Once pension commitments have been made, they are subject to the Pensions and Savings Act (Pensioen-en Spaarfondsenwet, PSW), which requires that pensions must be placed outside the company. This rule appears to reflect learning from the 1930s recession when various funds collapsed. Supervision is entrusted to the Insurance Board, which is a private regulatory agency that supervises pension funds and insurance companies. It enforces additional prudential rules concerning funding and valuation of assets.

The usual retirement age in occupational schemes is 65, as for the public pension. Nearly all plans are of the defined benefit type and most plans aim at a replacement rate of 70 per cent. Many plans also provide a survivor's benefit. The 70 per cent replacement rate takes into account the public pension through an adjustment technique known as AOW franchise. Occupational pension payments (4 per cent of Gross Domestic Product, GDP) are almost as large as AOW outlays (4.3 per cent). Both employers and employees pay into the funds, through contributions levied on wages above the franchise. The largest (with around 1 million active participants) is the funded pension plan for public servants, Algemeen Burgelijk Pensioenfonds (ABP), which was privatised in 1996. The plan for the health sector, PGGM, is second largest. As Table 3.1 demonstrates, compulsory industry pension

Table 3.1. Pension funds in the Netherlands, by category

	Plans		Members	
	Abso	**%**	**Abso**	**%**
Company pension funds	799	89.4	793,865	15.9
Compulsory industry pension funds*	72	6.9	4,276,811	77.3
Non-compulsory industry pension funds	20	1.8	300,117	5.9
Occupational pension funds	11	1.2	39,937	0.8
Company savings funds	6	0.6	92	0.0
Pension funds provided by law	1	0.1	3,395	0.1
Total	947	100	5,413,217	100

*Includes civil-service pension fund ABP.

Source: Insurance Chamber, 'pension monitor', situation as of 1 January 2002.

funds, although only a small fraction of all funds, account for over 77 per cent of total coverage. Most larger firms (e.g. Philips, Royal Dutch Shell, KLM, Heineken) provide their own funds.

3.2.3. Third Pillar Pensions

The third pillar of the Dutch pension system is based on private provision, for instance, through annuity insurance. Contributions are tax deductible provided that they do not result in a total pension entitlement being built up in 40 years exceeding 70 per cent of final earnings at the age of 65. Given that most supplementary pension schemes are designed to achieve 70 per cent of final earnings, this in reality leaves little room for the third pillar.

In short, the Dutch system is close to being a three pillar system, with a relatively small third pillar. In the mid-1990s total disposable income for persons aged 65–74 was around 80 per cent of that for people aged 51–64, but this may have fallen somewhat since (Carey 2002: 37). Table 3.2 shows the income sources of the elderly. The income share of the basic public pension is about 50 per cent for both single elderly and for (married) couples. Occupational pension schemes provide about 30 per cent, but somewhat less for the older cohorts. Annuities provide less

Table 3.2. Composition of retirement income in the Netherlands

	Public pensions[1]	**Occupational pensions**	**Asset income**[2]	**Other income**[3]
Singles				
65 years and over	49	28	19	4
of which:				
65–69 years	49	28	19	4
70–74 years	48	30	18	4
75–79 years	51	27	18	4
80 years and over	50	26	20	4
Couples[4]				
65 years and over	48	29	19	4
of which:				
65–69 years	44	32	16	8
70–74 years	48	29	20	3
75–79 years	49	28	19	4
80 years and over	51	24	20	5

[1] Excludes other public transfers.
[2] Includes income from owner-occupied housing.
[3] Includes wages, profits, and transfers.
[4] Both partners receive a public pension.

Source: Bovenberg and Meijdam (2001), data from CPB.

than 10 per cent. If asset income and income from owner-occupied housing is included, however, income from the third pillar amounts to about half the average size (20 per cent) of each of the other two pillars.

3.3. ASSET ALLOCATION IN DUTCH PENSION FUNDS

Compared to other countries in the Eurozone, Dutch pension funds are well developed (Clark and Bennett 2001: 32). Pension assets in 2001 were about as big as GDP. Worldwide, only Switzerland has larger pension assets in terms of GDP. Dutch pension funds in 2001 invested their assets mainly in equity and real estate (50 per cent of total assets) and bonds (32 per cent), mostly foreign. As a consequence, two-thirds of total assets of Dutch pension funds is invested abroad.

Table 3.3 shows that the portfolio composition of Dutch pension funds shifted dramatically in the 1990s. In 1992 private loans, mostly to the

Table 3.3. The changing asset composition of Dutch pension funds, 1992–2001

	Percentage of total assets[1]			Percentage invested abroad		Foreign assets as % total assets[4]
	Equity and real estate[2]	Bonds	Private loans[3]	Equity and real estate	Bonds	
1992	18	18	41	57	21	14
1993	22	19	37	57	21	16
1994	22	21	35	57	21	17
1995	26	22	30	58	23	20
1996	31	25	24	55	26	23
1997	35	27	19	57	39	31
1998[5]	42	27	14	60	55	40
1999	52	26	9	76	69	57
2000	49	31	6	81	75	63
2001	50	32	5	82	81	67

[1] Since not all investments categories (e.g. mortgages) are shown equity and real estate, bonds and loans do not add up to 100 per cent.
[2] Equity and real state: equity (around 40 per cent in 2001) includes private equity; real estate includes equities, convertible bonds, and investment in real estate.
[3] Private loans to governments, companies, and supranational institutions. Private loans were granted mostly to the Dutch government.
[4] Calculated as column (1)∗column (4) + column(2)∗column (5), assuming that the percentage of private loans, mortgages, etc., invested abroad is negligible.
[5] Statistical revision in 1998. The 'old' figures for 1998 for columns 1–6 are, respectively, 41, 28, 14, 59, 52, and 39 per cent.

Source: Own tabulations based on data from the Dutch Central Bank.

Dutch government, accounted for over 40 per cent of all investments, but by 2001 this percentage had fallen to 5 per cent. Over the same period, the share of investments in equities, real estate, and bonds together increased from 36 per cent in 1992 to 80 per cent in 2001.[2] Since an increasing proportion of these investments were abroad, this resulted in an internationalisation of the portfolio of Dutch pension funds. In 1992, by contrast, only 14 per cent of pension assets were invested abroad. Obviously, the increasing share of equities, real estate, and bonds in total pension investments and the internationalisation of these investments are closely related. The opportunities for spreading risks in financial markets are very limited in a small country like the Netherlands. Moreover, the EMU lowered transaction costs for risk spreading within the EU.

Over a third of the increase in the share of equity and real estate in total assets over the period 1992–2001 can be attributed to the change in investment strategy of the biggest pension fund—the ABP.[3] Until its privatisation in 1996, and unlike other pension funds, the government heavily regulated its investment strategy.[4] For example, the ABP was, until 1987, forbidden to invest abroad, and thus, granted the Dutch government a cheap pool of finance. In the second half of the 1980s, following the example of Anglo-Saxon pension funds, Dutch pension funds increasingly shifted their investments into bonds and equities. Because of its investment restrictions, the ABP could not follow this trend, and both the composition of its portfolio and the rate of return on its investment increasingly began to diverge downwards from other pension funds (ABP Annual Reports 1990; 1989).

The decision to privatise the ABP was taken in 1993. As privatisation would imply that all special investment restrictions for the ABP would be lifted, it was expected that investment policy would converge towards that of private pension funds. It was anticipated that by 2000 investment would shift to 40 per cent in equities and real estate and 60 per cent in fixed income (bonds, loans, and mortgages). The 1993 Annual Report endorsed simulation studies revealed that such a shift in composition would, over the longer term, lead to lower pension premiums (compared to the more one-sided composition of assets in the past) and do this with a more stable development of premiums (APB Annual Report 1993). Finally, after the privatisation in 1996, it was decided to speed up the shift in investment strategy of the ABP (ABP Annual Report 1997).

Initially, the new investment strategy after privatisation paid off: rates of returns on investment of the ABP were, on average, over 10 per cent during the period 1995–9. Other pension funds, which shifted to equity earlier, gained even more from the booming stock market. As a result, pension premiums paid to the ABP were frozen and the coverage ratio of the funds rapidly increased. Some company pension funds even enjoyed a premium holiday. However, things changed rapidly after the great stock market boom came to an end in the new millennium. The average rate of return on equities of Dutch pension funds fell to −1.5 per cent in 2000. Because of its increased share in total assets, this dragged down the rate of return on all investments from 15.5 per cent in 1999 to 2.5 per cent. Results for 2001 were even more dramatic (−2.8 per cent), and total pension assets even declined by €10 billion, causing a rapid fall of the pension coverage ratio. For 2002 the total rate of return on pension investment is expected to be −10 per cent.[5] The Dutch regulatory framework obliges pension funds to take action whenever their coverage ratio falls below 110 per cent. In July 2002, one-fifth of all pension funds were in this so-called danger zone.

Because almost all (97 per cent) active participants fall under DB chemes, the fall in the rate of return on investments has serious consequences for the pension funds.

Losses have to be shared between employers (higher premiums and/or additional contributions to the pension fund), active participants (higher premiums and/or de-indexation of accrued rights and/or a reduction of the aspiration level), and pensioners (de-indexation of pension benefits). Most pension funds try to restore their financial position in the short run by raising pension premiums and hoping for a recovery of stock markets (see ABP Annual Report 2001). Some companies have been forced to stock up their pension funds. De-indexation of accrued rights is only partly effective since a majority (57 per cent) of participants have a form of final pay scheme (where past service is automatically indexed). Although, in most schemes, indexation of supplementary pension benefits is conditional on the financial position of the fund, it is generally considered as an acquired right. Therefore de-indexation of pension benefits will meet fierce opposition from well-organised pensioners. It is clear that the fall in stock market prices will put the Dutch pension system under great pressure. Some pension funds are lobbying for an easing of the regulatory framework and argue that the 100 per cent pension coverage obligation should be lowered in view of the circumstances in 2002.

In addition to the short-term challenge of raising the pension–coverage ratio, the Dutch pension system, like any other welfare state, is confronted with the continuing challenges of changing labour markets and ageing populations.

3.4. LONG-TERM CHALLENGES FACING THE DUTCH PENSION SYSTEM

3.4.1. Labour Market Change

The Netherlands is sometimes praised for its 'employment miracle' (Schmid 1997; Visser and Hemerijck, 1997; Auer 2000). Between 1983 (ending a deep recession) and 2000 the number of jobs has increased at a rate of 2 per cent per year, far above the EU average. The expansion of part-time work was a strong contributory factor: three-quarters of the two million new jobs created since 1983 were part-time. Most of these went to women, and the female participation rate (in persons) jumped from 33 per cent in

1975 to 59 per cent in 1998, the largest rise in the EU (OECD 2000). Strong labour force growth (three times the EU average) explains why, in the 1980s, unemployment, which had reached a post-war record of 13 per cent in 1984, decreased only slowly. In the second half of the 1990s, however, strong job growth translated into a rising employment population rate and a rapid fall in unemployment. The unemployment rate in early 2001 dropped to 2.5 per cent, the second lowest rate in Europe (after Luxembourg).

As can be seen from Figure 3.1, the Netherlands is an outlier in Europe regarding part-time employment (Visser 2002). The incidence of

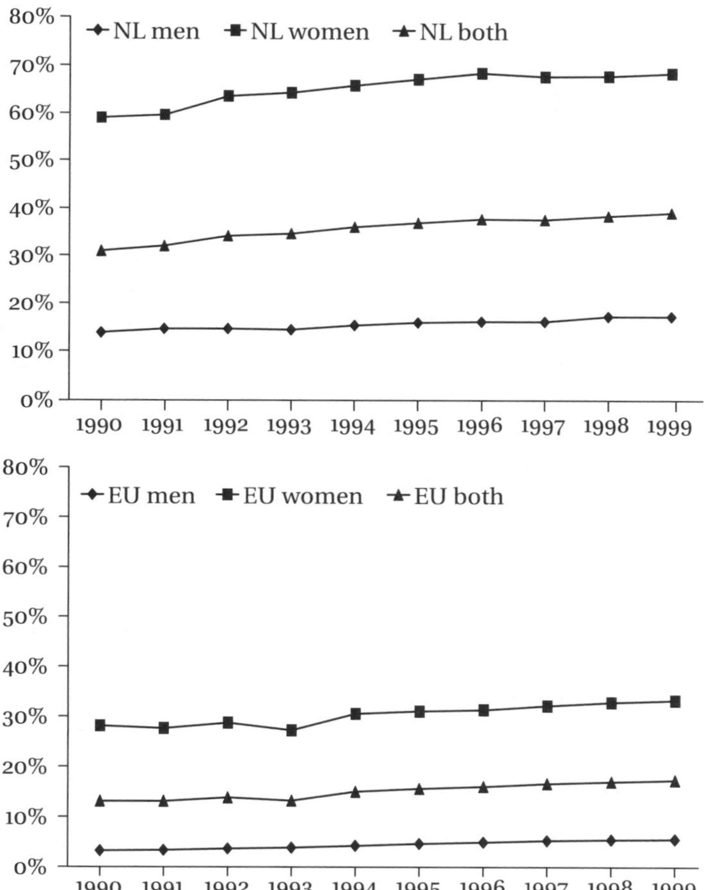

Fig. 3.1. Part-time employment in the Netherlands and the EU (as per cent of total employment).

Source: Eurostat (2001).

part-time jobs is 38 per cent, against 18 per cent in the EU. During the 1980s the growth of part-time employment accelerated in unison with the rise in female and service employment. The female share in total employment leaped from 25 per cent in 1977 to 39 per cent in 1999 (43 per cent if marginal jobs are included). In 1998, 68 per cent of all employed women worked part-time, compared to 45 per cent in 1981. Among men there was a rise from 3 per cent in 1981 to 17 per cent in 1997. Survey data show that Dutch employees more often prefer to work part-time than elsewhere in Europe. This may reflect the fact that the Dutch system facilitates part-time employment more than most other systems in the EU (Visser 2002).

But as a rule, part-time jobs tend to offer less than full-time ones in terms of job rights, pay, quality, and careers, and part-time workers do accumulate lower pension entitlement than full-time workers (O'Reilly and Fagan 1998). Therefore, because part-time jobs become the preserve for women's employment, their expansion may contradict EU equal opportunity policy (Rubery et al. 1999). In terms of labour law, employment protection, health insurance, and pension rights, part-time work poses a challenge for modernisation (Visser 2002). In a welfare state based on the notion of a breadwinner like the Netherlands, the same modernisation challenge is presented by the rising presence of women in the labour force and, in particular, mothers of young children. Another challenge—both for employment protection law and for social security legislation—is posed by the increased use of flexible contracts, interrupted careers, increased job (and employer) turnover, and shorter careers, in general. Due to more years of education and the use of pre- and early retirement provisions, fewer workers will have worked for 40 years.

In 1999, approximately 11.5 per cent of the Dutch employed had a temporary job when the average of the EU was 13.1 per cent, but the share of temporary workers is rising (Figure 3.2). Since 1992 the quantitative differences between the EU average and the Netherlands on this issue are small, but a qualitative difference remains. In the Netherlands more than half of people with temporary jobs (6.3 of the 11.5 per cent) were not interested in regular work, while in the EU only 10 per cent of the people who had a temporary job (1.3 of the 13.1 per cent) did so voluntarily (Eurostat 2001).

These changes in labour market behaviour and composition pose a challenge to the traditional philosophy and organisation of occupational pension systems, which evolved in the industrial age of the nineteenth

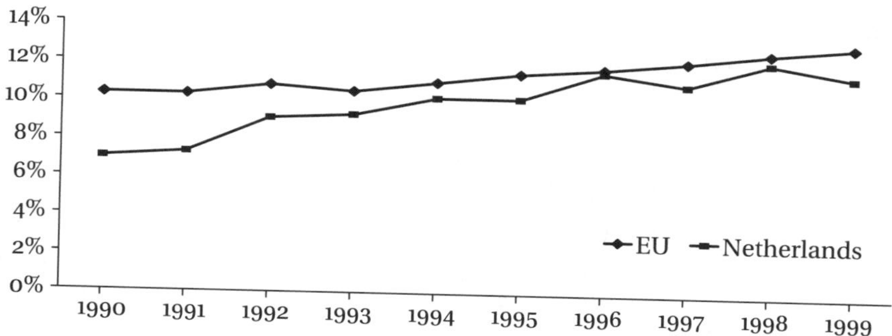

Fig. 3.2. Temporary employment in the Netherlands and the EU (as per cent of total employment).

Source: Eurostat (2001).

and twentieth centuries. Pension coverage for women, people working fewer hours, and provisions for persons with interrupted careers are likely to be inadequate. In addition to employment expansion, as the dominant policy response to the demographic challenge to pension systems there is a need for modernisation of pension systems in response to labour market and social change. We will come back to the Dutch response to that need in Section 3.5.

3.4.2. An Ageing Population

This section describes how the Dutch pension system is coping with an ageing population. As noted before, because of both the high rate of coverage of supplementary pensions and their funding, the Dutch pension system is unique among the Eurozone countries. For this reason, the Dutch pension system is often thought to be less vulnerable to ageing compared to pension systems in the rest of the Eurozone, which are mainly financed by PAYG-schemes. However, the vulnerability of pension systems not only depends on the specific mix of funded and PAYG-elements, but also on its generosity. This particularly applies to the Dutch pension system: first pillar pensions are slightly above the social minimum, and more importantly for future developments, indexed to earnings; second pillar pensions are of the DB type and most schemes are of the final-pay variant. These features make the Dutch pension system vulnerable to the impact of an ageing population, despite its well-balanced mix between funding and PAYG-elements.

Ageing and its impact on the labour market

Compared to other EU member states, the Dutch population is relatively young, having a old age dependency ratio (ADR) of 20 per cent—4 per cent below the EU average (EPC 2001: 111). Like other countries, a sharp fall in fertility rates since the 1970s, and to a lesser extent, rising life expectancy, will raise the old ADR in the first half of this century. However, the expected increase in the old age dependency ratio between 2000 and 2050 will be less than the EU average (21 per cent points against 25 per cent points increase for the EU (15) average). As a result, the old ADR will, in 2050, have fallen further below the EU average. According to Eurostat's baseline scenario, the Dutch labour force will not start to decline until 2016, which is 4 years later than the EU-average (Eurostat 2001). Projections of the future labour supply assume that the demographic effect will to some extent be compensated by a further increase in female participation rates (OECD 2002: 120).

Ageing and its impact on first pillar pensions

The EU's Economic Policy Committee (EPC) has, in cooperation with the Organisation for Economic Co-operation and Development (OECD), coordinated studies on the impact of ageing on the future costs of first pillar pensions (public expenditure as a percentage of Gross Domestic Product, GDP). For these studies, a set of commonly agreed demographic and macroeconomic assumptions have been used (see for details: EPC 2001). These studies, which were executed by experts from the member states, are made for a current (or unchanged) policy scenario. Table 3.4 shows the main results of these studies for the EU15. In order to identify driving forces behind the changes in projected expenditure, the results have been separated into four explanatory factors: population ageing, an employment effect, an eligibility effect, and a benefit effect.

The most surprising result is that, despite the relatively modest speed of ageing, first pillar expenditure in the Netherlands will converge from its current low level to the average EU level. The main factor behind this average increase of projected public pension expenditure is the benefit-effect. Under current rules, Dutch first pillar pensions are indexed to minimum wages. These are in turn coupled to general wages and therefore to productivity growth. As a result, benefits are assumed to grow in

Table 3.4. Breakdown of changes in old age public pension spending, 2000–50 (Level in percent GDP, changes in percentage points)

	Level (% GDP) 2000	2050	Increase 2000–50 (1)	Ageing (2)	Employment ratio (3)	Benefit ratio (4)	Eligibility ratio (5)
B	10	13.3	3.3	5.2	−0.9	−2	0.9
DK	10.5	13.3	2.8	4.1	−0.2	−1.7	0.5
D	11.8	16.9	5.1	6.2	−0.7	−2.7	2
EL	12.6	24.8	12.2	9.9	−3.6	4	1.4
E	9.4	17.3	7.9	8.2	−2.4	−0.3	2
F	12.1	15.9	3.8	7.7	−0.9	−3.6	0.7
IRL	4.6	9	4.4	4.5	−0.9	−0.7	1.4
I	13.8	14.1	0.3	9.5	−3.1	−4.9	−1.4
NL	7.9	13.6	5.7	5.4	−0.6	0.2	0.5
A	14.5	17	2.5	10.5	−2.2	−2.9	−3
P	9.8	13.2	3.4	6.7	−1.1	0.1	−2.4
FIN	11.3	15.9	4.6	6.6	−0.1	−0.1	−1.3
S	9	10.7	1.7	3.9	−0.5	−2.6	0.8
UK	5.5	4.4	1.1	2.4	0	−3.4	−0.1
EU15	10.4	13.3	2.9	6.4	−1.1	−2.8	0.6

Explanation (1) = (2) + (3) + (4) + (5); the decomposition is based on the following formula:

$$\frac{PPS}{GDP} = \frac{POP(55+)}{POP(20\text{–}64)} \times \frac{POP\ (20\text{–}64)}{EMPl} \times \frac{BEN}{PROD} \times \frac{PENS}{POP\ (55+)}$$

PPS is public pensions spending (which also coverages disability benefits and unemployment pensions: see for a detailed list EPC, op.cit.: 16). POP (55+) is the population older than 55, POP (20–64) is the population between 20 and 64, EMPL is employment. BEN is total spending divided by the number of pensioners. PROD is BBP/EMPL and PENS is the number of pensioners.

Source: Sociaal-Economische Raad (2002*a*), based on EPC (2001).

accordance with productivity growth and thus the general standard of living[6] whereas, in most other countries, benefits are expected to fall behind productivity growth. For example, as can be seen from Table 3.1, in both Italy and the United Kingdom, benefits are indexed only to prices and, as a consequence, will fall far behind productivity growth. This limits the effect of ageing on public pension expenditure in these countries. In addition, Italy assumes a big increase in the employment ratio, which neutralises the effect of ageing on the development of the labour force and through this, the growth of GDP. According to the calculations made by the European Commission (EC), the negative benefit effect of −2.8 in Table 3.3 for the EU15, implies that average net replacement rate in the EU will fall from its present level of 74 per cent down to 58 per cent in 2050 (CEC 2001*d*: 197).

Earlier projection of the public pension expenditure (e.g. Drees 1987) in the Netherlands assumed a similar long run discounting of benefits relative to earnings and productivity growth. This was because total wage growth was supposed to exceed contractual wage growth.[7] As benefits are indexed to contractual wage growth, their increases would be smaller than wage increases. Current projections assume first, that total wage growth equals contractual wage growth and second, that benefits are indexed to total wage growth. The Centraal Planbureau (Netherlands) (CPB), which made the calculations for the Netherlands (see also Van Ewijk et al. 2000) argues that the growth of extra-contractual wage premiums will be limited as relatively more people in the labour force reach their end of career. Moreover, in view of the increasing number of older voters, the CPB does not consider it realistic to assume that benefits will fall permanently behind average living standards (Van Ewijk 2001: 516–517). In addition to discounting benefits and lowering replacement rates, some countries hope to contain the cost of public pensions by tightening eligibility criteria. Given that public pensions are based on the residence principle, this policy option is not available in the Netherlands.

Therefore, the impact of an ageing population on public pensions in the Netherlands is neither mitigated through lower benefits nor through restricting eligibility. In contrast to most other EU-countries, ageing will almost proportionately increase the cost of public pensions. The question remains of course whether the de-indexation of benefits to general living standards in most other European countries is sustainable, as an increasing number of voters will face the consequences.[8]

Ageing and its effect on supplementary pensions

The CPB has also made projections concerning supplementary pension contributions as a percentage of wages (Van Ewijk et al. 2000: 99–104). According to these projections, contributions for supplementary pensions will increase slightly over the next decades from 6.8 per cent in 2001 to 8.0 per cent in 2060. This rise is the result of increases in life expectancy, which are not matched by later retirement. Again, these calculations were made on the assumption that current policy and rules will apply: that the DB nature of supplementary pensions is retained and pensions are indexed to wages, which is the case in periods in which the financial position is sound.

Given the funded nature of Dutch supplementary pensions, it is hardly surprising that supplementary pension contributions seem to be less vulnerable to demographic developments than public pensions.

However, obviously, funded pension schemes are prone to market and inflation risks. Because of the so-called leverage effect—defined as the ratio between the present value of accumulated pension rights over the total wage sum (the premium base)—ageing, in fact, increases the vulnerability of funded pensions to market risks.[9] This especially applies to DB schemes where, in order to meet a deficit on the balance sheet, surcharges will have to be placed on the contributions of ever fewer active members.[10] The vulnerability of Dutch supplementary pensions to market risks clearly emerges from sensitivity analyses applied to the calculations above. Assuming a 1 per cent lower real rate of return (4.8 per cent instead of 5.8 per cent), the CPB concludes that pension contributions would have to increase drastically.[11] According to the OECD, it is more realistic to assume that the long-term returns for Dutch pension funds will level at around 3.8 per cent instead of the 5.8 per cent assumed by the CPB. This implies that if pension funds do not exercise their right to partial or full indexation suspension, pension fund contributions would need to rise from 6.6 per cent in earnings in 2001 to 15 per cent in 2040 (OECD 2002: 131–2). Suspending indexation will be more difficult as pensioners become more numerous and—as is currently under discussion—are given seats on pension boards; Dutch pensioners are well organised and most of them view indexation as an acquired right. The majority of participants in Dutch pension schemes have some form of final pay scheme (57 per cent in 2001).[12] With final pay schemes, market risks are shifted to the pension fund.[13]

Age-related tax revenues

The picture that emerges from this cursory overview of the impact of ageing on the Dutch pension system is clearly less favourable than is often assumed. The reason for this is that attention has concentrated only on the expenditure side. Increasing retirement income from supplementary pensions, however, will increase tax revenues. Under current tax policies, pension premiums are tax deductible, and pension benefits will be taxed (although the elderly are taxed at a lower marginal rate than the marginal rate at which premiums are deductible). The CPB estimates the extra direct tax income as a result of increased pension income to be substantial: 3 per cent points of GDP between 2001 and 2060. In addition, extra revenues out of indirect taxation from the expenditure of the elderly population are projected to be 2 per cent GDP. Taken together age-related tax income is expected to compensate for the increased burden of public pensions. Thus, by increasing tax revenues, second pillar pensions will contribute to the financial sustainability of the Dutch pension system. However, net tax revenues are highly vulnerable to the market risks of pension funds. Higher contribution rates to compensate for lower real rates of return would, because of their tax deductibility, mean lower net tax revenues.

Dependency on foreign investment income

An increasing source for pension income will be foreign investment. The CPB and other studies assume that the net foreign asset position of the Netherlands will continue to increase substantially as a natural consequence of the trend towards ever more pension contributions being invested abroad (see Table 3.3). It is assumed that net income from foreign assets will increase by 1 per cent of GDP to more than 10 per cent in 2060.[14] According to these projections, the Netherlands will again be the renters-economy it once was.[15] Income from foreign investment will more than compensate for trade deficits. This reflects the increase in domestic demand relative to production due to population ageing. However, this means that the Netherlands will be increasingly dependent on developments in foreign markets.

Conclusion

This analysis challenges a number of perceived wisdoms about the robustness of pension systems in the face of demographic ageing. First, demographic ageing presents a risk for pension systems: There no magic formula. Second, after the specific mix of PAYG and funding, the relative generosity of the pensions system should be taken into account in any assessment of its financial sustainability and vulnerability to the impact of an ageing population. Third, the Dutch experience suggests the emergence of a more difficult trade-off between the generosity and financial sustainability of the pension system in the not too distant future.

3.5. POLICY RESPONSES

3.5.1. Overview: Work, Work, Work

The dominant policy response to welfare reform (including pensions) in the 1990s has been directed at increasing labour force participation

(Visser and Hemerijck 1997). In the late 1980s, policy-makers became aware that the low level of labor market participation was the Achilles' heel of the Dutch welfare state. In 1990 the Netherlands' Wetenschappelijke Raad voor het Regeringsbeleid published a very influential report, advocating a policy of maximising the rate of labour-market participation as the single most important labour market policy goal of any sustainable welfare state (WRR 1990). In spite of strong job growth and lower unemployment, the Netherlands was, at the time, still faced with low and declining employment rates of older workers, with rising numbers of disablement pensions and rising costs of social security. The indexation of pensions and benefits to contractual wages, which had been restored in 1989 when the Labour Party re-entered the government after years of opposition, again came under pressure (and was in fact suspended between 1992 and 1995). There was also considerable pressure, from the Christian Democratic coalition partner, to lower the statutory minimum wage and related social benefits. Reducing the volume of benefit claimants, through tightening eligibility criteria and less attractive conditions (for instance in the disability pension system) and increasing the volume of employment, came to be seen as the way forward. In response to the European Monetary System (EMS) recession of 1992–93, when job growth stagnated and unemployment was rising again, the government cajoled the social partners into an important central agreement on wage moderation. The new policy priority of participation began to make its imprint on all kinds of policy initiatives. Soon, it began to be seen as the preferred option of more unpleasant policy alternatives.

In run-up to the 1994 elections, the Christian Democrats suggested that benefit cuts, including old age benefits, might be unavoidable given the state of public finances (Metze 1995: 216). The political backlash was devastating: Many senior citizens, an important part of their core constituency, abandoned the party and voted for two newly founded elderly parties. Popular discontent over the issue of welfare reform dominated the 1994 elections. The Social Democrats were punished for their role in reducing the level and duration of disablement benefits, breaking an electoral promise in 1989. Though the party also lost a quarter of its seats in the new parliament, due to even larger losses of its Christian Democratic partner, Labour became the largest party and was able to forge a so-called purple coalition with two liberal parties. In its first period (1994–98) that coalition did not slow down in its reform effort, but Labour had a bottom line condition for its co-operation, drawing its lesson from the welfare reform crisis of the early 1990s. Committed to the defence of the level and duration of social benefits, the party was

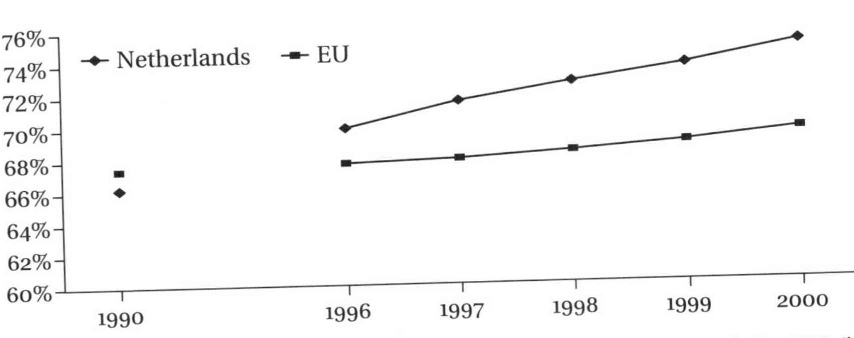

Fig. 3.3. Labour force participation rates in the Netherlands and the EU (in persons).

Source: Eurostat Labour Force Surveys (2001).

prepared to do everything possible to get the unemployed, young people, women (including single mothers), and older workers back into work. The new government's rallying slogan became 'jobs, jobs, and more jobs' (Visser and Hemerijck 1997).

The 'jobs, jobs, and more jobs' approach turned out to be successful as a political compromise between Labour and Liberals. The coalition returned to power in 1998, but slowing down its reform effort and ignoring other issues relevant to quality of life and public services, the purple coalition was defeated in 2002. Economically, and in terms of job and income growth, the years since 1994 have been extremely successful (see Figure 3.3). This explains, at least in part, why other policy responses to a possible pensions crisis in the future have had so little appeal. The memory of electoral punishment over the issue in 1994 is still vivid among politicians. The elderly parties have disappeared and the issue played no part in the 2002 elections.

The purple coalition and pension policy

In the wake of the extraordinary elections of 1994, the coalition between Social-Democrats and Liberals explictly committed itself to guarantee public pensions as a basic pension in the future. The goal of government was to enable public pensions to grow in line again with earnings. In order to achieve this, further policies directed at financing public pension expenditure were announced. These policy options were proposed in a policy memorandum published in 1996.[16] Its main presumption was that indexation of benefits to earnings could be preserved. The increase of the public burden could be dealt with by a number of measures: increasing labour force participation (especially by reducing early retirement schemes); lowering interest rate payments by public debt reduction; setting up a public pension-savings fund; and by broadening financing of Algemene Ouderdom Wet (AOW). The latter would be achieved by fixing pensions premiums at their 1997 level at 18.25 per cent.

With respect to supplementary pensions, reform efforts have concentrated on the modernisation of the pension system in response to demographic and economic change: labour market trends, cost-containment, and stronger work incentives in both the public and mandatory supplementary pension. The government intimated that, in the long run, individual pension provision should be given a greater role in the total pension package. In order to speed up the desired transition for final to average pay schemes, the government threatened to limit tax deductibility to average pay schemes only. A characteristic difference between average and final pay schemes is that pay increases do not have a retroactive effect in average pay schemes, whereas they do in final pay schemes, which means they are included for pension accrual. In addition, compulsory membership of sector-wide pension funds should also be limited to average pay schemes. At this point the 'shadow of hierarchy' (Visser and Hemerijck 1997) of Dutch industrial relations became highly visible. The background to the government's tough policy line was a number of concerns: about the effect of rising pension costs on general wage costs and employment; the effect of rising pension premiums on tax revenues due to tax deductibility rules; and the premiums the government itself had to pay for the civil servants' pension fund. Anxious to defend their much cherished sovereignty in supplementary pensions, the social partners formulated, in the Foundation of Labour, their own proposals for cost containment and the modernisation of supplementary pensions. They strongly opposed any forced changeover from final salary to average wage schemes. However, they did agree to increase coverage of supplementary pensions and to modernise benefit rules in order to increase flexibility and individual choice, as a way to control pension costs as the share of total labour costs (STAR 1997).

This, then, finally led to a covenant between social partners and government at the end of 1997.[17] In this covenant the government restated its goals concerning the preservation of the public pension as a fully fledged basic pension and the means to achieve this by extending employment. In addition, a public pension saving fund was set up. The government agreed not to change the fiscal treatment of supplementary pensions nor to change the law on mandatory extension of sector-wide pension funds.[18] In exchange, the social partners agreed to promote the modernisation of supplementary pension schemes without raising pension costs, to cost-containment of final pay schemes, to an the extension of the coverage of supplementary pensions, and to eradicate early retirement arrangements. In addition, several recommendations were made to bargainers at sectoral and company level to raise levels of participation of older workers. In short, the government received the commitment of the social partners to modernisation and cost-containment in supplementary pensions, and the closing off of early retirement avenues.

It had to give in, however, with respect to the proposed changeover to average pay schemes. The social partners, in turn, successfully defended their cherished autonomy in the fields of supplementary pensions. This was particularly important to employers. For the trade unions, the pledge to safeguard the basic income function of the public pension was crucial.

3.5.2. Explaining the Politics of Dutch Pension Policy Change

While it is not the case that the Dutch pension system is not vulnerable to the pressures of an ageing population, as we have argued above, we do observe a distinct lack of bold pension reform initiatives, especially in the area of public pensions. As a consequence, the basic structure of its multi-tiered design remains intact. Policy adjustments have largely concentrated on preventing the public pension system from becoming a burden to central government finance. This has been achieved mainly by broadening the financial base through raising levels of employment. In the second tier, policy changes have focused on containing pension costs as a component of labour costs and increasing work incentives, negotiated by the social partners, and by discouraging early exit from the labour market.

Pension reform offers an example of path-dependent policy change. There are huge hidden costs in whatever system obtains in any country. Politically, pension reform is an especially risky undertaking as it often challenges what is generally perceived as 'acquired rights'. Pension reforms that invoke losses for key groups are very likely to trigger veto powers against social policy reform (Pierson 1994; Bonoli 2000). The political feasibility of pension reforms depends to large degree on the institutional capacities of different governments' political systems to orchestrate a consensus for reform in the parliamentary arena (often including the opposition) and/or in the corporate arena between the government and the social partners. For the Dutch political economy, the politics of coalition governments, together with highly entrenched forms of corporatist intermediation between the social partners and governments in the area of industrial relations, more or less delineate the institutional capacities of Dutch policy-makers (Visser and Hemerijck 1997). By incorporating multiple parties in coalition governments as a result of proportional representation, and by rendering the social partners a semi-public status in public policy-making, the state can mobilise more resources and rally support for policy change. But divided coalitions and disagreement between the social partners can also inhibit change, precisely because of the need for extensive compromises in both the political and industrial arenas.

As a result, Dutch social and economic policy-making is, like all other negotiating policy systems, vulnerable to what Fritz Scharpf has called the joint-decision trap (Scharpf 1997) as a consequence of multiple powers of veto. Especially where the state is weak, disagreement among the social partners may lead to prolonged immobilisation. The interplay between the politics of accommodation and corporatist concertation goes a long way towards explaining the politics of pension reform (or lack thereof) in the Netherlands in 1990s. Ever since the critical elections of 1994, mainstream political parties have shied away from placing welfare retrenchment (including major policy reform in first pillar pension) on the political agenda. On the basis of the political hangover left by the disability pension crisis, the purple government was in no position to tamper with the level and duration of public pension benefits. Moreover, pensioner organisations were quite effective at the time in pursuing their interest in the legislative arena, backed by considerable electoral influence. From this defensive position, the coalition was committed to making the most of the 'job, jobs, and more jobs' policy approach. A broad cross-party political consensus, embraced by the social partners, was constructed around the need for further increases in the employment rate and public debt reduction. By way of broadening the financial base of a generous welfare state by increasing employment and bringing down interest payments through debt reduction, parametric reforms turned out to be, it would seem, to be unnecessary.

Compared to the parliamentary arena, with its relatively weak executive, the corporate arena, with its strongly institutionalised rules of interaction between the social partners and the government, is potentially an effective setting for pension reform, as long as cognitive understandings and normative orientations of actors coincide (Scharpf 1997). Moreover, political risks are inherently less prevalent in the supplementary tier because earnings-related pensions, negotiated by the social partners, are part and parcel of collective bargaining. The pension covenant is a good example of effective pension policy change. The Sociaal-Economische Raad (SER) and the Foundation of Labour (Stichting van de Arbeid), provided a forum for the government and the social partners, relatively insulated from electoral considerations, to work out a desired reform strategy. This was, however, achieved under a strong 'shadow of hierarchy'. The government threatened to alter the fiscal treatment of supplementary pensions and to suspend the mandatory extension of sectoral pension funds, if the social partners did reach an agreement—and this no doubt contributed to successful reform. It prevented the unions from pursuing a more narrowly based strategy of collective action. In order to raise the employment rate of elderly workers, unions agreed to a speedy transition of early retirement schemes to actuarially neutral pre-pension schemes. Central unions and employers federations agreed in the Foundation of Labour to advise negotiators at a lower level to abolish early retirement schemes. The outcome was a compromise in which governments promised not to reduce the tax deductibility of pensions premiums, while social partners promised to modernise pensions schemes and to mitigate final wage salaries schemes.

Finally, there is the element of fortuna, which in the long run may turn out to be a blessing in disguise. The increased reliance on occupational pensions and, as a consequence, capital funding under the highly favourable economic, financial, and labour market conditions of the 1990s, reinforced a belief that there was no longer a need for parametric reform or measures of cost containment.

3.6. WELL PREPARED TO MEET THE CHALLENGES?

3.6.1. Changing Labour Markets and Pension Coverage

In view of the rapid growth of part-time and temporary employment, pension coverage has upheld remarkably well. The percentage of employees without coverage even declined from 11 per cent in 1986 to 4.5 per cent in 1996 (SER 2001: 138–9). For most recent years no comparable data for the percentage of employees without supplementary pension coverage are available. However, the percentage of (mostly small) employers without a supplementary pension scheme declined from 22 per cent in 1996 to 16 per cent in 2001 (SER 2002*b*: 5). It is, therefore, likely that the percentage of empoyees without pension coverage continued to decline also after 2000.

The rise in pension coverage can be explained by two factors. First, since 1994 it has been illegal to exclude part-time workers from supplementary pension schemes. Second, as has been noted before, the social partners committed themselves in the pension covenant to raise pension coverage in general. This subsequently led to an agreement to increase pension coverage in the temporary work sector. Moreover, it has resulted in a lowering of age requirements for participation in supplementary pension schemes.

3.6.2. Debt Reduction and the Financial Sustainability of Public Pensions

One way of determining whether the challenge of ageing can be met is to look at the sustainability of public finances. The CPB has calculated, given their projections of public pension spending under current arrangements (see section on long-term challenge in the Dutch pension system), a time path for a sustainable development of public debt. This time path is based on two guiding principles: efficiency (tax smoothing) and equity (no externalisation of ageing cost to coming generations).[19] In addition to the costs of public pensions, the effect of ageing on public health costs have been taken into account. Further, the increase in tax revenues from the spending by pensioners has been considered. The resulting time path of public debt implies that debt should be redeemed within 25 years. The fall in future interest rate payments will be sufficient to compensate for the rising costs of ageing without raising tax and contribution rates. To achieve this, the so-called EMU surplus should be improved permanently by 0.7 per cent in 2001. For the first two decades of this century this implies, on average, a government surplus above 1.5 per cent which requires a high level of fiscal discipline by future governments. Postponing the necessary adjustment to make public finances sustainable requires tougher measures to balance the budget later on.

Public finances have deteriorated sharply because of the recent slowdown in growth. Given the strong pressures to increase spending on education and health, and taken into account the fall in tax revenues as a result of slower economic growth, it is now clear that the new government elected in May 2002 will not target a budget surplus over 1.5 per cent GDP annually. In fact, the strategy of debt redemption within 25 years has been effectively abandoned.

A public pension saving fund was set up in 1998 as a means of earmarking part of the debt reduction and savings on interest payments to finance a future rise in public pension expenditure. However, since essentially the fund only brings about a rearrangement of governments assets and liabilities, no actual pre-funding takes place (Van Ewijk et al. 2000: 58). In fact, by setting up the fund, only future expenditure for public pensions is earmarked. Politically, it was used to silence concerns by elderly parties over the credibility of the government's promise not to meddle with pension benefits or the legal retirement age.

3.6.3. Raising Participation Rates

The least painful way to achieve public debt redemption would be a rapid broadening of the tax base by increasing employment. Employment rates in the Netherlands still leave plenty of scope for further improvement: Participation rates of elderly (female) workers are still low and the female participation rate is—despite its hike over the last decade—still below the rates achieved in Scandinavia or the United States. However, the projections of public pensions costs discussed in Section 3.4, already take this into account: Female participation rates are assumed to rise in coming decades by 9 percentage points. This means that considerable efforts will have to be made to achieve any additional increases in participation rates.

While there is scope for further increases in labour force participation, pushing the employment rate above 75 per cent (as in Scandinavia or in the United States), may require policies for which political support may be lacking. There appears to be considerable hesitation over promoting longer hours and more participation among (single) mothers and married women. Given the preference for part-time work, as expressed in surveys, longer hours may find little support. Another difficult issue is how to increase the currently very low employment rate of ethnic minority immigrants, particularly the older generation with little education or language skills.

The activation of older workers, both native and immigrant, is another predicament. Replacing early retirement schemes by actuarially neutral pre-funded pre-pension arrangements has been a very important step in raising the employment rate of older workers. However, other exit routes from the labour market like disability insurance and unemployment insurance should be more effectively closed as well.

Dutch policy-makers now advocate 'active ageing' as an alternative to early retirement. The idea is to keep older people in the workforce by measures that make it possible to combine work and retirement. This calls for further reforms. In general, work-organisation and human resource policy needs to be more focused on an ageing workforce and the labour market position of older workers needs to be strengthened. There has been progress in this field, but clearly more has to be done to ensure that people will remain longer in the workforce and are willing to maintain their human capital (see also, Bovenberg 2001; Remery et al. 2001; OECD 2002: 139–41).

3.6.4. Reducing the Vulnerability of Supplementary Pensions

It was agreed in the pension covenant of 1997 that in order to contain pension costs with an eye to the ageing population, enhancements in final salary schemes should be contained. This was done by limiting the amount by which above average individual salary increases would be taken into account and by limiting the impact of wage increases just before retirement. In addition, the indexing of accrued rights in average pay schemes and of pension benefits should become to a greater extent conditional on the financial results of the pension fund. The review of the pension covenant in 2001 claims that on both issues the pension covenant has been successful (see STAR 2001).

It is fair to ask to what impact the abolition of pure final pay schemes and unconditional indexation have had in reducing the vulnerability of supplementary pension funds to market risks.[20] It should first be noted that the relevant percentages of pure final pay schemes and schemes with unconditional indexation of benefits were already low to begin with. More importantly, one may doubt whether these measures will be sufficient. Almost all supplementary pension schemes remain of the DB type and, despite the growing importance of average pay schemes, a majority of participants still falls under some variant of final pay schemes. Because they shift market risks to the pension fund, these are most vulnerable to the impact of an ageing population.

It has been noted in Section 3.4 that increasing supplementary pension contributions will affect net tax revenues. This is because the marginal tax rate at which pension premiums are deductable is lower than the marginal rate at which pension income is taxed. In this way the vulnerability of supplementary pension to the effects of ageing and the sustainability of public finances are linked.

3.7. CONCLUSIONS

Our answer to the question whether the Dutch pension system is well prepared to meet the challenges of changing labour markets and an ageing population is mixed. We certainly consider it remarkable that coverage of supplementary pensions has increased over time despite the increasing number of people working part-time or in temporary jobs. We also consider it important that incentives to early retirement have been phased out. This constrasts, for example, with the situation in Belgium or France, where any discussion on reversing the pathway of early retirement has been blocked (Ebbinghaus 2000).

Maintaining the high level of generosity in Dutch pensions from the perspective of an ageing population clearly has its price. Maybe the Dutch population is willing to pay this price. However, it is also possible that the increasing burden of the Dutch pension system puts the inter- and intragenerational solidarity, which is at the heart of the Dutch pension system, under pressure. This will certainly be the case if it is reinforced by societal trends such as increasing labour mobility and heterogeneous preferences of individuals which might limit the potential for risk-sharing in pension systems (see also, de Laat et al. 2000). As a result, it might become necessary to take the following measures (see Bovenberg 2001; Diamond 2001: 1–12; OECD 2002: 142–3.):

1. Limit implicit intergenerational transfers within the second pillar by applying actuarially fair and demographically neutral financing methods for supplementary pension schemes.
2. Make a greater appeal to intragenerational solidarity for financing public pensions by reducing the tax breaks for wealthy pensioners.
3. Spread market risks more equally in supplementary pensions between pensioners, active participants, and employers by a a more rapid changeover to conditionally indexed average pay schemes.[21]

4. Reduce the generosity of the Dutch pension system by gradually increasing the statutory and pivotal retirement age.

As a consequence, individuals who want to retire earlier should rely more on individual pension provision. In this way, future boundaries between public and private pension provision would gradually shift toward more third pillar pension provision.

This chapter has observed a lack of mould-breaking pension reforms in the Netherlands. This can be explained by the electoral revolt of pensioners in the early 1990s, the complacency of stakeholders and policymakers as a result of high and increasing rates of return of pension funds. In 2002 the stock market crisis began to expose the vulnerability of Dutch pension funds. As a result, higher premiums are necessary to compensate for falling pension coverage ratios. In addition, the slowdown of economic growth brings to the fore the political difficulty of continuing a strategy of debt-redemption under a recession. Thus, we expect the pressure for pension reform in the Netherlands to mount in the first decade of the twenty-first century.

NOTES

1. In 2000 the contribution rate was 17.95% of taxable earnings (except for earnings in the lowest income bracket) up to €27,009, only payable by employees and the self-employed.
2. The increase of the value of Dutch ownership of foreign equity has been a result of both an increase in volume as an increase in stock market prices. In contrast, the increase of the value of Dutch ownership of foreign bonds resulted exclusively from an increase in volume (Sparling 2002: 31, 34).
3. The growth rate of the share of equities and real estate in total assets over the period 1992–2001 is 1.79. This growth rate can be disaggregated to show the growth rate of the ABP and the rest (data for ABP form ABP annual reports 1992 and 2001). Own calculations show that 36% can be explained by the shift in asset-composition of the ABP. This is in accordance with the fact that over the whole period, the ABP owned about 35% of total pension assets.
4. In fact, restrictions on foreign investments and investments in equity were eased in 1988. In its Annual Report of 1990 argued successfully that its investment restrictions were not compatible with the liberalisation of capital markets in the EU in 1992 (ABP, Annual report 1990). As a result, investment restrictions were further eased in 1993.
5. NRC Handelsblad, 6 August 2002.
6. Actually, indexation rules are more complex and the degree of wage indexation varied over time. On average over the period 1961–93, there has almost been full indexation (Vording and Goudswaard 1997: 37–41). However, especially during the 1980s, public pension benefits have lagged behind wage growth (see also Bovenberg en Meijdam 2001: 44–5). Because supplementary pensions filled up the gap left by the public pension system to ensure that the ambition level of the pension system could be retained, boundaries between public and private pension provision have shifted to some degree over recent decades.

7. It was projected that extra-contractual wage increases would be 1% per year. As public pension benefits are indexed only to contractual wage developments, public pensions would over the long-term stay behind general welfare developments. As a result, according to Petersen (1988) in discounted terms benefits would fall by more than 40%.
8. See D'Amato and Galasso (2002); Van Ewijk (2001: 514–15) calculates that with indexation to real wage growth, the burden of Italian public pensions would rise with 12% points of Gross Domestic Product (GDP).
9. See for a formal exposition of the relation between the leverage ratio and the vulnerability to unforseen shocks: Van Ewijk et al. (2001: 108–11). The civil servant pension fund (ABP) expects the leverage ratio to increase from 6 to 9 over the coming 30 years (Ponds et al. 1999: 100). This implies that in the future a structural reduction of 1 percentage point in the rate of return will have to be compensated by a structural rise of 9 percentage points in contributions (cf. ABP annual report 2001: 27).
10. See Van Ewijk et al. (2001: 103–4). It is implicitly assumed in the text that general population ageing is reflected in the ageing of the members of the pension fund.
11. Van Ewijk et al. (2001: 68). See also Bettendorf, Bovenberg en Broer (2000). These authors examine the consequences of a possible fall of the real rate return as a consequense of ageing in OECD countries on Dutch supplementary pension funds.
12. The figure on final pay schemes is from Pensioen-& Verzekeringskamer (2002). Almost all of the final wage schemes include provisions that discourage strategic wage setting just before retirement. These schemes are therefore referred to as 'mitigated' final pay schemes.
13. See Jansweijer (1999) for a comparison between final pay schemes, average pay schemes, and defined contribution schemes regarding the coverage of various risks.
14. Van Ewijk et al. (2001: 63); Bettendorf et al. (2000: 68).
15. During the high-days of the Dutch renters-economy—at the end of the eighteenth century—investment income (government bonds) amounted to 12% of GDP. Half of this came from abroad (Zanden and van Riel 2000: 36).
16. Werken aan zekerheid, Tweede Kamer, vergaderjaar 1996–7, 25 010, nors. 1–2.
17. Convenant inzake arbeidspensioenen, Overeengekomen tussen het Kabinet en de Stichting van de Arbeid op 9 December 1997, Stichting van de Arbeid, publicatie 12/97.
18. However, fiscal treatment of early retirement schemes have been recently changed. The tax deductibility of early retirement schemes was phased out in 2022. In the future only those schemes will be eligible for tax deductibility which provide actuarially neutral adjustments to pensions for early or late retirement.
19. See for details Van Ewijk et al. 2000: 31 *ff.*; Van Ewijk 2001: 517–18. The timepath for a sustainable public debt has been confirmed by other Dutch studies (e.g. WRR 1999).
20. See also WRR (1999: 201–2).
21. This does not necessary mean a decline of the average generosity of the pension fund: see WRR (1999: 206).

CHAPTER

4

Facing the Pension Crisis in France

Bruno Palier

Translation by Chloe Flutter

4.1. INTRODUCTION: DEMOGRAPHIC TRENDS AND THE PENSION PROBLEM

The French system of old age insurance is a 'Pay-As-You-Go' (PAYG) pension scheme; it aims to maintain workers' income and guarantee relatively generous benefits for employees and their families. However, individual professional groups have maintained their own pension schemes, making the overall system highly fragmented. Furthermore, the French pension system, despite being compulsory, is not managed directly by the state. Instead, it is run by the social partners who represent those who benefit from and contribute to the system. Consequently, French pensions are not managed by a public bureaucracy, but by private social insurance funds that are required by law to provide a public service. Supplementary pensions can be added to compulsory pensions. These are provided by certain firms and sectors or are taken up voluntarily by individuals. Such pensions are either run within the firm (occupational) or offered by private insurers. As a result, while compulsory pensions are PAYG, some optional supplementary pensions are funded pension schemes. Debate about the structure of the French pension system is, therefore, not a question of a public system as opposed to a private system, but between compulsory and optional systems and between PAYG and funded pension schemes.

In France, the 1980s witnessed growing concern over the issue of financing the PAYG pension system. Between 1985 and 1993 a series of government reports were published.[1] All took a pessimistic view of the future of French pensions, and demanded cuts. In 1999, the Charpin Report demonstrated that the ageing of the French population is due to accelerate after 2006, when the baby-boom generation reaches the retirement age of 60. If current trends persist (relatively low fertility, low immigration, and a continuous lowering of the mortality rate), one French person in three will be over 60 by 2040. The dependency ratio of retired to active people will rise from 4 in 10 to 7 in 10. Even if falling numbers of children and unemployed release additional social security resources for pensions (in France, child allowances are substantially higher than in Britain) the financial viability of the PAYG pensions after 2010 is still suspect.[2]

An ageing population is revealing gaps in the financing of the French pension system and highlights a growing need for radical reform. Many of the system's characteristics make reform difficult, such as its generous benefits, its management by the social partners rather than the state and its corporatist fragmentation. To date, only one significant reform has occurred, in 1993. A window of opportunity for reform was opened briefly by the 1993 election and economic recession in the early 1990s during preparations for the single currency. However, the failure of Juppé's reform plan in 1995 and the subsequent change of government in 1997 quickly closed it. During the following 5 years (1997–2002), Jospin's government procrastinated over the pension issue for fear of the electoral consequences of such politically risky reform. The government elected in 2002 has announced its intention to reform pensions in spring 2003 without having much financial or political means to achieve it. Consequently, in France pension reforms are rare and highly contested, as in 1995 and in 2003.

Despite these debates failing to achieve consensus, they, nonetheless, demonstrate that the future of the French pension system as it stands is no longer assured. An analysis of the positions of the various French actors concerned with pension reform shows that it is widely believed that, in future, pensions will be based on a system of multiple pillars, mixing PAYG and funded schemes. The various plans that seek to reduce the generosity of PAYG pensions and policies aimed at implicitly promoting the development of pension savings all point in this direction. The French population seems to be taking heed of these changes without waiting for any explicit political decision. They are increasingly developing private savings to supplement the pension they will receive from the compulsory PAYG schemes, which—despite continuing to be financed—many believe is likely to diminish in future. As a result, the division between compulsory and optional pensions and between PAYG and funded pension schemes is in the process of being renegotiated in France, at the very least via changes in household behaviour if not because of explicit policy change.

4.2. A COMPLEX PENSION SYSTEM THAT IS DIFFICULT TO REFORM

French pensions are based almost exclusively on compulsory social insurance, which operates on a PAYG basis and provides retirement benefits to those with the requisite contributions. The system is primarily funded by joint social contributions made by employers and employees and is managed by administrative councils of their representatives. Collective schemes guarantee a pension with a replacement rate of between 70 and 75 per cent of wages on average. The system is very fragmented. It involves a dominant regime, *le régime général*, which covers private sector employees in industry and commerce; this accounts for approximately 60 per cent of the population. However, at the end of the Second World War, when the general regime was created, many occupational groups opted to maintain their own separate pension schemes. Their established pensions were either more generous than the general regime (e.g. the public sector and employees of public enterprises such as the railways—Société Nationale des Chemins de Fer Français, SNCF, and the Régie Autonome des Transports Parisiens, RATP and the Paris Metro) or involved lower contributions (as was the case with the liberal professions and agricultural workers).

For those covered by the general regime, the basic benefit level (a maximum 50 per cent of a reference wage, calculated over the 25 best years) is increased by a complementary pension, which is also compulsory and also operates on a PAYG basis. The complementary pension regimes are more numerous. They are arranged by economic sector (agriculture, commerce, industry, etc.), as well as by job type. For example, complementary pensions for managers are different to those for other employees (L'Association Générale des Institutions de Retraite des Cadres, AGIRC is for managers and Association des Régimes de Retraite Complémentaire, ARRCO for employees). While the general regime is based on defined benefits, the complementary regimes are based on defined contributions—employees receive points in return for contributions. The social partners regularly decide the value of these points with reference to economic conditions and demography, and their total over an individual's working life determines the value of the final pension.

Other types of pensions supplement this system; although currently marginal, these are now developing rapidly. A minimum state pension exists for those who have not paid sufficient contributions, or who have very low incomes.[3] Additional optional supplementary pensions are also available from provident societies to top up compulsory pensions. These additional pensions are also PAYG schemes, based on defined contributions and often established through collective branch agreements or at firm level. In principle, therefore, the overall system leaves little space for funded pension schemes. However, some professional groups have chosen to create voluntary supplementary pensions that are funded. These include Caisse nationale de prévoyance de la fonction publique (PREFON), established in 1967, Fonds de pension des élus locaux (FONPEL) established in 1993, and Contrats de Complément de Retraite Volontaire Agricole (COREVA), which was established in 1990 for agricultural workers but blocked by the European Court of Justice. Since 1994, tax deductions have been available for savings schemes that are for pension or general provident purposes. Finally, there has also been a rapid increase since the mid-1990s in additional supplementary pensions, called '*chapeaux*',[4] created by large corporations and run as funded pension schemes (e.g. the additional supplementary pensions in insurance societies and banks) (Babeau 1997). However, while state employees and liberal professionals are able to take advantage of funded pensions, no funded pension schemes exist for employees covered by the general regime, who constitute the majority of the French work force.

Pension reform is one of the most sensitive political issues in France. Any suggestion of reducing pensions encounters strong public opposition; the French are strongly attached to their social security schemes in general, their pension schemes in particular, because of the high replacement rate assured under compulsory regimes. Beyond their generosity, French pensions also enjoy high levels of public legitimacy. Their embodiment of social rights, their benefits, their financial structure and their representative systems of management—all reinforce their popularity. In France, social rights are acquired by paying social contributions directly out of wages; pension benefits are calculated according to the 25 best years of salary earned and/or the amount contributed, on an individual (not a collective) basis. These are difficult to challenge retrospectively and have an advantage over means-tested or more redistributive pension schemes because they do not undermine personal incentives to save. Further, under this individual and relatively accurate reference system, users are considerably more sensitive to any modification than under a flat-rate scheme. Hence, resistance to any reduction in pensions is strong. The method of financing pensions has also met resistance: social insurance contributions are perceived by workers as a personal investment for a retirement income, as the term 'deferred wage' (used to describe pension payments) indicates. By comparison, tax-funded pensions suffer from all the criticisms aimed at taxation. Unlike social contributions, money taken in tax is rarely hypothecated; in France as elsewhere, tax revenues disappear into the general public coffers. As individual pensions are financed through contributions, not taxes, the French would prefer to see social contributions raised rather than their pensions cut back (Gaxie et al. 1990; Palier 2002).

Historical research on the French pension regimes shows how they were established through progressive negotiation. As various exceptions emerged—particular, autonomous, or special schemes—numerous socio-professional categories have ensured that their specific interests are well defended (Guillemard 1980, 1986; Dumons and Pollet 1994; Friot 1994). This corporatist fragmentation into hundreds of distinct regimes reinforces its resistance to change. Specific socio-professional groups seek to preserve their particular advantages, requiring the government to negotiate with representatives of each group if they wish to initiate reforms. Since the mid-1980s, both left- and right-wing governments have tried to reduce PAYG pensions. French wage earners are represented by trade unions and their positions, if not united, were relatively homogenous throughout those years. The trade unions mobilised public opinion in defence of social security and emerged as the defenders of the status quo against official initiatives that appeared to threaten pensions.[5] Trade unions have been veritable 'veto players' (Tsebelis 1995; see also Immergut 1992) in French social protection ever since. Their support is essential for change to take place. Analysis of the last 20 years shows that it is not possible to reform French social security in the absence of any agreement with—or at the least the tacit consent of—the social partners (or at least some of them).

This 'corporatist-conservative' (Esping-Andersen 1990) configuration of French pension institutions explains their considerable resistance to change, in contrast for example, to Britain. The institutional features of the French system, established in 1945, appear to block reform, despite arguments in its favour dating from the late 1970s. However, the French system has not remained fixed. Certain economic events and policies have contributed to opening a pathway to change.

4.3. MUCH DEBATE, LITTLE REFORM

At the end of the 1980s, the future financing of pensions became an important issue in France. Numerous reports were commissioned to determine demographic projections and propose solutions (see note 1). Their projections, which were roughly similar, showed that for the pension system to remain in equilibrium in 2025, contributions had to increase by 170 per cent or benefits had to be halved (Ruellan 1993: 911–12). The reports highlighted the importance of ensuring the future long-term financial viability of the pension system, most notably by changing the way pensions were calculated. Several options were proposed: increasing the contributory period for a full pension, changing the reference salary used to calculate the pension due, and changing the method of indexation to revalue pensions. However, during the 1980s and up until 1993, no pension reforms were implemented despite the constant deficits in the general regime and pessimistic predictions about its future viability.

Faced with these difficulties, governments preferred to postpone the implementation of the proposed reforms and reverted to a standard and politically safer solution. Between 1985 and 1991, employee pension contributions rose from 4.7 to 6.55 per cent of the social security ceiling. The social partners themselves adopted the classic method when they adjusted the compulsory complementary pension systems (AGRIC and ARRCO) in 1993 and 1994. They increased social contributions and slightly reduced the pension amount by indexing the pension to prices instead of gross wages. Since the mid-1980s, to counter trade union defence of established pension schemes, public policy has consisted chiefly of commissioning reports and information campaigns to focus on the effects of an ageing population, the growing imbalance between active and non-active members of society and the catastrophic consequences for French pension futures.

In March 1993, a political window of opportunity opened up the pension debate. Legislative elections returned a strong majority to the Union pour la démocratie française—Rassemblement pour la République, UDF-RPR (right-wing) coalition, in an atmosphere of apparent crisis for the state of social security. Subsequently, the Balladur Government sought to implement recommendations from the various reports and introduced a reform to the general pension regime for employees in private industry and commerce. This reform was made possible because of concessions made by the government to the trade unions (Bonoli 1997).

The 1993 reform modified the method of calculating pensions, as well as the method for indexation.[6] The reform severed the previous link between contributions and benefits, like all reforms of Bismarckian systems of social protection, and generated a reduction in the replacement rate of pensions under the general regime (from 50 to 33 per cent of the reference salary, Babeau 1997). To promote acceptance of this reduction in benefits, the government announced a second part to the reform, which separated pensions based on social insurance from those based on 'solidarity'. 'Fonds de solidarité vieillesse' (FSV) financed benefits for retirees who had made insufficient contributions to the system during their working lives. These benefits were now no longer the financial liability of the social insurance budget.

In trying to impose the same kind of reforms to public sector employees, Alain Juppé demonstrated that he lacked the political savvy of Édouard Balladur. His inability to do so doubtless explains his loss of the 1997 election. The reform expounded by Édouard Balladur and Simone Veil only concerned the general regime (employees in private industry and commerce). It did not cover the special regimes for public servants or employees of public enterprises (SNCF; RATP; EDF-GDF; etc.), where union membership rates are the highest in France and for whom the method of calculating pensions is more generous than for private sector employees. In a plan presented on 15 November 1995, Alain Juppé announced the reform of these special pension regimes. He wished to extend the rules for calculating pensions from the private systems to the public ones, notably to increase the contribution period for a full pension from 37.5 to 40 years. Alain Juppé believed his political position[7] was strong enough to develop his social security reform plans in secret, without any negotiation with the social partners: he feared that prenegotiations would erode the overall social reform package. Responses to his proposed public pension reform were never heard. From the 23 November onwards, massive strikes occurred in the public sector (particularly at SNCF and RATP) and large-scale protests multiplied until 22 December 1995. Given the extent of social protest, which also focused on the plan to restructure SNCF, the government withdrew its pension reform plan.[8] The window of opportunity had closed until 2003.

Between 1997 and 2002, the Jospin Government did not attempt any major pension reform. Lionel Jospin learnt from Alain Juppé's failure. Instead, he devoted these years to preparing the ground for future pension reforms. He has also taken several measures to protect PAYG pensions, while simultaneously preparing the ground for future funded pension schemes. In 1999, the Prime Minister asked the *Commissariat au Plan* to consider possible reforms to pensions. The Charpin Report (1999) ensued. It was presented to the Prime Minister on 29 April 1999 and followed on from the previous reports published during the 1990s. As cited in the introduction to this paper, it showed how, if no changes are made, the future of the PAYG pensions will be undermined by 2010. Consequently, the Charpin Report again proposed to reform the general regime by extending the period of contribution necessary to obtain a full pension to 42.5 years. It also proposed to align the future of public employees (and associates) with those of the private sector. This report, however, did not generate consensus amongst all key players. While CFDT (a reformist trade union) approved the report and CNPF (the employers' association, renamed MEDEF in 1999) went one further, calling for the years of contribution to increase to 45 years, other trade unions were opposed to its conclusions.

Further reports were published during this period. In contrast to the homogeneity of expert opinion in the 1990s, these reports adopted a range of approaches.[9] A report by the Copernic Foundation[10] was published several months after the Charpin Report and contested the idea that a demographic shock threatened the pension system. It pointed out that, according to the Charpin report, pension spending needed to increase from the current level of 12 per cent of GDP to 16 per cent by 2040. This rise in pension spending, however, is only a small increase compared with the rise that has occurred from the 1950s, since when pension spending has doubled. The Copernic Foundation also contested the view that any increase in pension contributions was impossible (they could be partly financed from future productivity gains), especially, given that increased contributions could save the PAYG pension system without changing the replacement rate of future pensions. Furthermore, the report highlighted that the ageing of the population, which threatened the pension system, would concurrently result in a reduction in the number of children, young people, and most likely the unemployed,[11] and, hence, the amount spent on social security for them. These future savings could be spent on pensions so that their generosity could be maintained.

Faced with these two extreme positions, the Prime Minister preferred to seek further expert opinions rather than chose a solution that was too entrenched. Hence, in September 1999, Dominique Taddéi (2000) made a study for the Conseil d'analyse économique.[12] The report highlighted the contradiction between increasing the length of contributions and the continuing use of early retirement. In France, the effective retirement age is 57, not 60. Furthermore, people are entering the labour market at higher ages. Extending the length of contributions made it is impossible for many to work the number of years required to get a full pension. Dominique Taddéi, instead, recommended starting *à la carte* pensions by implementing a progressive system of transition from full activity to retirement, which allowed people to combine revenue from employment with retirement income.

Several months later, René Teulade wrote a report on pensions for the *Conseil économique et social* (Teulade 2000). Reflecting the main attitudes found in this *Conseil* (especially among trade unionists), the report stressed the level of uncertainty in 40-year demographic projections and, instead, opted for a 5-year perspective. This report also contested the proposal to increase the contribution period, given high unemployment and low activity rates amongst people over 50. Unlike the Charpin Report, this report proposed increasing the level of pensions in exchange for indexing private pensions to prices and taking more account of periods outside formal employment when calculating pension rights (unemployment, training, education, children, etc.). It disagreed with the idea of aligning the special regimes with the general regime. To assure the financial viability of PAYG pensions, the report recommended increasing the reserve fund and the state's role in financing non-contribution related pension rights. The Teulade Report, like the Taddéi Report, favoured an economic approach over a financial or demographic approach to the pension problem, noting that any solutions should be based on stronger economic growth and on higher employment rates amongst older workers.

Pensions are the object of an important, at times contradictory and always high profile debate. Therefore, Lionel Jospin has prudently preferred to wait until after the elections in 2002 before reaching any major decision. However, to show his commitment to preserving, not undermining, the PAYG pension system, the Jospin government created a reserve fund under the '*loi de financement de la Sécurité sociale*' (voted in 1998). This law was implemented at the start of 1999 with an initial contribution of 2 billion FF to the reserve fund. It will be supplemented with future surpluses in the social regimes (National agency for old age insurance (France), CNAV; Retirement solidarity fund (France) FSV; and *Contribution sociale de solidarité des sociétés*), half of all earnings from social deductions paid on inheritance income and with any exceptional revenue. Capital in the fund is currently increasing incrementally via government decisions. By 2003, it had risen to €20 billion, when more than €150 billion would be needed. The source of payments into the fund as well as its use (where it could be invested) have not yet been firmly decided by government.

In order to gain the consensus the Charpin Report had failed to achieve, Lionel Jospin (the Prime Minister at the time) also announced the creation of the '*Conseil d'orientation des retraites*' (COR) in April 2000. The council was made up of experts and representatives of the social partners (MEDEF,[13] notably, refused to take part). In April 2001, COR organised a seminar on the theme 'Age and Work' which sought to combine attempts to increase the length of contributions with raising the employment rate. In fall 2001, the COR published its first report, in which it promoted the lengthening of contribution period to obtain a full pension as the main solution for pension, as well as increase in the employment rate.

However, Lionel Jospin did not find a basis for compromise that would allow him to introduce such reforms without them being highly contested. Employers were also faced with protests from trade unions and the general population when they tried to extend the length of contribution required for complementary pensions. As part of a new negotiated social agreement Mouvement des entreprises de France (MEDEF) wanted to alter the rules for calculating complementary pensions in the AGIRC and ARRCO regimes, to extend the contributory period to 45 years. To promote this cause, MEDEF asked its members to stop paying contributions to the ASF.[14] However, this tactic, which could be seen as blackmail on the part of MEDEF, caused trade unions to mobilise in defence of complementary pension schemes. Several days later on 25 January 2001, the trade unions organised a protest of more than 300,000 people against MEDEF. Reneging on its position, MEDEF signed an accord with three Trade Unions. This accord froze contribution rates to AGIRC and ARRCO until December 2002 and brought the two complementary regimes more into line with each other. The accord also urged the government to undertake a full reform of pensions, including both the public and private regimes. During the electoral campaign for presidential election in Spring 2002, the two supposedly front-running candidates (Lionel Jospin and Jacques Chirac) promised rapid pension reform in order to save the PAYG system. The Raffarin government (which won the election) announced this reform for Summer 2003. It is designed to align the public sector with the private one. This involves an increase in the contribution period for public sector employees (up to 40 years, and after 2012 a progressive increase for all up to 42 years exchange for a new basis for calculating the replacement rate of the pension). Meanwhile, the government is trying to close down pre-retirement schemes and to promote private savings.

Despite the government being armed with new instruments (the reserve fund) and new slogans (raising the employment rate), the formula for preserving the future of PAYG pensions always rests on increasing the contribution period necessary to acquire the right to a full pension. It implies either an increase in the effective age of retirement or a reduction in the size of the pension paid, compared with what would have been paid had previous legislation remained in place. As there is no current trend towards a longer working life despite French commitments at the European level, this indicates a progressive reduction in the level of pensions paid out by the compulsory PAYG pension regimes. Expected reductions in public pensions create opportunities for an increase in private pension saving.

4.4. TOWARDS PENSION SAVINGS

The 1993 and 2003 reforms are the chief causes of the weakening of the French PAYG pension scheme. Due to these reforms, future pensions will be significantly lower than they are now. The most optimistic perspective, proposed by COR, show that the 1993 reforms imply a decrease in the replacement rate from 78 to 64 per cent in 2040 (COR 2001). Henceforth, private sector workers will no longer be able to rely as much on their basic pension and will have to supplement it with other sources to enjoy an equivalent level of retirement income.

This first reform, however, did not go far enough because the reform of the general regime and the plan to align public service (and associated) pensions with those in the private sector remained unresolved (a conclusion of the Charpin Report). The Raffarin government wants to introduce another reform. In order to win political support, reform is being preceded by a new phase of scare mongering about the state of French pensions. This reflects the 1980s when several reports predicted that the pension system would be doomed by the end of the 1990s (see notes 1 and 2). Several demographic and economic analyses have highlighted the future weakness of PAYG pensions. These predictions have had a significant impact on the French population. Indeed, the growing number of reports, publications, and media and government campaigns concerned with population ageing and its supposedly catastrophic effect on the pension regime, have contributed to sapping public confidence in PAYG pensions. Consequently, the French population strongly believes that the current system will not provide an appropriate pension for future generations, and surveys confirm that the French are anxious about the level of future pensions. In a survey for *Le Parisien* in 1999, the future level of pensions ranked as the third greatest preoccupation.[15] In other surveys of employees, the percentage expressing concern about their own pensions and the future of the pension scheme ranged from to 70 to 85 per cent.

These survey results and the positions of various actors show that there is an ambiguous consensus about the content of pension reform: Reform is a matter of establishing a mixed system where funded pensions supplement the PAYG scheme. While funded schemes were taboo for many involved with social protection in the 1970s (especially trade unions and left-wing parties), politicians and trade unionists today are increasingly ready to consider a role for funded schemes to supplement PAYG pensions.

There is, however, still no consensus over the form funded pension schemes should take. Consensus only concerns the principle that supplementary funded pensions should be developed in conjunction with (and not in the place of) PAYG pensions. This, nonetheless, represents a significant step forward in the debate, especially as, for a long time, it was pitched between supporters of either PAYG pensions or funded schemes. There is now agreement on the general framework within which debate must occur. Future debate will be significantly more concerned with the form of a mixed system than with the principle itself. One sign of this consensus is agreement by the majority of protagonists over the use of the term 'pension savings', which has been substituted for the term 'pension funds', a term considered tainted by the behaviour of the powerful British and American pension fund institutions.[16]

The reasons for this agreement over the development of pension savings differ widely. Insurers, mutual banks, credit agencies, commercial banks, and employers have wanted to develop pension funds for a long time. However, while they all would like to develop funded pensions, they disagree about the way funded pensions should be organised.[17] In 1991, soon after the publication of the white paper on pensions, insurers represented by the *Fédération française des sociétés d'assurance* (FFSA) published their proposal for 'ensuring the future of pensions'. The insurers suggested not one way of funding pensions, but two: One provided individual contracts for supplementary pensions and the other created a 'pension fund *à la française*'. The aim of the first was to encourage individual initiatives, freedom for anyone to apply for withdrawals solely transferable into annuities, including terms of revertibility. Since then, the FFSA has modified its thinking and proposed the option of partial withdrawals of capital. As for 'pension funds *à la française*', the FFSA proposed developing a collective fund (combining employees by sector, firm, or profession), which would be established by contract with optional membership. The system would be tax deductible and managed through integrated capitalisation (with transferable rights), overseen by the social partners (who would control administration and financing of contributions). This system would also require termination in an annuity, with rights transferable to the surviving spouse.

Fifteen months after the insurers' report, mutual banks and credit agencies joined together to form an Association de Recherche et d'Études pour l'Épargne et la Retraite (AREPPER). This association aimed to differentiate itself from the private insurers' proposals and to offer a mutualist-based proposal founded on the principle of creating a balance between solidarity and insurance. This included developing pension savings funds in 'tight collaboration between the social partners'. The pension savings fund would include firm or enterprise funds, not managed by the firm but by professional mutual societies controlled by the traditional players (the managers of social insurance: employer and employee representatives). The other notable difference from the FFSA proposal concerns withdrawals. Under the FFSA proposal, withdrawals are only by annuities. Under the other proposal, there are various options for withdrawals.

In October 1992, approximately 60 of France's biggest companies united together under the banner of the *Association française des entreprises privées* (French association of private firms). The president was Ambroise Roux, the honorary president of Alcatel-Alsthom. He proposed measures allowing the 'provision of supplementary pensions'. The objective would be to invest at firm level, allowing returns to augment the original savings fund. This involved a fund created by employers, to which they were the sole contributors. The management of the fund would be internal to the firm and returns would be accounted for on the balance sheet, as has long been the case in Germany. Withdrawals at the time of retirement would be made only in the form of a life annuity.

In July 1993, the banks (non-mutuals) presented their own proposal entitled '*Fonds d'épargne retraite*'. In France, the banks already have a presence in niche life insurance markets, managing salaried workers' savings schemes. The banks proposed that workers' savings schemes should be extended, either on the firm's initiative (firm funds or interfirm funds between SMEs), or on the initiative of authorised organisations. This system would allow individual membership (liberal professions and crafts). Membership would be optional and the employer would not be obliged to make a financial contribution. Management would be external to the firm, with the possibility of internal management for very big companies. The investment rules would allow quoted and non-quoted shares. They would also allow portable pension rights to remove restrictions on the working population and encourage transparent management. Benefits would be paid as life annuities or as a lump sum on retirement. The main difference compared with previous proposals is that it is possible for employers to exempt themselves from contributing to the funds and the possibility for fund management to remain internal to big companies.

Given these numerous concurrent developments, the representative organisation for French employers attempted to generate a single coherent strategy and to reach a compromise. It set up a commission involving industrialists, bankers and insurers, including the authors of the previous proposals. According to the working group, the creation of pension funds would contribute to the better 'functioning of the economy'. However, they remained vague about concrete methods for organising the funds. The pension system should be consolidated and reinforced by proper pension funds and the quasi-funds within firms and, in so doing, develop French capital markets. In 1999, Denis Kessler, a spokesperson for pension funds in France, became president of the *Fédération française des assurances* and deputy head of MEDEF (he subsequently quit at the end of 2002). His arrival in two of the highest posts in employer organisations implied that pensions had become a priority for French employers. The reasons used by Kessler to promote the development of pension funds were not the immediate interests of insurance companies or banks who would benefit from the expansion of this significant market, but the importance of developing a French and European capital market and, consequently, giving French and European firms greater financial capacity.

Political parties on the right were the first to adopt the employers' proposals. Three laws concerning the creation of pension savings funds were put before parliament between April 1993 and May 1996. The Right argued in favour of creating pension funds using similar arguments to those used by French employers, but recently adding arguments concerning 'sovereignty'. Beyond just the interests of business, Jacques Chirac argued the case for pension funds as a matter of national interest to France, given the current power of foreign investors—British and American pension funds: 'We must create a system of pension funds . . . so that French pensioners and workers can once again own their firms'.[18] During his electoral campaign in Spring 2002, Chirac promised the development of '*fonds de pension à la française*'. However, this project has been postponed both because of the stock market crisis and the budgetary difficulties of the French government.

At the end of the 1990s, members of the Socialist Party, like many trade unionists, also became sensitive to anti-American arguments, which they could advocate more easily than economic arguments in favour of pension funds. Nicole Notat, the Secretary General of CFDT, used this argument: 'European and French workers must ask themselves if they will continue to let Anglo-Saxon pension funds . . . continue to have the monopoly over intervention in the capital of French and European enterprises'.[19] François Morin (2000) showed that French firms required capital from French pension funds if they were to no longer to be dictated to by American pension funds.

A second argument used by the left to justify the development of workers' pension savings is that the creation of pension savings funds within firms is a way of reinforcing the power of the workers. In a report by Michel Sapin (2000), this argument is refined. 'For us, it is a means for the views of workers to penetrate the firm that is different to the "pension fund shareholder" method or to those of management.'[20] For some on the Left and for some trade unionists, pension saving funds managed collectively by workers, constitute a way for them to strengthen their control and decision-making power within the firm, thereby justifying the establishment of pension funds in France.

Most players in the pension debate now support a mixed pension regime, whereby a funded element is introduced into the regime to supplement PAYG pensions. However, they support it for different, even contradictory, reasons. This issue remains the object of staunch opposition from some trade unions and the Communist Party, while most of the trade unions, the reformist left, the right and employers are promoting a mixed system. The idea also seems to have the support of most French people. Surveys concerning the future of pensions show that, as a result of the prospect of lower PAYG pensions in future, people are prepared to save for their retirement in order to supplement their PAYG pension. Between November 1996 and December 1999, numerous surveys showed that a majority of those questioned (between 43 and 80 per cent, nearly two-thirds on average) favoured the creation of a pension savings regime that complemented PAYG pensions (Palier and Bonoli, 2000).

It is fair to conclude that most of the important players in the pension reform debate and a majority of the French public (two-thirds of those surveyed) now think that the French pension system will become a mixed system combining PAYG and funded pensions. However, further analysis of the positions of funded pensions shows that there is still insufficient agreement on the characteristics of pension savings (Should they be compulsory or voluntary? How should they be financed? Who manages them? Should they offer withdrawals through annuities or a capital lump sum? etc.). A first, essentially qualitative, step is about to be taken involving the formal introduction of funded pensions into the French pension system.

Beyond these debates, there are several indicators that show that France is already in the process of developing pension savings funds. Optional funded pensions already exist in certain professions.[21] A first tentative piece of legislation to extend optional private pension funds was introduced in 1997 (loi Thomas). This law was not implemented because of a change in the government. In 1997, the Juppé Government wanted to create the opportunity to establish optional pension savings funds, organised within the firm, for workers in commerce and industry. The law passed on 25 March 1997 sought to institute a pension savings system for 14.5 million workers in the private and agricultural sectors in France. The system would have been financed by member employees and eventually by employers who wished to contribute. It should have allowed withdrawals as annuities and eventually partly as capital. The reform package would have been made attractive by exemption from taxes and social charges. The law could only be applied after the publication of decrees precisely defining the conditions of its implementation. This should have occurred in June 1997. However, the dissolution of the National Assembly and the arrival of a new majority government interrupted the process. The then new Prime Minister, Lionel Jospin, announced that he would look again into the proposed system which risked 'putting in danger the PAYG system' because employers, who contributed to these funds, would be exempted from their social contribution, creating a deficit in the PAYG pension system. The decree to apply this law was blocked by the Jospin Government in 1997 and the law was repealed in the summer of 2001.

The Jospin Government, however, also helped pave the way for the creation of these types of pensions. Despite repealing the 'loi Thomas' and not openly wishing to develop pension funds, the Minister for the Economy and Finance in the Jospin Government, Laurent Fabius, had parliament adopt a plan to establish 'voluntary wage savings partnership plans'. These provided those workers who wished to save with a long-term savings plan (10 years or more as collective negotiation would determine) that was tax exempt and to which employers could eventually contribute. Amounts saved by workers would be payable as capital or as more flexible payments—politicians wanted to avoid using the notion of an annuity. This is a funded system in all but name; it aims to return power to French workers and to provide French savings funds for use in French firms. It is not explicitly designed to supplement all French pensions. However, it makes a contribution, as revealed in a slip of the tongue, by Fabius, who called wage savings plans 'pension savings plans' on television in January 2001. The right-wing government is now waiting for an opportunity to introduce new legislation favouring private savings.

Even though no comprehensive system of fully funded pensions has yet been put in place by the public authorities, pension savings are developing in France through changes in individual behaviour. The French population have already responded to the prospect of a future fall in PAYG pensions. The savings rate in pension products grew throughout the 1990s even though purchasing power did not change. If we analyse changes in the composition of French households' expenditure, we see that the amount relating to pension savings (life insurance and pension savings in the strict sense) rose steadily during the 1990s; a period of intense debate about of the PAYG pension system. Consequently, while only 31 per cent of French households owned one of these products in 1986, 46.6 per cent did so in 2000 (INSEE 2001).

Today, nearly one household in two saves for their retirement. Strictly defined pension savings (the institutional forms of which are poorly developed, as we have seen) are used by 20 per cent of households aged between 40 and 50. In the case of those in liberal professions, the rate rises to 31 per cent. It is approaching 24 per cent for agricultural workers and commercial artisans and nearly 20 per cent for managers (INSEE 1999: 294). For want of proper pension funds, life insurance is the substitute most used by households to prepare for retirement. This product provides a reasonably good return on capital (the return was 5.4 per cent in 1999) and has tax exemption. Investment in life insurance plans has steadily increased through the 1990s. 'In 1997, life insurance represented 18 per cent of total investment, compared with less than 5 per cent ten years earlier' (INSEE 2001: 147). More generally, 'the role of financial products (bank savings, stocks and shares, life insurance, etc.) has increased over the last 20 years and today represents half of the wealth of individuals, given that regional variations have diminished continuously during the period (3.5 per cent in 1997)' (INSEE 1999: 279).

Even before the government has adopted any laws to extend the take-up of pension savings funds, such savings are developing independently because individuals anticipate that PAYG pensions will fall. The main question today is whether the future funded pension system will receive contributions from the state and from employers. The development of private pension savings, which is already well underway in French households, is not the issue. In this, France is merely following the same path as other developed countries.

4.5. CHANGING THE BALANCE BETWEEN PUBLIC AND PRIVATE PENSIONS

The French pension situation is following the path of most Bismarckian pension institutions; it has long maintained a relative status quo despite several difficult reforms. Bismarckian pension institutions are very difficult to reform because change confronts the special interests of various privileged groups of workers. In order for the reforms to pass they must be negotiated with the social partners. Reforms have strengthened the link between contribution and benefits. Old age insurance no longer functions as a deferred salary, but more as salary savings. As the amount people have to contribute directly to their pensions increases, the level and the coverage of the PAYG pensions decreases. This retrenchment in the cover offered by basic old age insurance regimes results in the development of individual pension savings and, for those with insufficient contributions, increased dependence on means-tested benefits. This outcome emerges at a time when there is significant long-term unemployment, a greater number of interruptions in people's careers, and more insecure and part-time employment.

These reforms are based on an actuarial[22] logic which increasingly pervades social insurance, ensuring that it increasingly resembles private individual insurance: The amount of pension received upon retirement is calculated more and more with reference to the level of contribution paid and less according to the level of previous earnings salary. This logic implies a reduction in the redistribution function of old age pensions (those most disadvantaged by these reforms are workers with uneven and interrupted careers, most notably women). We find here again the same dynamic of progressive marketisation of social insurance that characterised changes in Anglo-Saxon systems of social protection (Pierson 2001: 455). The French situation is, however, still a long way from the British situation.

However, in order to appreciate the changes underway, one needs to look beyond reforms (achieved to a greater or lesser extent) to the compulsory public pension systems. An analysis of the French situation that takes into account changes in household behaviour indicates that, despite the French system being one of the more difficult to reform, profound changes are, nonetheless, taking place and these tend towards the development of private pensions. This trend only becomes apparent if the relationship between compulsory funded pensions and private savings for pensions is considered. It is in estimating how the public/private divide will change that we see what the future of French pensions will hold.

There are interconnections between compulsory PAYG pension systems and voluntary funded insurance schemes. Generally, the pension reforms that occurred in Europe during the 1990s have provided an opportunity to not only adapt but also to restructure pension systems, giving funded pension schemes a greater role. Despite considerable institutional differences between European countries, developments in the 1990s are based on a common logic. Under this logic, there is a relative reduction in the importance of PAYG systems as a method of income-transfer towards the aged, benefiting funded schemes (Palier and Bonoli 2000). Each country follows its own path in reforming its pension system. However, this path runs through a new and common landscape, structured by a global model of pension systems where funded pensions play an important role.

All national pension systems in Europe are being progressively transformed through the same interconnected mechanism. This proceeds at two speeds. First, the replacement rate offered by basic collective pensions is reduced. This reduction in the basic pension creates the space for developing supplementary funded pensions. Given reductions in benefits under the basic regimes, one can expect an expansion in the role of funded pensions, or at the least considerable pressure to go in this direction. This process has effectively been underway since the 1980s in many European countries.

Given the uncertainty about the future of PAYG pensions, there was an increase in private spending on old age pensions during the 1980s and 1990s. Increasing negative demographic and financial predictions, political scare-mongering that surrounds these predictions, and the progressive reduction in the projected benefits offered, all contributed to this uncertainty. While reform of the PAYG pension regimes to assure their financial viability, now and in the future, is the highest priority, these changes also contribute to the development of private pensions by reducing the replacement rate.

It is clear that new forms of private and voluntary pension forms will develop in France in the coming years. However, it is still difficult to assess the implication these developments will have for international finance. Indeed, France has taken a step towards the development of private pension funds in a system that was previously almost exclusively based on PAYG. This step was merely a political one, the difficulty having been to convince all the players that this should be done, and to find different arguments in favour of these developments. This chapter has analysed the content of the debates and the reforms that led to this new step. However, it is still unclear when and what type of pension funds will develop, who will be in charge of them, how they will be invested. Once the political decision has been taken, a practical way forward will need to be found. Whatever form these supplementary private pensions eventually take, they will have to take on board the social issues in parallel to the economic and political reasons put forward to support them.

4.6. CONCLUSIONS: THE SOCIAL CONSEQUENCES OF THE NEW PUBLIC–PRIVATE DIVIDE

Throughout Europe, the generosity of PAYG pensions is falling. Reforms have reduced old age benefits for future generations of pensioners, resulting in the expansion of funded pension schemes. This is likely to happen independently of government policy: not only in France but also in Germany, increases in spending on private old age insurance (through funded schemes) occurred in the 1980s before any significant legislative change in the area. On a Europe-wide scale, the main issue concerning pension policy no longer seems to be the choice between PAYG and funded pension schemes. It seems that the principle of combining the two systems has been adopted in all countries, as much because it is occurring already through individual economic decisions as through decisions by governments.

In Bismarckian systems, workers benefit from a level of redistribution (through, for example, credit for contributions, benefits calculated on the basis of 10 best years' salary, and a floor below which pension benefits do not fall). The goal of redistribution is put at risk by increasing the contribution-related nature of PAYG systems.[23] Furthermore, mechanisms for redistribution do not exist in funded pension schemes. This is a problem that must be dealt with if the object of pension reform is to create a system that is not just financially, but also socially sustainable.

The main issue in future decades will concern less the establishment of pension funds, and more the regulation of these funds. If pension funds develop without regulation, the logic of the market alone may have significant social implications. We can expect higher contributions for women, because they live longer than men, proportionally higher administrative costs on the pensions for low-income earners because charges are set at a fixed rate, and greater risk to pensions because they will be invested on the stock market. The development of pension funds without appropriate regulation could result in increased inequality and significant problems for atypical workers, whose working lives are increasingly becoming the norm. Part-time workers, often those on the lowest salaries, and those who have had numerous interruptions in their careers (especially women) will be the biggest losers.

ACKNOWLEDGEMENTS

Part of this text is based on work undertaken with Giuliano Bonoli (see Bonoli and Palier 2000 and Palier and Bonoli 2000). I would also like to thank Christelle Mandin for her research assistance, Chloe Flutter for her remarkable translation, and Noel Whiteside for her thoughtful editing work.

NOTES

1. Schopflin (1987); Etats généraux de la Sécurité sociale (1987); INSEE (1990); *Livre blanc sur les retraite* (1991); unpublished report on pension by Bernard Brunhes (1992) and Robert Cottave (1991).
2. See Davanne (1998); Charpin (1999) but also Teulade (2000); Taddéi, (2000); Conseil D'orientation des Retraites (2001).
3. In 2002, the minimum pension was €6,832.58 per year for a single person and 12,257.01 for a couple.
4. Translator's note: the English equivalent term might be 'umbrella' schemes.
5. This situation is not found in the German system even though the institutional structures are relatively similar. There is a legal obligation in Germany for the social partners managing social security funds to take measures to balance their funds' accounts as soon as a deficit is predicted. Social insurance accounts are 'automatically balanced' in Germany without government intervention.
6. Since this reform, pensions are calculated with reference to the 25 best years' salary (previously, it was the 10 best years'). To be paid a full pension (50% of the reference salary up until the fixed social security ceiling), one must contributed for 40 years (160 trimesters) instead of 37.5 years previously (150 trimesters). This extension of the length of contribution required will be introduced progressively (one extra trimester per year: people who retired in 1994 had to contribute for 151 trimesters, etc. The full reform will

be fully implemented in 2004). Furthermore, increases to pensions are no longer indexed to gross wages but to prices. This last change was adopted for 5 years in 1993, but has since been extended by the succeeding Governments.

7. The President of the Republic, the National Assembly and the Senate were all held by the same party. Electoral failure seemed unlikely and Juppé had 3 years before the next election.
8. The method for calculating public sector pensions remains unchanged: 37.5 years of contributions must be paid to receive a full pension. The pension is calculated from the salary paid over the last six months of the public servants' career (discounting bonuses), the period usually highest. The pension regimes for public servants provide a replacement rate in the order of 75% of the last salary.
9. For further information on these debates see Bozec and Mays (2001).
10. Made up of academics opposed to the neoliberalism and trade unions opposed to Juppé's reform plan (Kahlka 2001).
11. The Charpin Report based its projections on the hypothesis that the unemployment rate would stabilise between 6 and 9% of the active population. This rate was contested by the foundation because it showed that the public authorities had abandoned the goal of full employment.
12. A committee of economist established to undertake research on the request of the Prime Minister.
13. Former CNPF, the principle employers' organisation.
14. ASF was created in 1983 to finance complementary pensions taken at the age of 60.
15. After the future for children and fear of unemployment.
16. One argument in favour of establishing pension funds in France is to create a counterbalance to British and American pension funds. To construct this argument, it was first necessary to show how powerful these Anglo-Saxon pension funds were. However, in doing this, a negative image was associated with the term 'pension fund' which it is hoped will be forgotten through the use of another term.
17. The positions of the various groups presented here are analysed in further detail in Charpentier (1997: 306–12).
18. Speech by the President of the Republic, 14 July 1999.
19. *Libération*, 14 September 1999: p. 15.
20. Interview with M. Sapin in *Le Monde*, 5 January 2000: p. 5.
21. See above.
22. This term acknowledges that public pensions are increasingly calculated according to an actuarial model, usually used by private insurance. This model calculates the rate of annuity as a function of contributions paid, interest rates earned on these savings, economic conditions, and the life expectancy of the person receiving the annuity at the time of the first payment.
23. All the reforms to PAYG pensions are based on the actuarial logic of social insurance. This logic implies a reduction in the redistributative function of old age insurance, bringing it closer to the logic of private insurance.

CHAPTER

5

Private Pensions as Partial Substitute for Public Pensions in Germany

Winfried Schmähl

5.1. INTRODUCTION: THE PUBLIC–PRIVATE DIVIDE IN GERMANY'S PENSION DEBATES

For some years the public–private divide in pensions in Germany has been closely linked to the different methods of financing pensions: capital funding and Pay-As-You-Go (PAYG). This has not always been the case. On the contrary, from the introduction of statutory social pension insurance in Germany in 1889 until 1956, this branch of social insurance was—according to official statements—based on capital funding. Various economic and political circumstances made it necessary to run the scheme on a PAYG basis for longer periods than intended, and prevented the accumulation of reserve funds from gaining an adequate amount according to actuarial calculations. As a consequence, the level of public pensions remained low. During all these years, occupational arrangements (whether lump-sum payments or pensions) and additional private saving for old age were always a supplement to social insurance pensions.

During the Nazi period, the accumulated funds of the public pension scheme were used to finance public expenditure, which included military purposes. Funds were almost totally lost after the collapse of the Nazi regime. Nevertheless, the accumulation of funds within the social pension insurance scheme started again after the Second World War. This money was primarily used for financing investment in housing. Despite the dominant views in ministries and in pension administration, economic arguments in favour of PAYG financing of the compulsory public pension scheme gained political influence in the 1950s.[1] The shift from capital funding of the public scheme to PAYG was not fully realised in the great pension reform of 1957, although the reserve requirement of the public scheme was reduced to cover expenditure of one year at the end of a 10-year calculation period. In 1969, the reserve requirement was again reduced to cover expenditure of 3 months, later on to only one month, in 2002 to 0.8 months, and in 2003 even to 0.5 months.

Although over the last decades there have been several proposals for accumulating funds within the public scheme as a means for tunnelling the emerging pension mountain (i.e. to increase contributions above the level that would be necessary to balance the budget and to use the funds later in order to prevent a rapid increase in the contribution rate), the current view in Germany is that capital funding should only be realised in the private sector. One important argument is that accumulated reserves within the public sector are an incentive to increase expenditure. It is hardly surprising that players in the financial markets are in favour of a separation of (private) capital funding from (public) PAYG financing. So, discussion of the public–private divide in Germany also means considering the relative weight of funding compared to PAYG financing.

The 1957 pension reform led to an important change in public pension policy. By inserting dynamic elements into the social insurance pension scheme, the pension level was linked to the growth rate of average gross earnings, and pensions were increased by about 70 per cent on average within one year. One major objective of the 1957 reform was that pensions should replace the individual's earnings in relation to their earnings during their working career and, hence, should not only be regarded as an instrument for avoiding poverty in old age. Pensioners should also be able to participate in the fruits of economic development. This paradigm shift resulted in an increase in public pension expenditure as a percentage of GNP from 4.2 per cent in 1956 to 5.6 per cent in 1957. There was a strong resistance by the Federal Reserve Bank (Bundesbank) as well as by employers and other industrial organisations who argued that this would push up the inflation rate and undermine the ability and willingness to save for old age. These fears proved to be wrong. The remarkable increase in social insurance pensions did not result in inflation and did not crowd out occupational or individual private provision for old age. There was no negative effect on private saving.

It has been well known in Germany for many decades that the age structure of the population is going to change and to become a challenge for pension policy and other areas of social and economic life. The ageing population has been seen as an economic 'burden'. The fact that social insurance contributions are shared between employees and employers[2] results in rising non-wage labour costs if the contribution rate increases.[3] Not surprisingly, employers and their organisations call for a reduction rather than an increase in contribution rates. This became a powerful political argument in Germany because of growing labour market problems.

There are several ways to reduce contribution rates. A common one in the 1990s was to increase revenues from the federal budget in order to cover the pension expenditure in social insurance that was directed at interpersonal redistribution of income. This—as well as a reduction of this type of expenditure—strengthened the contribution–benefit link within the German pension insurance scheme.

This development was in contrast to a transformation of the public pension scheme from an earnings-related scheme (based for the most part on the idea of equivalence and reciprocity) to a flat-rate pension scheme, based on the idea of citizenship, as it was sometimes proposed in Germany. The role of the state as a provider of pensions was to diminish and private (capital funded) provision was planned to supplement a PAYG financed flat-rate pension. But these proposals—published during the last decades by the Freie Demokratische Partei (FDP), the Green Party as well as by some members of the Christian-Democratic Party[4]—never gained much political support.[5] The most recent proposals for changing the public–private mix in pensions and financing did not focus on the issue of 'earnings-related' versus 'flat-rate', although this may again become an issue in the future.

There are several political and economic reasons for a new public–private divide in German pension policy. One is the change in normative positions related to the role of the state. Since economists changed their approach to economic policy—from a Keynesian macroeconomic demand-oriented policy to a supply-oriented neoclassical microeconomic policy—public expenditure and its financing was increasingly viewed as a hindrance to market forces. The process of German unification required an increase in public expenditure, including social expenditure. The high ratio of public expenditure as well as public debt is often criticised. The Maastricht criteria have also resulted in political pressure to reduce public expenditure.

Shifting expenditure from public to private provision has added attractions, because many citizens do not fully recognise that additional private saving or private expenditure is needed if public expenditure as provision for old age is to be reduced. A shift of this sort will reduce the burden to the public budget but not necessarily the burden for the private household. There are many players interested in channelling pension money via capital markets, promising greater efficiency in private as opposed to public activities, and higher rates of return.

The public debate was framed by the argument that demographic changes will bring about a 'pension crisis': the burden of public pension insurance will become unbearable—especially for the younger generation. 'Generational equity', thus, became an important and powerful catchword in the public debate. The conclusion that public pensions cannot remain at the present level was widely believed: Pensions have to be reduced and they will no longer be sufficient to maintain 'standard of living' in old age in the future. Only a shift from public to pensions could relieve the burden on younger generations. These opinions prepared the ground for a pension reform that was finally agreed in 2001.[6] The 2001 reform measures are important for the new public– private mix in pensions that is now emerging in Germany. These pension reform measures are based on a paradigm shift in pension policy, in line with the mainstream of the international pension debate—which argues for a new mix of public and private pension provision and, linked to this, a new mix of financing methods.

This chapter deals with these new developments in Germany. The chapter starts with a brief outline of the institutional structure of Germany's system of old age protection (Section 5.2). Then the framing of the recent pension debate in Germany is discussed (Section 5.3). Major elements and some of the effects of the 2001 pension reform are explored in Section 5.4. The effects of the new measures on benefit level and financing are highlighted, as well as new rules for private and occupational pension arrangements. The chapter concludes (Section 5.5) with some reflections on future development and economic effects.

5.2. INSTITUTIONAL STRUCTURE AND OBJECTIVES OF GERMANY'S PENSION SCHEMES

5.2.1. The Institutional Structure Prior to the 2001 Pension Reform

As in most industrialised countries, in Germany formal pension arrangements[7] have been based on different tiers for a long time. These tiers include:

- mandatory basic schemes (first tier);
- supplementary occupational schemes (second tier); and
- additional private provision for old age (third tier).

The German pension scheme has public and private as well as mandatory and voluntary elements, often linked to tax incentives. The basic first tier of the German pension system is not a single scheme covering all citizens, but consists of several elements. The core element of the first tier as well as of the whole pension system in Germany is the statutory social pension insurance, covering all white- and blue-collar workers and some groups of the self-employed (see Figure 5.1). It is by far the most important pension scheme in Germany in terms of coverage as well as expenditure. Therefore, political debates as well as public attention are primarily focused on the scope and design of this scheme.

Social pension insurance consists mainly of three branches: for blue-collar workers, for white-collar workers, and for miners. Pension calculation and financing are identical for the first two branches. There are fiscal equalisation rules between the two branches and for miners there are some additional rules and benefits. Other first tier pension schemes apply to other specific groups—civil servants, farmers, and members of professional organisations. The financing of pensions in social pension insurance is on a PAYG basis by contribution payments of employees and employers from gross earnings up to a ceiling of 180 per cent of average earnings (200 per cent since 2003), and by general tax revenue which covers about 20 per cent of pension expenditure for blue- and white-collar workers and about 70 per cent for miners.

The calculation of social insurance pensions is based on the relative gross earnings (i.e. individual gross earnings compared to the average gross earnings of all employees) for all the years of the contributor's earning career. Pension claims are accumulated in individual accounts, making it a defined benefit (DB) pension scheme.

The second tier consists of supplementary occupational pension schemes in the private and public sector. In the public sector, in principle, all blue- and white-collar workers are covered on the basis of collective agreements. These DB schemes were integrated with social pension insurance, realising a certain percentage of final earnings as pension benefit, depending on years of service, as for civil servants. A recent agreement abolished the linkage between final earnings and pension benefit.

In the private sector, voluntary schemes have dominated.[8] Coverage in the private sector is only about 50 per cent and is very uneven, varying

	Self-employed not covered mandatorily	Professions	Farmers	Craftsmen, artists, and other self-employed covered mandatorily	Miners	Others		Civil servants***
3rd tier (additional)	**Non-certified private old age provision**							
	Voluntary social insurance			**Certified private pension plans**				
2nd tier (supplementary)					Miners' pension insurance	Occupational pensions	Public sector schemes (for all employees) (collective agreement)	**Civil servants' pension scheme**
1st tier (base)		**Pension schemes of professional associations** **	**Old age pension schemes for farmers***	Special schemes or rules for self-employed within statutory old-age pension		Pension insurance for blue- and white-collar workers		
				Statutory old age pension insurance				
	Means-tested basic protection							
Covered groups of persons	*Self-employed not covered mandatorily*	*Professions*	*Farmers*	*Craftsmen, artists, and other self-employed covered mandatorily*	*Miners*	*Others*		*Civil servants****
					Blue- and white-collar workers			
	Self-employed				*Employees*			
	Private sector						*Public sector*	

* Including family workers. This scheme is designed as partial old age security beside income from the former farm.
** Partly also for employees of the respective branches.
*** Including judges and professional soldiers.

Fig. 5.1. Old age pension schemes for various groups of the population in the Federal Republic of Germany.

Source: Own chart (based on earlier versions).

with the size of the firms and with significant differences between male and female employees depending on where they are employed. Occupational pension schemes were mostly of the DB type,[9] and there is a considerable variation in their design. They were financed in the main by employers, on a capital funding basis. There are also different organisational structures for these schemes both within the firm and outsourced by legally independent organisations.[10]

Collective agreements on pensions in the private sector were exceptional until the 2001 reform,[11] in contrast, for example, to the Netherlands. Since the 2001 reform, this is changing. During the 1990s, a decline in occupational pension arrangements was a consequence of giving less favourable conditions to new employees or closing schemes to newly hired employees, and coverage declined. The role of pensions in increasing labour costs and tax conditions are cited by firms as reasons for the downward trend in occupational pensions. It seems also that occupational pensions have lost their importance as an instrument for attracting qualified labour because of high unemployment in the labour market.

Table 5.1 shows the macroeconomic significance of pension expenditure in Germany in 1999 as well as of different institutions.[12] About 80 per cent of all pension benefits are from the first tier, and 10 per cent each are from the second and the third tier. That means, broadly speaking, that about 80 per cent of pensions are based on PAYG and 20 per cent on capital funding. To change this ratio is a major objective of recent reform measures.

Public transfer payments and social insurance pensions are, by far, the most important source of income for the majority of elderly people in Germany: This is so in West Germany and even more so in East Germany (see Table 5.2). This difference has arisen because in the former GDR there were no occupational or private pensions as sources of income in old age (Schmähl 1991*a*). The introduction of funded elements for old age security will take a long time before it becomes an effective instrument for financing retirement. Income from assets other than pension claims is generally low in Germany.

The standard of living in old age is not only dependent on income from pension schemes and assets: a number of other factors are relevant too. There may be intrafamily transfer payments and sometimes income from work or self-employment, but health and long-term care insurance, and the cost of contributions to these, as well as direct tax are particularly important. If in health insurance, for example, premiums are increased or the policy does not cover specific expenditure, then

Table 5.1. Pension expenditure, Germany, 1999

Expenditure for	**Per cent of GDP**[1]	**Per cent of total expenditure**
Old age	11.5	81.0
Survivors	0.4	2.8
Disability	2.3	16.2
Total[2]	14.2	100.0
Expenditure by (institutions)		
Social pension insurance	10.6	68.8
Civil servants	1.6	10.4
Farmers	0.2	1.3
Professions	0.1	0.7
Occupational pension schemes		
Private sector	0.7	4.5
Public sector	0.4	2.6
Subtotal	13.6	88.3
Life insurance and private pension insurance[3]	1.8	11.7
Total	15.4	100.0

[1] GDP 1999 = 3,86,1200 million DM.
[2] Without life insurance.
[3] Calculated according to estimation by Sachverständigenrat (2001), p. 159.
Source: All other figures Bundesministerium für Arbeit und Sozialordming (2001), pp. 21, 44.

people have to spend more out of their income to cover illness. If people need long-term care and especially costly residential care, it is crucial that benefits from mandatory long-term care insurance—introduced in 1995—develop in line with costs of long-term care. Where this is not the case—as in Germany at present—the frail elderly have to spend increasing amounts of their income to cover costs. If their own income and assets are not sufficient, social assistance payments are needed.[13]

The adequacy of pension benefits for financing old age is clearly influenced by the development of benefits in health and long-term care insurance, as well as by contributions and taxes. In addition, there are direct fiscal links between social pension insurance, and insurance for health, long-term care, and unemployment. Changes in other branches of the social security system influence revenue and expenditure of the pension scheme as well as the net pension benefits of pensioners. These

Table 5.2. Income of pensioners[1] from different sources, Germany, 1998: percentage of gross household income

(Gross) income from	Single-person households		2-Person households	
	West	East	West	East
Public transfer payments	82.3	95.8	77.8	93.4
Private transfer payments (incl. occupational pensions)	8.9	1.6	9.2	1.6
Employment	2.2	0.9	4.4	3.1
Private life insurance	1.7	0.4	3.3	0.4
Assets[2]	4.9	1.3	5.4	1.6

[1] Pensioner = person age 60 and over; dominating income source not from employment; in 2-person households: the first person with these characteristics.
[2] Without imputed income from living in own house or flat.

Source: Statistisches Bundesamt (2001) (own calculations).

interactions have to be taken into consideration in any analysis of German pension schemes and their effects.

5.2.2. The 2001 Reform: Two New Elements in the German Pension System

Two new elements were introduced into the German pension system in the reforms of 2001, to cope with the challenges facing Germany's pension schemes (see Figure 5.1):

1. A means-tested transfer payment where income is insufficient for persons aged 65 and older as well as for the disabled. The benefit amount is calculated in the same way as means-tested social assistance, but with one major difference: Children are not (as is case with social assistance) obliged to pay back the whole or part of the sum[14] where their own income is below €100,000 per year, if their parents claim this new means-tested benefit.

2. The second element is a subsidy for contributions to a private pension. These schemes have to meet certain restrictive criteria in order to get the certificate that is the pre-requisite for subsidies. The Social Democratic and Green Party coalition government describes this as the 'heart' of their concept for 'modernizing' the pension scheme.

5.3. FRAMING THE PENSION DEBATE

Pension schemes have to be adapted in response to changes in the environment in which these schemes are embedded. Changes in demography, economic conditions, household structures and also in political objectives and normative positions have a bearing as well as the effects of pension schemes themselves—such as incentives on the labour market. Until the beginning of the 1990s, there was a broad political consensus on the key elements of pension policy between the big political parties, Christlich Demokratischen Union/Christlich-Soziale Union (CDU/CSU) and Sozialdemokratische Partei Deutschlands (SPD), which now unfortunately no longer exists.[15] At the centre of the debate in Germany as in many other countries are PAYG financed schemes.

Germany faces a pronounced demographic ageing, resulting from a low fertility rate (which is one-third below the replacement level) and a rising life expectancy. The latter is a positive development, although in public debate it is usually described as a burden that results in additional costs for pensions, health and long-term care insurance. As an indicator illustrating demographic ageing, old age dependency ratios (ADR) are often used as a starting point or even as a proxy for a system dependency ratio (pensioner ratio) which is decisive for issues of financing and is influenced by many factors besides demographics (Schmähl 1981, 1989, 1990*a*). Table 5.3 is based on official population projection and indicates very clearly that ADR:

(1) depends on its definition (i.e. the beginning and end of the working phase of the life cycle), which is largely related to conditions in a country;[16]
(2) is increasing over time;
(3) is not changed fundamentally by migration (assuming realistic numbers of migrants);[17] and
(4) can develop more smoothly over time if the beginning of the retirement phase starts later.

Another important challenge results from economic conditions, especially from the high unemployment rate in Germany. This affects expenditure through early retirement, as well as revenue, both of which increase the demand for additional financing by contribution revenue, and/or federal grant. Difficult labour market conditions, particularly in East Germany after unification, are part of the problem. The different economic

Table 5.3. Old age dependency ratios (ADR) based on official population projections

Year	**ADR definition**[1]	**Variant**	
		1 (Migration 100,000 per year)	**2 (Migration 200,000 per year)**
1998	20/60	39.86	39.86
2030	20/60	74.33	70.71
	20/62	63.51	60.50
	20/63	58.26	55.56
2040	20/60	76.53	71.88
	20/62	67.42	63.28
	20/63	63.39	59.48

[1] Definition: ADR (20/60), (persons 20–59 years)/(persons 60+); ADR (20/62), retirement phase starts at age 62; ADR (20/63), retirement phase starts at age 63.

Source: Own calculation based on 9th Coordinated Population Projection of the Federal Statistical Office.

conditions in East and West Germany cause transfer payments from West to East Germany, which is also the case with social pension insurance. As a result, the contribution rate of pension insurance has increased by about one percentage point in both parts of Germany over recent years and it is expected that this will continue for many years to come.

Pension insurance was used for a long time as an instrument of labour market policy, resulting in several pathways to early retirement without deductions from the full pension (Schmähl and Jacobs 1989; Schmähl 1992*a*; Schmähl et al. 1996). This policy was based on a broad consensus between government, trade unions, and employers' organisations, and influenced the expectations of employees regarding their retirement age as well as their behaviour. Firms made extensive use of these options for reducing and rejuvenating the work force, and this in turn increased the contribution rate. But high contribution rates—at present around 19 per cent[18]—are now under attack, especially by employers, as an element in the high non-wage labour costs that has a negative impact on economic competitiveness.[19]

The reduction of non-wage labour costs is high on the agenda of politicians, employers, and industrial organisations,[20] and pension reform will lessen the increase of the contribution rate. It was argued that this would improve the international competitiveness of German firms, as well as the take-home pay of employees, with the result that employees would have the option of making additional savings for old age.

The demands to reduce public debt, reduce PAYG schemes and their 'implicit debt', and balance the public budget were (and still are) often based on the vague concept of intergenerational equity. There is no political party that does not claim that their proposals are in favour of intergenerational equity or that the present PAYG scheme is a violation of it. Intergenerational equity became one of the most widely used catchwords in the public debate in Germany. The different rates of return to be realised in public PAYG and private capital funded pension schemes were often the main argument.

PAYG pension schemes—in particular social insurance, but also civil servants' pension schemes[21]—remain under severe political pressure. The major reform alternative for solving future problems in the PAYG pension schemes was seen to be a radical shift towards capital funding. While in Germany the introduction of funded elements into a public scheme in general has been rejected, proposals for more capital funding are linked to proposals for privatising at least a part of old age security. It is hardly surprising that the insurance industry, banks, and investments funds were in favour of these reform strategies.

5.4. THE 2001 PENSION REFORM: A PARADIGM SHIFT AND A CHANGE IN THE PUBLIC–PRIVATE MIX

5.4.1. Key Features and Objectives of the Social Insurance Pension Prior to the 2001 Reform

To understand the changes that were introduced in the 2001 pension reform, it is helpful to outline the social pension insurance scheme as it existed before the reforms. In 1957 an earnings-related dynamic pension scheme was introduced in Germany. This scheme was later adapted several times to changing conditions, especially by reform measures agreed in 1989 which came into effect in 1992.[22] Key features of the social insurance pension scheme outlined below are important.

The pension insurance scheme is an earnings-related DB scheme. Individual pension benefits are linked to former earnings of the individual pensioner. The contributor acquires pension claims—in an individual account—according to the relative amount of his/her gross earnings compared to average gross earnings of all employees during each year of employment. If an individual's earnings in a year are average, they get one Earnings Point. At retirement, the sum of individual Earnings Points of all years of insurance is multiplied by a factor representing the value (in German marks, now in Euro) of one Earnings Point. This gives the pension benefit per month. This factor is the dynamic element in the German pension formula. In 1992 this factor was linked to the development of average net earnings instead of the development of average gross earnings, which had been the rule for indexing pensions since in 1957. The rate of change of this factor is used for adjusting all pensions calculated in previous years. Therefore, pensioners with the same sum of Earnings Points receive an identical pension benefit per month (or per year) irrespective of the year of retirement.[23]

In relation to the distributional objectives underlying the German social insurance pension scheme, a key aim is to smooth income or consumption over the life cycle by implementing a relatively close relationship between contribution payment and pension benefits.[24] That means that intertemporal redistribution over the life cycle dominates the design of the scheme and not interpersonal redistribution, which should be financed by general tax revenue from the federal budget.[25] The German social insurance pension scheme differs from many public PAYG financed pension schemes in other countries because of its relatively low degree of interpersonal income redistribution. Other countries (e.g. Sweden or Austria) are now planning to reduce interpersonal redistribution in order to realise a closer contribution–benefit link.

The negative effects of some risks like unemployment or illness (and an interruption to contribution payment record) on pension claims are in part avoided within the social pension insurance scheme: other social insurance branches pay contributions to pension insurance, in the case of unemployment and illness. Contributions are paid from the federal budget to social pension insurance for those periods that are credited for caring for children.[26] Contribution rates and pension calculation are identical for men and women which creates interpersonal—or 'intersexual'—redistribution in contrast the equivalence of contributions and benefits in voluntary private insurance.

5.4.2. Strategies for Reducing Public Expenditure in the 2001 Reform

In the autumn of 1998, the new coalition government of Social Democrats and Green Party declared—as the previous government did—that without reform measures a 'dramatic' situation would exist in pension insurance around the year 2030. The contribution rate necessary to balance the budget of the social insurance scheme was projected to rise from the current 19 per cent to about 24 per cent in 2030 which was deemed to be much too high. The government decided on target contribution rates: Up to 2020, contribution rates should not exceed 20 per cent, rising to a maximum of 22 per cent in 2030.

To achieve this objective several strategies were adopted to reduce public expenditure on the one hand and stimulate private—including occupational—pensions by tax and transfer incentives on the other. A brief outline of these measures follows.

Redesigning the pension formula

A central element for change was a redefinition of the pension adjustment formula aiming at a general reduction of the pension level. For example, the pension level for the standard pensioner (45 Earnings Points) will be reduced from 70 to 64 per cent in 2030. The emerging income gap is to be filled by subsidised voluntary private saving up to a maximum saving rate of 4 per cent from gross earnings if it fulfills various criteria (see below). This subsidised saving rate will be increased in four steps (starting with one percentage point in 2002, and ending in 2008). This notional contribution rate is implemented into the pension adjustment formula and in the period of phasing in reduces the adjustment rate and the pension level as well.

When evaluating the effect of a generally reduced pension level, the points below need to be taken into consideration: (a) the full pension will be paid in the near future only if the insured person retires at 65. Average retirement age today is about 60. A reduction of 3.6 per cent of the pension benefit per year of early retirement will apply. From 2012 on, the earliest retirement age will be 62, equal for men and women; and (b) A full social assistance benefit amounting to about 40 per cent of net average earnings today.

Table 5.4 shows the ratio of pensions to net average earnings if the pension level for the standard pensioner (45 Earnings Points) is reduced to 64 per cent as the result of the new formula. We can see, for example, that a pensioner with 35 Earnings Points retiring at 62 has a net pension level that is only slightly higher than the social assistance level. If the pension level is reduced, a higher number of Earnings Points will be needed to receive a pension at social assistance level, at present about 25 Earnings Points (at a standard pension level of 70 per cent) if retirement

Table 5.4. Social insurance pension as a percentage of average net earnings: standard pension level 64 per cent

Earnings Points	Retirement at	
	65	62
45	**64.0**	57.1
40	56.9	50.7
35	49.8	44.0
28.1	**40**	
31.5		**40**

Source: Own calculation.

is at 65. In the future, when the standard pension level is reduced to 64 per cent, about 28 Earnings Points will be needed and almost 32 if retirement is to be at 62.

How many Earnings Points a pensioner can accumulate during his/her working life is dependent not only on labour market conditions, periods of unemployment, part-time or full-time employment and earnings he/she received, but also on the legal rules for crediting benefits.

It is worth looking at the distribution of pension claims today and comparing it to social assistance as well as to the pension level of the 'standard pensioner'. Figures 5.2 (a, b) shed some interesting light on this. There is a remarkable difference between men and women, and (not shown here) between blue- and white-collar workers, and East and West Germany. In each square of the diagrams the absolute number of the respective Earnings Points (average Earnings Points accumulated over the life cycle multiplied by number of insurance years) is shown. There are three curves showing different combinations of years of insurance and Earnings Points per year of insurance: (a) for pensions to be at social assistance level in case of (ai) a standard pension level of 70 per cent and (aii) of 64 per cent, respectively; and (b) for the standard pension (45 Earnings Points). This standard pension is the main focus of public debate in Germany.

It can be seen that very few women get the standard pension and that substantial numbers of male pensioners also get less than the standard pension. A high percentage of women, even today, have a pension lower than social assistance, and reducing the pension level would increase this percentage.[27]

It is relatively easy for the government to make changes to the parameter of the pension formula to continue the reduction of the benefit level. The notional contribution rate for private pensions can be

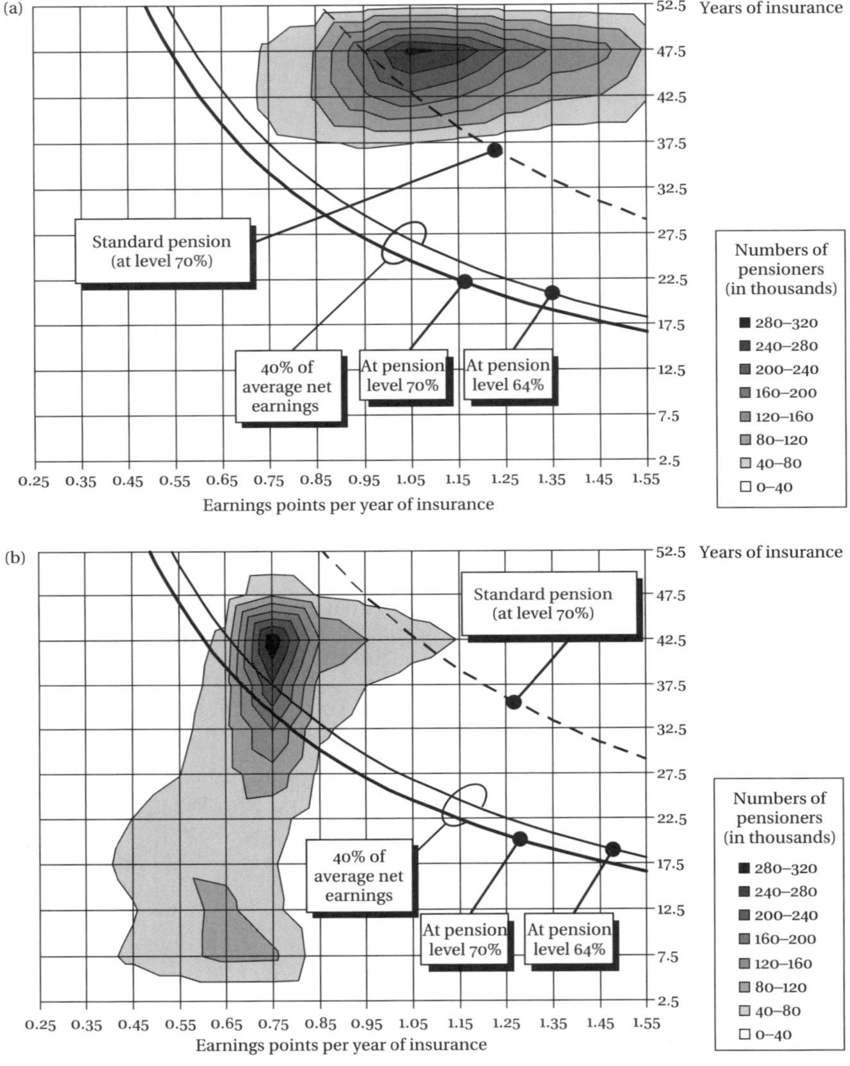

Fig. 5.2. Old age pensions by number of insurance years and average level of earned income over a working lifetime, Germany 2000: (a) male pensioners; (b) female pensioners. (My thanks to Dr Holger Viebrok for his work in designing this figure.)

Sources for data: Verband Deutscher Rentenversicherungsträger, Department of Statistics, 2001: 'Rentenbestand am 31.12.2000, Renten mit Rentenberechnung nach SGB VI wegen Alters', tables 311.01 G/311.02 G ('Verteilung der Nichtvertragsrenten nach durchschnittlichen Entgeltpunkten je Jahr an Beitragszeiten und beitragsfreien Zeiten sowie nach der Höhe der angerechneten Beitragszeiten und beitragsfreien Zeiten'), Frankfurt (CD-ROM); Calculation of pensions: §§63, 64 SGB VI (Code of Social Law).

increased, which would have the effect of lowering the adjustment rate, and therefore, the level of public pensions—an idea already floated by the Minister of Labour and advisors to the government. This would undermine (once more) confidence in the public pension. It is not unrealistic to speculate that this is a hidden aim of some players in the pension arena.

Reducing widow/er's pensions

The benefit level of widow's and widower's pensions is reduced even more, by two effects:

1. A widow/er's pension is a percentage of the insurance pensions of the former spouse. The level of the insurance pensions will be reduced and in addition the widow/er's pension will be 55 instead of 60 per cent of the insurance pension.[28] While pensions for the insured persons will be reduced by 8.5 per cent, the reduction for a widow/er's pension is 16.2 per cent.
2. There is an additional effect: If the survivor's pension is above a certain level, an income test, which now is based on the earnings and pension of the surviving spouse, is applied. In future, this will be extended to all kinds of income (except the new subsidised private pension).

The idea behind this development is that widow/ers' pensions should be phased out in favour of own pension claims from earnings and additional credits for child care (today 3 Earnings Points per child are credited).[29] It is an open question as to whether the new percentage of 55 will be further reduced or the parameters of the allowance changed. The allowance remains dynamic, linked to the development of average gross earnings.[30]

Effect on contribution rates and rates of return

The new rules in the social insurance pension scheme have only a moderate effect on the development of the contribution rate in social

---

Explanation referring to Fig. 5.2. On both axes of this diagram, the mid-points of classes are marked. The intervals amount to 0.1 earnings points (x-axis) and 5 years of contributions (y-axis). The frequencies refer to the width of one class (e.g. the frequency of pensions with 1—less than 1.1 earnings points per year and 40—less than 45 insurance years) (see Viebrok 2001: 231–3 (in German) for further details).

Table 5.5. Contributions for old age pensions

Year	Contribution rates social pension insurance (in per cent)		Additional contribution rate for private pension (in per cent)	'Total contribution rate' (in per cent)		
	Without Pension Reform Act 2001	Pension Reform Act 2001		Total	employer share	employee share
2001	19.1	19.1	—	19.1	9.55	9.55
2002	19.2	19.1	1	20.1	9.55	10.55
2003	19.1	18.8	1	19.8	9.4	10.4
2004	19.2	18.9	2	20.9	9.45	11.45
2005	19.1	18.7	2	20.7	9.35	11.35
2010	19.5	18.5	4	22.5	9.25	13.25
2020	20.6	19.6	4	23.6	9.8	13.8
2030	23.6	22.0	4	26.0	11.0	15.0

Source: Bundestags-Drucksache 14/5146.

insurance (see Table 5.5). According to official projections, the contribution rate required in 2010 will be one percentage point lower because of the reform measures, and in 2030, 1.6 percentage points below the contribution rate necessary for financing pension benefits according to the 'old' rules and their higher level of benefit. Prior to the reform, a contribution rate of about 24 per cent was thought to be too high—now 26 per cent seems to be politically acceptable. Has the 'demographic crisis' of the pension scheme disappeared?

Clearly, the division of contribution payments between employers and employees is set to change.[31] The reduction of the employer's contribution is, however, moderate: 11 per cent instead of 12 per cent in 2030. That means that the effect on non-wage labour costs is marginal. Although the burden for employees will be reduced by subsidies, the partial substitution of public by private pensions will impose an additional burden on private households for a long time. An additional effect of the partial substitution of PAYG financing by capital funding is that birth cohorts will be affected in different ways. People who are already pensioners or near retirement have no chance of compensating for future reduction in

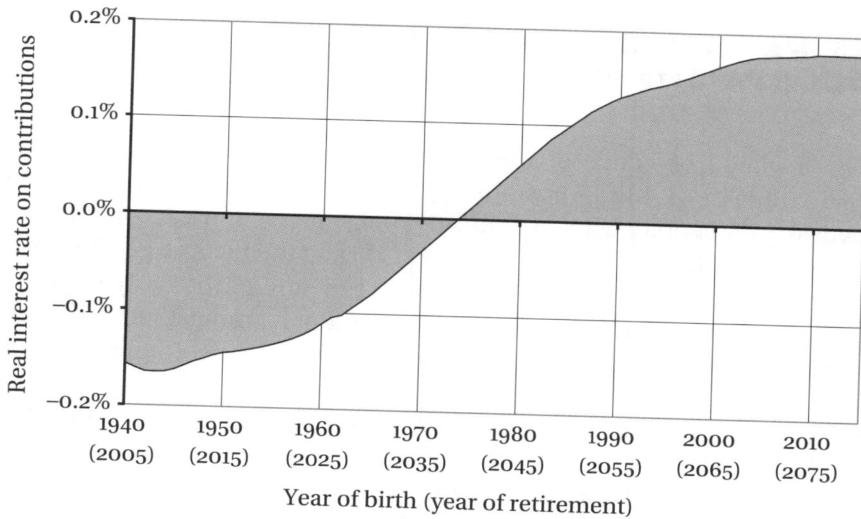

Fig. 5.3. Advantages and disadvantages of the Pension Reform Act 2001 by birth cohorts. *Basic assumptions:* Average earner, 45 years of insurance, 15 years receiving pension, additional 5 years widow's pensions, 2 children, retirement at age 65. Real interest rate on contributions for private pension 3 per cent p.a., real average gross earnings growth 1.5 per cent p.a.

Source: Own graph.

public pensions, whereas younger cohorts will gain from the new options (see Figure 5.3). However, the difference in rates of return resulting from reform measures is, at maximum, 0.2 percentage points only.

The 2001 reform: A summary

The main elements of the changes introduced by the 2001 pension reform are:

1. Limiting the contribution rate becomes the key objective. It is a shift from an 'expenditure-orientated revenue policy' towards a 'revenue-orientated' one. If the contribution objective cannot be achieved, the benefit level is likely to be further reduced.
2. Subsidised private pensions are no longer a supplement but a substitute for part of the public pension. There is a direct link between contributions for private pension provision and the level of public pensions via the pension formula of social pension insurance.

5.5. NEW RULES FOR PRIVATE AND OCCUPATIONAL PENSIONS

The declared objective of the government is to compensate for the reduction in public pensions by stimulating additional private pensions.[32] People who are already pensioners or near retirement, however, will have little or no chance of closing the income gap by additional saving for old age. In response to pressure particularly by trade unions, saving in some types of occupational arrangements is now subsidised as well. The employee has the right to convert 4 per cent of earnings up to the ceiling for social insurance contributions (about 180 per cent, resp. 200 per cent since 2003, of average gross earnings) into occupational schemes. While products for private pensions need a certificate (see below) some types of occupational pension arrangements do not need this to be eligible for subsidies.

5.5.1. Private Subsidised Pensions

Saving products have to fulfil several criteria to get the certificate, which is the precondition for becoming eligible for financial incentives. These criteria—together with incentives—will prevent some negative distributional effects.

The regulation of the certified products has attracted much criticism. As of the beginning of 2002, products with certificates can be offered by insurance companies, banks, and investment funds. The supervisory authority for insurance companies awards the certificate which means that the product fulfils the criteria. It says nothing, however, about the quality of the product.

Employees are now confronted with a huge number of different products. Insurance companies offering certified products often see it as a 'foot in the door' for additional products they want to sell and first experiences with mis-selling have been reported. Complaints include a lack of transparency about the costs of the different products and intensified competition between the different suppliers of certified products. It will be interesting to see how private pensions and occupational plans fare in the future: how much is saved via private pensions and how much via occupational plans—the costs of which should be lower than costs of individual contracts.

5.5.2. New Options in Occupational Pension Arrangements

One of the decisions of the 2001 reform package was to reduce the vesting period for pension claims based on employers' contributions from 10 to 5 years. In addition, new options for occupational pensions were created: a new right for earnings conversion, and the introduction of 'pension funds'. These measures are designed to stimulate the sluggish development of occupational pensions.

Earnings up to 4 per cent of the contribution ceiling in social pension insurance can be converted into a pension claim.[33] These earnings components may also be exempt not only from income tax but also from social insurance contributions until 2008. The effect will be to reduce the individual public pension and contribution revenue in addition to the reduction in general benefit—a change that has hardly been recognised in the German debate, thus far.[34]

In the private sector few collective agreements on occupational pension arrangements existed prior to 2001. This is changing in a number of important industries (e.g. the chemical and metal industries) and social partners have already negotiated collective agreements based on the option of earnings conversion. Because of the attractive conditions of arrangements via the firm or even a branch of industry in comparison to individual contracts (lower costs and information provided for investment), it is likely that many employees will choose this route instead of opting for a private pension. There is, however, no empirical data yet on how employees will decide.

Employees are now faced with a great number of new alternatives for subsidised saving for old age (see Table 5.6). Saving can be:

(1) private saving—up to 1 per cent of earnings (2002) increasing to 4 per cent (2008)—from net earnings in certified products eligible for subsidy or tax exemption (in Germany these pensions are named 'Riester-pension' after the Minister of Labour who introduced the reform);

(2) saving via conversion of earnings up to 4 per cent of the contribution ceiling either in specific occupational schemes, also eligible for the subsidy or tax exemption;

(3) saving from gross earnings (exempted from income tax and social insurance contributions up to 2008) also in specific types of occupational schemes; and

(4) saving in direct insurance with a flat rate tax of 20 per cent (instead of individual tax) and without paying social insurance contributions (up to 2008 and only for lump sums).

Table 5.6. Alternatives in subsidised saving for old age

Private saving	**Earnings conversion**		
(1% (2002) up to 4% (2008) of earnings)	**(Up to 4% of earnings at the ceiling for social insurance contributions)**		**(Up to 3.25% of earnings at the ceiling for social insurance contributions)**
		Only until 2008	
Saving is in principle from net earnings (after tax and contributions), but eligible for (a) subsidy or (b) tax exemption	Saving is in principle from net earnings (after tax and contributions), but eligible for (a) subsidy or (b) tax exemption	Saving from gross earnings (exempted from tax and contributions)	Saving only from lump-sum payments (single payments) instead of individual income tax rate of 20% no social insurance contributions (only until 2008)
If saving is in certified products	If saving is in direct insurance pension insurance funds pension funds	If saving is in direct insurance pension insurance funds support funds pension funds	If saving is in direct insurance pension insurance funds (only if tax- and contribution-free saving in pension insurance funds or pension funds is already exhausted)
New alternatives	New alternatives	—	Already existing alternative

Source: Own chart.

Pension funds have become established as a fifth type of occupational pension. In contrast to existing forms, these new funds have no cap on the amount of money that can be invested in various types of assets. They can, for example, invest 100 per cent in equities.[35] Companies with direct pension commitments based on book reserves have the option of outsourcing pension liabilities without negative effects regarding taxation. Meanwhile, the collective agreement on the public sector has also changed. Instead of the PAYG-financed DB scheme guaranteeing the employee a certain percentage of final earnings as pension income from social insurance, employees will have the option of saving in a defined contribution (DC) type of pension eligible for subsidies. That means, of course, that in future there will be no guaranteed benefit level.

5.6. CONCLUSIONS: IMPLICATIONS OF THE SHIFT TOWARDS PRIVATE AND OCCUPATIONAL PENSIONS

The new rules for pension policy in Germany came into force from the beginning of 2002, and will be phased in over the next few years. While it is too early for a comprehensive evaluation of the reform, some effects are already becoming apparent. There is a clear trend towards reducing the benefit level in social insurance, achieved by a general reduction of the pension level via the pension adjustment formula, and by changing conditions for disability and survivor's pensions. Private pensions as a substitute for public pensions are at present voluntary. But particularly where there is low participation of employees in the new options for saving, the issue of making private pensions mandatory—through industry-wide collective agreements or by law—will be put on the political agenda.

A combination of low public PAYG financed pensions and mandatory privately funded elements is to be seen in many countries. This is in line with the strategy the World Bank (1994) is proposing worldwide, with modifications depending on country-specific circumstances. A further push towards reducing public PAYG pensions can be expected at the European level. The Maastricht stability criteria and the requirement to reduce public debt and balance public budgets is an additional source of pressure.

Another influence at European level may be the result of the ongoing process of implementing an 'open method of coordination' in pension policy. Member states need to decide on common goals in pension policy and a set of indicators to form the basis for benchmarking pension policy. It may be, for example, that indicators like public pensions as a percentage of Gross Domestic Product (GDP) will play an important role. Clearly, the Ministers of Finance will be looking at the 'burden' for public households, rather than the 'burden' for private households if there is a shift from PAYG to capital funding in various private forms. The set of indicators chosen will be decisive in how the pension arrangements in the member countries are evaluated. This process is not yet complete, but may become a decisive element in the national pension debate and have a direct influence on the mix of pension schemes at national level.[36]

It does not seem unrealistic to assume that in the near future there will be a further demand to reduce the benefit level of public pensions in Germany, especially if the target contribution rate in social insurance is in danger of not being realised. Any further reduction in benefit level would make the conflict between pension level and desired structure of the scheme even more marked. The question is whether it will be politically possible to achieve a close contribution–benefit link in a mandatory scheme if the benefit level is so low that a great number of employees—even after a long period of contributing—can only expect a pension at or below the social assistance level. The development of basic pensions with strong redistributive elements will then be a realistic option.

Germany today is still a country with an earnings-related public pension scheme designed to smooth income over the life cycle and not only to avoid poverty in old age. It may not be totally unrealistic to anticipate that a shift in the first tier towards the primary objective of the avoidance of poverty will take place, allowing the second tier to move towards becoming mandatory (see Figure 5.4). These developments may influence each other. This model of flat-rate public pensions or a low pension level together with mandatory second tier can be seen in many countries such as the Netherlands or Switzerland,[37] and is often proposed as an attractive model for Germany.[38]

The private and occupational pension arrangements now emerging in Germany are complex and complicated and it may be that after these early experiences of the new system changes will take place. Employees are faced by very complex decisions. It is not unrealistic to assume that many employees will choose the route of earnings conversion into occupational pension schemes and employer-based pension arrangements because of lower costs and higher incentives, at least in the next few years. Occupational pension arrangements have already become, after the 2001 reforms, an important element in collective bargaining.

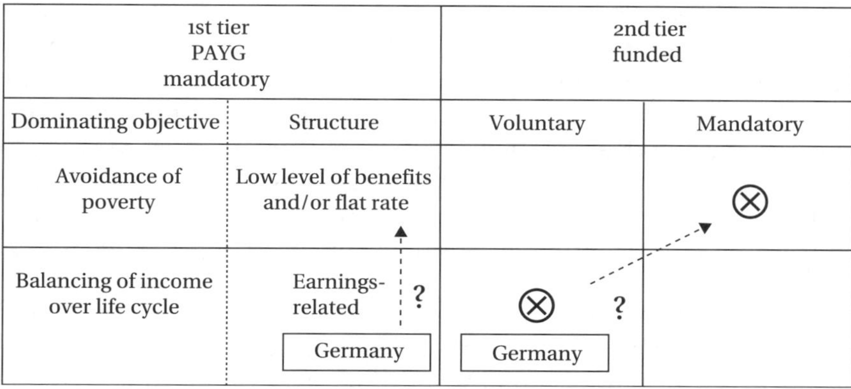

Fig. 5.4. Germany's position within a typology of pension schemes.
Source: Own chart.

For a long time trade unions had little interest in occupational pensions. Now they see a new field for activity in a period of decreasing influence. This interest in occupational pension arrangements based on collective agreements may also be important because of the scope it offers for influencing investment decisions in the new industry-wide pension funds that are to be established. Will we see a trend towards 'pension fund capitalism' which Peter Drucker (1976) described some decades ago?

The structure of occupational schemes in the private as well as in the public sector is changing from DB to DC. The financing of occupational pensions will now be mostly by employees instead of by employers as it was in the past. The movement towards DB will shift the risk from employers to employees.

The new strategy for pension policy in Germany will have a number of significant effects in relation to social policy and income distribution. Whether the shift towards funded private pensions of the DC type will result in adequate pensions in old age remains an open question. It can, however, be expected that the distribution of income in old age will become more diversified and inequality in old age will increase. The developments in the United Kingdom give some indication of this.

Many factors impact on personal income distribution: options for saving and the take-up of various subsidies, investment decisions and their return, as well as the costs linked to lower and higher amounts of saving. It remains an open question as to whether *additional* saving can be expected as a result of the new incentives, and how much this might amount to. Players in the financial markets anticipate a shift between types of saving in favour of equities, and that the trend towards privately funded pensions will fuel the stock market. They had pressed for a reduction in PAYG financing as well as occupational pensions based on book reserves, and a shift towards capital funding. This pressure—supported by many politicians as well as academics and the mass media—has clearly been successful. There are, however, already demands for moving further in this direction, including making private pensions compulsory.[39]

Those who can afford to save will profit from the incentives for building private pensions. This, however, requires an income that is high enough to use the range of options. Individuals on a low income may not have enough money to save in these privileged types of saving. A significant percentage of all German households (at present about nine per cent) are heavily indebted and cannot meet their current financial liabilities. If they have any spare money, they would be better off reducing their debt instead of saving, albeit in a subsidised form.

These incentives have to be financed too—a point often overlooked in public discussion. If tax expenditure for incentives to save is financed mostly by indirect taxes (like value added tax (VAT) or tax on petrol, etc.), all households have to finance the incentives, including households with low incomes and households that are not able to profit from the subsidies. Households with many children already face a relatively high burden through indirect taxation, and this will nullify part of the benefit they may get via the subsidies.

There remain many unanswered questions about the effects of the new strategy for Germany's pension policy, and the debate on pension policy in Germany will be ongoing. One reason is that at least two important areas were explicitly excluded from the 2001 reform package: changes in retirement ages and income tax rules on pensions—which will have to be changed because of a decision of the Constitutional Court. There is—after the reform decisions taken in 2001—a debate at national as well as European level on the participation of older workers in the labour force. In view of increasing life expectancy, an increase in retirement ages for claiming the full pension would seem to be a necessary measure for coping with the challenges of demographic ageing.[40]

Germany's pension arrangements are in the process of transition. The key question is whether in the future a further movement towards private pensions will be an adequate substitute for public pensions. Germany seems to have passed a crossroad. But how far we will go in this direction—one which politicians have now determined as the only way to solve future problems in pension policy—will depend on future economic and political developments.

NOTES

1. These economic arguments were already developed in a think tank during the late 1930s and the early 1940s, but when presented after the war this was not mentioned at all. On the origins see Schmähl (1981).
2. This is so for pension insurance, health, and long-term care insurance, as well as unemployment insurance. Only in accident insurance do employers pay the total contribution themselves.
3. However, there is a difference between paying a contribution and being burdened by the contribution payment (effects of forward or backward shifting). With regards to shifting, it is argued that opportunities for firms to shift costs have become much more difficult due to intensified international competition.
4. Most prominently by Kurt Biedenkopf, who became Prime Minister of the state of Saxonia after German unification.
5. Schmähl (1993*a*) gives an overview of proposals for flat-rate pensions in Germany to be financed by taxes or contributions. A very early proposal in Germany for a contribution-financed 'poor man's insurance' was made by Leopold Krug in 1810; see Schmähl (1997*b*).
6. The political process resulting finally in the reform package with many interesting and surprising features is discussed in Schmähl (2003).
7. N.B., formal, in contrast to informal, arrangements—especially intrafamily pension provision.
8. Social insurance for miners is an integrated scheme of first and second tier. The same is true for civil servants' pensions. However, pension calculation differs between these two schemes.
9. The vesting period—10 years—was relatively long compared to other countries. This is reduced by the 2001 pension reform to 5 years.
10. Four different types of occupational schemes existed in Germany's private sector before the 2001 reform:

    1. Direct pension commitments made by the employer and financed within the firm based on book reserves. This was an important instrument for internal (self-) financing of (big) firms particularly in the period of reconstructing the German economy after the Second World War.
    2. The Pension Insurance Funds (Pensionskassen) are legally independent institutions in the form of mutual insurance associations. Financing is by the employer, but the employee can also contribute.
    3. Support Funds (Unterstützungskassen) are also legally independent institutions, mostly registered associations, financed only by the employer.
    4. In the case of Direct Insurance the employer is the policyholder and takes out individual or group life insurance for the employee. Financing is by the employer, sometimes supplemented by the employee.

    For 1997 it was estimated that funds in occupational schemes to cover pension claims were about 531,000 million German Mark (DM). Regarding the different types of occupational schemes, 56.5% of the funds are in book reserves, 22.4% in Pension Insurance Funds, 13% in Direct Insurance and 8.1% in Support Funds. The total volume of funds compared to GDP is 14.5% including book reserves, without book reserves

6.3%. Compared to macroeconomic weight of occupational schemes in the Netherlands, the United Kingdom or the United States, Germany looks underdeveloped. However, this also reflects the quantitative importance of the social insurance pension scheme and the benefit level provided compared to the basic first tier arrangements in the Netherlands, the United Kingdom, or the United States. For a detailed analysis of occupational schemes and its links to the first tier pension schemes, see Schmähl (1997*a*) with further references.

11. This has existed in particular in the building industry for some decades.
12. The data is based on the official 'Social Budget' of the Federal Government. It does not include tax expenditure linked to pension arrangements or private provision for old age, saving, life insurance, etc. (the third tier). In addition, Table 5.1 gives an estimate of private saving for old age via life insurance.
13. In Germany, long-term care insurance was introduced in order to avoid social assistance in cases where a person needs long-term care (Schmähl and Rothgang 1996). While the number of people who need social assistance declined after the introduction of the new mandatory insurance, the number is already increasing because the benefits of long-term care insurance have been unchanged since its introduction in 1995.
14. Depending on income and assets of children.
15. For several phases of post-war pension reform in Germany see Schmähl (1998).
16. At present average retirement age is just below 60, while the entrance into the labour market is, however, above 20. Average retirement age is not identical with the average age of exit from the labour force because of pre-retirement possibilities. In Schmähl et al. (1996) the different pathways out of the labour force are discussed. The average retirement age is also influenced by the number of cohort members which has to be taken into account when looking at its development over time.
17. (Net-)Migration can reduce the ADR if the age structure of migrants is 'younger' than the population living already in the country of those who emigrate. Based on recent experience such an effect can be assumed. However, regarding the Pensioner Ratio it is essential that these people can be integrated into the labour market.
18. Contribution rate for social pension insurance (blue- and white-collar workers) 19.2% (1996), 20.3% (1997, 1998 and first quarter of 1999), 19.5% (1999 as of 1st April), 19.3% (2000), 19.1% (2001 and 2002).
19. For a discussion of this argument, see Schmähl (1995).
20. The Federal Government's declared objective is to reduce total social insurance contributions to below 40% (in 2001 it was 42.2%).
21. In the public debate civil servants' pensions hardly feature. That does not mean that there are no changes. On the contrary, these pensions are reduced much in line with reductions of social insurance pensions. That means the developments in social insurance has become a guideline for retrenchment, while during the phase of expanding pension schemes, rules for civil servants were the guideline for developing social insurance pensions.
22. The new rules became effective in West Germany in 1992, but the main elements had already been introduced in the then German Democratic Republic in July 1990, while unification was in October 1990. The major elements of the 1992 reform are discussed in Schmähl (1990*b*, 1993*b*), and the transformation of the pension scheme in the GDR in Schmähl (1992*b*).
23. For a formal presentation of the pension formula see Schmähl (1999).
24. There is no general minimum pension, except an upgrading of pension claims in certain conditions for contributors who have many years of insurance but low wages. This especially favours women. The rules for pension payments on minimum income levels have been changed several times since its introduction in 1972.
25. It covers about 20% of all expenditure of social pension insurance.

26. That is, for 3 years on the base of average gross earnings. For a detailed analysis of various links between social pension insurance and another public budgets, see Schmähl (2001*a*).
27. Whether these pensioners are or will be eligible for means-tested social assistance or the new means-tested transfer payment in old age, depends on the income (and assets) of the household. However, this information seems highly relevant with regard to willingness to contribute to the scheme and the acceptance of such a mandatory scheme.
28. For those who have raised children, a bonus is introduced as an element of family policy, financed, however, from revenue from pension insurance and not from the federal budget.
29. A detailed discussion on pensions for women is in Schmähl and Michaelis (2000).
30. Original plans of the government were to freeze the absolute amount of the allowance. It now remains earnings-related.
31. The question of shifting employer's contributions backwards to employees or forward into prices is not discussed here as well as the question whether trade unions will try to compensate increases in the private pension contributions by wage negotiations.
32. Nevertheless, the government rejects the idea that private pensions should be a part substitute for public pensions. The official statement describes these pensions as a supplement to the public pension.
33. The contribution ceiling is about 180% of average gross earnings. Therefore, a saving of 4% of earnings at the ceiling is about 7% of average earnings.
34. Only for those employees with earnings above the ceiling this exemption of private saving from contribution payment does not affect the Earnings Points in the year because he gets by his earnings, only the maximum Earnings Points (1.8, 2.0 since 2003) in one year. For the part of earnings above the ceiling no contributions have to be paid, but also no Earnings Points can be accumulated.
35. While, for example, a pension insurance fund only can invest up to 35% in equities.
36. For more aspects concerning this process, see Schmähl (2002).
37. For a comparison based on this typology, see Schmähl (1991*b*).
38. For example, the basic tier (AHV) in Switzerland is often mentioned because it covers the whole population and is highly redistributive. Its financing is earnings-related with little difference between lowest and highest pension (100%). The fact that the avoidance of poverty is achieved much less by the AHV in comparison to the earnings-related social insurance pension in Germany is often overlooked, as is the fact that occupational pensions are mandatory.
39. In this sense an 'institute'—named 'German Institute of old-age provision' (Deutsches Institut für Altersvorsorge)—has been established and financed by the Deutsche Bank.
40. The author proposed linking retirement age to the increase in life expectancy to divide additional years of life between working years and years in retirement. Changing the retirement age, however, requires several preconditions in order to become effective and socially acceptable, among other things further education and retraining of older workers. For a discussion of this topic, see Schmähl and Viebrok (2000) and Schmähl (2001*b*), with further references.

CHAPTER

6

Pension Reform in Sweden and the Changing Boundaries between Public and Private

Joakim Palme

6.1. INTRODUCTION

In June 1994, the Swedish Parliament took a decision about guidelines for pension reform. Four years later, the implementation of the actual legislation started and in November 2001 the first benefits generated under the new systems were paid out. The new legislation is reshaping all parts of the pension system. It is introducing notional defined contribution (DC) accounts as the first-tier, funded DC accounts with private fund managers within the public framework, and a new way of guaranteeing basic security for elderly people. The reform has provoked considerable interest, surprise, and confusion in the international community of pension scholars and policy-makers. This is due to the radical and innovative character of the reform, as well as to its complex nature.

There are a number of reasons why the Swedish pension reform is interesting to people beyond the country's own borders. The current understanding of social policy change during the crisis of mature welfare states has been largely informed by studies of conservative retrenchment of liberal welfare states (e.g. Pierson 1994). The Swedish welfare state is different, and so is the politics of the pension reform. Even if there are elements of privatisation, the reform does not represent a clear-cut retrenchment of public commitments—quite the contrary. Instead, it can be seen as a response the fundamental criticisms of modern welfare states for eroding incentive structures and lacking cost control, a response that tries to deal with these issues within a basically public framework. It is also an interesting test case for studying how welfare state institutions serve as a basis for interest formation and coalition building, as well as for creating their own legacies. The fact that the boundaries between public and private are reaffirmed generates a special interest in the context of the present book. This is also true for the fact that the reform has implications for how pension funds are integrated in European and global financial markets.

The proponents of the Swedish pension reform, moreover, claim that the reform is a solution to the demographic, financial, and political pressures on old age security. That the reform has influenced reforms in other countries is evident from both the Latvian and Polish cases (Fox and Palmer 1999). Whether there is scope for a further diffusion of the logic of the Swedish reform remains an open question. However, it is important to recognise that the reform has also provoked considerable confusion, as well as clear criticism. Obviously, many commentators have difficulties in understanding the technical aspects, as well as the social policy content of the reform, while others are just critical of the design of reformed system. This suggests that descriptive accounts of the reform are warranted. In addition, the reforms have implications for the public–private mix and for the wider political economy of the welfare states which, so far, have not been discussed very much.

The chapter addresses first, the background to the reform (Section 6.2). Then the content of it is described (Section 6.3) from the benefit side including the funded component and its organisation. Section 6.4 discusses the different forms of integration with international financial markets that is generated by the changes in the funding of the public system. Then follows (Section 6.5) a section on other aspects on the public–private interplay in the provision of pensions. The chapter concludes (Section 6.6) with a discussion of the future of nation-based welfare state from a Swedish perspective.

6.2. THE BACKGROUND TO THE REFORM

Pension reforms in mature welfare states are reactions to the problems and achievements of the existing systems of old age security, as well as to the different interests generated by them. This is also true for the Swedish pension reform. Even if the reform is radical in many respects, the legacy of the pension history of the twentieth century was strong.

Arguably, it is necessary to consider the historical development, not only to understand why the reform happened, but also why it was designed in such a way.

The first public pension reform, beyond systems design for specific groups like military officers and civil servants, can be dated back to 1913. It has been portrayed as the origin of the Swedish universality in social protection. This label is correct in some respects, but in others it is highly problematic. First of all, it did not provide universal benefits. The first-tier of the system was a universal and compulsory, fully funded contributory plan that would eventually pay benefits for those who contributed. The reform also included means-tested, so called 'supplementary', benefits that were targeted at low income pensioners (Elmér 1960). Another deviation from a strictly universal model was that it did not include state employees, who instead continued to have separate programmes.

It turned out that the funded benefits never became very big and that the means-tested supplements became of much greater importance. This was a result, not only of the modest size of the premiums and of the failure of the funded benefits to keep pace with inflation, but also of a gradually more generous application of means testing. Thus, in the early 1930s, a large majority of those above statutory pension age actually received some sort of public pension (Palme 1990). The debate in this era was about allowing groups, other than the state employees, to opt out of the system if their employer guaranteed them a private pension plan. The political answer to this was no further contracting out, and instead state employees became insured under the universal system in 1935 (Berge 1999).

The truly universal system, giving equal benefits to all persons above pension age, was established only after the Second World War, when means testing was completely abolished by the legislation of a universal 'People's Pension' in 1946 (Elmér 1960). This form of a truer universality also provided a new platform for policy-making in the pension area. The entire population was not only integrated in the same system of social protection but also provided with equal benefits. The growing importance of occupational plans among white-collar employees in the private sector (beside the existing programmes for public employees) became part of the platform for policy-making in the post-war era. It also raised the issue of earnings-related benefits for blue-collar workers in the private sector. Thus, the situation was similar to the British one after the war, to what Richard Titmuss (1955) labelled 'two nations of welfare' and the solution he saw was compulsory earnings-related pensions.

Whereas the People's Pension reform received unanimous support in parliament (Elmér 1960), the next step in the formation of the public pension system was accompanied by the most acute political conflicts in Swedish post-war political history (Heclo 1974). It was implemented only after a referendum that divided political life into different camps, and in parliament it passed with the smallest possible margin. The result was the Allmän Tilläggspension (ATP) plan that was enacted in 1959. In 1960 the population of working age started to earn entitlements to supplementary earnings-related benefits on top of their Flexiblare pensioneringssystem (FP). Whereas the FP was financed out of the general revenue, the ATP was entirely financed by employer contributions, originally with the same ceiling applying for both contributions and benefit purposes. Well above 90 per cent of the labour force had earnings below that ceiling.

The ATP programme was designed according to the Pay-As-You-Go (PAYG) and defined benefit (DB) principles. A benefit formula was applied where 30 years gave the right to full benefits based on the fifteen best years of earnings. The target level was set at 60 per cent of past earnings. Past contributions as well as outgoing pensions were indexed to the development of a consumer price based index—the so-called base amount. The same index was used for the FP benefits. Special transition rules were applied which meant that the first cohorts did not have to work more than 20 years for a full pension. This meant that the system started to mature in the early 1980s. However, as the ATP benefits began to be paid out, they triggered compensatory demands for higher benefits for those with only FP benefits. Following the Norwegian example, Pensionstillskott (PT) were introduced for those with no or very low ATP benefits (but with no other income testing). These supplements were graduated in relation to a fixed target level. This in fact made small ATP entitlements worthless, which is something we will return to in the context of the recent pension reform.[1]

Figure 6.1 presents a rough outline of what the old Swedish system looked like on the benefit side. It describes the size of the pension benefit from the person with the lowest state pension to that of the person with the highest state pension. The reader has to imagine that we have rank-ordered all elderly on the *x*-axis with the person with lowest public pension to the left and the person with the highest pension to the right. The *y*-axis measures the size of the pension. We see that we all pensioners receive the same basic benefit (FP). Most people have the earnings-related (ATP) benefits because most people have an employment record. For those who have only earned a small ATP benefit, or none at all, there is a supplement (PT).

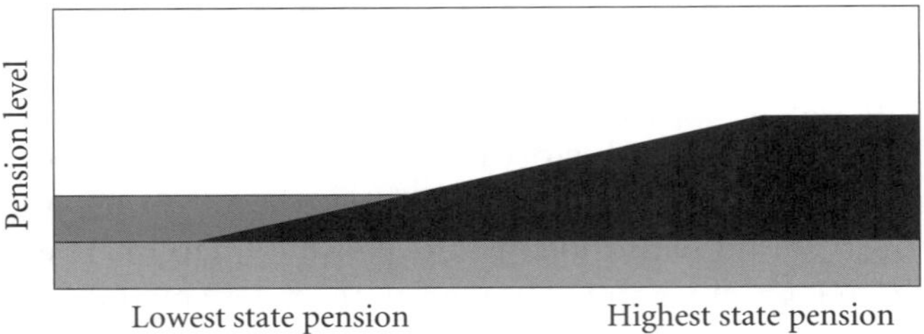

Fig. 6.1. People's Pension (FP), Earnings-Related Supplements (ATP), and Special Pension Supplements (STP).

In some respects, the data from the 1980s show a remarkable performance of the Swedish pension system. Not only had the ATP reform trebled the replacement rate of the public pension of a retiring worker in the 1980s compared to the situation in 1960, but the basic benefits had also almost doubled in relation to average earnings (Palme 1990). This development also had an impact on the relative economic position of the elderly population. In terms of poverty and inequality, only the Finnish and Norwegian systems, with similar designs, appeared to match the Swedish in terms of reducing inequality among the elderly (Korpi and Palme 1998). When the Organisation for Economic Cooperation and Development (OECD) launched its report, 'Reforming old age pensions', in the late 1980s (OECD 1988), the costs of the Swedish pension system were high as a percentage of Gross Domestic Product (GDP) but other countries had even higher expenditures. If expenditure levels were standardised by the relative size of the elderly population the levels appear modest by comparison. It is also interesting to note that when Jürgen Kohl (1988) concluded his comprehensive comparative study of pension systems he portrayed the Swedish system as the most successful in terms of achieving social policy goals.

With this background it is legitimate to ask, why was a system with such good track record so radically reformed? The need for change had become obvious, despite the good social policy performance. To explain the nature of the change is more complicated. The urgency of changes in the existing system had actually been recognised in the early 1980s and resulted in the formation of a parliamentary pension commission that was appointed in 1984. There were two outcomes of that commission. One outcome was very concrete; widow's pensions were to be phased out and replaced by time-limited survivors benefits for both men and women. This was a reflection of the fact that the dual-earner model had gained an almost universal foothold in Swedish society, but it also represented a reduced public commitment. The other outcome was more indirect in terms of changing policy and consisted of a comprehensive report into the status of the pension system (Report of the Government Commissions (SOU) 1990: 76). It was intended to serve as a basis for the further debate on the pension system.

The old age pension part of the system was under-funded and, given the increased demographic pressure that could easily be projected, these problems were going to be aggravated. The system was kept going by the interests from the buffer funds. However, the funds would have to be substantially reduced or even emptied to keep the system going, unless benefits were reduced or contributions increased. It had become clear that the price indexing of the system meant that the system was unstable in not only financial terms, but also when it came to the social policy goals. Financial instability was evident in the forecasts from the National Social Insurance Board. If growth was going to be low or zero, contribution rates would have to be increased to match the entitlements to such an extent that it would be unbearable for the population of working age.

The system of indexing that guided the Swedish social insurance system for decades has been admired for its simplicity and transparency. However, the ceiling for benefits purposes had been set at 7.5 of the so called 'base amounts' (used for the price-indexing of the social insurance system) in 1960 and with real wage growth this meant that more and more people had earnings above that ceiling. This process was slowed down by the fact that wage distribution had became more compressed during the 1960s and 1970s and real wages fell in the early 1980s. Towards the end of the 1980s, it was, nevertheless, evident that the gradual transformation of the entire earnings-related component of the pension system into a basic security flat-rate programme could be rapid if nothing was done. The price indexing of the basic benefits FP and PT had also resulted in frequent adjustments of the percentage of PT, but left it subject to the discretionary decisions of parliament. However, this was generally seen as a less serious problem.

In this context, problems with prevailing inequities should be added. The primary focus in the debate had been directed towards the benefit formula, where the thirty out of fifteen rules penalised those with a long working career and flat earnings profile over the life cycle, a typical trajectory of low income persons. Less attention was given to the fact that the gradual increase of PT meant that the past (employer) contributions of those with very low ATP in fact became worthless. The unintended effect of this coordination of basic and income security benefits nevertheless became an issue in the following work on reform. As part of a tightening of fiscal policies in connection with high unemployment and problems with increasing public deficits, both Centre-Conservative and Social Democratic governments had adjusted the indexing of the system, or, to put it bluntly, manipulated it. This had contributed to undermining the confidence in the pension system, despite the fact that previous cuts had been restored by the end of the 1980s.

Part of the background to the pension reform is the role of the private pension sector. It is useful here to distinguish between occupational and individual plans. Sweden is often associated with a social policy model that has crowded out private solutions. In the pension sector, this is somewhat misleading and warrants some qualification. The fact is that the occupational sector is among the most comprehensive in the Western Hemisphere, perhaps the most universal. This is due to the fact that different sectors in society are covered by collective agreements and they all have high levels of unionisation. State employees have a long tradition of being granted pensions as part of work contracts, and a special authority in charge of this plan, 'the State Pension Authority' (SPV). The municipality sector was very fragmented until the early 1970s when an important unification of these plans was carried through, which resulted in the setting up of 'the Pension Authority of the Municipalities' (KPA). The white-collar employees had their Industrins och handelns tilläggspension (ITP) plan organised by SPP with roots in the early twentieth century, the coverage of which actually had been spurred on by the implementation of ATP. The blue-collar workers in the private sector were last to go when they got their STP plan, managed by AMF, in the early 1970s. The degree of funding differed between sectors. There was virtually no funding in the programmes for public employees (with some exceptions for a few municipalities where pre-funding was used before the unification of the sector). The blue-collar plan was partially funded in the sense that the collective each year pre-funded the future pensions of the cohort retiring that year. The white-collar plan was a fully funded DB plan. In the 1980s, an important ingredient was added in a DC supplement (ITP-K). It became equal to 2 per cent of earnings and the insured person could choose between competing fund managers (Kangas and Palme 1991, 1993). As will become clear below, this is a model similar to the one applied in the public pension reform of 1990s.

Private individual insurance decreased in terms of the number of policies in the 1960s and 1970s. This can be interpreted as a decline in the perceived need for additional insurance in the wake of the ATP reform. Then, contrary to the expectations generated by the previous development, the number of policies started to increase in the 1980s. In 1980 about 5 per cent of the population of working age were active contributors to such plans and in 1989 this figure was above 15 per cent (Grip 2001). This can be seen as a reaction to the incentives provided by a system with high marginal tax rates and deductible premiums to private insurance plans. In my view, there are two important aspects of the development in the 1980s for how the public pension reform was designed (in addition to the ITP-K). One is the increased coverage and importance of private pensions for future generations of pensioners. I think this made it easier for the politicians to put a ceiling on future financing of pensions since old people could be expected to get improved incomes from additional sources. The other is the historically good return on capital. This made funded elements look very favourable (Myles and Pierson 2001).

In short, the pension system was not reformed because it had failed to deliver either basic pensions or income security to the retired population. Rather, it was reformed because it was tied to the development of prices and not the underlying real economy, which meant that the system was unstable from both a financial and social policy perspective. To understand the nature of the actual reform and the process that led to this outcome requires a more extensive analysis than can be offered within the context of the present paper (Palme 2001). It appears that behind the reform we have to see underlying processes of 'credit claiming' and 'blame avoidance' (Pierson 1994), as well as of 'making vice into virtue' (Levy 1999, 2001), concepts that have been elaborated in the retrenchment literature.

6.3. THE CONTENT OF THE REFORM

The Swedish reform is fundamental when it comes to the policy instruments. It is reshaping both the income and basic security components of the system, as well as the role and forms of pre-funding. Since it has no predecessor elsewhere in the world, it necessary to describe the basic elements in order to understand it, as well as its implications for the public–private boundaries. Since the reform has both micro- and macroeconomic implications, this is vital for understanding the implications for the economy at large. In short, the reform, first, is replacing the old earnings-related DB system with a DC system where basically 18.5 per cent of earnings is the financial basis of the old age pension system (cf. Palmer 2000 and Settergren 2001). Sixteen per cent will go into notional accounts (NDC) and form the basis of the income pension and 2.5 per cent will go into fully funded individual accounts (FDC). Both kinds of accounts are converted into annuities at the date of retirement, albeit these annuities have different forms. Second, basic security is ensured by a universal guarantee pension that replaces the old combination of FP and PT. The size of this guarantee is graduated in relation to the two contributory public retirement benefits (NDC and FDC). We will start the description with the income pension since it forms the first tier of the reformed system, continue with the guarantee pension, and conclude with the description of the fully funded component.

6.3.1. Income Pension According to the Notional Defined Contribution Principle

When it comes to the basis for determining the size of benefits, the reform introduces a number of changes. One fundamental change is that the earnings-related component becomes the first tier. Another fundamental change is that the benefit formula is to follow the principle of DC. Here, it is important to recognise that the total size of the contributions (18.5 per cent) has been determined with the underlying ambition of maintaining the replacement levels of the old system.[2] In expenditure terms, the reform implied an increase roughly equal to a scenario where the ceiling of the old system would be indexed to earnings. The concept of a notional account means that the PAYG character of the system is retained in this part and the size of the contributions going to the notional account was defined at a level high enough to cover the earned entitlements in the old system.

The reform introduces a new logic for determining the size of benefits. The principle is that all contributions are accumulated and attributed a rate of return which is equal to the growth in average annual pensionable income of all insured persons. Even if there is no fixed retirement age in the new system, the pension cannot be drawn before the age of 61 and there is no legal right for employees to continue their employment beyond the age of 67. The withdrawal is flexible not only beyond the age of 67, but also in terms of percentage. It can be drawn at 25, 50, 75, or 100 per cent. The accumulated notional wealth and the life expectancy of the cohort determines the size of the pension (but it is life-long for each individual). The annuity from this part of the system is calculated at an interest rate of 1.6 per cent. This interest rate has been imputed in the conversion of the accumulated notional wealth in order to get a more even income during retirement. There is a transitional period, which means that persons born in 1954 and later will have their pensions fully calculated according to the new benefit formula. Pensions of persons born between 1938 and 1953 will be determined according to a mix of old and new rules. The cost of administration has been calculated to 0.7 per cent of contributions or 0.02 per cent of notional capital.

In practice, the system is much more complicated, which has to do with the fact that there might be changes in employment and earnings, which means that the accumulation of pension entitlement in this notional system is not matched by future contributions. This is handled by the buffer fund of the notional system and the application of the automatic balancing mechanism. With the buffer funds it is also possible to handle demographic and economic shocks to the system, at least when it comes to the financial stability of the system and generational equity (Settergren and Mikula 2001).

The design of the benefit formula follows the principle of making lifetime earnings the basis for determining the size of the future pension. A strong motive here is to provide a good incentive structure to increase labour supply. An important feature of the reformed system is that it attempts to make all kinds of redistribution that occurs within the system explicit and motivated by social policy considerations. Thus, earnings not only give future entitlements to income pension, but also to a number of other incomes such as social insurance benefits. Credits are given for having small children, engaging in tertiary education and doing national service. Child rearing is a special motive for giving pension entitlements beside income and earnings. There are three different ways of calculating additional entitlements on top or in addition to the entitlements generated by the parental leave benefits. The most favourable way of calculating these entitlements is applied automatically. Common to all three mechanisms is that the credits only apply until the youngest child is 4 years old. In addition, military service and tertiary education can give additional pension credits. Since the incomes associated with these activities tend to be low, this will also be the case with the additional pension credits.

The old benefit formula had some implicit redistributive elements in it. It allowed those who stayed outside the labour market and/or worked part-time for some time still to earn a decent public pension because of the 30/15 rules. This was something that particularly benefited the large number of women who had interrupted work records and/or part-time jobs for long periods of time. For persons who had experienced extended periods of unemployment or sickness the old system also gave some leeway. At the same time, the old formula delivered a fair amount of unintended redistribution in favour of those who had chosen to work less for their own welfare.

6.3.2. Guaranteed Pension

The strongest element of redistribution is associated with the provisions for low-income pensioners. As indicated above, the old mechanism of providing basic pensions were the Flexiblare pensioneringssystem (FP) and the Pensionstillskott (PT) is now replaced by the guaranteed pension (GP). The GP is co-ordinated with the IP. This means that only those who lack an IP will get a GP at the maximum rate. Those who have an IP below the guaranteed level will get a supplement of GP. A difference compared to the old system is hence that those who have earned entitlements to IP will get a slightly higher total public pension (sum of GP and IP) than those with only a GP. This is an application of a Finnish innovation when it comes to co-ordinating basic pension and other benefits (Kangas and Palme 1991).

The universality of the basic provisions is important when it comes to the classical social policy goal of combating poverty. It also of vital importance in terms of the public and private boundaries of old age security and the interplay between these two spheres. The reformed public system is insulated from what happens with private provisions since the GP is only co-ordinated with IP (including the funded component) and not with private pensions, whether occupational or individual. In principle this is not new. However, in one respect, related to the tax system, the universality has been strengthened. This means that private pension savings will not have any effect on present and future public pension benefits. As will be argued shortly, this is important in the sense that it strengthens the motives for private savings without reducing the public commitments. This diverges from what happens elsewhere in the world in terms of strengthening the means testing of basic provisions.

Figure 6.2 presents the reformed pension system using the same method as in Figure 6.1 above. We see that there is a universal guarantee in the reformed Swedish system that no one should fall below. However, the reformed system is primarily an income-related system based on contributions. Most people will have contributory benefits because most people have been employed. For those who have only earned small contributory benefits there will be a supplement. So even if they have

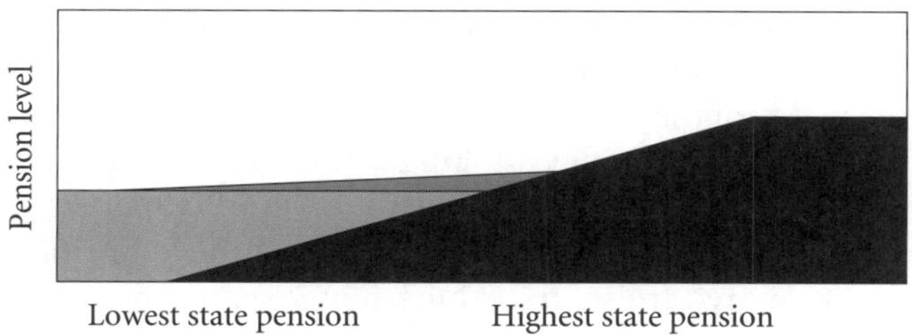

Fig. 6.2. Income Pension (IP) and Guarantee Pension (GP) in the reformed pension system.

not reached the guaranteed level on the basis of their past contributions, they will get some credit for past contributions and get a higher total pension, indicated by the grey part of the figure.

6.3.3. Fully Funded Individual Accounts within a Public Framework

This part of the reform is the clearest example of the changing boundaries of public and private in the system of old age security. It opens up the possibility of private fund managers handling individual contributors within a public framework, where public authorities both collect contributions and pay out the pensions. Moreover, it introduces individual risk taking within social insurance, where programmes are usually designed for collective risk-sharing. As indicated above, the size of the total contribution rate to the new system was guided by an ambition to secure the same benefit levels as in the old system, and the size of the notional accounts were determined by the explicit goal of maintaining earned entitlements. This left 2.5 per cent for a pre-funded element. The design is an outcome of a political compromise, where the centre–right accepted a higher contribution rate than required by the past commitments, only if an individual solution was found with regard to the funded component.

In contrast to the German pension reform, the contributions to the Swedish system are compulsory. They are collected jointly with the other contributions by Riksskatteverket (RSV). Until the final assessment of a person's taxable income is made, the National Debt. Office (Riksgäldskontoret) manages the funds. Then the money is transferred to Premiepensionsmyndigheten (PPM). The PPM manages the individual accounts of all contributors to the system. In 2000, this number was more than 4 million and it is expected to rise to 6 million in the foreseeable future. Each individual can choose a maximum of five different fund managers for their accumulated funds and fund managers can be switched each day of the working week without cost. The PPM aggregates all individual choices every day and trades them with the fund managers. This means that savers are anonymous to the fund managers. The accumulated funds of the individual are equal to the contributions and annual return on investment (plus inheritance gains and minus administrative costs). Funds can be withdrawn from the system starting at the age of 61 but can be postponed as long as the contributor wishes. The withdrawal is always in the form of an annuity—fixed interest or variable—that is provided by PPM. The proportion of the funds that is withdrawn is flexible (25, 50, 75, or 100 per cent of funds). The administration costs of the PPM is currently about 0.3 per cent of assets. To this about 0.5 per cent of administrative costs of the fund managers should be added.

6.4. PRE-FUNDING AND INTEGRATION WITH GLOBAL FINANCIAL MARKETS

The funding issue has been the subject of heated debate ever since the AP funds were established in connection with the implementation of the ATP programme in 1960. It is not funding as such which has been the big controversy, but rather the public control over it. In the 1950s, the political centre–right had proposed fully funded individual solutions outside public control. The funding issue also became important because the size of the funds became very large, even by international standards. As the ATP programme started to mature in the 1980s, the size of funds equalled 5–6 times the yearly expenditures of the supplementary earnings-related benefits. In all these respects the issue of funding emerged as critical in the reform process in the 1990s. Worries about the savings rate of the increased public commitment to old age security and a need to create buffers to smooth the effects of demographic changes, show that the macroeconomic concerns that were important motives in the early history of public pension funds in Sweden continue to be so (Government Report 2001/02: 180).

There were clear restrictions regarding the investment of the three AP funds from the beginning. The funds were mostly placed in Swedish, mainly government, bonds and used for investment in the housing sector. However, the importance of investments in the stock market grew, especially with the establishment of the fourth and fifth AP funds in 1974 and 1988, respectively. In 1996, a sixth fund was set up and directed towards emerging business, particularly small- and medium-sized firms. This supply of investment capital has been considered as important from time to time. This was, for example, the case when the third AP fund got its new and more liberal instructions. It coincided with a downward pressure on the prices on the Stockholm Stock Exchange, and was, therefore, welcomed by the private sector. However, the proposal by the Social Democratic Party at the time of the 1991 election, to liberalise the investment restrictions on the public pension funds, and thus, allow a larger share of assets in stocks and a larger share in individual companies, was heavily criticised by the political centre–right.

A central feature of the pension reform is that it separates old age pensions from the invalidity, or early retirement pensions, thus creating separate systems for managing the risks of ill health and old age. This may have important implications for various interest groups in society but this aspect of the reform will not be dealt with further in this chapter. However, one aspect is important to point out in relation to the issue of funding. A major achievement of the pension reform was to solve the long-term under financing of the old age pension system, partly by fixing contribution rates and linking entitlements strictly to contributions, partly by increasing contribution rates. The AP funds could not, however, be seen to be designed exclusively for coping with old age pensions. Rather, their purpose was to cover for fluctuations in both invalidity and old age, and it therefore seemed reasonable to use part of the funding to strengthening the general revenue, since the expenditure on invalidity pension now became a responsibility for the general revenue. The size of the sum to be transferred to the general revenue has been subject to discussion and some controversy. The view of the Ministry of Finance was that as much as possible should be transferred. For those who defended the pension system the obvious restriction here was that there was a clear need for a buffer fund if the automatic balancing mechanism was not to kick in. It was decided that in the first round 200,000 million SEK were to be transferred to the general revenue and that a check should be made in 2004, and then it should be decided if more money could be transferred. By the end of 2001, 565,300 million SEK remained within the AP fund system (Government Report 2001/02: 180).

In the future, the size of the AP funds is intended to vary and be dependent on, among other things, demographic development. The fact that the size of the pension funds will decline from time to time is not really a new feature, since they were originally designed as buffer funds. By international comparison they will not be small in the future either, but relative to the individually linked funds and to private pension funds they will lose in relative importance quite considerably. The PPM system is likely to generate assets of more than 700,000 million SEK.

The direct implications of any changes of the Swedish public and private pension systems are likely to be modest given the small size of the country's population and the size of funds. It may still be of relevance to study the different forms of integration, since the Swedish reform might continue to stand as an example in the pension debate internationally. Two different forms of integration have emerged in the wake of the pension reform. The first is the integration of international fund managers on the Swedish market as a result of the implementation of the PPM system. It represents a direct form of integration in the sense that international managers have been registered and approved with the PPM system and contributors have chosen these managers. This is also an inroad into the Swedish savings market. The PPM system offers one way of marketing these firms and presumably the same fund managers can offer their product to the voluntary markets. So far, the advances on the private savings/insurance markets have been modest if not negligible according to the observers of these markets.

The fact that the PPM system was opened up to all kinds of fund managers, including international ones, was to a large extent a result of pressure from the EU. The fact that the occupational plans are not (yet) open to fund managers, to the same extent as the PPM system, will probably serve as a brake to the penetration of the Swedish market by international players. It should be recognised that the size of the funds accumulated in the occupational sector can be projected to exceed the PPM related funds given the coverage and size of contributions applied. However, the integration in the world economy is not restricted to the foreign fund manager. On the contrary, the Swedish fund managers that are registered with PPM often do so with an investment profile that goes beyond Swedish borders. Hence, there are different funds specialising in, for example, Russia, Southeast Asia, and North America.

The other form of integration of financial markets goes in the opposite direction and is not a result of the PPM system, but an outcome of the reform of the AP fund system. These funds now have the explicit and sole purpose of maximising the returns to the old age pension system. Given the small size of the Swedish economy and the dominance of a fairly small number of multinational corporations, it has been seen as prudent to spread risks beyond the Swedish borders. There still are restrictions on what the AP funds can do and the different AP funds have chosen different strategies within the common framework.

Again, the Swedish pension funds are not of the magnitude that this will have any major impact on the international market. Still, it represents a form of integration of public pension funds that is important to recognise not only because it represents something new in Sweden, but also because it is a break with the patterns established elsewhere. This new direction of public pension fund investment has not been implemented without debate. Views diverge, not surprisingly, about the merits of the new system. Whereas trade union leaders and people from industry have claimed that the new openness is diverting Swedish capital, and is therefore, lowering investment in Sweden with implications for employment growth, others claim that the new order is necessary as any other directives would not only make the job of the AP funds difficult, but also make the pensions lower than they would otherwise be.

Another criticism concerns the macroeconomic implications of the large sums of money that have been going outside Sweden: that this outflow has put considerable pressure on the Swedish currency. The fact that the Swedish krona has developed poorly in relation to the US dollar as well as to the Euro and British pound during this outflow period has been interpreted as support for this hypothesis. The Prime Minister has, among others, expressed clear worries in this direction. Yet, as pointed out by some observers, most of the international investments have been hedged to insure the investment against changes in exchanges rates, which suggests that there may be other factors that accounts for the poor development of the Swedish currency. The conclusion of the Government Report (2001/02: 180) released in May 2002, is that the application of the new framework has been implemented without generating market disturbances.

A common feature of all pension funds is that they (at least until mid-2002) suffered extensively from the very poor returns on the international stock markets since 2000. This has actually lead to a decline of the nominal value of these investments and it is likely to have contributed to the low level of interest among the population in becoming active on this market. This is evident in the PPM system. Whereas more than 70 per cent made active choices in the first round in the year 2000, only 14 per cent of the newcomers in 2002 made active choices (PPM Press release, 23 April 2002).

6.5. CHANGING PUBLIC–PRIVATE BOUNDARIES

It can be argued that the pension reform has changed the public–private boundaries in several ways. As pointed out above, the most clear example is how the funds of the fully funded component of the public system are managed: not only do private fund managers manage the pension contributions, but there is also an open registration procedure and a free choice for the contributors. This should, however, not be confused with an entire privatisation of pension provision. There are a number of important differences that deserve to be emphasised in this context. First of all, the system is entirely anonymous since the fund managers do not know the identity of those who have chosen their fund. Second, the payments from the fully funded component are public in the sense that PPM pays the annuities to the contributors, even if this part is also subject to choice in terms of the start date, duration, amount (in percentage), and form of benefit. It is also important to point out that contributions are compulsory and not voluntary, as is usually the case with private pensions. Moreover, there is a default fund with public management of the funds for those who do not actively choose a private fund manager. Depending on how their skills in management are perceived by contributors, this fund has the potential to be of great importance.

The private–public interplay is however changing in other ways, too. What is the character of this interplay? Are they crowding each other out or are they mutually reinforcing? Historically, both kinds of mechanisms can be observed. In preparatory work for the 1913 reform, the representative from the private insurance market expressed fears that a major public commitment to old age security would eventually crowd out the market for private insurance (Elmér 1960). In some senses his worries were well-founded, even if the development is not as straightforward as one might have suspected, given the drastic expansion of public pension entitlements. The fact that the first reform was inadequate in terms of providing decent benefits was one contributing factor. The abolition of the means-testing of benefits, on the one hand, decreased the motive for saving since it guaranteed every old person a basic pension. On the other hand, it became rational to save, since an individual's future income in the form of interests or private pensions would not reduce the future public pension. The ATP reform became a worse threat, in the sense that it provided income security for fairly large segments of the labour force that otherwise would have had wherewithal, in terms of motivation and higher incomes, to save in private pension plans. Yet the occupational programmes continued to expand and were also redesigned to be better coordinated with public provision. It appears that the existence of public provision reduced shortsightedness among the population, and made other solutions affordable.

The relative importance of private solutions has been on the increase for over two decades. This shows very clearly when we compare expenditure levels for social insurance with those for occupational and private individual insurance for the 1990s. Even if the expenditure on old age pensions increased in real terms in the public systems, the growth was higher in both absolute and relative terms in the private sphere (Grip 2001). A more forward-looking way of understanding the importance of funding in the different sectors is to examine the inflows to the systems in terms of contributions. Note that this comparing different things. Contributions to the PAYG plan generated future entitlement but are, at the same, time used for expenditure on current pensions, but this does not apply to funded solutions. The most recent data (for 1998)[3] showed contributions of 124,826 million SEK to the public PAYG scheme and 21,660 million SEK to the public funded component. In 1998, the occupational pension plans in the public sector were predominantly PAYG and generated 31,000 million SEK in contributions whereas the funded occupational plans collected 50,590 million SEK. This compares with 25,957 million SEK which were generated for private individual plans. Turning to the coverage of the various kinds of provisions, available data gave the following picture for 1998[4]: both the public PAYG and funded schemes covered virtually 100 per cent of the labour force and more than 80 per cent of the population of working age (20–64). The funded occupational plans covered more than 60 and 50 per cent of the labour force and the population of working age, respectively. The corresponding figures for the PAYG occupational plans were 30 and 25 per cent. The number of contributors to private individual plans equalled about one-third of the population of working age; this proportion more than doubled during the 1990s (see above).

The design of pension reform has consequences for the coordination with private sector benefits. It is difficult, or at least potentially very expensive, to run DB plans on top of public DC plans. The pressure on (and desire of) employers to get a grip on costs has pushed development in the occupational pension sector in the same direction. The DC plans offer a solution. Here, it is interesting to note that the occupational plans include redistribution, for example, by giving credits during periods of parental leave, showing that these sorts of elements can also be a part of private pensions. It should be emphasised that the collective plans in the public sector have moved towards more extensive funding since 1998. The move towards more funding started with the reform of the blue-collar workers' scheme in the private sector which is converting the plans to individual DC. It continued with a reform of the municipality sector with a new agreement in 1998, and further developed with a new agreement for a funded component for state employees in 2002. Negotiations have been progressing in the fourth and last area, the ITP plan for private white-collar workers where the plans are fully funded but where employers are pushing for a change towards DCs. In all areas changes have been made to include employees with temporary contracts in order to improve coverage. The coverage has also been improved by lowering the age for earning entitlements in the occupational plans.

When we assess the incentive structure in the wake of the pension reform the methods of coordinating basic provision (the guaranteed pension), with other income are important features. The coordination of basic benefits with earnings-related ones in the reformed system gives incentives also for low-income persons to earn additional pension credits. Another important aspect of the pension system is that it is insulated in relation to private pensions. The universal guarantee is not affected by income other than contributory public pensions. This gives good incentives for private savings. In many countries, the minimum guarantees might actually be higher than the contributory benefits, which provides very little incentive for people to take part in the public system. A means-tested minimum provides a disincentive for savings because people who have saved will not get the basic pension. These micro-motives might very well have negative macro-effects on the rate of savings. My conclusion is that the design of the pension reform has the potential to foster interplay between public and private pension provisions, which is mutually reinforcing rather than mutually exclusive. This is also related to the fact that the replacement levels delivered by the income pension are likely to be lower than desired for most people, especially if increased longevity will continue to exert a downward pressure on public benefits. The yearly statements of the individual pension entitlement that the Swedish population receives will probably increase the awareness of this. The financial stability of the system should reduce shortsighted behaviour and increase long-term savings.

6.6. CONCLUSIONS: THE FUTURE FOR NATION-BASED WELFARE STATES

Even if it is clear that the future of the nation-based welfare state will be determined by the development in other parts of the systems of social protection as well as other external factors, the pensions system forms a sort of backbone to the Swedish welfare state. This is partly expressed in expenditure terms, where the pension sector is only matched by health care and education, and partly in terms of social risks, where it is evident that the risk of old age is something that all groups in society share. Given the general demographic scenario of an increasing proportion of the population moving above normal pension age, the importance of the pension systems is not likely to diminish. Since old age is a period where dependence on others is greater (regardless whether this is family, state, or the market), there is a growing number of people who are likely to be interested in how the nation-based welfare state is organised in the future. How these interests are articulated, organised, and mobilised is likely to be at least partially dependent on the how the nation-based welfare states are organised in the first place (Kangas and Palme 1996; Korpi and Palme 2003).

What can be seen as a crisis for the nation-based welfare state is related to a number of different issues. Key elements are the current financial crisis and the sustainability of existing commitments. This, in turn, has implications for the legitimacy of the system. There is also an ideological component, in the sense that the desirability of existing institutions has been called into question. Interrelated with all this is a political crisis raising questions about the ability of democratically elected governments to handle the situation. The Swedish development, not least during the 1990s, is a good illustration of these different symptoms of a crisis. The Swedish pension reform can be seen as an attempt to solve this in a critical area of social policy. The reform could be seen as an example of the potential of politics in enabling democratic institutions to solve the kind of long-term challenges they face in the twenty-first century.

In terms of putting the pension system onto a financially stable footing, there is no doubt that the reform has been successful in the long and short term. The system is actually stable, irrespective of demographic and economic developments. In this respect, the nation-based welfare state appears to be on safer ground than before the reform. Will the reform increase legitimacy of the nation-based welfare state? This question is, of course, more open than that of financial stability. One problem is related to the fixed contribution rate that is in effect shifting the financial risk onto the retired population (Pedersen et al. 2001). The question is whether pension levels will be seen as offering a decent living to retired people even if longevity increases substantially.

The individual risk-taking in the FDC part of the reform is another aspect that limits the risk-sharing introduced by the reform. Whether this will contribute to the erosion of solidarity that typically underpins nation-based welfare states, remains an open question. This is also the case with the exit option in the funded component of the reformed system. Potentially, if solutions outside the typical boundaries of the national welfare states appear attractive to a majority of the population, this might increase political demands for moving further in the same direction in pensions, and in other areas of social policy.

The major part of the welfare state is outside the pension system, and not pre-funded. The dependence on employment and growth is direct. The critical question from this perspective is whether the reform increases output. While Barr (2002) has recently argued that the critical issue is not whether the pension systems are funded or not, it still seems reasonable to assume that improved incentives can make at least some contribution to increased output. In this context, it appears warranted to mention North's (1990) point about the importance of stable institutions for growth. Arguably, making the pension system financially stable, and carrying the reform with over 80 per cent of the votes in parliament is relevant in this context.

There are parallel trends in developments in other sectors of the Swedish welfare state. The importance of private provision and choice has also increased elsewhere. This could be interpreted as a strategy for legitimising a continued commitment to a generous welfare state by giving some leeway for individual choice and, thus, increasing the legitimacy of the system. However, it might also be that the exit option provided by the choice offered in voucher-like systems, whether in the pension system or in health care, will erode the support of systems based on social solidarity and that the individual choices will reinforce social divisions more markedly. In other words, the Swedish model after the pension reform is different from what was before, but this is the result of a number of factors additional to the pension reform itself.

Does politics matter? This is a question related to the issue of the future of nation-based welfare states which has been asked before in other contexts. The fact that the reform was supported both by the Centre/Right coalition and the Social Democratic opposition might be interpreted as supporting the view that party politics do not matter any longer, implying that the driving forces behind current changes in mature welfare states are different from the expansion during the 'golden age of capitalism'. However, this interpretation fails on several grounds. First, consensus in final decision making does not actually mean that there is no impact from party politics as such. If the decision is a compromise, the final agreement might hide an underlying conflict, both in terms of interest and ideology. It might also be the case that the circumstances more or less forces some parties to comply with decisions that are going to be taken in any case. It would, for example, have been difficult for one of the coalition parties not to agree, given that they would like to stay in government. What, in my view, emerges most clearly is that existing institutions appear to have reshaped the interests and expectations of the population, thus limiting the degree of freedom of movement for the politicians. That the reform addressed the issue of entitlements both of the retired population and the population of working age, is one expression of the importance of these interests. The question of earned rights is of course central, and in this respect the reform implies a continuation of the commitments of the nation-based welfare state.

All social policy programmes affect interests and the formation of coalitions (Korpi 1980). This implies that changes in social policy programmes have the potential for changing the formation of interests and coalitions, and here the reform raises several issues. The first is the separation of the financing of old age and invalidity pensions. This is problematic from a distributional point of view. The financial base for the invalidity pension (which primarily goes to low income people) is thinner in terms of forming risk coalitions. The pension reform solves the problems of financing the old age pension part of the system, while it leaves the invalidity pensions to be financed out of general revenue. Second, the shift in terms of making the income pension the first tier of the system reflects changes in the employment structure, including the increased female participation in the labour force. It is also a way of dealing with the equity and incentive problems inherent in the old benefit formula and of the coordination of basic and earnings-related benefits. These changes may enhance the legitimacy of the system, and the wage indexing of the ceiling guarantees a continued broad base of commitment to the system. The fact that the basic provisions are supplementary forms a second tier, and narrows the level of commitment to this benefit. Universality is retained, but the changes may have implications for the extent to which the Swedish people are prepared to subscribe to the system. The indexing to prices of the universal guarantee is also likely to create tensions. Furthermore, those living on other benefits will get credits, which in turn, means that there will be very few with only the guaranteed level. These are projections, however; there is nothing so far to indicate that developments will take this direction.[5]

No other part of the welfare state is likely to have as great a degree of inertia as old age pensions: the contributory systems build up entitlements over long periods of time, and young and old are involved at the same time. This means that it is difficult, but not impossible, to change existing institutions. There is no determinism in institutions. Even if the design of institutions is important for how interests are organised, and make some scenarios more likely than others, it is still the case that the future of specific institutions lies in the hands of people who are free to choose. Moreover, every kind of change may trigger different kinds of mobilisation with different consequences for the viability of the institutions themselves. The conclusion is that the Swedish pension reform, like all pension reforms, represents both continuity and change. The reason for continuity, when there is a change in the overriding purpose of a reform, lies in the fact that the state also has to deal with both those who have already retired and those who have earned entitlements in the existing systems. The Swedish reform also represents continuity in that it maintains the social policy goals of basic security, income security, and redistribution, although the means have been changed dramatically. The drama is not about the level of benefits, but how the different parts of the system are coordinated and how redistribution is achieved.

NOTES

1. In addition to these benefits, housing benefits paid by the municipalities (KBT) were paid to pensioners with low incomes. Despite the fact that it was expected that these benefits would disappear more or less automatically as the pension system matured, these benefits have remained of great importance for low-income pensioners and have been found to be important in the reduction of poverty among the elderly.
2. The assumption is a contribution record of 40 years, same life expectancy as in 1994 and a 2% annual growth in average income.
3. *Sources*: Statistics Sweden and Finance Inspection (Finansinspektionen) FM17 SM 0002; National Social Insurance Board (RFV) Statistikinformation Is-I 1999:007; Direct information from the National Tax Board (RSV), and the different organisations for the occupational plans AMF, KPA, SPP, and SPV.
4. Comprehensive data has not been available. Figures have been estimated, using direct information from the various authorities, except for the labour force data from Statistics Sweden.
5. As an illustration, I will give an example in an anecdotal form. In 1993, the 80th anniversary of the 1913 'People's Pension Law' was celebrated with a seminar. I gave a presentation on the historical development of pensions from a comparative perspective, but ended with some reflections on the consequences of fewer and fewer elderly people being dependent on the basic benefits only. This is a result of the fact that new retirees had earned their pensions to a larger degree, and the others were dying off. I concluded that this might reduce motivation for defending the basic benefit. The first proposal for a pension reform which had been published in 1992, made this situation even more acute. What some saw as a problem was the replacement of a truly universal basic

benefit for everybody, with a universal guarantee (only to be paid to those who had not earned enough contributory pension entitlements). The fact that only a minority of the elderly population in the future were likely to be affected by the universal guarantee, since they would have 'earned their pension', would, in principle, mean that only a minority would be interested in defending the guaranteed level which, some argued, stood in sharp contrast to the conditions under the old regime. One possible scenario would be an introduction of means-testing for the guaranteed level on the assumption that the interest base in the country would be too weak to counter such a move. However, in reality, a comment (not a proposal) to such a scenario by the Minister of Social Insurance in a television interview triggered the most spectacular storm of protest of the 1990s. The actual reduction of child benefits, sickness insurance, and invalidity benefits at the time, had much less impact. I am not arguing that anything goes—just that we have to be careful in drawing conclusions about the future of political mobilisation.

CHAPTER

7

Pension Reform in the United Kingdom: Increasing the Role of Private Provision?

Carl Emmerson

7.1. INTRODUCTION

The UK pension system is particularly interesting due to the frequent and significant reform that it has undergone over the last 25 years. The incomes of the current generation of pensioners comprise state support together with a slightly smaller but very significant amount from private sources. This is in sharp contrast to many other EU countries such as France, Germany, and Italy where a much larger proportion of pensioner income comes from the state (Disney and Johnson 2001).

The number of pensioners is forecast to grow by just over 40 per cent in the next 50 years while the working age population is expected to remain approximately constant. Given that the public pension system in the United Kingdom is financed on a Pay-As-You-Go (PAYG) basis, this ageing of the population might have been expected to lead to financing problems in the future. This is not the case. The reforms introduced in the United Kingdom since 1980 have left the state system sustainable in terms of future costs. These have taken the form of reductions in the future generosity of the state system—through increases in the state pension age for women, reductions in the earnings-related component of the public pension system, and the formal price indexation of the flat-rate pension. When additional state spending has been made available it has often been focused at lower-income pensioners through increasing means-tested benefits. The result is that means-tested benefits form a very important part of the state system.

While no-one is, at present, allowed to opt out of the Basic State Pension, the UK pension system allows employees a large degree of choice over their second tier pension coverage. Historically, this reflects the fact that a significant earnings-related state pension scheme was only introduced in 1978 by when the coverage of occupational pension schemes was already high. Employees have to be a member of a pension scheme, but if offered the chance to join their employers' scheme they are free to decide whether to accept this offer, or to remain in the State Earnings Related Pension Scheme (SERPS), or alternatively, whether to make their own individual arrangements. Higher earners are much more likely to be members of an occupational pension scheme. Coverage of personal pensions is highest among those in the middle of the earnings distribution. Those who have chosen to remain in the state scheme tend to have lower earnings. The latest reforms to SERPS, the first stage of which was introduced in April 2002, will eventually lead to even greater incentives for those on middle and high earnings to join a private pension scheme.

The current system is certainly not without problems and further reform is likely. It remains to be seen whether the UK public pension system will prove to be sustainable politically, with future projected state expenditures remaining broadly constant as a share of national income despite increasing proportions of the electorate being above the state pension age. Furthermore, the frequent reforms have left the UK system looking very complex. This complexity and the regularity with which the system is reformed will hinder individuals who are trying to make appropriate decisions over how much, and in which form, to save. The reliance on means-tested rather than universal benefits leads to problems with some pensioners falling through the social security safety net, since they do not claim the benefits that they are entitled to. It also means that those individuals who expect to be on a relatively low income in retirement will face a disincentive to save through the high marginal withdrawal rates arising from potential eligibility to a number of means-tested benefits.

This chapter starts by discussing the demographic changes expected in the United Kingdom over the next 50 years (Section 7.2) and provides an outline of the United Kingdom pension system (Section 7.3). Section 7.4 looks at the expected costs of both the current pension system and the system of means-tested support to pensioners, and recent proposals from both the Labour government and the opposition Conservative Party. Section 7.5 looks at the private pension arrangements that individuals have made and how these vary by characteristics such as age and earnings. It also discusses the difficulty in trying to extend coverage of private pensions further down the earnings distribution. Section 7.6 discusses the important issue of transferability of pension funds and how this might affect both competition among pension providers and also improve labour market flexibility.

7.2. DEMOGRAPHIC TRENDS

The latest demographic forecasts from the Government Actuary's Department are shown in Table 7.1. The number of pensioners in the United Kingdom is set to increase from 10.5 million in 2000 to 14.4 million in 2050. Over the same period the number of individuals aged below the state pension age is set to fall slightly from 36.3 million to 35.8 million. This is despite the planned increase in the state pension age for women from 60 in 2010 to 65 in 2020.[1] These trends reflect both previous birth rates and also improving life expectancies.[2]

Also shown in Table 7.1 is the number of people expected to be contributing to the UK's National Insurance fund and the corresponding number of people expected to be claiming a pension. The latter is higher

Table 7.1. Demographic forecasts for the UK population, 2000–50

	Year					
	2000	**2010**	**2020**	**2030**	**2040**	**2050**
Working age population (million)[1]	36.3	37.3	38.8	37.3	36.2	35.8
Pensioner population (million)[1]	10.5	11.5	11.5	13.8	14.9	14.4
Ratio of working age to pension age[1]	3.46	3.23	3.38	2.71	2.42	2.50
Ratio without equal retirement ages	3.46	3.23	2.76	2.22	2.08	2.10
Contributors (millions)	20.2	21.6	22.2	21.5	21.4	21.3
Pensioners (millions)	11.0	12.3	12.6	15.2	16.4	15.8
Support ratio	1.8	1.8	1.8	1.4	1.3	1.3

[1] State pension age for women is set to be increased from 60 in 2010 by sixth months every year so that it reaches 65 in 2020.

Source: Government Actuary's Department (1999).

than the number of people in the United Kingdom over the state pension age due to the pension claims of individuals who have moved overseas. The ratio of contributors to pensioners is set to fall from around 1.8 today to 1.3 by the mid-century.

The expected ageing of the UK population over the coming century is not as severe as that expected in many other countries. For example, the percentage of the UK population aged over 65 is forecast to increase by 14.7 percentage points between 1990 and 2030 (from 24.0 per cent in 1990 to 38.7 per cent in 2030). This compares to increases of 27.5 percentage points in Germany, 18.3 percentage points in France, and 17.7 percentage points in the US (Bos et al. 1994).

This ageing of the population is likely to have a number of effects on the public finances. The extent to which it is healthy or unhealthy ageing will be a major determinant of the future demands placed on the National Health Service and the demand for long-term care. Initial work suggests that the increase in demands on the NHS over the next 50 years from changing demographics may be around the same magnitude as the increase seen over the last 50 years (Emmerson et al. 2000). Increasing numbers of the population at older working ages, and whether ageing is healthy or unhealthy will also have implications for numbers of recipients of disability benefits. In contrast, with regards to education spending, the effect of demographics is actually likely to reduce pressures (HM Treasury 1999). As is shown in Section 7.4 the costs of the UK State pension system, in its current guise at least, is sustainable in terms of cost in that large future tax increases are not expected to be needed. This is despite the expected increase in pensioner numbers and the fact that it is financed on a PAYG basis. Whether the system is politically sustainable remains to be seen.

7.3. THE CURRENT UK PENSION SYSTEM

The UK pension system is very complicated due to numerous reforms over the last quarter of a century. Figure 7.1 provides a simplified picture of the current UK pension system, which can be split into three main tiers. The first tier is mandatory, flat-rate, and publicly funded on a PAYG basis. There is also a significant, and growing, amount of means-tested benefits available to lower income pensioners. The second tier is also mandatory to employees although individuals are faced with a large degree of choice over the type of pension that they can accumulate.

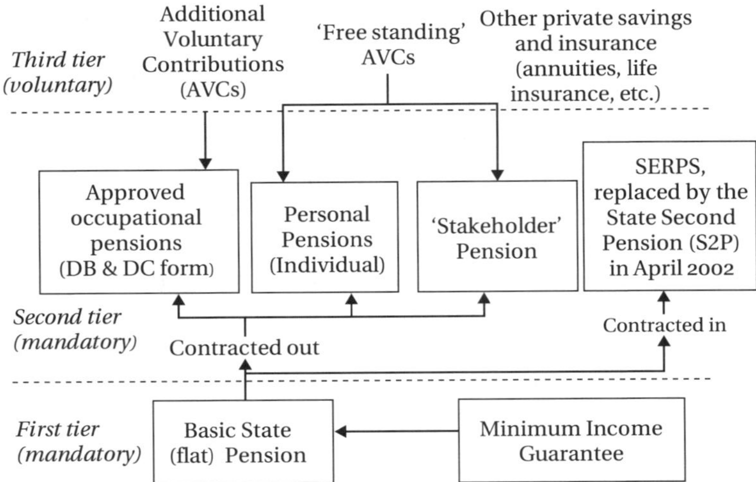

Fig. 7.1. Schema of the UK pension system, 2002.

The state second-tier pension is financed on a PAYG basis, as are most of the occupational pension schemes that are offered to public sector workers. Private sector occupational schemes, personal pensions, and Stakeholder Pensions are all financed on a funded basis. The third tier consists entirely of voluntary private savings, again all of which operate on an individual and funded basis. This subsection provides a brief outline of each tier in turn—more detailed descriptions can be found in, for example, Disney (1996), Disney et al. (1999), and Disney et al. (2001).

7.3.1. The First Tier of Pension Coverage

This tier is entirely publicly provided and funded on a PAYG basis. The largest single item of Government expenditure is the Basic State Pension, which for a single pensioner will be worth £75.50 a week from April 2002. Over the period from 1948 to 1975 it was increased and actually grew relative to average earnings. The Social Security Act of 1975 formally linked the Basic State Pension to the greater of either growth in prices or average earnings and this lasted until the early 1980s. Since then it has been automatically been increased in line with prices, although occasionally above inflation increases have been announced, for example, in April 2001 and April 2002.[3]

The structure of the Basic State Pension has largely been unreformed since it was introduced in 1948. It is a flat-rate benefit payable to men from the age of 65 and to women from the age of 60. In contrast to the pension systems of many European countries the Basic State Pension is payable, regardless whether individuals have actually retired or not.[4] Rights to the Basic State Pension are established through National Insurance Contributions (NICs). All those who earn over the primary earnings threshold (PET, £89 a week in 2002–3) have to pay NICs. Those earning between the lower earnings limit (LEL, £75 a week in 2002–3) and the primary earnings threshold have contributions made on their behalf. This is also true of those in periods of illness, unemployment, and disability. In order to qualify for the full amount individuals need to have contributions for 90 per cent of their working lives (44 years for men and 39 years for women) though this can be reduced through years spent looking after a dependent. If only one partner in a couple qualifies for the Basic State Pension then they receive an extra dependant's addition worth around 60 per cent of the single allowance for their partner.

In theory at least, no individual is left reliant on just the Basic State Pension for income in retirement. This is due to the level of means-tested benefits being higher than that the level of the Basic State Pension. This has generally been the case over the last 50 years, although this was not the original pension system envisaged by Beveridge nor the one established in 1948 when the Basic State Pension was £1.30 a week and the national assistance level of support set at £1.20 a week. In April 2002 the Minimum Income Guarantee (MIG) is worth £98.15 a week for a single person aged 60 or over, some 25 per cent higher than then level of the Basic State Pension. Those over the state pension age may also claim other benefits such as housing benefit and council tax benefit or, depending on their health, certain disability related benefits. The last 20 years has also seen a large increase in the numbers of people receiving disability benefits prior to reaching the state pension age (Blundell and Johnson 1998).

7.3.2. The Second Tier of Pension Coverage

The next tier is compulsory to all those in paid employment who earn above the Lower Earnings Limit (LEL) (although not the self-employed). Individuals have a significant amount of choice over the way in which they save within this tier. The default is for individuals is to be a member of the state scheme which, like the Basic State Pension, is funded on a PAYG basis. Contributions made since April 2002 accrue rights to the State Second Pension which initially will be an earnings-related pension, although the Government has stated that in the near future this will become a flat-rate top up to the Basic State Pension (Department of Social Security 1998). It is more generous towards lower-earners than its predecessor, the SERPS.[5] SERPS was introduced in 1978 and individuals were able to accrue rights to the scheme up until March 2002. The change will mean that SERPS payments will continue to be made for a considerable time to come. This highlights the fact that a pension reform that does not create losers will often lead to extremely long transition periods—for example, an individual aged 20 in 2000 will not reach the state pension age until 2045 but may still have accrued a small entitlement to SERPS.

Since SERPS was first introduced in 1978, individuals have been able to opt out of the state scheme into a private pension. Between 1978 and 1988 this had to be a defined benefit (DB) (final salary) scheme that guaranteed to pay at least as generous a pension as the state alternative. Over this period individuals whose employer offered them the chance to join an occupational pension scheme had to join that scheme. In return for forgoing their rights to SERPS individuals and their employers paid a lower rate of National Insurance (NI) contribution.

From 1988 onwards individuals were able to choose instead to opt out of the state scheme into a defined contribution (DC) (money purchase) pension scheme. More controversially, individuals were also allowed to choose not to join their employers pension scheme, and instead choose to open their own personal pension or instead to revert to the state scheme. These DC schemes could either be provided by employers or on an individual basis in accounts known as 'approved personal pensions'. Since these schemes could not guarantee to pay a certain pension, the Government instead paid part of individuals' NICs directly into their fund.[6] In retirement, this part of the pension fund is used to purchase a protected rights annuity (the rates on which do not vary by gender).

From April 2001, individuals could also choose to opt out into a Stakeholder Pension. This is a no-frills personal pension with a regulated cost and charging structure. Employers currently have to designate a scheme to their employees and enable them to make contributions directly from their pay.[7] There is no requirement, as yet, for employers to make any contribution to these schemes.

While personal pension and Stakeholder Pensions operate on a DC (money purchase) basis, the majority of occupational pension schemes (weighted by membership of scheme) still operate on a DB (final salary) basis.

7.3.3. The Third Tier of Pension Coverage

Individuals can also make additional contributions (up to a limit depending on their age and earnings) to a private pension. Contributions are made from income before tax; there is no income tax or capital gains tax on any returns to the fund and one-quarter of the fund can be taken tax-free on withdrawal. The remaining three-quarters of the fund has to be used to purchase an annuity before the individual reaches 75, the income from which is subject to income tax.[8]

Individuals can also save for their retirement in many other tax-privileged ways such as housing or in an Individual Savings Account (ISA). Returns to funds held in an ISA are not subject to income tax or capital gains tax, and there is a 10 per cent dividend tax credit on any dividends received from UK equities, at least until April 2004. Funds held in an ISA have the advantage of being more liquid than those held in a private pension and there is no requirement to annuitise funds. Offsetting this is the fact that tax advantages are, at least for those individuals who expect not to be on means-tested benefits in retirement, not as great as those given to savings held in a private pension (Emmerson and Tanner 2000).

The UK pension system provides individuals with a large degree of choice over their pension arrangements. This choice comes at the expense of an extremely complicated pension system. The next section looks at the financial costs of the state part of the current system, including the relatively large expenditures on means-tested benefits. The clear attractiveness of this system in terms of its ability to focus state expenditures on those with the lowest incomes in retirement is also highlighted.

7.4. THE FRAMEWORK OF DEBATE

7.4.1. The Costs of the Current System

The current UK pension system certainly does not need further reform to make it sustainable in terms of its likely cost. Despite the forecast ageing of the population, spending as a share of national income is expected to remain relatively stable over the next 40 years, while NIC rates should actually be able to fall. This is shown in Table 7.2. This is due to the assumed indexing of the Basic State Pension to prices (which rise more slowly than national income), the planned increase in the state pension age of women, and two reforms to SERPS which substantially reduced its future generosity and hence the expenditure on it.[9] The Basic State Pension, worth £75.50 in 2002–3, would have been worth slightly over £100 a week had it been indexed to earnings since 1981–2. While the Basic State Pension is forecast to cost £51.2 billion, in 2050 this would more than double (to approximately £108.8 billion) if it were continually increased in line with earnings instead of prices.

There are several reasons why the figures presented in Table 7.2 understate government expenditure on future generations of pensioners.

First, the NI rebates are paid to individuals who have chosen to opt out of SERPS or the State Second Pension. In the past these have been more generous than would have been required to provide an incentive for individuals to opt out of the state scheme. In part this reflected the drive to move towards privatisation of part of the second tier of pension coverage. The cost of reduced NICs, after netting off the reduced

Table 7.2. Forecast state expenditures on pensioners, 2000–50

	Year					
	2000	**2010**	**2020**	**2030**	**2040**	**2050**
Basic State Pension (£ billion)	34.4	38.0	41.3	49.4	52.8	51.2
SERPS/State Second Pension (£ billion)	4.9	9.5	12.8	17.8	22.5	30.2
Total State Pension (£ billion)	39.3	47.5	54.1	67.2	75.3	81.4
Total NI expenditure (% of GDP)	5.4	5.5	5.4	5.6	5.3	4.9
Required NIC rate (%) (employers and employees)	20.2	19.0	18.2	19.2	18.5	17.7
GDP per pensioner spending (1999–2000, 100)	98.7	92.2	88.1	78.8	70.7	68.3

Note: Total NI cost includes some non-pension expenditure such as Incapacity Benefit and Jobseekers Allowance. Figures exclude the cost of expenditure on means-tested benefits to pensioners. Cost of the Basic State Pension excludes the cost of the above inflation increases in April 2001 and April 2002 that were announced in the November 2000 Pre-Budget Report. It also excludes the November 2001 Pre-Budget Report commitment to increase the Basic State Pension by a minimum of 2.5 per cent if inflation falls below this level. Neither of these increases in generosity is sufficient to significantly change the long-run picture.

Source: Government Actuary's Department (1999; 2000); Authors' calculations.

entitlement to SERPS, was £5.9 billion for the period 1988 to 1993.[10] In 1999–2000 National Insurance Contributions were £8.8 billion (1 per cent of GDP) lower than they would have been in the absence of the contracting out arrangements. This is equivalent to between a 2.5 and 3 percentage point increase in the NI contribution rate (Disney et al. 2002).

Second, these estimates, like any other projections, are subject to forecasting errors. In the past these have tended to underestimate future numbers of pensioners due to an underestimate of future improvements in mortality (Disney 1998). For example, the 1996 population projections published by the Government Actuary's Department forecast that there would be 8.2 million people aged over 75 in 2051 compared to a forecast of 8.7 million made just 2 years later (Emmerson et al. 2000).

Third, the Government Actuary's projections, shown in Table 7.2, do not include the cost of means-tested benefit and other (non means-tested) benefits that go to pensioners. Table 7.3 shows that a total of £60.3 billion (6.0 per cent of GDP) is spent on benefits to those above working age, of which only £42.0 billion (4.2 per cent of GDP) is on the flat-rate and earnings-related pension schemes. Other than these, the biggest items are expenditure on the MIG (£4.4 billion) and housing benefit (also £4.4 billion). How these expenditures change in future will depend on whether the Government's aspiration to increase the MIG in line with earnings is fulfilled and the private incomes of future generations of

Table 7.3. State spending on those over working age, 2001–2

Payment	£ billion	% of GDP
Retirement Pension—basic	36,470	3.6
Retirement Pension—earnings-related	5,500	0.5
MIG	4,405	0.4
Housing Benefit	4,365	0.4
Attendance Allowance	3,130	0.3
Disability Living Allowance	2,100	0.2
Winter Fuel Payments	1,700	0.2
Council Tax Benefit	1,365	0.1
Over 75 TV Licence	370	0.0
Other	880	0.1
Total	60,285	6.0

Note: Figures are for estimated out-turns. Largest 9 items of spending listed separately—the remainder have been grouped in other.

Source: Department of Social Security (2002).

pensioners. The latter will depend on how much these individuals save for their retirement and the return that they receive on those funds. Further reform represents a further increase in spending on means-tested benefits of around £2 billion a year. It is also the case that pensioners will benefit disproportionately from some other aspects of state spending such as that on the NHS and subsidised public transport.

The increasing reliance on means-tested benefits has been due to the Government concentrating additional resources on low-income pensioners. This has come with at least two possible disadvantages. First, many pensioners do not take up the means-tested benefits to which they are entitled. The result is that the poorest pensioners are those left reliant on a level of income below the means-tested floor. The most recent Government estimates suggest that only between 64 and 78 per cent of eligible pensioners claim the MIG.[11] Second, the presence of increased reliance on means testing will lead to some individuals having a reduced incentive to save for their own retirement.

Rather than increasing the generosity of the state pension system, the successive Conservative Governments from 1979 to 1997 tended to focus any additional resources on means-tested support for pensioners. The Labour government since 1997 have increased state spending on pensioners by a greater extent, and again a very large proportion of this has been targeted at lower-income pensioners. Interestingly, the large increase in means-tested income safety net for pensioners has not led to an increase in the number of people aged 60 or over on income support (or its successor) (Brewer et al. 2002). Given that take-up rates have been relatively stable, this is probably due to younger cohorts having higher private incomes then previous generations.

For a government wanting to target additional resources at low-income pensioners, increasing the MIG rather than the Basic State Pension is attractive because all the funds will go to the low-income target group. Figure 7.2 shows the gains across the income distribution from increasing the Basic State Pension to the level of the MIG. In total this measure would cost around £5.5 billion (0.5 per cent of GDP). Those pensioners with no private income except the Basic State Pension, who currently receive the MIG, would not gain at all since it is currently withdrawn with a 100 per cent taper. The biggest cash gains would go to pensioner couples who are not in receipt of any means-tested benefits.[12] In particular, those couples where both individuals have full pension entitlement in their own right will receive the biggest cash gains. These are more likely to be found towards the top of the pensioner income distribution. The poorest 20 per cent of pensioners would gain an average of

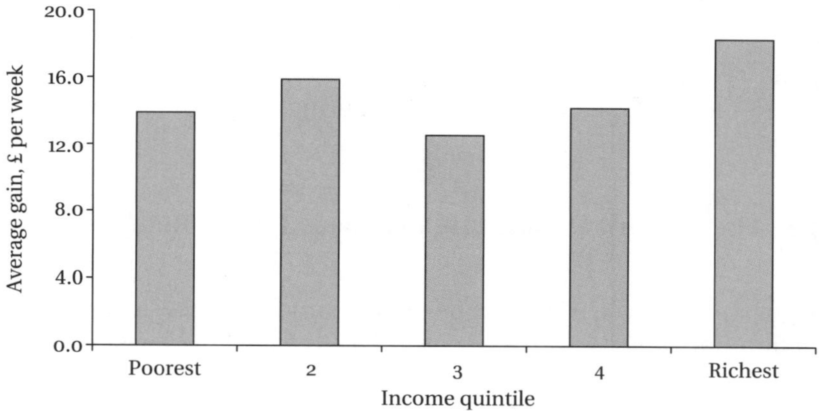

Fig. 7.2. Average gain from increasing the Basic State Pension to the level of the Minimum Income Guarantee (MIG), £ per week.

Notes: Income quintiles are calculated by dividing the pensioner population into five equally sized groups according to the income of their family (adjusted for family size). The 1st quintile contains the poorest 20 per cent of pensioners, the 2nd the next poorest 20 per cent of pensioners up to the 5th quintile which contains the richest 20 per cent of pensioners. An important caveat to this modelling is that the methodology will understate the gains to those pensioners who are not claiming means-tested benefits to which they are not entitled. These will be disproportionately found in lower income quintiles.

Source: IFS tax and benefit model, TAXBEN, using data from the 1999–2000 Family Resources Survey and the April 2002 tax and benefit system.

£14 a week compared to £18 a week among the richest 20 per cent of pensioners. An important consideration is that many of the poorest pensioners do not take-up the benefit to which they are entitled. The modelling below does not capture this non-take-up, and hence, the gains to the bottom quintile in particular will be understated. However, the picture clearly shows that a significant part of the additional spending goes to the top of the income distribution which, if the objective is to help the poorest pensioners, is badly targeted.

Future reform, or at least more expenditure than that implied by the current plans, might become politically necessary. State expenditures remaining broadly constant as a share of national income during a period of increases in the proportion of the population aged over the state pension age, imply that the proportion of national income publicly spent on each pensioner is set to fall. Table 7.2 shows that by 2050 state expenditure on each pensioner per unit of national income will be just 68.3 per cent of the level seen in 1999–2000. Without the replacement of SERPS with the more expensive State Second Pension, this figure would have further fallen to 56.2 per cent. Whether this is politically sustainable is likely to depend on the views of the increasing proportion of the electorate aged above or near the state pension age. More specifically, it may depend on how the retirement income that they receive from the state compares to the expectations they held during their working lives.

7.4.2. The Current Debate and Proposed Future Reform

The government will, from October 2003, introduce a new means-tested benefit to individuals aged 65 or over. This is called the Pension Credit. The motivation behind this is that under the present system the 100 per cent withdrawal rate on the MIG means that a pensioner with a small amount of private income will not necessarily be any better off in retirement than someone with no private income. The Pension Credit will remove this feature, since it will introduce a withdrawal rate of 40 per cent. (Retired women aged 60–64 will not receive the Pension Credit. Furthermore those with non-means-tested income of less than full Basic State Pension entitlement will still face a 100 per cent withdrawal rate, at least on part of their income.) The Pension Credit will cost around an additional £2 billion a year from 2004–5 onwards.[13] Naturally, as the generosity of means-tested benefits is increased, this will lead to more people being eligible. The result will mean that while 53 per cent of over 65 year olds are currently in families who are entitled to at least one means-tested benefit, this will rise to 61 per cent as a result of the introduction of the Pension Credit.

A different direction of reform was suggested by the Conservatives at the 2001 general election, with a proposal that individuals should be allowed to 'opt out' of the Basic State Pension.[14] This would have increased further, the amount of privately provided pension provision and would also have increased further, the amount of choice that individuals had over their pension savings. The effect on the public finances would be a deterioration in the short run due to the NI rebate on offer, but an improvement in the long run arising from the reduced future state expenditures. The overall effect on the public finances is ambiguous since it depends on what level of government contribution is required to persuade individuals to forgo their entitlement to the Basic State Pension. It would also have the effect of shifting further away from a PAYG pension system towards a funded pension system. The desirability of this reform depends in part on attitudes towards individual choice and risk taking and also the possible advantages from portfolio diversification from at least a portion of future state pension liabilities being paid for on a PAYG basis (Emmerson 2001).

The next section turns to examine in more detail current coverage of private pensions and assesses the difficulty that the government faces in its attempts to extend coverage of private pensions further down the earnings distribution.

7.5. REDRAWING THE PUBLIC–PRIVATE DIVIDE: DOMESTIC ISSUES

7.5.1. Current Coverage in the UK

The UK State pension system appears to be financially sustainable. As discussed, this has been achieved by large reductions in future state expenditures. In fact, by international standards, there has always been a relatively low level of UK State expenditure going on the pension system. Alongside this, there has always been a significant amount of private pension provision. State spending on pensions as a share of national income increased from 2.5 per cent of GDP in 1957 to just over 5 per cent in 1982 and has fallen since (Banks and Emmerson 2000).

Membership of occupational pension schemes fluctuated around 50 per cent of employees from the late 1960s to the late 1980s (Government Actuary's Department 2001). This has translated into a relatively high proportion of pensioners' income coming from private sources. Currently, around 40 per cent of pensioner income is from private sources and the remainder from public sources. The 1998 Green Paper stated that the government wanted to reverse this by the middle of the current century (Department of Social Security 1998). One of the mechanisms by which this is to be achieved is through the introduction of Stakeholder Pensions. The government hopes that these will be more suitable for individuals with lower earnings and therefore will extend private pension coverage further down the earnings distribution.

Current coverage of private pensions, by age, gender, and type of employment is shown in Figure 7.3. Among full-time employees, 54 per cent of men and 58 per cent of women have an occupational pension, with coverage highest among the 35–44 year old age group (as shown in the left-hand panel). The higher level of coverage among full-time women is due to the fact that they are more likely to work for employers that offer such schemes—for example, women are more likely to work in the public sector.

Coverage of personal pensions is lower; with 23 per cent of men and 14 per cent of women employed full-time having made their own arrangements in this way (as shown in the right-hand panel). The average age of individuals with a personal pension is younger than those with an occupational pension. The relatively young age of those who have chosen to open a personal pension is, perhaps, unsurprising since these schemes have only been around since 1988. In addition, younger workers were initially provided with a far stronger incentive through the original NI rebates to opt out of SERPS (Disney and Whitehouse 1992).

Coverage of private pensions also varies considerably by earnings level. This is shown in Figure 7.4 using data from the 9th wave (1999) of the British Household Panel Survey. In total 46 per cent of those in paid employment report being a member of an occupational pension scheme, with a further 7.4 per cent reporting that they also have a personal pension in that year[15] and 10.1 per cent having just a personal pension. Those with higher earnings are much more likely to be members of an occupational pension scheme with 82.1 per cent of those in the highest earning 10 per cent of the population having either an occupational scheme or an occupational scheme and a personal pension. This may

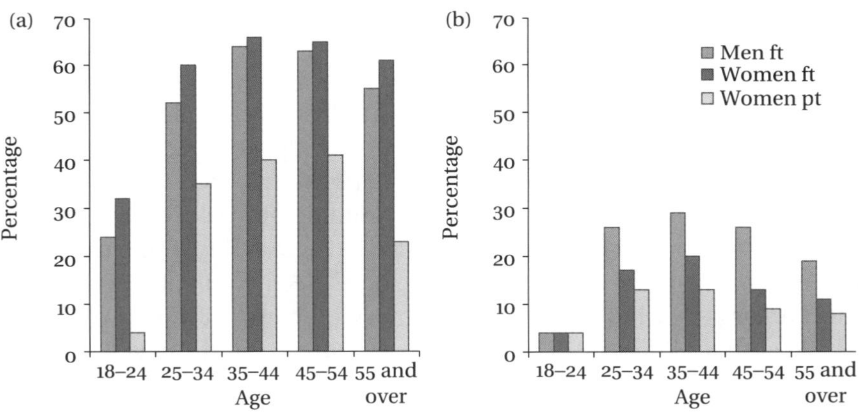

Fig. 7.3. Private pension coverage among employees in the UK, by age, gender, and type of employment, 2000. (a) Occupational pensions (b) Personal pensions.

Note: Only a small proportion of men work part time in the UK, and therefore, are excluded from the analysis.

Source: Office for National Statistics (2001) using data from the 2000–1 General Household Survey.

appear counterintuitive, since those employers that offer an occupational pension might have been expected to pay less since the overall package could still be as attractive to employees as that offered by other firms who do not offer an occupational pension. Empirical evidence suggests that this is not the case. Gustman and Steinmeier (1993), using US data, show that even among the same individuals, jobs that offer occupational pensions tend to be better paid. Disney and Emmerson (2002) find a similar result using data from the United Kingdom.

In contrast to occupational pensions, with personal pensions there is not a monotonic increase of coverage with regards to earnings level. Those with lower levels of earnings are less likely to have a private pension arrangement. These people will either be contracted into SERPS (and from April 2002 the State Second Pension), or will have earnings below the LEL, and hence, will not be accruing any second-tier pension rights.[16]

It is important to note that Figure 7.4 only provides a snapshot of pension coverage at a point in time. As shown by Disney et al. (2001),

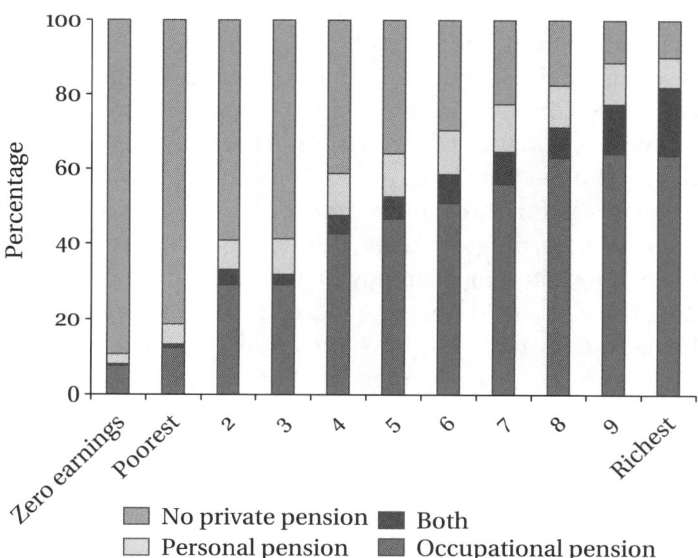

Fig. 7.4. Private pension coverage in the UK, by earnings decile, 1999.

Note: Sample includes only individuals aged 20–59 who are not currently self-employed. Total sample size is 9,342, individuals. These are split between 2,422 in the zero earnings category and 692 in each of the ten earnings deciles.

Source: British Household Panel Survey (1999).

60 per cent of employees accrued rights to more than one type of pension scheme over the 7-year period from 1991 to 1998.

7.5.2. Are Further Increases in Coverage of Private Pensions Likely or Desirable?

The government has stated that it would like to increase private pension coverage further. Stakeholder Pensions, introduced in April 2001, were intended to be primarily targeted at 'middle earners', defined as those individuals who earn between £9,000 and £18,500 a year who do not already have a private pension. This would represent a further shift towards individual funded provision rather than collective provision financed on a PAYG basis. The fact that employment status, earnings, and pension status change considerably over time suggests that there are likely to be problems with a pension policy that is designed on the basis of each individual's current earnings and pension status. Life cycle models of retirement saving suggest that as well as current income, individuals would need to take into account a whole range of other considerations. These include the income that they expect to receive in the future as well as their current and future consumption needs (Attanasio 1999). With these concerns in mind, the next paragraph turns to look at empirical evidence on the characteristics of those in government's target group for stakeholder pensions.

The target group for Stakeholder Pensions is very small. The majority of people whose earnings were in the target earnings range at some point between 1992 and 1995 already had some form of private pension. In addition, those who did not were more likely to experience periods of unemployment and tended to have no, or very low levels of, savings. If they were able to save, then it might well be more appropriate for them to hold these savings in a relatively liquid form rather than tie them away for retirement. This is discussed further in Disney et al. (1999).

The decision to exclude smaller employers from having to designate a stakeholder scheme is likely to reduce take up of Stakeholder Pensions among the target group. This is particularly true since those earning between £9,000 and £18,500 without a private pension are more likely to work for a smaller employer than those not in this group (Emmerson and Tanner 1999).

While the current target group for Stakeholder Pensions is small, demand from future generations could be considerably larger. For example, many individuals in the current population who purchased a personal pension with up-front costs may not be well advised to switch provider but perhaps would have taken out a Stakeholder Pension in the first place had that option been available to them. This might be particularly true of those who are more likely to experience periods of unemployment, since the flexibility of contributions that stakeholder schemes have to offer will be more attractive to those who are less able to commit to regular contributions. Of course, this will still only apply to those who feel that they do want to lock their savings up until retirement rather than hold them in a more liquid form.

One important factor that could potentially hinder the Government's efforts to increase take-up of private pensions further down the earnings distribution is the significant amount of means-tested support for lower income pensioners. Individuals who expect to retire on a relatively low income in retirement will face a disincentive to save due to the high marginal withdrawal rates arising from combinations of means-tested benefits. The MIG is currently withdrawn at a rate of 100 per cent; the Pension Credit will be withdrawn at a rate of 40 per cent. While this will reduce the marginal withdrawal rate faced by many lower-income pensioners it will also bring more people onto means-tested benefits, and hence, increase their withdrawal rate. In addition, many pensioners will be eligible for council tax benefit and housing benefit which even postreform will combine to produce high marginal withdrawal rates. Around 30 per cent of the current generation of pensioners are expected to face a withdrawal rate of greater than 50 per cent once the Pension Credit reform is in place (Clark T. 2002). Whether this really matters will depend on how much these individuals would have saved in the absence of the high withdrawal rate.

Before the Pension Credit reform, and assuming that the government's aspiration of earnings indexation of the MIG was met, a 65-year-old retiring in 2050 with no other income would receive just over £250 a week, in today's prices, indexed to earnings for the remainder of their life (assuming real earnings growth of 2 per cent a year). If they were to live for 14 years then, assuming a real discount rate of 4 per cent, this would be worth nearly £170,000. If receipt of typical housing benefit and council tax benefit (£40 and £5 a week, respectively, again indexed to earnings) are also included then this rises to over £240,000. Those who had a contributory record of 49 years would be able to receive the maximum amount of Basic State Pension and State Second Pension. This would provide an income of £240 a week in today's prices, indexed to prices (i.e. not to earnings) for the remainder of their life. Hence, it would start at over £10 a week below the level provided by the MIG with the difference widening over time. The value of the stream of income provided by the Basic State Pension and the State Second Pension would be worth around £140,000, some £30,000 less than the amount provided by the MIG alone.

While the introduction of the Pension Credit will mean that someone with just the full Basic State Pension will not face a 100 per cent withdrawal rate, some individuals will face a disincentive to save—in particular, those who expect to be eligible for housing benefit and council tax benefit on top of the Pension Credit. Those who are eligible for all three benefits will face a 91 per cent marginal withdrawal rate on any additional income.

An interesting question for future research is the decision facing individuals who are taxpayers during their working lives who expect to receive the Pension Credit once they reach 65. One option would be to save in a private pension, but it might be the case that they would be best advised to save in an ISA. If the latter does turn out to be the case for many individuals, then the government may wish to consider more changes to the pension system. One possibility would be to look at the generosity of the State Second Pension. If this were to be made more generous it would reduce the number of people who will end up on high marginal withdrawal rates in retirement. Originally, the State Second Pension was set at a level intended to ensure that individuals with a full contribution record would not be reliant on the MIG in retirement.[17] Given that the MIG is now more generous than it was when the State Second Pension was introduced, the government might decide to increase the size of the compulsory second tier of state provision. The fact that to receive the maximum amount of State Second Pension requires a full (49-year) contribution record might also need to be reconsidered given that many individuals will not be able to achieve this. For example, those who remain in education beyond the compulsory school leaving age of 16 will be unable to achieve the maximum award of State Second Pension.

An alternative proposal that has been suggested is to remove the State Second Pension and the Pension Credit and instead increase the Basic State Pension to the level of the MIG and uprate it in line with earnings rather than prices (Brooks et al. 2002). This would certainly achieve a much simpler state pension system that should aid individuals trying to make appropriate saving decisions. The biggest gainers in terms of percentage increase in income would be those pensioners who currently receive just the Basic State Pension, since they do not take up the means-tested benefit to which they are entitled. It would, however, not benefit those lower-income pensioners who are in receipt of the full MIG. Many lower-income pensioners would also lose out from the loss of the Pension Credit. Given that over 50 per cent of pensioners will be entitled to the Pension Credit, it is extremely difficult to think of any reform that would achieve simplification of the UK pension system while not being considered prohibitively expensive or leaving some of those eligible for the Pension Credit worse off. The proposed removal the State Second Pension would also lead to the removal of the current contracting out arrangements—and the implications of this on the current private pension arrangements would need to be carefully considered.

So far, the analysis of pension reforms has focused on their implication for the government's finances and the incomes of pensioners, both today and in the future. Recent trends in pension coverage—for example, towards greater funding and saving on an individual rather than a collective basis (through either the state or an employer) will potentially have a wide range of other economic effects. The next section discusses some of these.

7.6. REDRAWING THE PUBLIC–PRIVATE DIVIDE: INTERNATIONAL ISSUES

The 1986 Social Security Act, which extended the right to contract out of SERPS by allowing individuals to choose instead to save in a DC (money purchase) scheme has a wide range of potentially interesting effects. These include the overall effect on public finances, changes in saving rates, changes in retirement behaviour, and potentially, changes in labour market flexibility (Disney et al. 2003). The shift from state and occupational pension coverage towards greater take-up of personal and stakeholder pensions is a shift from collective pension provision to individual forms of saving for retirement. Moving from DB (final salary) schemes towards DC (money purchase) schemes might also increase labour market flexibility, since it potentially removes the prospect of pension loss from a change of employer. Occupational pension schemes in the UK typically operate on final salary schemes which tend to reward more highly those with long job tenures. The issue of pension portability and its potential consequence for labour market mobility is not just a domestic one—it is also of importance at the level of the European Union (EU) as it tries to promote greater labour market flexibility.

The issue of pension portability (whether there is a pension loss when an individual changes employer) and pension transferability (whether funds held in a pension can be transferred to another provider) are not the same. Some types of pensions will have very low levels of transferability but might not be expected to have any effect on job mobility. For example, pension rights accumulated in the SERPS or the State Second Pension are not transferable, since accrued funds cannot be transferred into a private pension. However, this lack of transferability of the funds should not have any implications for labour market mobility, since individuals can accrue rights to these pensions when they change employers.

On the other hand, the situation with pension rights accrued in occupational pension schemes is often very different. While funds can be transferable between schemes, they can still act as a deterrent on labour market mobility due to the way in which funds build up in the fund over time. Occupational pension funds in the United Kingdom generally (in the private sector at least) operate at the firm level. They also often work on a final salary rather than (for example) a career average salary. This has the effect of tending to reward longer stayers at the relative expense of those with shorter job tenures.

Part of the motivation behind the introduction of personal pensions was the potential impact on labour market mobility. This is confirmed by the 1985 Green Paper which stated that a 'major factor in the demand for personal pensions has always been that they should be fully portable. People must be able to take their own pensions with them without any loss when they change jobs. The Government are committed to ensuring that barriers in pensions do not affect job mobility' (Department of Social Security 1985).

Like SERPS and the new State Second Pension, membership of a personal pension or a stakeholder pension might not be expected to reduce labour market mobility, since individuals can continue to contribute to the same scheme, regardless of whether they switch employer. Unlike the UK State pension schemes, funds held in a personal pension can be moved between different providers. However, this might often not be an optimal retirement savings strategy due to the charging structure of personal pensions. The obvious example is an individual who paid significant up-front costs when they opened a personal pension who subsequently decided to transfer the funds to another scheme. It seems likely, at least with hindsight, that this was not an optimal strategy. Furthermore, personal pensions may charge individuals exit charges—again restricting transferability of funds.

The regulated charging structure imposed on Stakeholder Pensions, by only allowing funds to charge up to 1 per cent of the fund each year, allows individuals to transfer funds, without costs, between schemes.

Indeed, it is precisely this type of switching, or at least the threat of this type of switching, that the government hopes will aid competition and place downward pressure on charges. If the introduction of Stakeholder Pensions does succeed in these aims, then it is likely to also place downward pressure on the charges in personal pensions since providers of Stakeholder Pensions and personal pensions are likely to be competing for individuals' pension funds (Emmerson and Tanner 1999).

In addition to these theoretical arguments about the potential impact of different types of pension schemes on labour market mobility, there is also some recent empirical evidence looking at job mobility within (although not yet between) different EU countries. Andrietti (2001) looks at the effect of pension coverage on labour market mobility using the European Community Household Panel (ECHP) survey in Denmark, Ireland, the Netherlands, and the United Kingdom. He finds that pension-covered workers are only less likely to move jobs in the United Kingdom. This is perhaps unsurprising for Denmark, where the majority of occupational schemes are DC schemes and for the Netherlands where the schemes are typically arranged at the industry level rather than at the company level. In the Dutch case, we would only expect to see job moves between industries being affected by pension coverage rather than job moves between employers within the same industry.

Another test of whether pension-covered workers are less likely to move job, is provided by Disney and Emmerson (2002). This uses data from the British Household Panel Survey to look at the subsequent labour market mobility of the group of individuals who were offered the opportunity to join their employers' pension scheme, but choose instead to make their own arrangements. They find that (after controlling for other important covariates, such as age and the estimated potential wage advantages of changing job) those who choose to open a personal pension instead of joining their employers scheme are 5.6 percentage points more likely to change job in the subsequent period. This gives some evidence that employer provided pension schemes might lead to lower job mobility. Given that the majority of individuals who were a member of an occupational pension scheme during the period of their study would have been members of a DB rather than a DC scheme, it is also evidence that this effect is from the incentives in these schemes.

Further research is required to unpack whether it is individuals who suspected that they might move job who chose not to join their employers pension scheme or whether it is because they did not join the scheme that they were subsequently more prepared to move job. The latter case would mean that further moves away from employer provided pension schemes, and more specifically, moves away from DB schemes, would increase labour market mobility and, through an improved match between workers and employers, potentially increase economic efficiency.

7.7. CONCLUSIONS

Future reform of the UK pension system is not needed to make it sustainable in terms of its cost. Forecast expenditures can be met without tax increases. This has been achieved by large cuts to the state pension system over the last 20 years, in particular through the price indexation of the Basic State Pension, the planned increase in the state pension age for women, and the reforms to the second tier of state pension provision that were carried out in 1986 and 1995 (which reduced future SERPS expenditure to around a quarter of what it would have been). It remains to be seen whether the current system is politically sustainable. Despite the recent introduction of the State Second Pension, which will increase future state expenditures, state spending per pensioner relative to national income is expected to be less than 70 per cent of its current level by the middle of this century. Given that an increasing proportion of the electorate will be aged over the state pension age, what they expect in terms of retirement income from the state may play a very important part in determining whether the current arrangements prove to be politically sustainable.

The reforms have also dramatically increased the amount of choice that today's working population has over their retirement savings. Employees who are offered the chance to join their employers' scheme can either choose to accept, or to decline and open a personal pension or a stakeholder pension, or decide to remain in the state scheme. If they have their own savings that they want to invest, they will want to consider whether they should tie up their savings in a private pension or whether they would be better off saving in a more liquid form such as an ISA. The appropriate strategy for the majority of people has tended to be that the tax-treatment of private pensions makes them a more attractive retirement savings vehicle than other tax-favoured accounts. This choice is complicated by the increasing reliance on means-tested benefits in retirement. These provide a disincentive to save in a private pension for individuals who expect to be receiving benefits with high marginal withdrawal rates in retirement.

The increased choice that individuals now face also means that the current UK pension system is very complicated, perhaps overly so. It has also been frequently reformed in a way that makes it less, rather than more, easy to understand: reforms have tended to add new parts to the system without removing existing parts. At least in part, this is due to a desire not to create immediate losers from any reform. It is now difficult to think of a simplifying reform to the UK state pension system that would not be considered prohibitively expensive or leave some lower income pensioners worse off. This complexity, and the frequency with which the system is reformed, make it harder for individuals to make appropriate retirement savings decisions (Banks and Emmerson 2000).

The Government has a stated objective of increasing the proportion of pensioner income that comes from private saving. The majority of middle earners already have a private pension. Those who do not tend to have characteristics that suggest that they might be better advised to save in a more liquid form. Recent large increases in the MIG and also the introduction of the (means-tested) Pension Credit represent an increase in future state expenditures on lower income pensioners. These will make it more difficult for the Government to meets its stated objective to increase the proportion of pensioners' incomes that comes from private sources.

While membership of occupational pension schemes is still relatively high, it has been falling. One of the justifications used to introduce personal pensions was that it might help to reduce barriers to job mobility. Increasing labour market mobility is also a very important policy issue for the European Union. A potential constraint on this is the way in which pension rights accrue. Evidence from the United Kingdom suggests that movements away from occupational pensions (and probably from final salary DB schemes) might lead to increases in labour mobility due to the reduction of pension losses arising from job changes.

Given the frequency of pension reform in the United Kingdom, more reform is not unlikely. One possible reform is to increase further the generosity of the State Second Pension in order to ensure that individuals with full contribution records during their working lives are less likely to be on relatively high withdrawal rates in retirement. If further reform is to occur it would seem sensible to consider ways in which the current system can be simplified so as to make it easier for individuals to make sensible decisions over how much, and in which form, they should save.

NOTES

1. This increase in the state pension age for women is to achieved by it being increased by 6 months every year between 2010 and 2020. The state pension age for men is set to remain unchanged at 65.
2. Banks and Emmerson (2000) provide more details of trends in birth rates and life expectancies.
3. Banks and Emmerson (2000) provide details of the level of the Basic State Pension in real terms and relative to average earnings over time.
4. An earnings test did exist until October 1989 See Disney and Smith (2000) for more details.
5. For a more detailed discussion of SERPS see Disney and Johnson (2001). The State Second Pension is discussed in detail in Agulnik (1999) and Disney et al. (1999).
6. For more details see Disney and Whitehouse (1992), Dilnot et al. (1994), and Disney et al. (2001).
7. Employers who employ less than 5 employees and those who offer membership of an occupational pension scheme or a contribution to a group personal pension scheme are exempt from this.
8. For more details see Banks and Emmerson (1999) or Inland Revenue and Department for Work and Pensions (2002).
9. See Johnson et al. (1996) for more details of the cuts to SERPS announced in the Social Security Acts of 1986 and 1995.
10. See Budd and Campbell (1998) for more details. The voluntary nature of contracting out means that the arrangements are likely to cost more than the savings to the state from the reduced future pension expenditure (Disney et al. 2001).
11. Figures for 1999–2000. Take-up by expenditure is estimated to be higher at between 74% to 86%. Pensioners are found to have a lower take-up rate than non-pensioners. Source: Department of Social Security (2001).
12. Since income from the Basic State Pension is taxable basic rate taxpaying pensioners would gain more in cash terms than the relatively small (but growing) number of higher-rate taxpaying pensioners.
13. For a discussion of the reform, including distributional effects, see T. Clark (2001; 2002). Estimates of its long-term costs can be found in Department for Work and Pensions (2002*a*).
14. A similar policy was proposed by the Conservatives at the time of the 1997 election (basic pension plus), but this was to be compulsory for new entrants to the labour market. It was proposed that the transition would be paid for by a move from taxation of pensions in payment (EET) towards taxation of contributions to pensions (TEE).
15. There are several possible explanations for individuals reporting that they have contributed to more than one type of pension. Perhaps most obviously some will have have changed pension status at some point during the last 12 months (for example, if they have moved jobs). Another explanation is that those who are members of a group personal pension might report that are both a member of a scheme offered by their employer and also a member of a personal pension.
16. The State Second Pension also provides credits for recipients of invalid care allowance and those caring for individuals receiving attendance allowance or disability living allowance, and those receiving child benefit where their youngest child is aged under 5.
17. Since the MIG is increased in line with earnings whereas once in payment the State Second Pension only increases in line with prices, individuals with a full contribution record but no private income would have expected to be eligible for the MIG at around age 75 (Disney et al. 1999).

CHAPTER

8

Restructuring Pensions for the Twenty-first Century: The United States' Social Security Debate

Alicia H. Munnell

8.1. INTRODUCTION

This chapter focuses on the debate about privatising Social Security in the United States. Social Security in the United States has a much narrower meaning than it does in Europe and other developed countries. It refers only to the government-sponsored 'Old-Age, Survivors and Disability Insurance' programme. This programme covers virtually the entire workforce, provides benefits based on lifetime earnings, and adjusts payments after retirement in line with inflation. The benefit structure is progressive so that the average earner retiring at age 65 receives benefits equal to about 40 per cent of previous earnings; low-wage workers receive 53 per cent; and those with maximum taxable earnings receive 24 per cent.[1]

In the United States, the public Pay-As-You-Go (PAYG) Social Security programme is only one component of a three-tiered retirement system. The second tier consists of employer-provided supplementary pensions, which are fully prefunded. These tax-subsidised plans are sponsored by private employers, by the federal government for its employees, and by state and local governments for their workers. They play an important role in assuring a comfortable retirement, but the percentage of the private sector workforce covered by an employer-sponsored pension plan at any given point in time has remained around 50 per cent since the 1970s. This constancy obscures two changes, however. First, pension coverage has increased for women and declined for men. Second, a major shift has occurred in the types of plans from defined benefit (DB) to defined contribution (DC). DB plans—like Social Security—generally provide retired workers with a set amount based on their salary history, while benefits under DC plans depend on the accumulated amount in a worker's account.

The third tier of the US retirement income system is individual saving. Those 65 and older currently receive roughly half of their non-earned income from Social Security, one quarter from employer-provided pensions, and one quarter from private saving. Not surprisingly, Social Security accounts for virtually all retirement income at the low-end of the income scale, and income from assets accounts for the bulk at the high end.

Although tier 2, the private pension system, and tier 3, individual saving, raise a host of interesting questions, 'privatizing' tier 1, Social Security, is the topic of this study. As in other countries, the consensus on the value of PAYG social insurance has broken down in the United States. Critics argue that Social Security costs too much, hurts the economy, and reflects an out-moded social philosophy. They contend that workers—to a much greater extent than they do now—should decide how much, when, and in what form to protect themselves once they stop working. Advocates for change say that privatisation will boost private saving, control costs as the baby-boom generation retires, and reflect changes in social philosophy about the relative importance of individual and collective effort.

This chapter explores the critics' case and assesses the extent to which the United States is likely to restructure its public pension system for the twenty-first century. The discussion addresses three questions. First, how is the United States dealing with the demographic, financial, and political pressure on its public pension system? Second, to what extent will these pressures redraw the boundaries between public and private responsibilities? Third, how would such shifts, if they should occur, affect individuals, financial markets, and future low-wage workers?

Four conclusions emerge from this analysis. First, the United States faces a relatively manageable financial challenge. Second, the push for shifting responsibilities for retirement income from the public to the private sector emerges from the political climate and the 1990s stock market boom rather than from the demographics. Third, privatisation alone—that is, the introduction of private accounts without additional funding—will not improve the Social Security's finances or raise returns on individuals' payroll tax contributions. Finally, private accounts shift the financial risk of the basic pension to the individual and contain the seeds for unravelling the US social insurance system.

8.2. DEMOGRAPHIC, FINANCIAL, AND POLITICAL PRESSURES ON PENSIONS IN THE UNITED STATES

Like other developed countries, the United States faces an ageing population that will increase the costs of its PAYG Social Security system. Like other developed countries, the United States is engaged in a major debate about restructuring its national retirement programme. What is unique to the United States is that the financing problems facing its Social Security system are relatively modest, and political rather than economic considerations are driving the debate on privatisation. Nevertheless, the debate culminated with President Bush establishing a commission to come up with specific recommendations to privatise at least a portion of the programme. The Commission reported on 21 December 2001 with three alternative proposals to introduce private accounts into the existing Social Security system.

8.2.1. United States' Social Security Problems are Modest

The Social Security financing problems in the United States are relatively modest for three reasons. First, as discussed in the introduction, Social Security plays a limited role; it is only one portion of the nation's retirement system.[2] As a result, public social insurance benefits—and therefore costs—are lower in the United States than elsewhere. Second, while the US population is ageing, the demographic shifts are much more muted than in other developed countries. Finally, economic growth is somewhat higher in the United States, which helps control programme costs. Let us take a closer look at each of these factors.

Because the United States relies heavily on the private sector and individual saving for the provision of retirement, it provides relatively modest Social Security benefits.[3] Several studies have examined the replacement rates (ratio of benefits to pre-retirement earnings) for various social security programmes throughout the world, and the United States consistently comes out on the low end (e.g. see US Social Security Administration 1999 and Weaver 1998). Figure 8.1 reports the most recent of these replacement rate comparisons and, with the exception of Canada, the United States shows the lowest benefit levels relative to earnings. The US replacement rate of 41 per cent is less than half that in France and the Netherlands, both 91 per cent. It is also significantly below that in Belgium (77 per cent), Italy (75 per cent), Spain (63 per cent), and Germany (62 per cent) (Gruber and Wise 1999).[4] Another dimension of programme generosity is the adjustment to benefits after retirement. Adjusting for inflation, as the United States does, allows retirees to retain the purchasing power of their benefits, but as retirees age their position declines relative to workers whose earnings reflect productivity gains as well as inflation. Some countries provide more generous adjustments that allow retirees to retain their relative position, but adjusting benefits for the growth in wages or Gross Domestic Product (GDP) is quite expensive. The United States does not incur this additional expense; rather, it starts with modest benefits and adjusts them after retirement only for changes in prices.

In addition to having a less costly Social Security programme today, the United States faces less dramatic demographic shifts in the

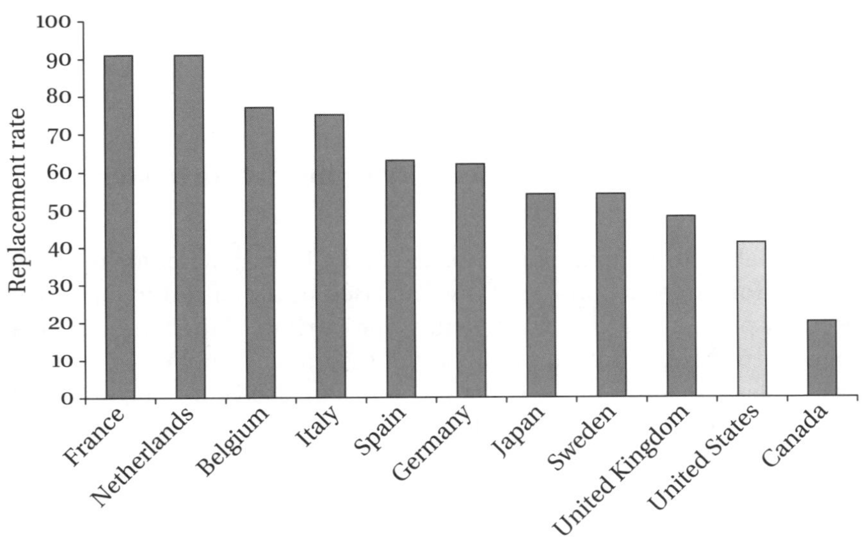

Fig. 8.1. Replacement rate at early retirement age, 1999. Many of these countries have undergone recent pension reform, see note 3.

Source: Gruber, J. and Wise, D. (eds) (1999). *Social Security and Retirement Around the World.* National Bureau of Economic Research. Chicago, IL: University of Chicago Press, table 1, p. 29.

future—and therefore less increase in costs—than other countries. Demographics affect the cost of any PAYG social insurance programme, and the United States is no exception. Like in other countries, the number of beneficiaries per 100 workers has already increased, from 20 in 1960 to 30 today, and is scheduled to rise, to 40 by 2020 and 56 by 2080. An increasing ratio of retirees to workers brings commensurate increases in PAYG costs. Indeed, costs as a per cent of taxable payrolls are projected to rise from 10.5 per cent today to 20.1 per cent in 2080 (OASDI 2002).[5]

Although the projected increase in beneficiaries in the United States is significant, the beneficiary/worker ratio is lower today and is projected to remain lower than in other developed countries. One important reason for the more moderate burden is that the fertility rate in the United States remains at two children per woman—the level required to keep the population from declining (Figure 8.2). In contrast, fertility rates are significantly below replacement for a large number of developed countries. At the same time, life expectancy at age 65 in the United States is roughly the same as the average for the other developed countries for men and less than average for women. Higher fertility and less than

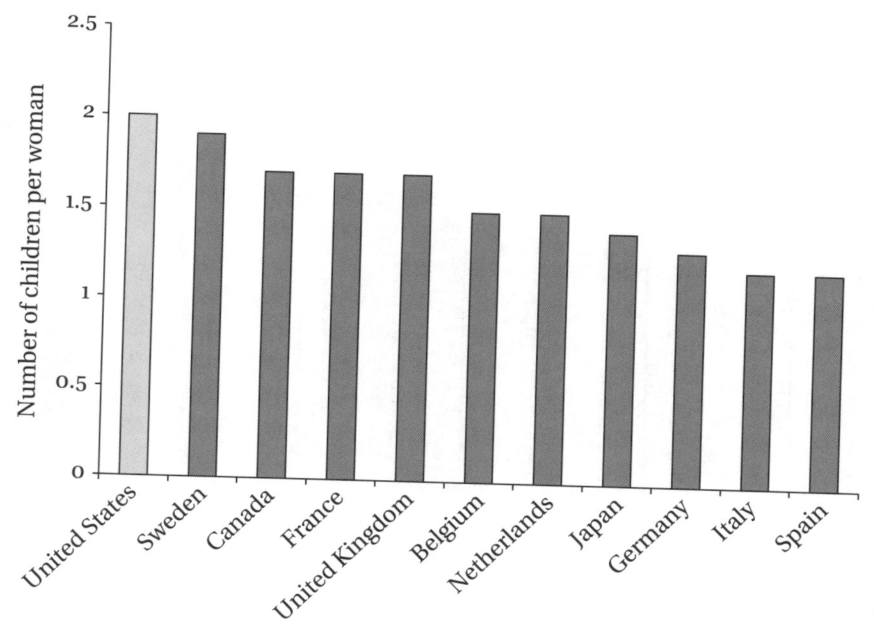

Fig. 8.2. Fertility rates, by country, 1996.

Source: United Nations Department of Economic and Social Affairs (1996). *Demographic Yearbook 1996*, United Nations.

average life expectancy means that the population shifts will be less dramatic in the United States than elsewhere.

The United States not only faces less challenging demographics, it also has a greater proportion of older workers in the labour force than other countries. If older people continue working, they contribute to the pensions of retirees rather than drawing benefits. Although US analysts often emphasise the dramatic decline in labour force participation of older men from 82 per cent in the 1960s to 53 per cent today, the current labour force activity of older workers is high compared to European countries. Figure 8.3 shows the average labour force participation rates today for men aged 55–65. The greater labour force participation in the United States eases the burden in a PAYG system.

Although economics are not as important as demographics in Social Security's finances, US economic performance also serves to ease the burden. Economic growth in large part reflects the growth in output per worker—that is, labour productivity. Higher productivity growth leads to lower programme costs, although it is important not to exaggerate its impact. Higher economic growth initially increases tax receipts, which are based on wages, but not payments to those already retired, which are

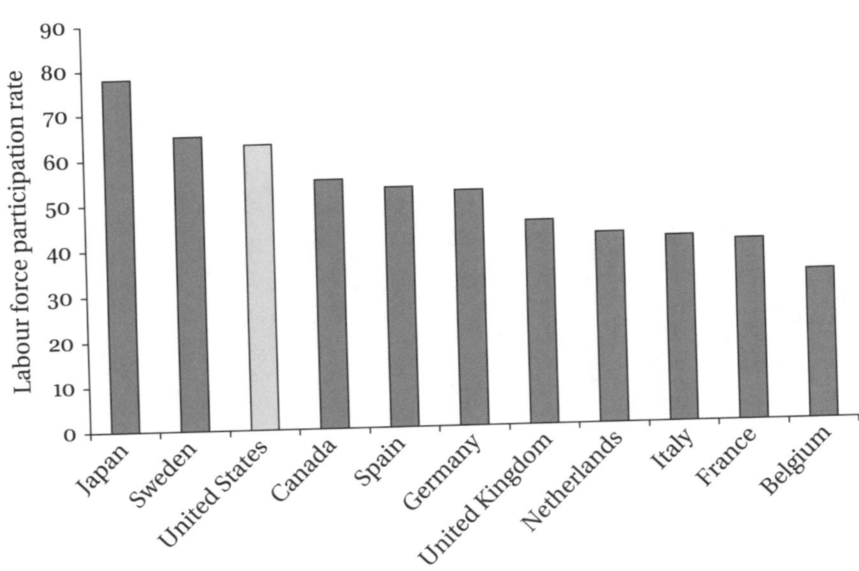

Fig. 8.3. Average labour force participation rate for men aged 55–65, 1999.

Source: Gruber, J. and Wise, D. (eds) (1999). *Social Security and Retirement Around the World*. National Bureau of Economic Research. Chicago, IL: University of Chicago Press, table 1, p. 29.

adjusted only for changes in prices. Thus, the initial impact on programme is very favourable. After time, however, benefit levels for the next generation, which are tied to the new higher level of wages, will rise and offset some of the initial gains. Nevertheless, on balance higher productivity growth reduces costs, and as shown in Figure 8.4, productivity growth in the United States has been higher than in most other countries.[6]

Although US Social Security costs are relatively low, any PAYG programme needs a committed stream of income to be financially sound. While today's payroll taxes are more than adequate to cover current benefits and the programme is running substantial annual surpluses, the US Social Security system faces a shortfall when looked at over the 75-year projection period. How big is that shortfall? According to the most recent official projections, between now and 2017 the US Social Security system will bring in more tax revenues than it pays out. From 2017 to 2027, adding interest on trust fund assets to tax receipts produces enough revenues to cover benefit payments. After 2027, the government can meet the benefit commitments by drawing down trust fund assets until the funds are exhausted in 2041 (The 2002 Annual

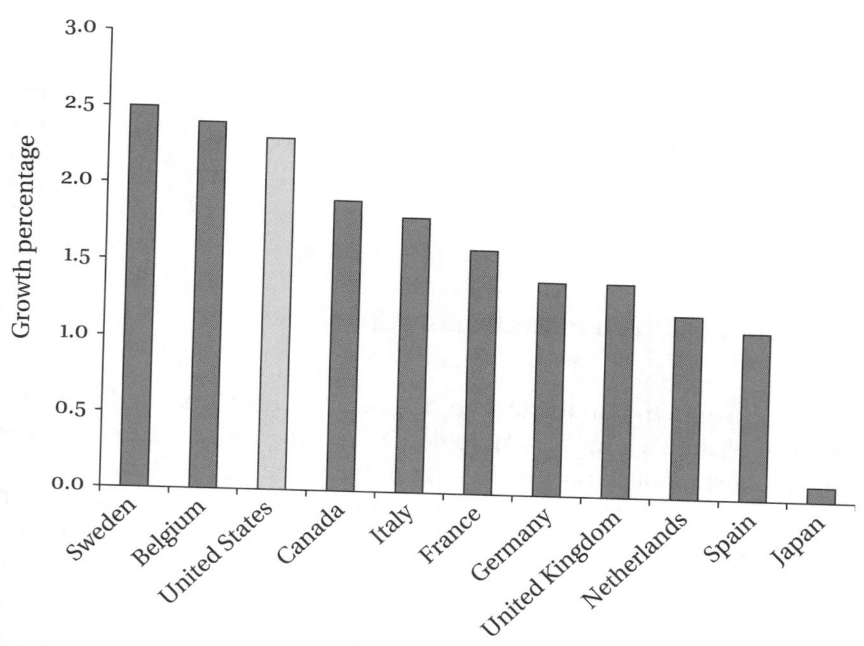

Fig. 8.4. Average productivity growth, 1995–2000.
Source: OECD (2001). *OECD Economic Outlook* 70 (December), Annex table 13.

Report).[7] The exhaustion of the trust funds does not mean the programme ends; even if no tax or benefit changes were made, current payroll tax rates and benefit taxation would provide enough money to cover more than 70 per cent of benefits thereafter.

Over the next 75 years, Social Security's long-run deficit is projected to equal 1.87 per cent of covered payroll earnings. That figure means that if the payroll tax rate were raised immediately by roughly 2 percentage points—1 percentage point each for the employee and the employer—the government would be able to pay the current package of benefits for everyone who reaches retirement age at least through 2076.[8]

To put the US shortfall in perspective, it is helpful to compare it with that of other countries. In 1996, OECD economists estimated the net present value of pension contributions, expenditure, and unfunded liability for the major social security systems. The US unfunded liability for Social Security over the 75-year projection period was equal to 23 per cent of 1994 GDP, approximately where it remains today. The comparable burden was three or four times larger for most of the other countries studied. Some countries, such as Canada and Sweden, have undertaken major reforms since the 1996 study, so their numbers are no longer relevant. Nevertheless, the fact is that the US Social Security system faces one of the smallest financing shortfalls of any developed country.[9]

In short, modest benefits and relatively favourable demographics means that the United States does not face the same financial challenge as other developed countries. Nevertheless, proposals abound to replace at least a portion of the current Social Security programme with private accounts.

8.2.2. Political Push to Restructure Social Security

Despite the benign outlook for the US Social Security system, President Bush established a commission to come up with specific recommendations for cutting back on the existing programme and replacing a portion of the programme with private accounts. The Commission's report in December 2001 included three alternative private account proposals. In each case, individuals would contribute part of their payroll taxes to these accounts and invest the tax payments in private sector assets. At retirement, people would receive some of their income from the traditional Social Security programme and some from the accumulated assets in the private account. Why the enthusiasm for dramatically restructuring the programme given the modest size of the problem? The answer rests in a confluence of events and politics and the special role played by the 1994–96 Advisory Council on Social Security.

At least six factors have been driving support for private accounts—the emergence of a long-term deficit, the maturation of the system and decline in returns, the 1990s stock market boom, Wall Street's interest in this potential market, the desire to increase national saving, and the appeal of an asset development social policy.

Emergence of a Deficit. Social Security would in all probability not be on the national agenda if the system were in actuarial balance, instead of facing a deficit over the 75-year projection period. The reemergence of a deficit was particularly disconcerting in the wake of the 1983 Amendments that were supposed to keep the Social Security system solvent for 75 years and produce positive trust fund balances through 2060. Yet, only a year after the 1983 legislation the Trustees began to project a small deficit, and the deficit grew more or less steadily for the next decade (Figure 8.5). The reemergence of a deficit made Social Security vulnerable to critics' attacks, and the critics often exaggerated the problems in order to justify dramatic solutions.

Maturation of the System and Decline in Returns. A modest deficit by itself would probably not have been enough to stimulate a major

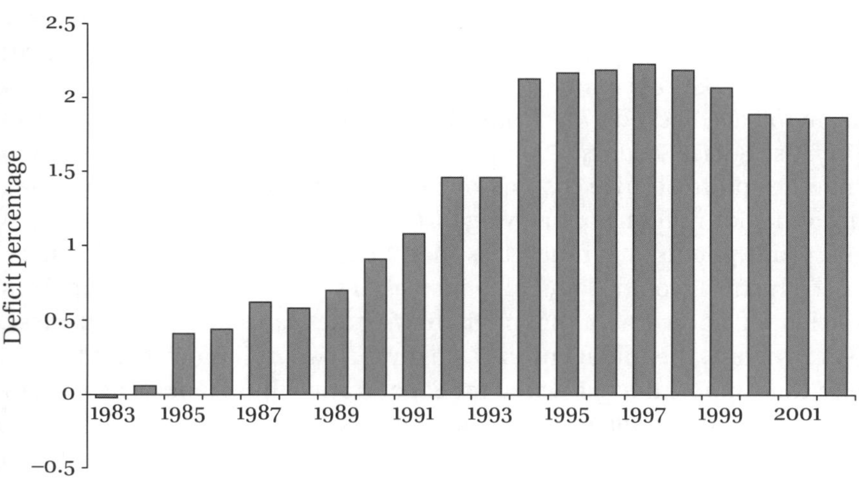

Fig. 8.5. Social Security deficit, 1983–2001.

Source: *The 2002 Annual Report of the Board of Trustees of the Federal Old-Age and Survivors Insurance and Disability Insurance Trust Funds* (2002). Washington, DC: US Government Printing Office.

movement to restructure Social Security. The deficit emerged, however, just as the system matured, making apparent the full cost of the programme and the low expected returns on Social Security contributions as compared to those available on market investments—the so-called 'money's worth' issue. Since raising taxes or reducing benefits only worsen returns, almost all reform plans involve some form of equity investment.[10] Given that equity investment is desirable, those who do not have confidence in government-administered investment plans conclude that private accounts are the only mechanism through which to achieve financial diversification.

A Booming Stock Market. At the same time that it became clear that Social Security required more money and that returns on contributions had declined, the stock market started to boom. Real (inflation-adjusted) returns on equities, which had averaged 7.4 per cent between 1926 and 1995, surged to 18.8 per cent between 1995 and 2000 (Ibbotson 2001). The stock market clearly looked like a more attractive option than Social Security. The simultaneous rise of DC pension plans in the private sector also increased the number of people who participated in the stock market. Many who observed rapidly rising balances in their pension accounts believed that they were brilliant investors and could do much better saving on their own.

Wall Street. The potential for 'making the system private' quickly caught the attention of the nation's financial institutions, and they have been supportive of conservative think tanks leading the charge towards privatisation. Interestingly, financial institutions, which once thought that private DC accounts would be an attractive line of business, now seem to have backed away from wholehearted endorsement of efforts to privatise Social Security. Their reversal appears to reflect the recognition that the administrative costs associated with setting up and maintaining accounts for millions of low-wage workers would be very high and that the profit potential is much less than originally envisioned. Moreover, such an effort would likely bring increased scrutiny and regulation from the federal government that might harm other aspects of their business. Nevertheless, the initial enthusiasm on the part of financial institutions and the support they provided for conservative think tanks was a major factor behind the push for private accounts.

Desire to Increase National Saving. Longer life expectancies and a rapidly ageing population will greatly increase the cost of supporting the aged, and almost everyone agrees that it is prudent to save in anticipation of such an event. Like the debate about government investing in equities, however, the issue is whether saving can be done at the government level. Supporters of the current programme argue that it is politically possible to save through Social Security trust funds, particularly if Social Security accounts are separated from the rest of the budget; advocates of private accounts disagree.

Asset Development Social Policy. Some researchers and policy-makers increasingly view asset accumulation by low-income households as a valuable social policy goal (e.g. Sherraden 1991).[11] They argue that financial assets can help alleviate poverty by increasing people's capacity to initiate new or expanded ventures. Accumulated assets can also serve as a protection against risks, and as a means to withstand crises and cope with transitions. Millions of Americans currently have no appreciable financial assets, and proponents contend that introducing private accounts as part of Social Security would help this population. The salience of this argument is evident in the fact that the final report of President Bush's Commission to Strengthen Social Security is entitled, 'Strengthening Social Security and *Creating Personal Wealth for All Americans*' (emphasis added).

While these broad trends laid the groundwork for the privatisation debate, the role of the 1994–96 Advisory Council on Social Security was pivotal. This group was appointed by President Clinton's Secretary of Health and Human Services under a statute requiring a quadrennial review of Social Security.[12] The report of the 1994–96 Advisory Council was the first official document to include privatisation proposals. Conservative analysts in the United States, who placed great weight on the merits of private control, had advocated privatisation of Social Security during the 1970s and 1980s, but such proposals were viewed as extreme and garnered little support. The Advisory Council report was also the first attempt to cost out the financial implications of moving from the current system to one with funded DC accounts, fully recognising the burden of the transition.

The Council took up its work in 1994 just as Social Security's 75-year deficit, which had increased very gradually between 1983 and 1991, suddenly doubled. The Council quickly recognised that the tax increases or benefit cuts required to eliminate the growing deficit would further reduce returns on payroll tax contributions, which had already declined sharply as the system had matured. Council members also saw that equity investment in one form or another would provide additional revenue, and reduce the magnitude of the tax increases or benefit cuts needed to restore solvency. The question was how to introduce equity investment into the programme, but the Council was sharply divided and unable to agree on a single proposal. Instead, it issued a report with three separate alternatives. One option attempted to solve the problem within the DB structure. The second cut benefits to fit within the existing payroll tax, and then created supplementary savings accounts equal to 2 per cent of taxable payrolls. The third called for a dramatic restructuring of the system, by diverting 5 percentage points of the 12.4 per cent payroll tax into mandatory personal security accounts. Unlike the second alternative, where the accounts would be held by the government and annuitised upon retirement, these accounts would be invested privately at the discretion of the individual, and individuals would have the choice of when and how they were paid out after retirement age. With these three alternatives on the table, the debate over privatising Social Security began in earnest. Many argued that the time had come to redraw the boundaries between public and private responsibilities in the provision of retirement income.

8.3. REDRAWING THE BOUNDARIES BETWEEN PUBLIC AND PRIVATE RESPONSIBILITIES?

Most proponents of redrawing the boundaries between public and private provision of retirement income—that is, privatising a portion of the programme—couch their arguments in terms of 'saving Social Security'. To what extent would privatising save Social Security? That depends on the nature of Social Security's problems. One problem, certainly, is the 75-year deficit; it undermines confidence in the programme and should be eliminated. A second problem is the increase in future PAYG payroll tax rates that place a large burden on the next generation. A third problem could be the low return on Social Security contributions, which allows critics to say that people are not getting their 'money's worth' from their payroll tax payments. Restoring balance requires improving the programme's cash flows. Reducing the burden on the next generation requires some prefunding of future benefit commitments; and improving returns on payroll tax contributions requires diversifying investment options to include private sector assets, such as equities. How would privatisation contribute to the financing, prefunding, and diversification efforts? In fact, privatisation alone would do nothing to restore balance to the programme, and prefunding and diversification can be accomplished in the existing programme as well as in private accounts.

8.3.1. Private Accounts on their Own Do Not Help Financing

Although the debate in the United States over private accounts occurs in the context of restoring balance to the Social Security programme over the next 75 years, proponents rarely articulate how shifting responsibilities from the public to the private sector will contribute to the financing effort. Restoring balance to a system where expenditures are projected to exceed revenues requires changes in cash flows. The only ways to improve cash flows are to increase revenues, lower benefits, or improve returns on trust fund assets. Notice that the list of options does not include 'private accounts'. They are not on the list because, by themselves, private accounts do nothing to improve cash flows. In other words, the creation of private accounts alone—that is, without prefunding or diversifying investments—will not help restore financial balance of the Social Security programme.

Consider what it means to introduce private accounts without making any changes in cash flows. Currently about 75 per cent of Social Security revenues go out immediately to pay benefits and cover other expenses. This transfer of funds is necessary because past Congresses authorised larger benefits for retirees than their payroll taxes could justify. No one—neither supporters of Social Security or advocates of private accounts—suggests that benefits payable to current retirees or those soon to retire should be cut significantly. Thus, workers must continue to transfer an amount equal to 75 per cent of current payroll taxes to maintain these benefits, regardless of whether the nation retains Social Security or partially replaces it with private accounts.

The relevant scenario for establishing private accounts without increasing the programme's prefunding is one where the payroll tax not currently used to finance benefits—about 25 per cent of the total—is diverted into private accounts. (Assume for now that private accounts like the trust funds are invested in bonds.) Such a shift would not change the amount of prefunding, since the accumulation of assets in private accounts would simply replace the accumulation of reserves in the Social Security trust funds. In addition, since annual revenues exceed current outlays such a shift would have no immediate impact on the programme's ability to pay benefits. Down the road, fewer Social Security reserves would be available to pay benefits, but public benefits could be cut by a roughly equivalent amount to reflect the payments from the accumulation in the private accounts. The net long-run impact on the system would be zero. Thus, the creation of private accounts, without prefunding or diversifying investments, would do nothing to close the current 75-year financing gap.

The legitimate case for private accounts as a means of improving Social Security's long-term financing rests on identifying a political link between private accounts and the methods listed for improving Social Security cash flows. For example, Edward Gramlich, former Chair of the 1994–96 Advisory Council on Social Security, favoured private accounts, because he thought that the only way to get Congress to legislate a payroll tax increase was to have the increased tax revenue go into private accounts.

Similarly, private accounts might be a device to improve the political chances of cutting future benefits. If some payroll tax revenues are diverted into private accounts, then there is clear logic for making some cuts in benefits in anticipation of the benefits that will be financed by the money in the private accounts. If the cuts in benefits exceed what can be plausibly financed from the accounts for some future workers, then this becomes a political device for cutting benefits.

Alternatively, private accounts might be viewed as a politically acceptable way of broadening investment options. Indeed, most observers would like to see Social Security participants—particularly those with no other assets—have access to the higher returns associated with equities. Some conclude that the only way to broaden the investment option is to have workers invest their payroll tax contributions individually. This issue will be discussed further below.

The point is that simply introducing private accounts will not bring more money into the system or reduce outflows from the programme. Private accounts—in economic terms—are not a solution to Social Security's 75-year financial shortfall. Geanakoplos et al. (1998) clarified this point in an important paper, and all serious analysts—whether they support or oppose private accounts—acknowledge that privatisation alone does not solve the financing problem. The case for private accounts must rest on the contention that their introduction will facilitate the needed changes in cash flows. Needless to say, careful analysis often gets swept away in the heat of political debate.

8.3.2. Private Accounts Not the Only Way to Prefund Social Security

In addition to restoring balance, many involved in the Social Security debate would like to see some prefunding of the system's benefit commitments. Prefunding would reduce the required payroll tax increases down the road and ease the burden on future generations. Advocates of private accounts see privatisation as the only way to accumulate 'real' reserves. Supporters of the current programme conclude that the Social Security trust funds have already accumulated economically meaningful reserves, and can continue to do so in the future.

The primary purpose of prefunding in the United States is to reduce the burden on future generations. That burden will depend on two factors: (1) the portion of future output of goods and services that future workers will have to give up to support the retired; and (2) the total amount of goods and services produced at that time. The portion going to the elderly can be reduced through explicit benefit cuts or the more politically acceptable option of increasing the retirement age. Prefunding can increase the size of future output.

Prefunding increases future output by increasing national saving, assuming that the accumulation of pension reserves is not offset by a decline in other government, personal, or business saving. Given that the United States has highly efficient capital markets, virtually everyone involved in the US debate assumes that increased saving will be allocated to the most productive investment. If prefunding increases national saving, and that saving is transformed into productive investment, it will increase the size of the capital stock and future output. Greater future output means that for any given share, workers will have more left over after they transfer resources to the elderly.

Note that it does not matter from an economic perspective whether the elderly's claim on output, in say 2040, is in the form of accrued rights under Social Security or in the form of purchasing power gained through the sale of accumulated assets (Thompson 1998). Given the size of the total national output, the question is simply how much the working population in 2040 will have to transfer to the elderly and how much of total output will be left over for their own consumption. In other words, prefunding does not affect the burden by changing the nature of retirees' claims, but rather by increasing future output.

Prefunding not only adds to national saving, but also would avoid the high PAYG costs projected for the current system. Under current law, the costs for retirement and disability benefits are scheduled to rise from 10.5 per cent of payroll today to 20.1 per cent in 2080. Many conclude that the high payroll tax may be politically unacceptable, and thereby put the programme in jeopardy. By providing interest income, prefunding would reduce the required payroll tax rates in the future.

Moving from PAYG finance to the buildup of reserves within either the Social Security system or private accounts is designed to increase national saving. For this effort to be meaningful, however, the current generation of workers will have to forego some current consumption. That means that they will in effect pay twice: they already have to reduce their consumption to cover promised benefits for the retired and those about to retire; now they will also have to reduce consumption to build up assets either collectively or individually. This is an inescapable outcome of the decision to move from a PAYG system to prefunding.

Some advocates of privatisation tend to gloss over this fact and characterise the transition to private accounts as essentially painless. For example, Martin Feldstein, a Harvard economist and early supporter of individual accounts, has offered a series of plans that he claims would place no additional burden on individuals (e.g. Feldstein and Samwick 1998*a, b*).[13] Initially, Feldstein would have used the budget surpluses that emerged in the late 1990s (and have since disappeared!) to fund a 2 per cent contribution to private accounts. Once the surpluses were exhausted, he would turn to a big boost in corporate income taxes to cover tax credits for individual contributions. The boost in corporate tax revenues arises from his assumption that private accounts would increase national saving, investment, and corporate profits. This is controversial since it rests on the contention that in the absence of private accounts, the government would spend the money on tax cuts or programme increases. Advocates of maintaining the current structure of Social Security argue that the more relevant counterfactual would be for the government to accumulate assets in the trust funds, in which case private accounts create no increase in saving.

Other advocates of private accounts address the issue of transition costs head on. Members of the 1994–96 Social Security Advisory Council acknowledged that the transition to their proposed 'Personal Savings Accounts' would require additional revenues equal to 3 per cent of pay for 35 years, or as they proposed, 1.5 per cent for 70 years. If the prefunding were undertaken within the current programme, it would require a burden on the current generation. To accomplish real saving requires a cutback in current consumption. Despite the additional burden on the current generation, policy-makers generally view some prefunding as desirable.

If the decision is made that prefunding is desirable, does that mean that responsibility for pensions has to be reallocated from the public to the private sector? That is, are individually controlled private accounts the only option for accumulating reserves in anticipation of benefit payments? Certainly, those who do not have confidence in the government's ability to administer pension assets conclude that private accounts are the only mechanism to prefund benefit commitments. In fact, the desire to prefund, along with a preference for equity investment, is probably the main motivation for privatisation proposal (Samwick 1999). Feldstein has used this argument repeatedly in his writings, and the desire for prefunding and equity investment was a major factor influencing the pro-privatisation members of the 1994–96 Advisory Council on Social Security. Most recently, President Bush's Commission to Strengthen Social Security (2001) repeated the rationale. Two of the Commission's primary findings were 'Partial advance funding of Social Security should be a goal of any effort to strengthen the system' and 'Advance funding within Social Security can best be accomplished through personal accounts rather than direct government investment.'

Supporters of the existing programme believe that it is possible to accumulate reserves within the Social Security trust funds. In fact, the US Social Security programme has already begun to amass reserves. Since 1983, payroll taxes have exceeded benefit payments, and the trust funds now hold reserves equal to 2.5 times annual outlays. One political impediment to the further accumulation of trust fund reserves is the debate in the United States about the extent to which these surpluses are economically meaningful—that is, the extent to which they constitute 'real' prefunding. Large deficits in the overall budget during the 1980s and most of the 1990s made it difficult for many to appreciate that Social Security surpluses had increased national saving. Critics contended that surpluses in Social Security simply went to cover deficits in the rest of the budget, and had no impact on government or national saving. They were wrong, of course; reducing government deficits is just as important in economic terms as increasing government surpluses.

In the late 1990s, the fiscal outlook changed in a fashion that was particularly conducive to clarifying the contribution of Social Security reserves to saving. The budget had reached the point where both the non-Social Security and Social Security portion were in surplus, and Congress decided that it was important to keep the two accounts separate. In fact, it created a 'lock box' to ensure that revenues covered outlays in the non-Social Security portion of the budget, freeing up Social Security surpluses to pay down the outstanding government debt. This separation of accounts would make it very clear that real prefunding was occurring.

Two factors eroded this separation of accounts. The first was a massive tax cut enacted in May 2001 that sharply reduced non-Social Security revenues; the second was the terrorist attack of September 11 that further weakened a faltering economy and led to a major increase in spending.

As a result, the non-Social Security portion of the budget is in deficit, and is borrowing funds from Social Security to cover the shortfall. Even in the new environment, of course, Social Security reserves continue to add to national saving, because, as just noted, reducing a budget deficit is just as important as increasing a surplus.[14] Nevertheless, the deterioration in the overall budget condition makes it difficult, once again, to convince the public that the accumulation of Social Security reserves increases national saving and actually prefunds future benefit commitments. But this is a political and public relations problem, not an economic barrier to prefunding a government retirement programme.

Less controversial evidence that government entities in the United States can prefund benefits comes from the experience of state governments. In addition to their general operations, these governments accumulate reserves to fund pension obligations for their employees. They generally balance their budgets excluding the retirement systems, and run annual surpluses in their retirement funds of around 1 per cent of GDP. Thus, states are clearly prefunding their pensions and adding to national saving through the accumulation of pension reserves.

In short, prefunding some of the US pension obligations has widespread support from both supporters and opponents of privatisation. The debate centres on whether prefunding requires a shift from public to private responsibility for providing retirement income.

8.3.3. Public Versus Private Responsibility for Equity Investment

The debate over public versus private responsibility really heats up when the question of prefunding is combined with the possibility of diversification—that is, the possibility of investing accumulated Social Security reserves in equities. Supporters of private accounts claim that allowing Congress into the investment business will result in government interference in private sector activities. But supporters of the existing structure believe that it is possible for the government to accumulate reserves in advance of benefit payments and to invest part of those reserves in equities without political interference (Advisory Council on Social Security Reform, 1997; Munnell and Balduzzi 1998; and Aaron and Reischauer 2001).

Everyone involved in the debate in the United States agrees that having the federal government in the business of picking winners and losers in the stock market and voting on corporate proposals is undesirable. Thus, allowing the Social Security trust funds to purchase equities would require establishing mechanisms to ensure that the government does not interfere in private sector decisions. One such mechanism would involve indexing trust fund equity investments to a broad market average to avoid picking individual stocks. Another would require establishing an expert investment board to select the index, to choose portfolio managers for the accounts, and to monitor the performance of the managers. To ensure that government ownership does not disrupt corporate governance, most proposals require that voting rights be given to the asset managers, not voted at all, or voted in the same fashion as the other shareholders, which is equivalent to not voting at all.

Two types of government pensions in the United States already invest in equities with no apparent ill effects. The federal Thrift Savings Plan (TSP) for government employees has established a highly efficient stock index fund. TSP designers insulated investment decisions by setting up an independent investment board, narrowing investment choices, and requiring strict fiduciary duties. The TSP also operates in a political culture of noninterference. Its creators made clear from the beginning that economic, not social or political, goals were to be the sole purpose of the investment board (Cavanaugh 1998).

State and local pension funds also invest in equities. Some opponents of trust fund investment in equities contend that state and local pensions interfere in private sector activities (Greenspan 1999). The contention is that these funds often undertake investments that achieve political or social goals, divest stocks to demonstrate that they do not support some perceived immoral or unethical behavior, and interfere with corporate activity by voting proxies and other activities. Recent research, however, documents that political considerations have had almost no effect on investment decisions at the state and local level (Munnell and Sunden 2000). Indeed, public pension plans appear to be performing as well as private plans.

In addition to the US examples, several countries—most notably Canada, Japan, and Sweden—have undertaken prefunding of their social security systems and broadened their investment options to include equities. Perhaps, the most relevant example for the United States is Canada, since its Social Security system is similar to that in the United States. In the early 1990s, Canada's public PAYG pension plan known as the Canada Pension Plan (CPP) was in serious financial trouble. In response, the Canadian federal and provincial finance ministers decided to re-examine the current programme and make changes to ensure its solvency. In the resulting reforms, Canada increased payroll contributions and took the radical step of investing its public pension funds in the stock market to raise pension returns. In order to ensure that the investments were undertaken in 'the best interests of the contributors and beneficiaries of the plan', the government created the Canada Pension Plan Investment Board (CPPIB).[15]

The Canadian programme is up and running, and board members have already started to move from passive investment to partially active investment.[16] According to the most recent figures, by the end of their fiscal year 2001, the CPPIB had C$7.1 billion in equity assets under management. This amounts to about 14 per cent of all consolidated public pension assets available in Canada.[17] And that number is expected to grow in the near future; according to CPPIB estimates, the value of assets under management is expected to exceed C$130 billion by 2011. Although CPPIB experienced a loss due to market fluctuations in fiscal 2001, the CPPIB is highly confident that its equity investments will eventually produce returns that meet or exceed their long-term targets (CPPIB 2001).

To summarise, the debate in the United States is not about the desirability of prefunding, nor is it about broadening investment options. Most observers would like to see some prefunding of benefit commitments and would like to see Social Security participants—particularly those with no other assets—have access to the higher returns associated with equities. Rather, the debate is about the ability of the public sector to accomplish prefunding and diversification. In practical terms, achieving the economic goals of restoring balance to the system, raising return on system assets, and increasing the amount of prefunding does not require a shift from the public to the private sector. These goals could be accomplished within the current structure by increasing the accumulation of reserves in the Social Security trust funds and investing part of those reserves in private stocks and bonds.

Nevertheless, until recently, the politics in the United States appeared to favour shifting responsibilities for the provision of retirement income toward the private sector. Not only did the political climate support individual over collective responsibility, but also there was—and still is—considerable opposition to broadening investment options within the Social Security system. Alan Greenspan's rejection of the notion of investing the Social Security trust funds in equities is particularly important. His allegation that government investment in equities will hurt private sector rates of returns makes it extremely difficult to achieve the funding and diversification goals within Social Security. My sense is that in the wake of the sharp decline in the stock market, interest will wane in introducing equities in any form into the Social Security system. At the same time, efforts to restore long-run balance to the programme will also be deferred.

8.4. HOW WOULD PRIVATISATION AFFECT INDIVIDUALS, FINANCIAL MARKETS, AND THE NATION?

If the government and the private sector were equally capable of providing benefits to retired and disabled workers, the debate would not be so intense. However, the nature of the pension promise changes fundamentally depending on whether the benefits are provided through social insurance or through private accounts. Private accounts shift substantial investment risk to the individual. This increased risk might be worthwhile if privatisation increased returns that individuals could earn on their Social Security contributions or greatly improved financial markets, but neither is the case. Moreover, privatisation contains the seeds of unravelling the entire social insurance structure in the United States, and thereby putting the welfare of future generations of low-income individuals at risk.

8.4.1. Impact of Private Accounts on the Welfare of Individuals

Private accounts shift risks to individuals. This may be fine for supplementary retirement income, but is harder to justify for people's basic retirement benefit. Moreover, individuals do not earn higher returns in exchange for this increased risk.

The current Social Security pension promise is a DB based on lifetime earnings, paid out as a lifetime annuity, and fully adjusted for inflation after retirement. Private accounts are DC plans where benefits depend on contributions and investment returns. The change in the benefit commitment shifts substantial risks to the individuals and makes the benefits unpredictable. Such a shift is inconsistent with the goals of the Social Security programme; the whole point of having a Social Security system is to provide workers with a predictable basic retirement income to which they can add income from private pensions and other sources. If it is appropriate for the government to interfere with private sector decisions to ensure a basic level of retirement income, it does not make sense for that basic amount to be uncertain, reflecting one's good luck or investment skills.[18]

In addition to the fundamental philosophical argument, private accounts raise a host of practical problems, including potential access before retirement, lack of automatic annuitisation, and cost.

Access Before Retirement. Private accounts create a very real political risk that account holders would pressure Congress for early access to these accounts, albeit for worthy purposes such as medical expenses, education, or home purchase. Although most proposals prohibit such withdrawals, experience with existing Individual Retirement Accounts (IRAs) and employer-provided DC plans suggests that holding the line is unlikely. To the extent that Congress acquiesces and allows early access—no matter how worthy the purpose—many retirees will end up with lower, and in some cases inadequate, retirement income.

Lack of Automatic Annuitisation. Another risk is that individuals stand a good chance of outliving their savings, unless the money accumulated in their private accounts is transformed into annuities. However, few people purchase private annuities, and costs are high in the private annuity market.[19] Even if costs were not high, the necessity of purchasing an annuity at retirement exposes individuals to interest rate risk; if rates are high when they retire, they will receive a large monthly amount, if rates are low, the amount will be much smaller. Moreover, the private annuity market does not offer full inflation-adjusted benefits. In contrast, by keeping participants together and forcing them to convert their funds into annuities, Social Security avoids adverse selection and is in a good position to provide inflation-adjusted benefits.

Cost. The 1994–96 Social Security Advisory Council estimated that the administrative costs for an IRA-type private account would amount to 100 basis points per year.[20] A 100-basis point annual charge sounds benign, but it would reduce total accumulations by roughly 20 per cent over a 40-year work life. Moreover, while the 100-basis-point estimate includes the cost of marketing, tracking, and maintaining the account, it does not include brokerage fees. If the individual does not select an index fund, then transaction costs may be twice as high. Indeed, the United Kingdom, which has a system of personal saving accounts, has experienced considerably higher costs (Murthi et al. 1999). Finally, unless prohibited by regulation, these transaction costs involve a flat charge per account that will be considerably more burdensome for low-income participants than for those with higher incomes.

Many advocates of personal accounts have now recognised the very high administrative costs of the IRA approach and have fallen back to a more pooled approach. This would involve investing accumulated contributions in large pools, and limiting individuals' investment choices to a limited number of index funds. Costs would be substantially less under this alternative; President Bush's Commission estimated that their private account proposals would cost 30 basis points to administer. Even this reduced estimate, however, is substantially greater than the costs of the current Social Security programme. Moreover, for those concerned about government involvement, this approach has the government picking the appropriate equity funds and retaining control of the money.

In short, private accounts shift investment risk to the individual, are costly to administer, and raise a host of complex issues about how to deal with accumulated assets at retirement. It is virtually impossible for the private sector to duplicate the inflation-indexed annuity currently provided by the Social Security system. The increased risk and costs might be worthwhile if they brought higher returns and improved financial markets, but neither is the case.

8.4.2. The Impact of Private Accounts on Returns on Contributions

The creation of private accounts alone—that is, without prefunding or diversification—will have no effect on the returns earned by participants. It is true that the expected inflation-adjusted return on private-sector assets exceeds the expected return on Social Security taxes. Even the return on intermediate government bonds—2.2 per cent over the period 1926–2000—is better than the 1.3 per cent projected for Social Security. But that comparison ignores the fact that 75 per cent of revenues are dispensed immediately to cover promised benefits. The debate about rates of return should concern only whether returns on the remaining 25 per cent of Social Security income would be higher if they were invested in private accounts than in the Social Security trust fund. In fact, the two entities could hold the same securities and, before considering administrative costs, earn the same gross return. Once administrative costs were considered, however, the net returns would be higher under the trust fund approach, since it costs a lot less to invest aggregate trust fund assets than to set up 150 million private accounts.

Suppose that the funds transferred to private accounts were invested in equities instead of bonds. In that case, projected returns on privatised accounts would appear much higher than returns under the current system. But the comparison ignores the fact that stocks involve more risk than bonds, and returns need to be adjusted for risk. If all households held both stocks and bonds, they should value an additional dollar of stocks the same as an additional dollar of bonds, even though stocks have a much higher expected return before adjusting for their added risk. That is, the risk-adjusted return on stocks and bonds would be identical. This conclusion has to be modified to the extent that some households currently do not have access to equity investment. In this case, the risk-adjusted returns would be higher than those currently earned on the bonds held by Social Security.

The added returns could be secured without introducing private accounts, however. As discussed above, the revenues not required for current benefits could be invested in equities by private fund managers on behalf of the Social Security trust fund. Although the two approaches would appear quite different from the perspective of participants, the impact on *gross* returns would be equivalent. As noted earlier, for any given investment, private accounts always earn lower *net* returns because of the administrative costs.

Consider a second scenario where individuals transfer not only the 25 per cent of payroll taxes not required for current benefits, but also an additional 25 per cent that is earmarked for current benefits. That is, suppose they send 50 per cent of their payroll taxes to Merrill Lynch or Fidelity rather than the US Treasury. Assume that, like the rest of the funds, this additional 25 per cent is invested in intermediate government bonds, which return 2.2 per cent. That return seems like an improvement over the 1.3 per cent projected for Social Security, but a simple comparison of returns is not the end of the story. Because workers invest payroll tax contributions that were earmarked to pay current benefits, the government needs to find some way to pay off promised benefits to current retirees and those nearing retirement (since, as noted above, no one suggests reneging on these commitments). One approach would be to borrow the money. The government, however, would have to raise new taxes to pay the interest on these bonds, and—for identical portfolios—the new taxes would exactly offset the higher returns on private accounts (Diamond 1998, 1999; Geanakoplos et al. 1998). In other words, participants gain nothing by diverting to private accounts payroll taxes earmarked for benefits.

In short, the introduction of private accounts alone cannot raise the return that workers earn on their payroll tax contributions. The only way to improve returns is to build up a trust fund so that people do not have to contribute so much in payroll taxes in the future. But building up reserves can take place in either the trust funds or private accounts. Either approach would eventually raise returns once the unfunded benefit commitment was paid off. Higher returns to future generations, however, would be gained at the expense of lower returns to current generations who have to pay twice, first to cover promised benefits for others and second to build up reserves in their own accounts. The question of how much to prefund requires weighing the welfare of one generation against that of another. Without prefunding, however, a shift to private accounts cannot raise returns. The implications for financial markets are similar; the introduction of private accounts without new funding has little impact.

8.4.3. The Impact of Private Accounts on Financial Markets

Two aspects of the interaction of private accounts and financial markets merit consideration. The first is the extent to which a shift from public to private provision of retirement income affects financial flows and relative rates of returns on bonds and equities. The second is the extent to which the introduction of private accounts fundamentally alters the level of government activity.

The introduction of private accounts without any additional funding would have virtually no effect on financial markets. Consider first, the case where both the trust funds and private accounts are invested in bonds. In this event, the increase in bond holdings from the private accounts would be exactly offset by the reduction in bond holdings by the trust funds. The transaction would have no impact at all on financial markets. Next consider the case where the private accounts were invested in equities. Even this scenario produces only a minimal effect on financial markets, since the shift would involve little more than a restructuring of portfolios. That is, individuals would purchase, say, $100 billion of equities through the private account component of the Social Security system, and the public would hold $100 billion less of equities outside of Social Security. Similarly, Social Security through the reduction in trust fund reserves would hold $100 less in bonds, and the public would own $100 billion more. From the perspective of financial markets, this is virtually the same transition that would occur if the trust fund investments were broadened to include equities. In both cases, the portfolio restructuring might have some effect on relative rates of return of equities and bonds, but the changes would be expected to be very small (Bohn 1998).

The alternative scenario is one where an increase in funding accompanies the creation of private accounts. This is more than a portfolio restructuring, and increased funding would affect real variables such as national saving. The primary impact of an increase in national saving would be a reduction in real interest rates due to the increased availability of funds. If the prefunding were accompanied by an increase in equity investment either through private accounts or the trust fund, relative rates of returns again might be affected slightly. But the primary impact of the prefunding would be lower rates, which would encourage investment and higher national income in the future.

Thus, private accounts alone do nothing to enhance Social Security financing, improve returns to individuals, or affect financial markets. Diversifying investments—that is, expanding Social Security investments to include equities—either through private accounts or through the trust funds—would increase the return on system assets but not by as much as first thought because of the necessary adjustment for risk. The only way to have a real impact on the economy is to increase the funding through the accumulation of reserves, and again this can be accomplished either through the trust funds or through private accounts. Prefunding—if not offset by decreased personal or business saving—will lower interest costs and encourage investment. It will also improve returns down the road once the system's current unfunded liability is paid off. In other words, prefunding is the key economic factor, not private accounts. Advocates of private accounts are often unclear about this fact.

Advocates of private accounts also exaggerate the political advantages to private accounts. Although proposals to introduce private accounts as compared to proposals to invest Social Security trust fund reserves in equities elicit very different responses from policy-makers, the two approaches are remarkably similar. As discussed earlier, the 1994–96 Social Security Advisory Council put three alternatives on the table. The most extreme—individually managed private accounts—has been all but eliminated from consideration because of the extremely high administrative costs. The remaining candidates are government-managed private accounts and direct trust fund investment. Government-managed private accounts would work very much like the existing TSP, where the federal government deposits workers' contributions in a private account and, following the workers' preferences, allocates the money among a designated series of index equity funds, bond funds, and fixed-income investments. Except for the worker direction, this process is virtually identical to what would occur in the case of direct trust fund investment, where the government would invest a portion of payroll tax receipts in an appropriate broad market index.

Those who fundamentally do not trust the government should find neither option appealing. Opponents of investing in equities through the trust funds contend that the government might use its equity holdings to directly influence corporate decisions and might also invest on the basis of social rather than risk and return considerations. For example, the current controversy over tobacco litigation might create pressure to take tobacco holdings out of the index. But note that a system of government-administered private accounts also requires the government to designate a series of index equity funds for investment. Hence, questions about which stocks to include in the indexes, and how shares are to be voted are just as much issues for the government-administered private accounts are as for the centrally managed approach. The only difference is that individuals have a propriety interest in their own account, and this interest might make the government more reluctant to interfere for its own purposes.

Not only are the mechanics of government-managed individual accounts and trust fund investment nearly identical, but also the introduction of private accounts does not mean that the government would be out of that portion of the retirement business. Government regulation of employer-sponsored plans, which as noted above in the United States provide about one quarter of retirement income, serves as a useful benchmark. The primary regulatory structure is the federal income tax system, reflecting the notion that pensions are tax preferences or indirect government expenditures. But regulation goes beyond the Internal Revenue Service, which administers the tax laws, and includes three other government agencies.[21] In addition to government agencies, the federal Courts and multiple sets of laws regulate the pension system. Some observers have suggested that firms that get involved in providing private accounts for Social Security may see the regulation of those accounts spill over to other aspects of their business.

To summarise, privatisation alone would have almost no impact on financial flows or rates of return. Only prefunding—by increasing national saving—would affect economic fundamentals. Similarly, the extent to which privatisation would eliminate government from retirement income activities is often exaggerated. In the most probable form of private account, the government would be required to select the equity indexes and decide how the shares should be voted, just as in the case of trust fund investment in equities. The government would also play a major regulatory role with regard to private accounts. At the same time that private accounts do not greatly diminish the role of government, they create a serious long-run threat to the stability of the US social insurance system.

8.4.4. Private Accounts Could Unravel the Social Security System

While private accounts are merely risky and costly for the average and above average worker, they could end up being disastrous for low-income workers in the future. The whole point of shifting funds to private accounts is to emphasise individual equity—that is, a fair return for the individual saver—rather than adequacy for all. Taking part of what the high earner makes to improve the return for the low earner would be contrary to the spirit of such a plan. To meet this objection many advocates of the DC approach provide either a flat-benefit amount or a healthy minimum benefit for low-wage workers. Although such provisions will protect low-income workers in the short term, opponents of these accounts believe that maintaining redistribution within the programme is unlikely to be sustainable.

A mixed system with a flat-benefit and a private account is likely to respond very differently to change over time than the existing DB arrangement. For example, suppose that the overall size of Social Security was viewed as too large as the retirement of the baby boom nears. Benefit cuts under the existing programme would likely affect all people at all points in the income distribution proportionately; for example, the extension of the normal retirement age from 65 to 67 in 1983 was a form of across-the-board cut. Congress might even attempt to protect the benefits of workers with low incomes. Cuts under a mixed system are likely to be very different. Congress is likely to view the private account component as individual saving and see little gain from cutting it back. The more plausible target would be the flat-minimum benefit, which goes to both those who need it and those who do not. Higher wage workers are going to find they get very little for their payroll tax dollar from such a residual Social Security programme and will withdraw their support. As the minimum is cut repeatedly, it will become inadequate for low-wage workers. In response, Congress is likely to replace the flat benefit with a means-tested programme.

Observers sometimes argue that the same economic outcome can be achieved either through means-tested benefits or through social insurance payments that are then taxed back. This conclusion ignores psychological, social, political, and institutional factors in the United States. Means-tested and social insurance programmes in the United States grow out of different historic traditions, have different impacts on their recipients, and are viewed very differently by the public. Social insurance reflects a long history of people getting together to help themselves. This self-help approach means that individuals have an earned right to benefits, since they receive payments based on contributions from their past earnings. The programmes involve no test of need, and programme benefits can be supplemented with income from saving or other sources. Means-tested programmes in the United States, on the other hand, grow out of the punitive and paternalistic poor-law tradition, which recognises only begrudgingly a public responsibility for providing for the impoverished. Means-tested benefits tend to be less adequate than those provided under social insurance programmes and have a stigma, which means that many who are eligible never claim their benefits. To the extent that people at the low end of the income distribution are forced to rely on means-tested benefits, they are likely to be worse off than they would be under the existing DB Social Security system.

8.5. CONCLUSION

How a nation arranges its public pension system can have profound effects on financial markets, on individuals, and on society as a whole. Much of the debate about pension arrangements both in the United States and in Europe is couched in terms of private versus public provision of retirement benefits. The economic dimensions, however, are the ones with real impact. The economic questions include how much advance funding should be undertaken, how that prefunding should be invested, and whether the programme should be structured as a DB plan or a mixed DB/DC arrangement. The public/private issue is important only to the extent that it influences the response to one of these questions. The lesson from the US Social Security debate is that words such as 'privatization' often obscure rather than clarify how proposed reforms will impact the economy.

NOTES

1. Most people retire before age 65, so actual replacement rates are lower.
2. Much of the US retirement system faces no financial problems. Employer-provided pensions—the second tier—are for the most part fully funded. The growth in assets in employer-provided plans has been remarkable. Pension assets have increased from barely over 1% of household wealth in 1945 to about 22% in 2001. In 2001, pension assets ($8.9 trillion) approached the market value of all household-owned real estate ($11.6 trillion) in the United States. The enormous growth in pension assets reflect two factors: (1) pensions were in their infancy in the 1940s, and (2) pension reserves reflect the large contributions made on behalf of the baby-boom generation. Individual saving, the third tier, is also fully funded by definition.
3. Esping-Andersen (1990) characterises the US Social welfare system as liberal in his hierarchy of regimes. Liberal welfare states, such as the United States, Canada, and Australia, are ones in which means-tested assistance, modest universal transfers, or modest social-insurance plans predominate. Instead, the state tries to encourage market mechanisms and institutions as a means of welfare. Full employment, not generous welfare benefits, provides the key to economic well being. Esping-Andersen contrasts liberal welfare states with the social democratic and the conservative. Social democratic welfare states (i.e. Scandinavia) promote a high level of social equality among their own citizens. These regimes, through heavy taxation, provide universal services and benefits at middle-class standards. Conservative welfare states (i.e. Southern European countries such as France, Germany, Italy, and Spain), due to strong religious histories, institutionalise the family by supporting the male breadwinner/female caregiver model with transfers. Here, a generous public welfare policy is a means to preserve status differences, as services and benefits improve with class and status.
4. Replacement rates are for the early retirement age of each respective country. Since the calculation of these rates by Gruber and Wise (1999), many of these countries have undergone pension reform that will effectively lower their replacement rates. For example, Belgium recently raised its normal retirement age to 65, which will lower the replacement rate to 60% at the typical retirement age. Italy has eliminated its seniority pensions, began applying a full actuarial reduction to early retirement benefits, created a private system of pensions through tax incentives to subsidise the basic government pensions, and reduced the level of benefits at the normal retirement age. These changes are projected to decrease the Italian replacement rate to 60%. In May 2001, Germany replaced the current system with a reduced PAYG pension and a tax-subsidised private pension system. The reform lowers the replacement rate at the normal retirement age of 65 from 70% to 63%. Sweden has made sweeping changes to its pension scheme.
5. A very different pattern of costs emerges when Social Security outlays are projected as a per cent of gross domestic product (GDP) rather than as a per cent of taxable payrolls. According to the intermediate projections of *The 2002 Annual Report of the Board of Trustees*, the cost of the programme is projected to rise from 4.5% of GDP today to 6.8% of GDP in 2035, where it roughly remains. The reason why costs as a per cent of GDP stabilise while costs as a per cent of taxable payrolls keep rising is that taxable payrolls are projected to decline as a share of total compensation due to a continued projected growth in fringe benefits. A 2%-of-GDP increase in Social Security costs is significant, but hardly qualifies as a 'demographic time bomb' (Peterson 1996). Budget changes equal to 2% of GDP in the United States are not uncommon; defense spending increased by 5% of GDP at the start of the cold war and declined by 2% between 1991 and 1998.

6. In the case of the US Social Security system, sensitivity analysis in *The 2002 Annual Report of the Board of Trustees* shows that each 0.5 percentage-point increase in the assumed 'real-wage differential' increases the 75-year actuarial balance by 0.51% of taxable payrolls. The 'real-wage differential' is closely related to the rate of productivity growth.
7. Social Security financing will put increasing pressure on the unified federal budget before the trust fund balances are exhausted. Although shortfalls between 2016 and 2038 can be met in a technical sense from the programme itself, first by drawing on the interest earned on the trust funds and then by drawing on the funds themselves, these actions will lead to a higher unified deficit unless the government raises taxes, reduces other spending, or increases federal borrowing. However, the fact that workers have paid taxes in excess of contributions since 1983 resulting in the accumulation of trust funds reserves means that the nation has more resources to meet these demands that it would have had otherwise. Social Security reserves represent an increase in government and national saving, and this increased saving encourages investment, which produces more national income.
8. Social Security's long-term financing problem is somewhat more complicated than just described. Under current law, the tax rate is fixed while costs are rising, and this pattern produces surpluses now and large deficits in the future. As a result of this profile, under present law, each year the 75-year projection period moves forward, another year with a large deficit is added to the 75-year deficit. Assuming nothing else changes, this phenomenon would increase the 75-year deficit slightly (0.08% of taxable payroll with today's deficits) each year. Many policy-makers believe that the system should not be left with a huge deficit in the 76th year.
9. A study by the International Monetary Fund (Chand and Jaeger 1996) came to very similar conclusions.
10. For example, all three proposals emerging from the 1994–96 Advisory Council on Social Security (1997) advocated equity investment.
11. In testimony before President Bush's Commission to Strengthen Social Security, Michael Sherraden of Washington University stated that 'For the vast majority of households, the pathway out of poverty is not through income and consumption but through saving and accumulation . . . When people begin to accumulate assets, their thinking and behavior changes as well. Accumulating assets leads to important psychological and social effects that are not achieved in the same degree by receiving and spending an equivalent amount of income' (Commission to Strengthen Social Security 2001). The Commission report includes a number of citations regarding the positive effects of asset accumulation on health, education, children's saving behaviour, etc.
12. The chair was Edward Gramlich, Dean of the School of Public Policy at the University of Michigan and currently a member of the Federal Reserve Board. Gramlich is probably best described as a liberal academic with some government experience who cares deeply about increasing national saving. The Secretary charged Gramlich and his council to look particularly at the long-run financing of the programme.
13. For a full listing of Feldstein's articles on privatisation see Feldstein and Leibman 2001.
14. The only way in which Social Security surpluses would not increase government saving is if Congress decided to increase spending or reduce taxes in the non-Social Security part of the budget because of the surplus in Social Security. As noted above, there is little evidence that such offsets have occurred to any significant degree in the past, and do not seem to be occurring now.
15. The Canada Pension Plan Investment Board operates independently from the Canada Pension Plan under legislation that gives it responsibility for all investment decisions. The Board's powers, however, are not unchecked. Rigorous corporate governance practices, code of conduct, and conflict of interest guidelines have been set up by the directors of the programme and are designed to set high standards for performance, disclosure, and ethical behaviour.

16. Initially, CPPIB was only allowed to invest passively in equity-indexed funds. By August 2000, the regulation was relaxed to allow up to 50% of the capital allocated to equities to be actively managed. The board's first major active decision was to reduce exposure to Nortel Networks, a stock that represented 28% of its current assets. This action avoided C$535 million in loses that would have otherwise occurred had the board not actively reduced their holdings.
17. Currently, all investments under the Canada Pension Plan control are in fixed-income portfolios.
18. Some proponents of private accounts acknowledge the advantages of DB plans, but contend that because DB and DC plans are subject to different types of risks, a system that combines the two approaches will function better than a system that relies on a single model (Shoven 1999). But the United States has never tried to provide retirement income through a single plan. By design, Social Security has provided inadequate income—particularly to middle- and upper-income individuals—in the expectation that they will supplement these benefits on their own. It has worked, at least in part; roughly half the work force is covered by supplementary pensions. Many of the supplementary plans started as DB plans, but increasingly have shifted to the DC model. On top of that, individuals can save independently through a variety of voluntary tax-subsidised Individual Retirement Accounts. In other words, the United States already has many tiers that combine the DB and DC approaches to providing retirement income. It does not have to privatise Social Security to create still another tier.
19. The reason for the high costs is adverse selection: people who think that they will live for a long time purchase annuities, whereas those with, say, a serious illness keep their cash. Private insurers have to raise premiums to address the adverse selection problem, and this makes the purchase of annuities very expensive for the average person.
20. In addition to costs, a study by the Employee Benefit Research Institute (Olsen and Salisbury 1998) raised real questions about the ability, in anything like the near term, to administer a system of individual accounts in a satisfactory way. Unlike the current Social Security programme that deals with the reporting of wage credits, a system of personal accounts would involve the transfer of real money. It is only reasonable that participants would care about every dollar, and therefore, employer errors in account names and numbers that arise under the current programme would create enormous public relations problems under a system of individual accounts.
21. The three agencies are: (1) the Department of Labour, which oversees rules relating to fiduciary conduct, disclosure of information to plan participants, and enforcement of rights; (2) the Pension Benefit Guarantee Corporation, which assures the security of benefits under DB plans; and (3) the Securities and Exchange Commission, which regulates investments products offered to individuals under DC plans.

CHAPTER

9

Twenty-first-century Pension (In)Security

Gordon L. Clark

9.1. INTRODUCTION

Throughout this book, we have been most concerned with how western European and Anglo-American countries have sought to accommodate the demographic and financial pressures related to the pending retirement of the baby-boom generation. Our expert contributors have addressed these issues in a variety of ways. We should hardly expect otherwise. The combination of different disciplinary perspectives and distinctive historical trajectories demands respect for the various styles and modes of analysis that are a strength of our book. Indeed, it is interesting to reflect upon the role and status of academic disciplines with respect to pension and retirement income policy amongst the countries surveyed in this book. Part of the intellectual ferment apparent in the field of pension analysis and policy has to do with the realisation that no one discipline has the scope and strength of analytical tools necessary to cope with the pressures being brought to bear on nation-state social security institutions. We might suppose that some disciplines have a close affinity with issues of social justice and equity whereas others have a close affinity with issues of funding and financing. But at the same time, if these affinities provide a point of analytical reference, we have asked our contributors to reach out beyond their normal affinities to a set of three questions that have no 'natural' disciplinary home.

Those questions were stated in the Preface of the book. The first simply asks about how nation-states are dealing with the apparent and increasing pressures on established national pension and retirement income institutions. Each answer begins with the past in one way or another and identifies the forces and responses. Each answer requires an appreciation of country-specific institutions and political alliances. But each answer also reaches out to European, international, and global imperatives. The second question asks contributors to explore the changing relationship between public and private pension and retirement income institutions. For some countries, notably the Anglo-American, private institutions are already in place even if they carry with them significant issues of income distribution, gender equality, and risk allocation. In a number of European countries, by contrast, private institutions barely exist—part of the story is the design and implementation of these types of institutions in the context of past political commitments to nation-state comprehensive institutions. In this context, the Dutch long experience with supplementary pension institutions coupled with the recent Swedish experience have important implications for France and Germany. But, of course, nothing is as simple as this statement implies (and as our contributors indicate). Finally, the last question asks for an assessment of the significance of these new arrangements for European and global financial markets. This is an immense topic, one of prospective thought rather than long experience in Europe. For the Europeans, however, it is a most vital question as Pochet and others indicate.

These are the issues and arguments explored in this chapter. Unlike the other chapters of the book, we look at the commonalities rather than the differences between pension systems, being global in perspective even if reliant upon US and UK experience for illustration.[1] By this account, the future of retirement income provision in Western economies is bound up with regulation of finance and the process of global financial market integration. Yet, at the moment, we have what Stiglitz (2002: 21) has called 'global governance without global government'. Making good on the promise of globalisation for the future incomes of retirees as opposed to its costs and vicissitudes is an essential ingredient in any comprehensive nation-state policy aimed at providing for pension security in the twenty-first century.

9.2. PENSION PROSPECTS IN THE GLOBAL ECONOMY

Through much of the nineteenth century, governments concerned about ageing and retirement income promoted individual and collective or mutual aid solutions rather than nation-state comprehensive solutions. Many of the related mutual aid societies survived into the twentieth century and reappear from time to time in debate about pensioner incomes as institutions worth emulating in the search for institutional innovation. Of course, the nineteenth century also saw the beginning of employer-sponsored pension plans in continental Europe, the United Kingdom, and the United States (being concentrated in the largest public and private employers, Clark 2000). In these ways, by the early years of the twentieth century some countries had stitched together mixed systems of pension provision albeit with many gaps and cracks through which those least able to look after themselves and those most vulnerable to the vicissitudes of capital and labour markets fell to certain poverty. One of the most remarkable achievements of the twentieth century was to create social institutions of relevance to every citizen's well being.

At the turn of the twenty-first century, the achievements of the twentieth century seem increasingly at risk to the gathering forces of global financial integration. The nation-state institutions of the second half of the twentieth century may be impossibly expensive if applied in the same form to the retirement of the baby-boom generation (Disney 2000). Indeed, that generation has an obligation to their children and grandchildren to ensure that successive generations are not enslaved or impoverished by excessive burdens on their incomes and accumulated capital. The balance between what is owed to retirees and what is owed to their children and grandchildren is surely a most emotional and yet profound economic and financial matter. In various ways, western governments have slowly discounted the value of prospective social security and pension obligations (OECD 2000). Recognising this fact, Europeans have looked again for retirement income through employer-sponsored pension plans and individual insurance and pension products.[2] However, just as nation-states have found capital markets to be severe constraints on their discretion, employers and individuals have found the market risks of such provision more significant than anticipated (referencing post-war experience).

Nation-states and individual citizens have come to recognise that their future income prospects are bound up with the performance of global financial markets. If markets were the enemy of social welfare through the nineteenth and twentieth centuries, markets are essential ingredients in any comprehensive solution to retirement income provision in the twenty-first century. For many, especially those enamoured with the social welfare institutions of the second half of the twentieth century, this argument is both horrifying and entirely implausible: invoked time and time again, in this respect, are theoretical arguments and empirical evidence to the effect that financial markets, like capitalism itself, is subject to recurrent episodes of crisis (Blackburn 2002). The technology, media, and telecommunication (TMT) boom, bubble, and bust is further evidence of the irrational exuberance and irrational pessimism associated with financial markets (Shiller 2002*a*). Even so, continental Europe has seen their financial systems caught up in the momentum of global financial markets; there is no refuge from the hegemony of finance. In that case, recipes for reform, for extending the scope and depth of global financial regulation, and for linking domestic social goals with financial imperatives have enormous contemporary importance (see Soros 2002).

9.3. EUROPEAN PENSION INCOME SECURITY

By reason of retirement or permanent disability, a pension is an expected flow of income directed to a designated recipient. In large part, it is designed to sustain that person's (and perhaps their family's) standard of living through their after-work years until death. There are other ways of defining a pension, many of which place pension institutions in a wider context considering nation-state welfare systems in particular (see generally OECD 1998).[3] Similarly, pension institutions could be related to employment contracts and the processes of collective bargaining (Clark 1993). At this point, however, we begin with a rather simple conception of a pension, emphasising the intimate connection between income, consumption, and standards of living (pace Esping-Andersen et al. 2001).

In some countries, pensions are designed to maintain beneficiaries' standards of living at close to their immediate past pre-retirement incomes. In this respect, pension income is directly related to a nation's policy of income replacement being a mechanism for ensuring that retirees share with working people the income benefits of economic growth and increasing labour productivity. In other countries, however, pension benefits are designed to ensure recipients have a minimum standard of living, presumably above commonly accepted measures of poverty in the relevant community. Crudely speaking, continental European countries have been committed to high income replacement rates whereas Anglo-American countries have been committed to insuring a minimum standard of living of retirees leaving retirees' total income to their own discretion, planning, and opportunities

(Budd and Campbell, 1998). Being committed to high income replacement rates has not meant that all European citizens actually attain such a lofty ideal. Similarly, pensioner poverty is an ever-present fact of life in the United Kingdom and the United States and elsewhere (see G. Clark 2002; and Emmerson on United Kingdom; and Munnell on United States, in this volume).

Whatever the goal of pension benefit provision, it is widely believed that pension systems should have four characteristics. In the first instance, pensions should be predictable since most retirees rely heavily upon the pension benefit for their standard of living. In the second instance, pensions should involve minimum risks to the recipient since retirees are poorly placed to compensate for any unanticipated shortfalls in expected income. In the third instance, pensions should be long-lasting, being viable and of sufficient value over the years of retirement until death. This is especially important considering the physical and mental agility of retirees progressively declines as they age; and finally, more often than not, pensions should be comprehensive in coverage, recognising the inequities of discrimination whether that be on the basis of gender, working life experience, ability, or disability. The extension of pension benefits to the community through the twentieth century was, in part, a response to the apparent social and urban crises of nineteenth century industrialisation (Whiteside, this volume).

Pensions protect and sustain retirees' consumption (Campbell and Viceira 2002). While there are other sources of retiree income and wealth including inheritance, property, and savings accounts, for the vast majority of people in advanced western economies, pensions are essential to their long-term quality of life. It should be noted, of course, that pension systems differ in many respects (Gillion et al. 2000). In some countries, people may claim a pension as an entitlement by virtue of their citizenship. In some countries pensions are a form of deferred earned income and are therefore proportional to lifetime earnings. In some countries pensions combine the notion of entitlement with deferred earned income in the form of social insurance. And in some countries, pensions are funded by the accumulation of assets over individuals' working lives whereas in other countries pensions are funded by virtue of intergenerational transfers of income administered by governments. Here, we refer to well-known differences between funded pension schemes (pillar II) common in the Anglo-American world and the Pay-As-You-Go (PAYG) social security systems (pillar I) of continental Europe explained elsewhere in this book and in the growing literature devoted to the topic (see, for further details, Feldstein 2002).

Nation-state sponsored social security was the core pension institution of the twentieth century. However funded, it can be thought of as an institutional and political commitment by government to provide current and future retirees with a well-defined and predictable income. In many cases, social-security pension entitlement has been highly regulated, using complex benefit formula and tests of eligibility based upon a wide variety of social and personal characteristics. Over time, antidiscrimination legislation and reference to conventions on human rights have ensured that such rules and regulations have become systematic rather than arbitrary. While often described as an income guarantee, social-security pension benefits should be also thought of as an implicit bond or a social contract made between the state and the individual or group designated as the eligible recipient. Over the 1990s, one of the most contested and disputed issues in social and economic policy has been the attributed value of long-term pension entitlements presumed guaranteed by the nation-state, but actually discounted in value by governments of all political persuasions.

In this sense, social-security pension benefits are not without risk. Just as individuals and companies may default on a bond and may violate the terms of a previously agreed contract to provide goods and services, so too may governments default, discount, and change the rules of entitlement and pension provision. In doing so, they may violate previously agreed commitments to provide retirement income that is predictable, stable, long-lasting, and comprehensive in coverage. As is widely appreciated, PAYG social security pension systems are very sensitive to the old age dependency ratio and the benefit ratio. Policies that encouraged earlier retirement combined with policies of increased benefit values over the 1980s have become substantial threats to the future of European PAYG social security systems (Gruber and Wise 1999).[4] Furthermore, the relative ageing of a nation's population can also have significant consequences for the affordability of promised pension benefits. In these circumstances, the discounting of pension benefit guarantees has prompted significant political conflict and debate; at the same time, it has been realised that the value and predictability of nation-state social-security pension benefits depends, in part, upon the financial integrity of the nation-state itself.

What determines the long-term financial integrity of the nation-state? This is a most complex and involved question not easily answered in the space of the paragraph or so. Indeed, it is a question debated and discussed by economists over the last 300 years (since at least Adam Smith). But let us make the following observations. If we are concerned about the long-term value and predictability of PAYG pension system wherein pension benefits are proportionate to current real income, it is reasonable to suggest that the rate of real income growth is closely related to the rate of economic growth and the rate of labour productivity. In a situation where there are fewer and fewer active workers compared to the numbers of retirees, and in a situation where there is a commitment to maintain the link between pension benefits and the growth in real income, the nation-state has an interest in increasing the rate of economic growth and their share of income growth in the form of taxes and ultimately intergenerational transfers of income. In other words, any pension benefit guarantees would be delivered by creaming-off a proportion of higher economic growth thereby managing the incipient conflict between the generations over the share of current income (Visco 2001).

But notice, in a multi-jurisdictional environment like Europe and in a world in which global economic integration is accelerating, the financial integrity of the nation-state also depends upon the following: in the first instance, a tax regime which is competitive, with tax rates less than that which would prompt capital flight and systematic tax avoidance by the employed; in the second instance, a regulatory regime which is conducive to innovation and entrepreneurship combined with incentive systems that would reward endogenous capital accumulation and investment; in the third instance, a trade policy within Europe and between Europe and the rest of the world which would be conducive to export growth, and thereby the generation of external income over and above that determined by current and prospective population and real income growth (market size and wealth).[5] In these ways, the value and predictability of retirees' social-security benefits is directly related to nation-state and European industry organisation, to policies determining income distribution, and to the performance of indigenous firms in the global economy. Recognising the relatively poor performance of European economies compared to the Anglo-American world over last two decades, it is arguable that PAYG social security pension benefits can only decline in real value over the coming 25 years (Clark 2003).

Consequently, there have been significant attempts at the European level to build an integrated economic framework consistent with long-term economic growth. This is most apparent in the long-term commitment to a single European market for goods and services. Here, the motivating imperative is the efficient allocation of resources across time and space thereby contributing to greater economies of scale and higher rates of labour productivity. This initiative has been followed by a less successful commitment to build an integrated capital market in the hope of offering companies greater access to cheaper capital and, perhaps, greater opportunities for individuals to become part of the 'equity culture'. At the national level, slowly but surely, governments have sought to introduce tax incentives to encourage individual savings for retirement as well as opportunities for employers to provide funded pension schemes in a manner consistent with Anglo-American experience. At the limit, the European Commission has argued that not only would private pensions provide an important supplement to nation-state social-security these kinds of schemes would also introduce into continental Europe new kinds of investment institutions able to manage the risks associated with global capitalism.[6]

9.4. EMPLOYER-SPONSORED SUPPLEMENTARY PENSIONS

Whereas nation-state social security provides UK and US retirees a base-level income supplemented by employer-sponsored pension funds and individual savings, in continental Europe social-security is the overwhelming source of retiree income. Furthermore, in contradiction to the neoliberal mantra dominating Anglo-American political discourse, social solidarity remains an important social and political commitment underpinning European welfare states. In fact, the nation-state and related representative institutions from civil society have had vital roles in setting (and limiting) options for pension reform even if continuing high levels of long-term unemployment would seem to threaten the legitimacy of such corporatist bargains. Until recently, employer-sponsored pension schemes were of limited significance in continental Europe (although each country has had various forms of such institutions over the twentieth century). But this is changing under the weight of forecast public pension liabilities and growing unease amongst the middle classes about their long-term retirement income prospects.

In this light, we should consider the extent to which funded pension schemes have been important in the Anglo-American world in ensuring pension security (predictable, stable, long-lasting, and comprehensive retirement income). The history of employer-sponsored pension funds in the Anglo-American world has been told a number of times (see Sass 1997). Likewise, recent trends in coverage rates, the balance between defined benefit (DB) and defined contribution (DC) plans, and the emergence of cash balance and stock-option related plans are part of an ongoing debate about the proper role of supplementary pensions in guaranteeing workers' retirement living standards (US Government 2002). Apart from Australia, Anglo-American countries do not require or mandate participation of all workers in supplementary pension schemes.[7] Historically, supplementary pension schemes were offered by larger employers in unionised manufacturing industries as well as by local, state, and national governments to their professional and administrative employees. Through much of the post-war period, employers used DB plans or final salary schemes that, in effect, promised a retirement income based upon age, years of service, and income.

In this respect, DB plans provided employees predictable, stable, and long-lasting pension income even if coverage rates were hardly ever above 40 per cent of the private workforce (Clark 2000). In relation to our previous discussion of the risks associated with the PAYG social-security systems, we should recognise three salient features of Anglo-American supplementary pensions. In the first instance, by convention and then later by regulation such schemes were required to be fully funded; expected future liabilities were required to be matched by financial assets that could, in principle, pay off those liabilities if forced to do so the immediate future. In the second instance, the embedded risks associated with meeting future pension obligations were borne by the employer not the employee. Until recently, it is arguable that firms and financial markets tended to distinguish short-term liabilities from long-term liabilities in valuing the sponsoring firm. In the third instance, as those plans came to maturity in the late 1980s, plan sponsors were then fortunate to participate in one of the most extraordinary speculative bubbles of all time (Shiller 2002*a*). Many plan sponsors took pension contribution 'holidays' over the 1990s while using excess returns on their invested pension assets to supplement reported corporate earnings (McConnell et al. 2001).

In the United States, the risks of default associated with employer-sponsored DB pension obligations are borne by taxpayers through the US government's Pension Benefit Guaranty Corporation (PBGC). On the continent there are similar kinds of institutions especially important in Germany and the Netherlands. In a world of national economies, and competitive stability between national corporations and whole industries, it was widely believed that these insurance institutions would face only idiosyncratic risks of default (isolated instances of corporate failure). However, as domestic manufacturing industries have been exposed to increasing international competition, it is apparent that these institutions have had to deal with large-scale systematic risks of default.[8] Furthermore, as the speculative bubble of the 1990s collapsed and as the value of stock market portfolios significantly declined many corporate DB plan sponsors reported large-scale shifts in the value of plan assets from 'surplus' to 'deficit'. The prospect of relatively lower stock market performance over the foreseeable future combined with the introduction of stricter national and international accounting rules on the matching of plan assets and liabilities have added to the systematic risks of default on DB pension promises.

While the contribution costs of DB pensions were absorbed by stock market growth over the 1990s, many DB plans were terminated, closed to new entrants, and if possible transformed into DC and hybrid stock plans. In the United States, whereas 25 years ago DB plans were predominant over DC plans (in terms of the total volume of employees covered) DC plans now dominate DB plans. See Table 9.1 (using 1998 data). These patterns are apparent throughout the Anglo-American world, and are especially important in the United Kingdom (at present) where the introduction of FRS 17 (an exacting accounting rule on pension assets valuation) combined with the precipitous decline in stock market prices has raised widespread concerns about the future of DB schemes. At the same time, over the 1990s many employers in new economy sectors introduced stock-option and stock-matching DC schemes designed to reward employee loyalty to the firm while discounting current wages and salaries with the promise of future wealth through stock market appreciation (Teece 2000).

It is difficult to be precise about the relative significance of the various causes driving the shift from DB schemes to DC schemes (see Paine 1993 for an early assessment of the emerging trends).[9] Clearly important has been the realisation amongst many employers that they (and their employees) have less interest than ever before in locking-in job tenure. At the same time, regulatory requirements have limited employers' discretion in their differential treatment of more and less valued employees. Thus, both the regulatory and compliance costs associated with DB schemes have increased significantly in many Anglo-American countries. Equally, estimates of increasing life expectancy have raised the long-term costs associated with DB plans. These are now often perceived as increasingly uncertain (but inevitably larger) and perhaps too significant given the separate strategic interests of corporate executives in remaking corporate form to respond to heightened global competition. In effect, employers have sought to separate pension

Table 9.1. Participants and assets by type of pension plan, United States, 1979–98

Year	Participants (thousands)			Assets ($ millions)[1]		
	Total	DB	DC	Total	DB	DC
1979	55,097	36,810	18,287	445,430	319,595	125,835
1980	57,903	37,979	19,924	563,551	401,455	162,096
1981	60,564	38,903	21,661	628,916	444,376	184,540
1982	63,243	38,633	24,610	788,987	553,419	235,567
1983	69,147	40,025	29,122	923,470	642,359	281,111
1984	73,895	40,980	32,915	1,044,592	700,669	343,922
1985	74,665	39,692	34,973	1,252,739	826,117	426,622
1986	76,672	39,989	36,682	1,382,910	895,073	487,837
1987	78,223	39,958	38,265	1,402,488	877,269	525,219
1988	77,685	40,722	36,963	1,503,635	911,982	591,653
1989	76,405	39,958	36,447	1,675,597	987,971	687,626
1990	76,924	38,832	38,091	1,674,139	961,904	712,236
1991	77,662	39,027	38,634	1,936,271	1,101,987	834,284
1992	81,914	39,531	42,383	2,094,087	1,146,798	947,289
1993	83,870	40,267	43,603	2,316,272	1,248,180	1,068,092
1994	85,117	40,338	44,778	2,298,556	1,210,856	1,087,700
1995	87,452	39,736	47,716	2,723,735	1,402,079	1,321,657
1996	91,716	41,111	50,605	3,136,281	1,585,397	1,550,884
1997	94,985	40,392	54,593	3,553,757	1,735,604	1,818,152
1998	99,455	41,552	57,903	4,021,849	1,936,600	2,085,250

Notes: DB: Defined Benefit; DC: Defined Contribution.

[1] Asset amounts shown exclude funds held by life insurance companies under allocated group insurance contracts for payment of retirement benefits. These excluded funds make up roughly 10 to 15 per cent of total private fund assets.

Source: US Government (2002, tables E5 & E11).

funding from the financial and competitive structure of the firm. In doing so, they have shifted to employees the risks associated with the provision of predictable, stable, and long-lived pension benefits. Most importantly, employees have been given the responsibility for the desired value of their retirement income.

Care should be taken not to exaggerate either the significance of DC schemes dominated by sponsors' stock or the spread of such schemes through US industry. The available evidence suggests that only a small fraction of employer-sponsored DC schemes have a significant stock-option component, and many of those plans are sponsored by bluechip firms. As well, in many cases the accumulated commitments were limited, given the short tenure of many participating employees. See Mitchell and Utkus (2002) and Munnell and Sunden (2002) for extensive treatment of the related issues.[10] The shift from DB to DC schemes, however, does remind us of two vital issues regarding pension policy in general. First, whereas employer-sponsored pensions have a vital place in Anglo-American retirement income policy, they are private employment institutions before they are public retirement income institutions. Second, their value for individual employees and their countries are a function of the integrity and performance of national and global financial markets. Neither should be taken for granted, as recent events have shown.

9.5. RISK AND RETURN IN GLOBAL STOCK MARKETS

The shift from DB to DC supplementary pensions means that employees' future retirement incomes are directly dependent upon national and global stock markets. Considering that Anglo-American state-sponsored social security schemes provide a minimum or basic pension benefit, we all have a stake in the effective and efficient performance of stock markets. To the extent to which the value of European PAYG nation-state social-security pensions are discounted and employers and individuals encouraged to rely upon their own savings and investment schemes, then stock market performance will be an important element in determining the predictability, stability, and long-lasting value of prospective retirees' incomes. Here, I suggest that not withstanding the extraordinary run-up in Anglo-American (and global) stock markets over the 1990s, informed commentators believe that stock market returns will be quite low over the immediate future and possibly low by historical standards over the coming 5–10 years.[11]

Conventional wisdom would have it that a diversified portfolio of assets is an essential ingredient in any long-term investment and retirement income strategy. Advocates of modern portfolio theory (Markowitz 1952) have showed this, theoretically at least. Diversification can take a number of forms, most obviously diversification between asset classes and diversification within asset classes, adjusted by the age of an investor (in the DC universe) and the maturity of a pension fund (in the DB universe). To the extent that younger people have access to stock markets, they may wish to carry the greatest risk, given their prospective lifetime earnings and the long time horizon over which investment strategies may be resolved. In middle-age, presumably investors should hold a relatively risky portfolio, given the security and high predictability of earned incomes. Older people, pending retirement and the need to build in predictability, stability, and long-lived income, should hold a portfolio characterised by low relative risk. Similarly, depending upon the average age of active participants and the balance between active and retired participants, DB plans may wish to hold more or less risky portfolios (as developed in detail by Campbell and Viceira 2002).

Over the 1990s, conventional wisdom was overtaken by what Shiller (2000: xii) termed 'irrational exuberance—wishful thinking on part of investors that blinds us to the truth of the situation'. It became obvious that the most significant determinant of the rate of return was the extent to which assets allocations were skewed towards equities. This had significant implications for DB schemes whatever their underlying maturity profiles, just as it had significant lessons for DC plan participants. Whereas many pension plan participants entered the 1990s with a balance between equities and bonds (for example), by the end of the 1990s many defined contribution portfolios were characterised by a strong bias towards US equities and a bias within equities towards TMT stocks. Equally, institutional investors responsible for DB plans, the investment of insurance company assets, foundations, and endowments systematically shifted towards high risk US equities as if risk had been resolved once and for all by the proclaimed certainties of a structural transformation in labour productivity associated with the new economy of Silicon Valley and other regions.

The TMT bubble may be just a footnote in the inevitable progress of modern capitalism (as implied by some optimists; see generally Dimson et al. 2002). But consider Shiller's (2000: xii) comment coming after his definition of irrational exuberance: 'if we exaggerate the present and future value of the stock market, then as a society we may invest too much in business start-ups and expansions, and too little in infrastructure, education, and other forms of human capital. If we think the market is worth more than it really is, we may become complacent in funding our pension plans, in maintaining our savings rate, in legislating an improved social security system, and in providing other forms of social insurance.' Perspicuous words indeed. There is no doubt that the TMT bubble was a most remarkable speculative bubble (according to the historical record). See Figure 9.1 where it is shown that the late 1990s were characterised by extraordinarily high price/earnings (*P*/*E*) ratios for S&P Composite stocks (and even higher values for firms listed on the NASDAQ) (Shiller 2002*b*). Combined with the 9/11 terrorist attacks, the collapse of the TMT bubble has brought to global economy to the brink of recession and perhaps long-term stagnation.

As the TMT bubble grew, investment strategy became fixated on the growth in stock prices. Notwithstanding the appeals of value investors, amateur and expert investors sought to capture the windfall benefits of successive successful bets on the stock market while promising to lock-in those gains by exquisite timing (relative to other investors seemingly overcommitted to an inevitable future value of the Dow Jones Index of

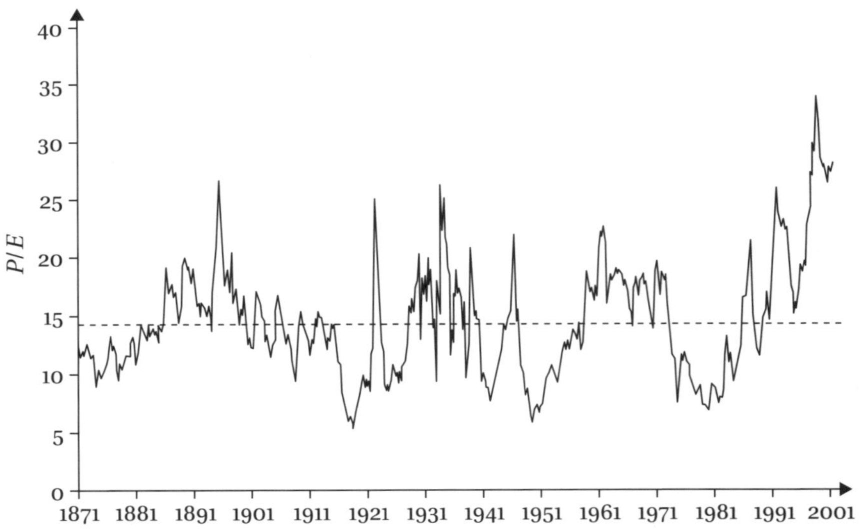

Fig. 9.1. Historical *P*/*E* ratios, US, 1871–2001.

Note: Ending month for 2001 is September.

Source: Siegel (2002).

30,000). Unrecognised by many, was the contemporaneous decline in the equity premium, explored in detail by Siegel (2002). Assuming a simple definition of the equity risk premium—'the difference between the real return for stocks and the real return for bonds and bills'—he showed that (a) real rates of return on stocks and bonds have varied considerably over post Second World War era, (b) the apparent variation is not always synchronised, (c) the equity risk premium (over bonds) was about 5 per cent for the period 1982–99, but (d) taking into account the years 1999–2001 the equity risk premium shrank to just less than 2 per cent for bonds and about 7 per cent for bills. See Table 9.2, which reproduces in a summary fashion his evidence. He concluded that the long-run real rate of return on equities would be about 5 per cent and the equity risk premium about 2 per cent.

There is an enormous debate about the existence, current status, and likely future of the equity risk premium.[12] At this point, we should recognise a number of points made by Siegel and others about the sensitivity of the risk premium to long-run and short-run circumstances. In the first instance, it should be noted that the historical price/earnings (*P*/*E*) average is about 15. Most recently, the highest *P*/*E* ratio was about 37.0. Thereafter, the *P*/*E* ratio has been declining. In the second instance, we should recognise that as speculation in the growth of stock prices drove the TMT bubble this was reflected in very high *P*/*E* ratios. However, even as stock prices declined in the aftermath of the bubble, reported earnings in a number of technology-related companies virtually collapsed maintaining relatively higher *P*/*E* ratios than might have been expected if earnings had remained constant. In the third instance, if we take seriously the underlying value of corporate stocks, declining investment and consumption spending will no doubt significantly affect the flow of earnings. By this account, the current crisis in global stock markets is the product of enormous downwards pressure on stock prices and the effects of a gathering recession on earnings. In the United States, at least, these two effects are related.

Some analysts are more pessimistic than Siegel. Some analysts would dispute, in any event, the future significance of equities given the ageing of western countries' populations and the concomitant increasing significance of fixed income products like bonds (Campbell and Viceira 2002). Other analysts, distrustful of financial markets and a world of financial flows largely unaccountable to nation-states and their citizens, would have us believe that current circumstances portend the unravelling of global finance. However, there are reasons to be more optimistic rather than pessimistic. Most importantly, recent research on the

Table 9.2. Historical returns and equity premiums, United States, 1802 to September 2001

Period	Real Return						Stock Excess Return			
	Stocks		Bonds		Bills		Bonds		Bills	
	Comp. %	Arith. %	Comp. %	Arith. %	Comp. %	Arith. %	Comp. %	Arith. %	Comp. %	Arith. %
1802–2001	6.8	8.4	3.5	3.9	2.9	3.1	3.4	4.5	3.9	5.3
1871–2001	6.8	8.5	2.8	3.2	1.7	1.8	3.9	5.3	5.0	6.6
Major subperiods										
1802–1870	7.0	8.3	4.8	5.1	5.1	5.4	2.2	3.2	1.9	2.9
1871–1925	6.6	7.9	3.7	3.9	3.2	3.3	2.9	4	3.5	4.7
1926–2001	6.9	8.9	2.2	2.7	0.7	0.8	4.7	6.2	6.1	8.0
Post Second World War										
1946–2001	7.0	8.5	1.3	1.9	0.6	0.7	5.7	6.6	6.4	7.8
1946–1965	10.0	11.4	−1.2	−1.0	−0.8	−0.7	11.2	12.3	10.9	12.1
1966–1981	−0.4	1.4	−4.2	−3.9	−0.2	−0.1	3.8	5.2	−0.2	1.5
1982–1999	13.6	14.3	8.4	9.3	2.9	2.9	5.2	5.0	10.7	11.4
1982–2001	10.2	11.2	8.5	9.4	2.8	2.8	1.7	1.9	7.4	8.4

Note: Comp.: compound; Arith.: arithmetic.
Source: Siegel (2002).

productivity effects of the new economy suggests that these positive effects are real, will be sustained over the long term, and will increase the long-term rate of inflation-neutral economic growth (Jorgenson 2001). When combined with the fact that workers' incomes are more stable than ever before, that labour market flexibility has proved to be more resilient than expected, and that macroeconomic management is sensitive to the risks of stagflation then there are good reasons to expect that real incomes will grow over the coming 5 years. Will that translate into increased corporate earnings (a crucial part of the equation affecting *P*/*E* ratios)? Here, issues of income distribution between the generations and the political economy of income distribution between owners and workers intrude being less amenable to analytical guesswork. Even if there is only a modest flow of increased real earnings into corporate earnings, further falls in stock market prices combined with stable and increasing corporate earnings could provide us a *P*/*E* ratio of about 20.0.

This scenario implies that all but the most hardy of TMT survivors will be ground out of the system. It implies that investment management (individual and institutional) will return to the so-called fundamental determinants of the value of stock market prices.[13] And it implies that the reemergence of a modest equity premium will encourage equity asset allocations. But fundamentals are vulnerable to the variable mix of sentiments, expectations, and modes of valuation that make up any stock market (Shleifer 2000). While some might suggest that recent circumstances have simply eradicated the irrational, all the evidence from behavioural finance and psychology suggest that the 'irrational' is ever-present in markets and life in general (Clark and Marshall 2002). Notice a most important implication: short-term market turmoil can translate into long-term market uncertainty profoundly affecting the accumulation of pension assets and ultimately the value of pension incomes. In this context, any policies that require private pension providers to meet minimum real rates of return on invested assets of 4 per cent or more year-upon-year (as is the case in a number of continental European countries) would appear impossibly prescriptive. Like the equity risk premium, real rates of return may be planned but are only resolved over time in particular circumstances (Clark 2000).

We have concentrated upon US equity markets to illustrate the uncertainties associated with market dependent pension incomes and to suggest that the windfall gains of the 1990s are unlikely to be repeated over the coming decades. There remains, however, a related question on which we have been silent: the relative significance of the US and UK markets compared to European markets. At issue here is the extent to which prospective

European retirees ought to take more seriously the opportunities afforded by the Anglo-American world compared to continental Europe. This is a most important issue of long-term economic welfare, and geopolitics.

There are four attributes of US and UK markets that make them attractive to European investors seeking long-term pension security. These markets are relatively cost-effective and efficient compared to European markets in part because of their large sizes, scope, and the embedded experience of the institutions that regulate and participate in those markets. These markets are more liquid, implying greater opportunities for the diversification of risk, surely a most important issue for individuals, pension plan sponsors, and those concerned with sustaining predictable and long-lived retirement incomes. Furthermore, the slow and tortuous path towards capital market integration in Europe suggests that London and New York will remain the most important markets in the global financial architecture. In the main, these markets are also more transparent and accountable than European markets. Recent evidence gleaned about the underlying structure and opaqueness of market prices for German stocks suggest that there remain significant issues of ownership and corporate governance that affect investors' choices and strategies (Clark and Wojcik 2003).

Most importantly, these two markets represent national and global opportunities for higher rates of economic growth, capital appreciation, and corporate earnings (perhaps reflected in stock market rates of return and the equity premium). More than European markets, the UK stock market provides investors around the world access to very different long-term demographic profiles implying, all things being equal, rather different economic growth trajectories. Similarly, New York markets provide international investors an opportunity to share in the economic benefits of a much younger demographic profile, higher rates of immigration, and continuing economic innovation characteristic of the US economy. When the prospects for technological innovation, invention and the knowledge economy (if not the 'new economy') are added to the argument, the United States, and to a lesser extent the United Kingdom, economies appear located at a higher rate of long-term economic growth. Given the existence of the larger pools of risk capital and greater experience in risk assessment especially in relation to entrepreneurship and firm formation, there may be significant benefits in mobilising European pension and retirement assets for investment in the United States and the United Kingdom and the global economy.

This argument is developed in more detail in Clark (2003), Feldstein (2002), and industry reports such as Lonergan and Hanson (2002).[14]

What remains to be determined is the nature and organisation of European investment in the Anglo-American world and the global economy: open for debate is the proper role of the nation-state, political elites, and collective organisations in the management of such investment institutions. In this respect, just as social security in the European context is best understood as an institution of nation-state welfare and social solidarity so too any debate about the accountability of European investment institutions must take into account the social context in which those institutions are formed and managed. Perhaps less abstractly, the extent to which European retirees will become part of the global economy will also depend a great deal upon the robustness of financial regulation. This point is illustrated below with reference to the Enron debacle.

9.6. REGULATION OF PENSION SECURITY

Recall that Enron failed as the unaccounted liabilities of its financial engineering were exposed by a combination of external scrutiny and internal 'whistle blowing'. Also recall that many Enron corporation employees lost their retirement savings because the company's 401(K) plan encouraged participants to hold company stock as a large proportion of their investment portfolios while discouraging and even disallowing participants to divest themselves of company stock except over a very long time horizon. In effect, Enron employees were both employed by the company and were locked-in shareholders unlike any other external investors (and senior executives of the firm) who bought and sold stock in accordance with market expectations. Against the advice of virtually all independent financial planners, Enron employees were encouraged to concentrate rather than diversify the risks associated with their current and future income streams.[15] As Enron's market price collapsed, employees could only watch as their jobs and retirement plan assets evaporated.[16]

Introducing the Democrats' 'Employee Pension Freedom Act' on 23 January 2002, George Miller (California) indicated that the 'measure . . . is urgently needed in the light of the recent Enron scandal and other threats to pension security affecting millions of American families'. Thereafter, he noted that the actions of Enron senior executives were an 'audacious assault on our pension security laws' offending 'the sense of fairness and justice in every American' (Congressional Record—House,

29 January 2002: H86). In essence, the Democrats' response to the Enron scandal was to propose legislation requiring the equal treatment of employees and senior executives, limits on lock-in and restrictive rules regarding employees disposal of sponsors' stock, the introduction of independent advice consistent with employees' life cycles, and most importantly employee representation on employer sponsored pension plans being a means of equalising the power between employers and employees in the design and administration of private pension plans. Overall, Democrats were most concerned with the diversification of risk and the management of risk in accordance with employees' long-term retirement income security (opposed to the various objectives of employers).

The Republicans' Enron response, the 'Pension Security Act', was introduced by John Boehner (Ohio) on 14 February 2002 (see Congressional Record—extension of remarks, 15 February 2002).[17] At the time, Boehner indicated that the bill represented President Bush's commitment to 'American workers' and the preservation and enhancement of their retirement savings. Key components of the bill included a 3-year vesting rule allowing for workers to divest themselves of company-sponsor stock thereafter over a period of 5 years, quarterly benefit account statements including advice on the benefits of diversification and their rights to do so, equal treatment of employees and senior executives during black-out periods (wherein administrative procedures do not allow for trading-out of company stock), and a clear distinction between the plan sponsor and those with a fiduciary duty to advise participating employees. In doing so, the House majority sought a balance between corporate interests in promoting stock compensation to their employees and employees' interests in an unfettered investment strategy. Closing his opening statement, Boehner noted that the 'private pension system is essential to the security of American workers, retirees, and their families. Congress should move decisively to restore worker confidence in the nation's retirement security and pension system' (p. E174).

For both the Democrats and the Republicans, the Enron debacle was an instance of theft. By their actions, senior executives acting on behalf of their own welfare deliberately misrepresented the true financial health of the firm to stock market investors and their own employees as workers and future retirees. Knowing the true situation, senior executives virtually extinguished the value of employees' retirement income savings. Being conscious of the existence of other similar 401(K) plans dominated by company-sponsor stock subject to onerous lock-in requirements and harsh penalties upon withdrawal, both Democrats and Republicans were concerned to avoid a repeat of the Enron debacle, and thereby secure the continuing significance of employer-sponsored pension and retirement income plans. Otherwise, as one Republican noted, given very low individual saving rates, the failure of pillar II pensions would guarantee retiree poverty. In these ways, the meaning of pension security ranged from protecting assets from theft through to protecting the integrity of the pension system itself.

Nevertheless, Republicans and Democrats fundamentally disagreed on the means by which pension security should be sustained. Being concerned about the theft of assets, the Democrats sought employee representation on pension plan boards. By contrast, the Republicans sought to engage the financial services industry as guardians of plan participants' welfare (ignoring evidence from the United Kingdom and elsewhere of poor advice, competing-interests, and so-called pension 'mis-selling' scandals). Whereas the Democrats returned time and time again to corporate governance, the Republicans sought to limit the scope of the issue to instances of individual wrong-doing. In these ways, pension security was conceived in narrow and expansive ways being mostly concerned about the administration, management and investment of pension plan assets. At no time during the debate did either side of the House consider pension security as an issue of stock market risk with respect to the current and final value of accumulated pension assets. Left out of the analysis was the value of final pension benefits.

There is no doubt that protection of the integrity of pension and retirement income institutions is an essential aspect of any comprehensive commitment to pension security. With respect to institutions, integrity can be thought to have three elements or components. In the first instance, there should be a coherent link between the means and ends of pension policy such that administrative and management functions are consistent with the goals of pension and retirement income. In the second instance, such institutions should be focused upon the welfare of beneficiaries, insulated from competing interests and claims on the resources and administrative decisions of those responsible for its functions. In the third instance, such institutions should be cost-efficient in the sense that the claims of independence from competing and external interests can only be justified if such pension and retirement income institutions are cost-effective in achieving their goals. Otherwise, those that sponsor and pay for such institutions might reasonably believe that their welfare is subservient to the welfare of others. Without some measure of efficiency, pension and retirement income systems may be systems of expropriation rather than welfare (Mitchell 1998).

9.7. IMPLICATIONS AND CONCLUSIONS

Clearly, ensuring the integrity of pension systems is a vital component of any comprehensive commitment to long-term pension and retirement income. But for many, pension security is more than an issue of system-wide and institutional integrity. Also in play, particularly in the political arena, is a commitment to pension security in the form of pension and retirement income guarantees. In this concluding section, I look at this issue beginning with individual pension and savings instruments (pillar III), moving on to employer-sponsored supplementary pension systems including defined contribution and defined benefit systems (pillar II), ending with nation-state sponsored social security whether a minimum benefit or an income replacement model or ideal type (pillar I). As will become apparent, I am not convinced that income guarantees are possible in pillar II and pillar III institutions and I have grave reservations about the plausibility of any nation-state social-security income guarantees.

Few would believe that pillar III pension and retirement income institutions are capable of providing income guarantees. In the main, these kinds of institutions are based squarely in financial markets and are based upon long-term rates of return from investment in a variety of financial instruments including government bonds, higher risk interest bearing bonds, and (to a lesser extent) equities (as well as other more exotic instruments). In some countries, to be designated as a preferred individual retirement income and savings product provider vendors have had to conform to well-defined restrictions upon asset allocation, year to year risk profiles, and certain restrictions upon the total cost of such products. In many countries, individual retirement savings products have included mutual funds, investment trusts, and other kinds of investment products some of which have offered minimum rates of return in relation to long-term government bonds. One way or another, and not withstanding the advertising of the financial services industry, any risks associated with the performance of such products are surely borne by the investors (that is, those saving for their retirement). Furthermore, the time-specific risks associated with transferring between investment and a guaranteed income stream in the form of an annuity is surely a most problematic moment with enormous long-term consequences.

Most significantly, the risks associated with domestic and global financial market performance have figured prominently in debate about who should properly bear the risk of employer-sponsored supplementary pensions (pillar II). Historically, defined benefit or final salary schemes dominated the provision of sponsored plans, being important in the Anglo-American world as well as in a number of countries in continental Europe (including Germany and the Netherlands, for example). Here, an explicit promise was made about the value of beneficiaries' pension benefits in accordance with standardised rules regarding seniority, age, and earned income. In this sense, pension security was to be found in the value of that promise, recognising that any risk associated with that promise was to be borne by the Plan sponsor. Of course, even if the financial risks embodied in such promises were not underwritten by the beneficiary, it was still underwritten by the sponsor firm, its shareholders, and even its employees. Indeed, there are many instances where pension security (the promised value of beneficiaries pensions) has been a financial burden imposed upon firm shareholders, debt holders, and creditors. In a number of countries, even bankruptcy may not extinguish the value of the promise pension benefit—in the end, taxpayers have had to bear the burden of such promises (Clark 1993).

As we have seen, defined contribution plans make no commitment about the final value of any derived pension. These schemes depend upon asset allocation between investment classes, the performance of particular investment products, and the costs associated with active as opposed to passive investment strategies offered by financial service providers. Overarching these factors is, of course, the more fundamental question of the long-term performance of global stock markets (and the existence or otherwise of the so-called equity premium). Moment by moment, judgments made about these issues vary according to market sentiment, institutional capacity, and other less easily quantified expectations and variables. Given the fact that individual and matching employer contributions in such schemes are often quite low relative to monthly earnings and the contributions associated with most DB plans (Choi et al. 2001), pension security, if understood as an issue of long-term pension value is very problematic.

In this context, it is arguable that, in the end, the nation-state is the ultimate guarantor of pension security (the final value of the pension and retirement income product). This view is widespread across continental Europe. But the combination of social security liabilities associated with the ageing of the baby-boom generation, relatively low rates of older-age labour force participation, and lower rates of economic growth suggests that no European nation-state would be able to shoulder of the risks associated with the failure of pillar II and pillar III pension and retirement income systems. Furthermore, it seems quite unlikely that European nation-state social-security systems will be able to deliver on promises of high income replacement. In fact, any reading of pension reform on the continent would surely lead analysts to conclude that those reforms have systematically discounted the value of those promises through by changing indexation, by increasing the years needed to attain maximum benefit, and by changing the reference wage in determining wage-related retirement benefits. Even here, the nation-state has stepped away from pension security if security is to be understood as a question of income guarantee. At the same time, however, the nation-state has become more active in regulating the integrity of pension and retirement income institutions. Pension security has been redefined in the face of global financial imperatives.

Whereas Anglo-American countries have had for many years mixed systems of pension and retirement income, relying upon different mechanisms to ameliorate and manage long-term income risk, there is a sense in which the performance of each component in such mixed systems of pension provision are converging upon just one kind of institution: domestic and global financial markets. Whereas many European countries have relied heavily upon nation-state sponsored social security, the introduction of tax preferred and private employer and institution-sponsored retirement plans have introduced greater uncertainty about citizens' long-term retirement incomes. Indeed, just as they are more exposed to the performance of domestic and global financial markets, their nation-state social-security institutions are also similarly exposed, if only because the nation states themselves find their fiscal and monetary discretion increasingly constrained according to the norms and conventions that dominate financial market expectations. Inevitably, there has been a retreat, albeit done quietly and under the cover of other sentiments such as European integration, from pension security as a form of income guarantee. Ordinary citizens increasingly appreciate this even if domestic political debate would have such retreat characterised as a betrayal of the working lives and expectations of the baby-boom generation.

ACKNOWLEDGEMENTS

This chapter was written with the support of the UK Economic and Social Research Council through the Future Governance programme administered by Professor Ed Page and in conjunction with my colleague Professor Adam Tickell from Bristol University. Research assistance was provided by Linda Atkinson and Isla Wright. Over the last few years, I have benefited from discussion about pension-related issues with my graduate students, including Chloe Flutter, Tessa Hebb, and Dariusz Wojcik. I have also benefited from the comments and advice of colleagues including Ronald Dore, David Merrill, Olivia Mitchell, Alicia Munnell, Mike Orszag, and Noel Whiteside. None of the above should be held responsible for the opinions expressed herein.

NOTES

1. There is widespread debate in the social sciences about the persistence of capitalist diversity (see, e.g. Crouch and Streeck 1997; Hall and Soskice 2001). For some, the western world is converging upon common modes of social organisation and market structure stripping-out from the past distinctive institutions and traditions at odds with the imperatives of global markets. For others, the rhetoric of convergence and apparent instances of convergence are superficial but unwarranted threats against progressive nation-state social commitments at odds with Anglo-American conventions (Dore 2000). Here, I tend to agree with Strange (1997: 182), who suggested that global capital and commodity market integration will not only drive convergence in 'national versions of capitalist production', but will also undercut nation-state power (over resources and the autonomy of policy setting) and relevance (for regulation, for the welfare of its older citizens, and for the long-term well-being of its employed citizens).
2. The baby-boom generation are increasingly uneasy about their long-term pension security. See, for more details, the results of a large cross-European survey of citizens' pension attitudes and expectations reported in Boeri et al. (2001).
3. Some pension policy analysts would have us believe that the embedded nature of nation-state pension institutions makes comparative study and, most especially, cross-country pension programmes of reform deeply problematic. See Reynaud (2000: 2) who noted the coexistence of 'widely differing institutional environments and traditions' going well beyond and deeper than the 'purely technical' aspects of managing pension benefits and funding systems.
4. It should be recognised that pensions have played a significant role in the management of private enterprise labour forces, being essential ingredients in corporate restructuring, downsizing, and changing corporate strategy (see Clark 1993). For Europe, PAYG public pension systems have played a similar role, managing national labour markets and in particular the entry of younger workers and the exit of older workers in the context of a limited supply of work. Pension policy, work, and the management of labour are important responsibilities distributed between the public and private sectors on the basis of inherited institutions.
5. There is a large and growing literature devoted to the consequences of globalisation and the putative competition between nation-states for increasing shares of global economic income. This is hardly the moment to look closely at the related debates over, for instance, claims and counter-claims made about the 'race to the bottom' and the 'race to the top'. These issues are treated in Clark and Tracey (2004).
6. See, for example, the proposals brought forward by the European Commission regarding the building of a pan-European framework consistent with the imperatives of the

'knowledge economy' (Bolkestein 2000). See also Allen and Gale (2000) and Davis and Steil (2001) for comparative analyses of Anglo-American and European financial systems.

7. It is arguable, in this context, that Australian pension policy is, therefore, more European than Anglo-American policy notwithstanding the adoption of a defined contribution model as opposed to a DB model with a high income replacement goal. This reflects, no doubt, the origin of Australian policy with the Labour government of the 1980s and the deliberate policy of managing macroeconomic stability through deferring wage growth to pension benefits. See Edey and Simon (1998) on the development of Australian policy.
8. While, nominally a model based upon risk premiums and collective insurance, the PBGC has had a roller-coaster existence at times teetering on bankruptcy at other times flush with the benefits of exploding stock market asset growth. In instances of industrial and economic restructuring (such as steel and other related manufacturing industries) these kinds of institutions have proven to be inadequate in the face of the enormous financial burdens imposed. See Clark (1993) on the PBGC and the US automotive and steel industries.
9. The patterns embedded in the data on the relative significance of DB and DC schemes are long-term in nature. While related to the burden of regulation and the transparency of DB costs in relation to financial imperatives, there are more complex issues involved including employees' preferences, the risk preferences of younger workers, and the expected job mobility and job tenure of young workers. The changing nature of the labour market, the increasing importance of contingent contracts and the expectations of job-switching and short-term job tenure are noted by many including Esping-Andersen (1999) for the United States and social welfare states and Supiot (2001) for Europe in particular.
10. There are fewer 401(K) plans that have such a significant component of sponsor's stock included in their portfolio than may be apparent from discussion in the media. For a broader assessment of defined contribution plans see the report US Government (2001).
11. Notice that I do not mean to imply that stock markets need be the only institution through which pension assets are invested and managed on behalf of current and potential retirees. There are other institutions, asset classes, and investment products. But it is clear that public markets as opposed to private and closed investment opportunities are deemed by many to be often more efficient and cost-effective. This is one aspect of the competition between whole systems of corporate governance discussed by Dore (2000) amongst others.
12. For theoretical surveys of the related issues, see Claus and Thomas (2001), Fama and French (2002), and Pastor and Stambaugh (2001).
13. Reflected, for example, in recent reports devoted to reassessing corporate earnings reports, industry-by-industry, and firm-by-firm (see McConnell 2002).
14. Notice that Lonergan and Hanson (2002) argue that the US economy is both more stable and on a higher growth trajectory than the Eurozone suggesting 'a high risk premium relative to the US.' By this account, the rate of return on European equities and the likely long-term rate of return on government bonds (reflecting the rate of economic growth) may be significantly lower than the United States and the United Kingdom.
15. Here, there are a number of issues of contrast and debate that can not be developed for reasons of limited space. Note that over the 1990s, German corporate-sponsored pension plans that relied upon book reserves (a form of self-investment) were widely criticised in the academic literature for concentrating risk. In response, greater external investment and management of workers' pension promises were introduced and a slow retreat from book reserve systems initiated (Clark 2003). In the United States, of

course, such concerns were swept away by enthusiasm for the promise of great wealth associated with the new economy. So significant was this movement that it effectively emasculated the Financial Accounting Standards Board's attempts to introduce rules regarding the current valuation of stock options and the like.

16. Similar issues were raised by the WorldCom debacle. As reported in *Pensions & Investments* (8 July 2002, pp.1, 33), WorldCom employees had on average about 40% their 401(K) assets in company stock. From a share price of $64.50 3 years previously, WorldCom stock was worth just $0.06 in July 2002. Some individual employees were severely affected. In the article, P&I reported one employee's 401(K) balance shrinking from $470,000 in 2000 to just $400 in 2002. Furthermore, reflecting the discounting of US equity markets, the frozen WorldCom DB plan went from being overfunded by $42 million in late 1999 to being underfunded by $21 million by year end 2001.
17. For a comparison of the competing Democrat and Republican versions of 'Pension Reform' in the context of the Enron debacle see the commentary provided by Orszag (2002).

BIBLIOGRAPHY

Aaron, H. J. and Reischauer, R. D. (2001), *Countdown to Reform: The Great Social Security Debate*, New York: The Century Foundation Press.

Abelshauser, W. (1996), 'Erhard ou Bismarck? L'orientation de la politique sociale allemande', in MIRE, Rencontres et Recherches (ed.), *Comparer les systemes de protection sociale en Europe, Vol. 2: Rencontres de Berlin* (pp. 115–45). Paris: MIRE.

Able-Smith, B. and Townsend, P. (1961), *The Poor and the Poorest*, London: Bell.

Advisory Council on Social Security. (1997), *Report of the 1994–1996 Advisory Council on Social Security*, Washington, DC: US Government Printing Office.

Agulnik, P. (1999), 'The Proposed State Second Pension', *Fiscal Studies*, 20/4: 409–22.

Allen, F. and Gale, D. (2000), *Comparing Financial Systems*, Cambridge, MA: MIT Press.

Anderson, K. M. (2002), 'The Europeanisation of Pension Arrangements: Convergence or Divergence?', in C. de la Porte and P. Pochet (eds.), *Building Social Europe through the Open Method of Co-ordination* (pp. 251–83). Brussels: P. I. E.-Peter Lang.

Andrietti, V. (2001), 'Occupational Pensions and Interfirm Job Mobility in the European Union. Evidence from the ECHP Survey', Working Paper No. 5/01. Turin: Center for Research on Pensions and Welfare Policies.

Aproberts, L. and Reynaud, E. (1992), *Les systèmes de retraite à l'étranger, Etats-Unis, Allemagne, Royaume-Uni*, Paris: IRES.

Arcq, E. and Pochet, P. (2002), 'UNICE and CEEP in 2001: Changes in prospect?', in E. Gabaglio and R. Hoffmann (eds.), *European Trade Union Yearbook 2001*, (pp. 205–22). Brussels: Institut Syndical Européen (European Trade Union Institute).

Attanasio, O. (1999). 'Consumption', in J. B. W. Taylor and M. Woodford (eds.), *Handbook of Macroeconomics, Vol. 1B* (pp. 741–812). Amsterdam: Elsevier Science.

Auer, P. (2000), *Employment Revival in Europe. Labour Market Success in Austria, Denmark, Ireland and the Netherlands*, Geneva: ILO.

Babeau, A. (1997), 'Problèmes posés par l'introduction des fonds de pension en France', in MIRE, Rencontres et Recherches (ed.), *Comparer les systèmes de protection sociale en Europe du sud, vol. 3: Recontres de Florences* (pp. 293–306). Paris: MIRE.

Baldwin, P. (1990), *The Politics of Social Solidarity: Class Bases of the European Welfare State, 1875–1975*, Cambridge: Cambridge University Press.

Banks, J. and Emmerson, C. (1999), *UK Annuitants*. Briefing Note No. 5, London: Institute for Fiscal Studies.

—— (2000), 'Public and Private Pension Spending: Principles, Practice and the Need for Reform', *Fiscal Studies*, 21: 1, 1–64.

Banque Centrale Européenne (BCE). (2000), 'Le vieillissement de la population et la politique budgétaire dans la zone euro', *Bulletin mensuel de la BCE*, July: 59–72.

Barr, N. (2002), 'Reforming Pensions: Myths, Truths, and Policy Choices', *International Social Security Review*, 55: 3–36.

Beau, P. (ed.) (1995), *L'Ouvre collective, 50 ans de sécurité sociale*, Paris: Espace Social Européen.

Berge, A. (1999), ' "People's Pensioner" in Sweden 1914–1954: On the Changing Moral Content of a Social Category', *Scandinavian Journal of History*, 24: 267–80.

Bettendorf, L. J. H., Bovenberg, A. L., and Broer, D. P. (2000), 'De gevolgen van de vergrijzing voor de economische ontwikkeling in Nederland', *OCFEB Studies in Economic Policy*, No. 3. Rotterdam: OCFEB.

Beveridge, W. H. (1909), *Unemployment: A Problem of Industry*, London: Longmans.

—— (1942), *Social Insurance and Allied Services* (usually known as *The Beveridge Report*), London: HMSO.

—— (1948), *Voluntary Action*, London: Allen and Unwin.

BIT (Bureau International du Travail). (1999), *Réforme des retraites et concertation sociale* (ed. Emmanuel Reynaud), Geneva: Bureau International du Travail.

Blackburn, R. (2000), 'The New Collectivism: Pension Reform, Grey Capitalism, and Complex Socialism', *New Left Review*, 233 (January/February): 3–65.

—— (2002), *Banking on Death or Investing in Life: the History and Future of Pensions*, London: Verso.

Blundell, R. and Johnson, P. (1998), 'Pensions and Labor Market Participation in the UK', *American Economic Review*, 88/2: 168–72.

Boehner, J. A. (2002), 'Introduction of the Pension Security Act', *Congressional Record—Extension of Remarks* 148 (15 February): E174.

Boeri, T., Borsch-Supan, A., and Tabellini, G. (2001), 'Would You Like to Shrink the Welfare State? The Opinions of European Citizens', *Economic Policy*, 16: 7–50.

Bohn, H. (1998), 'Social Security Reform and Financial Markets', in *Social Security Reform: Links to Saving, Investment, and Growth*, Boston: Federal Reserve Bank of Boston.

Bolkenstein, F. (2000), *Integration of Financial Markets in Europe*, Brussels: DG Single Market, European Commission.

—— (2001), 'Defusing Europe's Pensions Timebomb', Speech to the European Commission, 6 February (2001), Available online at: http://europa.eu.int/comm/internal_market/en/speeches/spch52.htm.

Bonoli, G. (1997), 'Pension politics in France: Patterns of Co-operation and Conflict in Two Recent Reforms', *West European Politics*, 20/4: 160–81.

—— (2000), *The Politics of Pension Reform: Institutions and Policy Change in Western Europe*, Cambridge: Cambridge University Press.

Bonoli, G. (2001), 'Political Institutions, Veto Points and the Process of Welfare State Adaptation', in P. Pierson (ed.), *The New Politics of the Welfare State*, Oxford: Oxford University Press.

—— and Palier, B. (1996), 'Reclaiming Welfare: The Politics of French Social Protection Reform', *South European Society and Politics*, 1: 240–59.

—— ——*a* (2000), 'From the Cradle to . . . Where? Current Pension Policy Trends in Western Europe', *Yearbook of European Administrative History*, 12.

—— ——*b* (2000), 'Pension Reforms and the Expansion of Private Pensions in Western Europe', *Yearbook of European Administrative History*, 12: 153–74.

Bos, E., Vu, M. T., Massiah, E., and Bulatao, R. O. (1994), *World Population Projections, 1994–95 Edition: Estimates and Projections with Related Demographic Statistics*, Baltimore, MD: John Hopkins University Press.

Bosco, A. (2000), ' "Vers une remise en cause des systèmes nationaux de protection sociale?", observations sur la jurisprudence récente de la Cour de Justice', *Problématiques européennes No. 7*. Paris: Groupement d'études et de recherches Notre Europe.

Bovenberg, A. L. (2001), *Hoe houden we de Pensioenpolder Droog?*, OCFEP Research Memorandum (0106), Rotterdam: Erasmus Universiteit.

—— and Meijdam, L. (2001), 'The Dutch Pension System', in A. H. Börsch-Supan and M. Miegel (eds.), *Pension Reform in Six Countries*, (pp. 39–67). Berlin: Springer.

Bozec, G. and Mays, M. (2001), *Pension Reform in France. Public Participation and the Pension Policy Process: The Citizen and Pension Reform (PEN-REF) Report D2-France*, Vienna: ICCR (Interdisciplinary Centre for Comparative Research in the Social Sciences).

Brewer, M., Clark, T., and Wakefield, M. (2002), 'Five Years of Social Security in the UK', Working Paper No. 02/12. London: Institute for Fiscal Studies.

Brooks, R., Regan, S., and Robinson, P. (2002), *A New Contract for Retirement*, London: Institute of Public Policy Research.

Brunhes, B. (1992), *Rapport sur les retraites*, Paris: Senat.

Budd, A. and Campbell, N. (1998), 'The Roles of the Public and Private Sectors in the UK Pension System', in M. Feldstein (ed.), *Privatizing Social Security* (pp. 99–127). National Bureau of Economic Research, Chicago: Chicago University Press.

Bundesministerium für Arbeit und Sozialordnung (BMA) (ed.) (2001), *Sozialbudget 2000—Tabellenauszug*, Berlin: BMA.

Byrne, J. and Davis, E. P. (2002), 'A Comparison of Balance Sheet Structures in Major EU Countries', *National Institute Economic Review*, 180: 83–94.

Caisse de Pensions et de Secours (CPS) (2001), *Des pensions sûres et viables, Rapport du Comité de la protection sociale sur l'évolution à venir de la protection sociale*, June (2001), Brussels : EU.

—— and Le Comité de Politique Economique (CPE). (2001), *Qualité et viabilité des pensions, Rapport conjoint du Comité de protection sociale et du Comité de politique économique sur les objectifs et méthodes de travail dans le domaine des pensions: application de la méthode ouverte de coordination*. No. 10672/01 ECOFIN 198 SOC 272, Novembre 2001. Brussels: EU.

Campbell, J. Y. and Viceira, L. (2002), *Strategic Asset Allocation: Portfolio Choice for Long-Term Investors*, Oxford: Oxford University Press.

Canada Pension Plan Investment Board (CPPIB). (2001), *Canada Pension Plan Investment Board Annual Report 2001*, Toronto, ON: CPP Investment Board.

Carey, D. (2002), 'Coping with Population Ageing in the Netherlands', OECD Economic Department Working Papers No. 325. Paris: OECD.

Cavanaugh, F. X. (1998), 'Discussion of Public Investment in Private Markets', in R. D. Arnold, A. J. Graetz, and A. H. Munnell (eds.), *Framing the Social Security Debate: Values, Politics and Economics* (pp. 319–29). Washington, DC: Brookings Institution Press for the National Academy of Social Insurance.

Centre Européen des Entreprises à Participation Publique (CEEP) (2001), *Opinion on "The Future Evolution of Social Protection from a Long-term Point of View: Safe and Sustainable Pensions"*, CEEP 2001/AVIS 13, 13 June (2001), Brussels: CEEP.

Cerny, P. G. (1997), 'International finance and the Erosion of Capitalist Diversity', in C. Crouch and W. Streeck (eds.), *Political Economy of Modern Capitalism* (pp. 173–80). London: Sage.

Chand, S. K. and Jaeger, A. (1996), *Aging Populations and Public Pension Schemes*, Washington, DC: International Monetary Fund.

Charpentier, F. (1997). *Retraites et fonds de pension, l'état de la question en France et à l'étranger*, 2nd edn, Paris: Economica.

Charpin, J.-M. (1999), *L'avenir de nos retraites. Commissariat général du Plan*, Paris: La Documentation Française.

Chassard, Y. (2001), 'European Integration and Social Protection: From the Spaak Report to the Open Method of Co-ordination', in D. G. Mayes, J. Berghman, and R. Salais (eds.), *Social Exclusion and European Policy* (pp. 231–321). Cheltenham: Edward Elgar Publishing.

Choi, J., Laibson, D., Madrian, B. C., and Metrick, A. (2001), 'The Path of Least Resistance in 401(K) Plans', NBER Working Paper No. w8655. Cambridge, MA: National Bureau of Economic Research.

Chomsky, N. (2000), *New Horizons in the Study of Language and Mind*, Cambridge: Cambridge University Press.

Clark, G. L. (1993), *Pensions and Corporate Restructuring in American Industry: A Crisis of Regulation*, Baltimore: Johns Hopkins University Press.

—— (2000), *Pension Fund Capitalism*, Oxford: Oxford University Press.

—— (2001), 'The Cocabulary of Europe: Code Words for the New Millennium', *Environment and Planning D: Society and Space*, 19: 697–717.

—— (2002), 'Pension Systems: A Comparative Perspective', in Lazonick, W. (ed.), *The International Encyclopedia of Business and Management: IEBM Handbook of Economics* (pp. 5194–204). London: Thompson.

—— (2003), *European Pensions & Global Finance*, Oxford: Oxford University Press.

—— and Bennett, P. (2001), 'Dutch Sector-wide Supplementary Pensions: Fund governance, European Competition Policy, and the Geography of Finance', *Environment and Planning A*, 33(1): 27–48.

—— and Marshall, J. (2002), 'Decision-making: models of Real World Expertise.' Working Papers in Economic Geography No. 02–04. Oxford: School of Geography and the Environment, Oxford University.

—— and Tracey, P. (2003), *Global and Regional Competitiveness*, forthcoming.

—— and Wojcik, D. (2003), 'An economic geography & global finance: Annals, Association of American Geographics 93:450–67.

Clark, T. (2001), 'Recent Pensions Policy and the Pension Credit', Briefing Note No. 17. London: Institute for Fiscal Studies.

—— (2002), 'Rewarding Saving and Alleviating Poverty?', Briefing Note No. 22. London: Institute for Fiscal Studies.

Claus, J. and Thomas, J. (2001), 'Equity Premia as Low as Three Percent? Evidence from Analysts' Earnings Forecasts for Domestic and International Stock Markets', *Journal of Finance*, 56: 1629–66.

Commission of the European Communities (CEC) (1997), 'Les retraites complémentaires dans le marché unique—Livre vert', Communication No. (1997) 283, 10 June 1997. Brussels: Commission of the European Communities.

—— (1999*a*), 'Une stratégie concertée pour moderniser la protection sociale', Communication No. (99) 347, 14 July 1999. Brussels: Commission of the European Communities.

—— (1999*b*), 'Vers un marché unique pour les retraites complémentaires—Résultats de la consultation relative au Livre vert sur les retraites complémentaires dans le Marché Unique', Communication No. (1999) 134. Brussels: Commission of the European Communities.

—— (1999*c*), 'Towards a Europe for all ages: promoting prosperity and intergenerational solidarity', Communication No. (1999) 221, May 1999. Brussels: Commission of the European Communities.

—— (2000), 'Communication from the Commission to the Council, to the European Parliament and to the Economic and Social Committee. The Future Evolution of Social Protection from a Long-term Point of View: Safe and Sustainable Pensions', Communication No. COM (2000) 622 Final. 11th October. Brussels: European Union.

—— (2000*a*), 'L'évolution à venir de la protection sociale dans une perspective à long terme: Des pensions sûres et viables', Communication No. (2000) 622, 11th October 2000. Brussels: Commission of the European Communities.

—— (2000*b*), 'Proposal for a directive on the activities of institutions for occupational retirement provision', Communication No. (2000) 507, 11 October 2000. Brussels: Commission of the European Communities.

—— (2001*a*), 'Réforme économique: rapport sur le fonctionnement des marchés communautaires des produits et des capitaux', Communication No. (2001) 736, 7 December 2001. Brussels: Commission of the European Communities.

—— (2001*b*), 'Une approche intégrée au service des stratégies nationales visant à garantir des pensions sûres et viables', Communication No. (2001) 362, 3 July 2001. Brussels: Commission of the European Communities.

—— (2001*c*), 'New Labour Markets, Open for All, with Access for All', Communication No. (2001) 11628, February 2001. Brussels: Commission of the European Communities.

—— (2001*d*), 'European Commission Reforms of Pension Systems in the EU—an Analysis of Policy Options. *European Economy*, 73: 189–94.

—— (2002*a*), 'Plan d'action de la Commission en matière de compétences et de mobilité', Communication No. 72, 13 February 2002. Brussels: Commission of the European Communities.

—— (2002*b*), 'Co-ordination of Economic Policies in the EU: A Presentation of Key Features of the Main Procedures', Euro Papers No. 45, July 2002. Brussels: Commission of the European Communities.

Commission to Strengthen Social Security. (2001), 'Strengthening Social Security and Creating Personal Wealth for All Americans', *Final Report of the Commission* (21 December, Washington, DC: Social Security Administration.

Conseil d'orientation des Retraites (COR). (2001), *Retraites: Renouveler le contrat social entre les générations*, Premier rapport du COR (Paris: La Documentation Française).

Cottave, R. (1992), *Rapport sur les retraites*, Paris: Senat.

Crossman, R. H. S. (1972), *The Politics of Pensions*, Eleanor Rathbone Memorial Lecture, Liverpool: Liverpool University Press.

Crouch, C. and Streeck, W. (1997), 'Introduction: The Future of Capitalist Diversity', in C. Crouch and W. Streeck (eds.), *Political Economy of Modern Capitalism* (pp. 1–18). London: Sage.

De Laat, E. A., Van Der Ven, M., and Canoy, M. (2000), *Solidariteit, Keuzevrijheid en Transparantie: De Toekomst van de Nederlandse Markt Voor Oudedagsvoorzieningen.* CPB Special Publication 23. Den Haag: Centraal Planbureau.

D'amato, M and Gelasso, V. (2002), 'Assessing the Political Sustainability of Parametric Social Security Reforms: the Case of Italy', CEPR Discussion Paper 3439. London: Centre for Economic Policy Research.

Davanne, O. (1998), *Retraites et Épargne*, Conseil d'analyse économique No. 7. Paris: La Documentation Française.

Davis, E. P. and Steil, B. (2001), *Institutional Investors*, Cambridge, MA: MIT Press.

Deacon, B. (1995), 'The Globalisation of Social Policy and the Socialisation of Global Politics', in J. Baldock and M. May. (eds.), *Social Policy Review Vol. 7.* Social Policy Association.

Dehousse, R. (2003), *La méthode ouverte de coordination: convergence et politiques dans I'UE*, Paris: L'Harmattan, forthcoming.

De La Porte, C. (2002*a*), 'Is the Open Method of Coordination Appropriate for Organising Activities at European Level in Sensitive Policy Areas?', *European Law Journal*, 8/1: 38–58.

—— —— (2002*b*), 'The Soft Open Method of Co-ordination in Social Protection', in E. Gabaglio and R. Hoffmann (eds.), *European Trade Union Yearbook 2001* (pp. 339–63). Brussels: Institut syndical européen.

—— and Pochet, P. (eds.) (2002*a*), *Building Social Europe through the Open Method of Co-ordination*, Brussels: P. I. E.-Peter Lan.

—— (2002*b*), 'Public Pension Reform: European Actors, Discourses and Outcomes', in C. de la Porte and P. Pochet (eds.), *Building Social Europe through the Open Method of Co-ordination* (pp. 223–50). Brussels: P. I.E.-Peter Lang.

De Ryck, K. (1996), *European Pension Funds: Their impact on European Capital Market and Competitiveness*, Report commissioned by the European Federation for Retirement Provision. Brussels: EFRP.

Department for Work and Pensions. (2002*a*), *The Pension Credit: Long-Term Projections*, London: Department for Work and Pensions.

—— (2002*b*), *The Government's Expenditure Plans 2002–03 to 2003–04*, Social Security Departmental Report Cm. 5424. London: Department for Work and Pensions.

Department of Social Security (1985), *Reform of Social Security: A Programme for Action*, Cm. 9691. London: HMSO.

Department of Social Security (1998), *A New Contract for Welfare: Partnership in Pensions*, Cm. (4179). London: HMSO.

—— (2001), *Income Related Benefits: Estimates of Take-up in 1999–2000*. London: HMSO.

Diamond, P. A. (1998), 'Economics of Social Security Reform: An Overview', in R. D. Arnold, M. J. Graetz, and A. H. Munnell (eds.), *Framing the Social Security Debate: Values, Politics and Economics*, Washington, DC: Brookings Institution Press for the National Academy of Social Insurance.

Diamond, P. A. (1999), *Issues in Privatizing Social Security*, Cambridge, MA: The MIT Press for the National Academy of Social Insurance.

—— (2001), 'Social Security Reform with a Focus on the Netherlands', *De Economist*, 149/1: 1–12.

Dilnot, A., Disney, R. Johnson, P., and Whitehouse, E. (1994), *Pensions Policy in Britain: An Economic Analysis*, London: Institute for Fiscal Studies.

Dimson, E., Marsh, P. and Staunton, M. (2002), *Triumph of the Optimists: 101 Years of Global Investment Returns*, Princeton: Princeton University Press.

Disney, R. (1996), *Can We Afford to Grow Older? A Perspective on the Economics of Ageing*, Cambridge, MA: MIT Press.

—— (1998), 'Social Security in the UK: A Voluntary Privatization', Social Reform: International Comparison's Conference. 16–17, March Rome.

—— (2000), 'Crises in Public Pension Programmes in OECD: What are the Reform Options?', *Economic Journal*, 110: F1–23.

—— and Emmerson, C. (2002), 'Choice of Pension Scheme and Job Mobility in Britain', IFS Working Paper No. 02/09. London: Institute for Fiscal Studies.

—— —— and Smith, S. (2002), 'Pension Reform and Economic Performance in Britain in the 1980s and 1990s', in R. Blundell, D. Card, and R. B. Freeman (eds.), *Seeking a Premier League Economy*, Chicago: University of Chicago Press.

—— —— and Tanner, S. (1999), 'Partnership in Pensions: An Assessment', Commentary No. 78. London: Institute for Fiscal Studies.

—— —— and Wakefield, M. (2001), 'Pension Reform and Saving in Britain', *Oxford Review of Economic Policy*, 17/1: 70–94.

—— and Johnson, P. (eds.) (2001), *Pension Systems and Retirement Incomes across OECD Countries*, Aldershot: Edward Elgar.

—— and Smith, S. (2000), 'The Abolition of the Earnings Rule for UK Pensioners', IFS Working Paper No. 00/13. London: Institute for Fiscal Studies.

—— and Whitehouse, E. (1992), *The Personal Pension Stampede*, London: Institute for Fiscal Studies.

Dore, R. (2000), *Stock Market Capitalism: Welfare Capitalism. Japan and Germany Versus the Anglo-Saxons*, Oxford: Oxford University Press.

Doublet, J. (1962), 'Les regimes complementaires a l'etranger', *Droit Sociale*, 25/7–8: 464–73.

Drees, W. B. (1987), *Gespiegeld in de tijd: De aow in de toekomst: Rapport van de commissie financiering oudedagsvoorziening*. Den Haag: Commissie Financiering Oudedagsvoorziening.

Drucker, P. F. (1976), *The Unseen Revolution: How Pension Fund Socialism Came to America*, New York: Harper Trade.

Dudek, C. and Omtzigt, P. (2001), 'The Role of Brussels in National Pension Reforms', EUI Working Papers No. 47. Florence: European University Institute.

Dumons, B. and Pollet, G. (1994), *L'État et Les Retraites: Genèse D'une Politique* (Paris: Belin).

Dupont, G. and Sterdyniak, H. (2000), *Quel Avenir Pour Nos Retraites?* (Paris: La Découverte, Collection Repères).

Ebbinghaus, B. (2000), 'Any Way Out of "Exit from Work". Reversing the Entrenched Pathways of Early Retirement', in F. W. Scharf and V. A. Schmidt (eds.), *Welfare and Work in the Open Economy* vol. 2 (pp. 511–53). Oxford: Oxford University Press.

Ecofin Council. (2001), 'Key Issues Paper on the 2001 Broad Economic Policy Guidelines' No. 7001/01 ECOFIN 77 SOC 113, 12 March. Brussels: EC.

Economic Policy Committee (EPC). (2000), 'Progress Report to the ECOFIN Council on the Impact of Ageing Populations on Public Pension Systems', No. EPC/ECFIN/581/00—Rev. 1, 6 November 2000. Brussels: EPC.

—— (2001), 'Budgetary Challenges Posed by Ageing Populations: The Impact of Public Spending on Pensions, Heath and Long Term Care for the Elderly and Possible Indicators of Long Term Sustainability of Public Finances', No. EPC/ECFIN/655/01-EN final, 24 October 2001. Brussels: EPC.

—— (2002), *Annual Report on Structural Reforms 2002.* No. ECFIN/EPC/117/02-EN, 5 March 2002. Brussels: EPC.

—— EFC and Commission (2001), *Report from the Commission and the (ECOFIN) Council to the European Council on the Contribution of Public Finances to Growth and Employment: Improving Quality and Sustainability,* No. UEM 55/ECOFIN 73/SOC 109, 23–24 March 2001. Stockholm: EPC.

Edey, M. and Simon, J. (1998), 'Australia's Retirement Income System', in M. Feldstein (ed), *Privatizing Social Security* (pp. 63–97). Chicago: University of Chicago Press.

Elmér, Å. (1960), *Folkpensioneringen i Sverige* (People's Pensions in Sweden), Lund: Gleerups.

Emmerson, C. (2001), 'Should We Let People Opt Out of the Basic State Pension?', IFS Election Briefing No. 12. London: Institute for Fiscal Studies.

—— Frayne, C. and Goodman, A. (2000), 'Pressures in UK healthcare: Challenges for the NHS', Commentary No. 81. London: Institute for Fiscal Studies.

—— and Tanner, S. (1999), 'The Government's Proposals for Stakeholder Pensions', Briefing Note No.1. London: Institute for Fiscal Studies.

—— —— (2000), 'A Note on the Tax Treatment of Private Pensions and Individual Savings Accounts', *Fiscal Studies,* 21: 65–74.

Eriksen, T. and Palmer, E. (1994), 'Deterioration of the Swedish Pension Model', in J. Hills, J. Ditch, and H. Glennerster (eds.), *Beveridge and Social Security: An International Retrospective,* Oxford: Clarendon Press.

Esping-Andersen, G. (1990), *Three Worlds of Welfare Capitalism,* Princeton, NJ: Princeton University Press.

—— (1996), *Welfare States in Transition, National Adaptations in Global Economies,* London: Sage.

—— (1999), *Social Foundations of Post-Industrial Economies,* Oxford: Oxford University Press.

—— Gallie, D., Hemerijck, A., and Myles, J. (2001), 'New Welfare Architecture for Europe? Lessons from Canada', Report to the Belgium Presidency of the European Union. Brussels.

—— —— —— —— (2002), *Why We Need a New Welfare State,* Oxford: Oxford University Press.

États Generaux de la Sécurité Sociale. (1987), *Rapport du comité des sages.* Ministère des Affaires Sociales. Paris: La Documentation Française.

European Round Table of Industrialists (ERT). (2000), *Pensions Schemes that Europe Can Really Afford*, A report by the European Round Table of Industrialists chaired by Carlo De Benedetti. Brussels: ERT.

—— (2001), *Monitoring "Slow" Pension Reforms in Europe: Progress in Pension Reforms Following "Pension Schemes that Europe Can Really Afford"* (January 2000). Brussels: ERT.

Eurostat. (2001), 'Regional Labour Force in the EU: Recent Patterns and Future Perspectives', *Statistics in Focus*, 2001/02: 1–8.

Fama, E. and French, K. R. (2002), 'The Equity Premium', *Journal of Finance*, 57: 637–59.

Farnetti, R. (1996), 'Le marché financier et les multinationales brittaniques: Royaume uni ou desuni?', *Economies et Sociétés*, 9/6: 153–91.

Feldstein, M. (2002), 'Introduction: An American Perspective', in M. Feldstein and H. Siebert (eds.), *Social Security Pension Reform in Europe* (pp. 1–9). Chicago: University of Chicago Press.

—— and Liebman, J. B. (2001), 'Social Security'. NBER Working Paper 8451. Cambridge, MA: National Bureau of Economics Research.

—— and Samwick, A. A. (1998*a*), 'The Transition Path in Privatizing Social Security', in M. S. Feldstein (ed.), *Privatizing Social Security* (pp. 215–60). Chicago: University of Chicago Press.

—— —— (1998*b*), 'Potential Effects of Two Per Cent Personal Retirement Accounts', *Tax Notes*, 79/5: 615–20.

—— and Siebert, H. (eds.). (2002), *Social Security Pension Reform in Europe*, Chicago: University of Chicago Press.

Fiedler, M. (1996), 'La "rationalisation sociale" de l'entreprise', in MIRE, Rencontres et Recherches (ed.), *Comparer les systemes de protection sociale en Europe, vol. 2, Rencontres de Berlin* (pp. 87–115). Paris: MIRE.

Fitoussi, J. P. and Le Cacheux, J. (2002), *Rapport sur l'État de l'Union européenne 2002*, Paris: Fayard/Presses de Sciences Po.

Fox, L. and Palmer, E. (1999), Lativan Pension Reform. Social Protection Paper No. 9922. Washington, DC: The World Bank.

Friot, B. (1994), Aux origines interprofessionnelles des régimes de retraite complémentaires français: la naissance de l'AGIRC. *La revue de l'IRES* (été): 105–21.

—— (1998), *Puissances du salariat, emploi et protection sociale à la française* (Paris: La Dispute).

Gamet, L. (2000), 'Towards a Definition of "Flexibility" in Labour Law?', in B. Stråth (ed.), *After Full Employment: Euopean Discourses on Work and Flexibility* (pp. 197–221). Brussels: Peter Laing.

Gaxie, D., Collovald, A., Gaïti, B., Lehingue, P., and Poirmeur, Y. (1990), *Le 'social' transfiguré: Sur la representation politique des préoccupations 'sociales'* (Paris: PUF).

Geanakoplos, J., Mitchell, O. S., and Zeldes, S. P. (1998), 'Would a Privatized Social Security System Really Pay a Higher Return?', in R. D. Arnold, M. J. Graetz, and A. H. Munnell (eds.), *Framing the Social Security Debate: Values, Politics and Economics* (pp. 137–56). Washington, DC: Brookings Institution Press for the National Academy of Social Insurance.

Gillion, C., Turner, J., and Latulippe, D. (eds.) (2000), *Social Security Pensions: Development and Reform*, Geneva: International Labour Office.

Ginn, J. (2001), 'From Security to Risk: Pension Privatisation and Gender Inequality', Catalyst Working Paper, December 2001. London: Catalyst.

—— Street, D., and Arber, S. (2001), *Women, Work and Pensions: International Issues and Prospects*, Buckingham: Open University Press.

Gough, I. (2000), *Global Capital, Human Needs and Social Policies: Selected Essays*, Basingstoke: Palgrave.

Government Actuary's Department. (1999), *National Insurance Fund Long Term Financial Estimates:* July. London: HMSO.

—— (2000), *National Insurance Fund Long Term Financial Estimates*: January. London: HMSO.

—— (2001), Occupational Pension Schemes 1995—Tenth Survey by the Government Actuary. London: HMSO.

Government Report. (2001), *Redovisning av AP-fondernas verksamhet år 2001.* (Report on the activities of the AP-funds in the year 2001.) Regeringens Skrivelse 2001/02: 180. Stockholm: The Swedish Government.

Greenspan, A. (1999), 'On investing the Trust Fund in Equities', Testimony before the Subcommittee on Finance and Hazardous Materials, Committee on Commerce, United States House of Representatives (3 March).

Grip, G. (2001), 'Social, avtalad och privat försäkring i Sverige under 1990-talet (Social, agreement-linked and private insurance in Sweden in the 1990s)'. In J. Fritzell and J. Palme (ed.), *Välfärdens finansiering och fördelning* (The Financing and Distribution of Welfare). Reports of the Government Commissions (SOU) 2001: 57. Stockholm: Fritzes.

Gruber, J. and Wise, D. (eds.) (1999), *Social Security and Retirement around the World National Bureau of Economic Research*, Chicago: University of Chicago Press.

Guillemard, A. -M. (1980), *La Viellesse et L'état* (Paris: PUF).

—— (1986), *Le Déclin Du Social* (Paris: PUF).

Gustman, A. L. and Steinmeier, T. L. (1993), 'Pension Portability and Labor Mobility: Evidence from the Survey of Income and Program Participation', *Journal of Public Economics*, 50: 299–323.

Hall, P. and Soskice, D. (eds.) (2001), *The Varieties of Capitalism: The Institutional Foundations of Comparative Advantage*, Oxford: Oxford University Press.

Hannah, L. (1986), *Inventing Retirement*, Cambridge: Cambridge University Press.

Harris, J. (1977), *William Beveridge: A Biography*, Oxford: Clarendon Press.

Haverland, M. (2001), 'Another Dutch Miracle? Explaining Dutch and German Pension Trajectories', *Journal of European Social Policy*, 11/4: 308–23.

Heclo, H. (1974), *Modern Social Politics in Britain and Sweden*, London: Yale University Press.

Hennock, E.P. (1987), *British Social Reform and German Procedures*, Oxford: Clarendon Press.

Hinrichs, K. (1998), 'Reforming the Public Pension Scheme in Germany: The End of the Traditional Consensus?', Bremen ZeS-Arbeitspapier No. 11/98. Bremen: Zentrum für Sozialpolitik, Universität Bremen.

—— (2001), 'Elephants on the Move: Patterns of Public Pension Reform in OECD Countries', in S. Leibfried (ed.), *Welfare State Futures*, Cambridge: Cambridge University Press.

HM Treasury. (1999), Economic and Fiscal Strategy Report, London: HMSO.

Hutton, W. (1995), *The State We're In* (London: Jonathon Cape).
—— (2002), *The World We're In*, London: Little Brown.
HypoVereinsbank. (2001), 'Age Wave: zur Demographieanfälligkeit von Aktienmärkten', *Policy-Brief*, 4: 1–8.
Ibbotson Associates, Inc. (2001), *Stocks, Bonds, Bills, and Inflation 2001 Yearbook*, Chicago: Ibbotson Associates.
Immergut, E. (1992), *Health Politics. Interests and Institutions in Western Europe*, Cambridge: Cambridge University Press.
Inland Revenue and Department for Work and Pensions (2002), Modernising Annuities; A consultation document, London: Inland Revenue.
Institut National de la Statistique et des Études Économiques (INSEE). (1990), *L'avenir des retraites* (Paris: La Documentation Française.
—— (1999), *Données sociales, la société française*, Paris: La Documentation Française.
—— (2001), *Revenus et patrimoine des ménages*. Paris: La Documentation Française.
Jansweijer, R. M. A. (1999), 'Pensioensystemen vergeleken: wie draagt welke risico's', in J. B. Kuné (ed.), *Studies Naar Defined Benefit- En Defined Contribution- Regelingen*. The Hague: Stichting Pensioenwetenschap.
Johnson, P. (1994), 'The Employment and Retirement of Older Men in England and Wales, 1881–1981', *Economic History Review*, 47/1: 106–28.
Johnson, P., Disney, R., and Stears, G. (1996), *Pensions 2000 and Beyond. Vol. 2: Analysis of Trends and Options*, London: Retirement Income Inquiry.
Jorgenson, D. W. (2001), 'Information Technology and the US Economy. *American Economic Review*, 91: 1–32.
Kahlka, P. (2001), *Les retraites au péril du libéralisme* (Paris: Syllepse).
Kangas, O. and Palme, J. (1991), 'The Public–Private Mix in Pension Policy' *International Journal of Sociology*, 20: 78–116.
—— —— (1993), 'Eroding Statism? Labour Market Benefits and the Challenges to the Scandinavian Welfare States', in R. Erikson, E. J. Hansen, S. Ringen, and H. Uusitalo (eds.), *Scandinavian Welfare Trends* (pp. 3–24). New Jersey: M. E. Sharpe.
—— —— (1996), 'The Development of Occupational Pensions in Finland and Sweden: Class Politics and Institutional Feedbacks', in M. Shalev (ed.), *The Privatization of Social Policy* (pp. 211–40). London: Macmillan.
King, D. (1998), *In the Name of Liberalism*, Oxford: Oxford University Press.
Kohl, J. (1988), 'Alterssicherung in Westeuropa: Struktur und Wirkungen', in M. G. Schmidt (ed.), *Staatstätigkeit. international und historich Vergleichende analysen*, Politische Vierteljahrschrift, Sonderheft 19, Opladen: Westdeutscher Verlag, 221–50.
—— (2002), 'Die deutsche Rentenreform im europäischen Kontext', in Verband Deutscher. Rentenversicherungsträger (ed.), *Offene Koordinierung Der Alterssicherung in Der Europäischen Union* Frankfurt: DRV-Schriften 34: 27–31.
Kohli, M., Guillemard, A.-M., Van Gunsteren, H., and Rein, M. (1991), *Time for Retirement*, Cambridge: Cambridge University Press.
Korpi, W. (1980), 'Social Policy and Distributional Conflict in the Capitalist Democracies. A Preliminary Comparative Framework', *West European Politics*, 3/3: 296–316.

—— and Palme, J. (1998), 'The paradox of redistribution and Strategies of Equality: Welfare State Institutions, Inequality and Poverty in the Western Countries', *American Sociological Review*, 63/5: 661–87.

—— —— (2003), 'New Politics and Class Politics in the Context of Austerity and Globalization: Welfare State Regress in 18 Countries, 1975–95', *American Political Science Review* 97: 3 September.

Labour Party. (1957), *National Superannuation*, London: Labour Party.

—— (1963), *New Frontiers for Social Security*, London: Labour Party.

Laroque, P. (1946), 'Le plan français de sécurité sociale', *Revue française du travail*, 1: 9–20.

—— (1962), *Haut Comité Consultatif de la Population, Rapport de la Commission d'études des problèmes de la vieillesse* (colloquially called 'Rapport Laroque'). Paris: La Documentation Française.

Levy, J. (1999), 'Vice into Virtue? Progressive Politics and Welfare Reform in Continental Europe', *Politics and Society*, 27/2: 239–74.

—— (2001), 'Partisan Politics and Welfare Adjustment: The Case of France', *Journal of European Public Policy*, 8/2: 265–85.

Lhernould, J.-P. (2000), 'Nouvelles dérives libérales de la CJCE en matière de retraites complémentaires—CJCE 12 septembre 2000', *Droit Social*, 12 (December): 1114–23.

Lion, H. (1962), 'La convention du 14 mars 1947 et son evolution', *Droit Social*, 25/7–8: 396–403.

Longergan, E. and Hanson, T. (2002), *The European Discount*, London: Global Economic Research, Cazenove.

Lordon, F. (2000), *Fonds de pension, piège à cons?* Paris: Raison d'agir.

Lyon-Caen, G. (1962), 'La co-ordination des regimes complementaires de retraites', *Droit Social*, 25/7–8: 457–63.

McConnell, P. (ed.) (2002), *Pro Forma Earnings: A Critical Perspective*, New York: Bear Stearns.

Macnicol, J. (1994), 'Beveridge and Old Age', in J. Hills, J. Ditch, and H. Glennerster (eds.), *Beveridge and Social Security: An International Retrospective* (pp. 73–97). Oxford, Clarendon Press.

—— (1998), *The Politics of Retirement in Britain, 1978–1948*. Cambridge: Cambridge University Press.

Mantel, J. (2000), 'Demographics and the Funded Pension System', *Debtquity*, London: Merrill Lynch & Co.

—— (2001), *Progress Report European Pension Reforms—Pension Reform Barometer for Europe*, London: Merril Lynch.

Markowitz, H. (1952), 'Portfolio Selection', *Journal of Finance*, 7: 77–91.

Math, A. (2001*a*), 'Les retraites par répartition dans le collimateur européen? A propos d'un rapport du Comité de politique économique sur l'impact du vieillissement sur les systèmes de retraite'. Working Paper No. 24. Brussels: Observatoire social européen.

—— (2001*b*), *Réformes des retraites et concurrence. Une analyse des rôles et stratégies des acteurs au niveau communautaire* Document de travail (No. 02. 04). Paris: Institut de Recherches Economiques et Sociales.

—— (2001*c*), 'Europe. Défense des intérêts patronaux au niveau européen: le cas des retraites'. *Chronique internationale de l'IRES* No. 72. Paris: Institut de Recherches Economiques et Sociales.

Math, A. and Pochet, P. (2001), 'Les pensions en Europe: Débats, acteurs et méthode', *Revue belge de sécurité sociale*, 2 (June): 345–62.

—— Pegg, J., and Zion, D. (2001), *Accounting Issues: Pension and other Retirement Benefits I*, New York: Bear Stearns.

Metze, M. (1995), *De Stranding*, Nijmegen: SUN.

Miller, D. (2000), *Citizenship and National Identity*, Cambridge: Polity Press.

Ministry of Health and Social Affairs. (1992), *Ett reformerat pensionssystem—Bakgrund, principer och skiss.* (A reformed pension system—Background, principles and outline.) Report from the Government No. 89, Stockholm: Allmänna Förlaget.

Mitchell, O. S. (1998), 'Administrative Costs in Public and Private Retirement Systems', in M. Feldstein (ed.), *Privatizing Social Security* (pp. 403–52). Chicago: University of Chicago Press.

—— and Utkus, S. P. (2002), *Company Stock and Retirement Plan Diversification*, Philadelphia: Pension Research Council, Wharton School, University of Pennsylvania.

Morin, F. (2000), *L'économie française face aux fonds de pension américains, quelles leçons pour le système de retraite?*, Report by Conseil d'analyse économique. Paris: La Documentation Française.

Munnell, A. H. and Pierluigi, B. (1998), Investing the Social Security Trust Funds in Equities. Public Policy Institute, American Association of Retired Persons (AARP), #9802 (March).

—— and Annika, S. (2000), Investment Practices of State and Local Pension Funds: Implications for Social Security Reform. in Olivia S. Mitchell and Edwin C. Hustead (eds.), *Pensions in the Public Sector*. Philadelphia, PA: University of Pennsylvania Press for the Pension Rights Council.

—— —— (2002), '401(K)s and company stock: How can we encourage diversification?' Issue in Brief No. 9. Chestnut Hill, MA: Center for Retirement Research at Boston College.

Murthi, M., Orszag, M., and Orszag, P. R. (1999), 'Administrative Costs and Individual Accounts: Lessons from the U.K. Experience'. Presented at Conference on 'New Ideas about Old Age Security'. The World Bank (February 1999).

Myles, J. (1984), *Old Age in the Welfare State. The Political Economy of Pensions*, Boston: Little Brown.

—— and Pierson, P. (2001), 'The Comparative Political Economy of Pension Reform', in P. Pierson (ed.), *The New Politics of the Welfare State* (pp. 305–33). Oxford: Oxford University Press.

—— and Quadagno, J. (1997), 'Recent Trends in Public Pension Reform: A Comparative View', in K. Banting and R. Broadway (eds.), *Reform of Retirement Income Policy. International and Canadian Perspectives*, Kingston, Ontario: Queen's University, School of Policy Studies.

National Social Insurance Board (RFV). (1999), Statistik Information IS-I 1999, Stockholm: RFV.

Neumann, M. J. M. (1998), 'Ein Einstieg in die Kapitaldeckung der gesetzlichen Rente ist das Gebot der Stunde', *Wirtschaftsdienst*, 78: 259–64.

North, D. C. (1990), *Institutions, Institutional Change and Economic Performance*, Cambridge: Cambridge University Press.

OASDI. (2001), *The 2001 Annual Report of the Board of Trustees of the Federal Old-Age and Survivors Insurance and Disability Insurance Trust Funds.* Washington, DC: US Government Printing Office.

—— (2002), *The 2002 Annual Report of the Board of Trustees of the Federal Old-Age and Survivors Insurance and Disability Insurance Trust Funds.* Washington, DC: US Government Printing Office.

Office for National Statistics. (2001), *Living in Britain: Results from the 2000/01 General Household Survey,* London: HMSO.

Olsen, K. A. and Salisbury, D. L. (1998), *Individual Social Security Accounts: Issues in Assessing Administrative Feasibility and Costs,* Special Report No. SR-34 and EBRI Issue Brief No. 203. Washington, DC: Employee Benefit Research Institute.

O'Reilly, J. and Fagan, C. (eds.) (1998), *Part-Time Prospects: An International Comparison of Part-Time Work in Europe, North-America and the Pacific Rim,* London: Routledge.

Organization for Economic Cooperation and Development (OECD). (1994), *OECD Jobs Study, May 1994,* Paris: OECD.

—— (1988), 'Reforming public pension', *Social Policy Studies* No. 5. Paris: OECD.

—— (1998), *Maintaining Prosperity in an Ageing Society,* Paris: OECD.

—— (2000), *Reforms for an Ageing Society: Social Issues,* Paris: OECD.

—— (2001), *OECD Economic Outlook.* Vol. 70 (December), Annex Table 13.

—— (2002), *Economic Survey: Netherlands,* Paris: OECD.

Orleans, A. (ed.) (1994), *Analyse Economique Des Conventions,* Paris: PUF.

Orloff, A. S. (1991), *The Politics of Pensions: A Comparative Analysis of Britain, Canada and the United-States,* Madison: University of Wisconsin Press.

Orszag, P. (2002), 'House "Enron" Pension Legislation Includes Troubling Provisions That Could Harm Rank-and-File Workers'. Mimeo. Washington DC: Brookings Institution.

Paine, T. H. (1993), 'The Changing Character of Pensions: Where Employers are Headed', in R. V. Burkhauser and D. I. Salisbury (eds.), *Employer Pensions in a Changing Economy* (pp. 33–40). Washington, DC: Employee Benefit Research Institute.

Palier, B. (2002), *Gouverner la sécurité sociale: les réformes du système français de protection sociale depuis 1945* (Paris: PUF).

—— and Bonoli, G. (2000), 'La montée en puissance des fonds de pension.' *L'Année de la régulation,* 4: 209–50.

—— and Viossat, L. C. (2001), *Politiques sociales et mondialisation* (Paris: Éditions Futuribles).

Palme, J. (1990), *Pension Rights in Welfare Capitalism. The Development of Old Age Pensions in 18 OECD Countries 1930–1985.* Dissertation Series No 14. Stockholm: Swedish Institute for Social Research.

—— (ed.) (2001), *Hur blev den stora kompromissen möjlig?* (How was the big compromise possible?), Stockholm: Pensionsforum.

Palmer, E. (2000), The Swedish Pension Reform Model: Framework and Issues. World Bank's Pension Reform Primer Social Protection Discussion Paper No. 0012. Washington, DC: The World Bank.

Pampel, F. C. and Williamson, J. B. (1989), *Age, Class, Politics, and the Welfare State,* New York: Cambridge University Press.

Pastor, L. and Stambaugh, R. F. (2001), 'The Equity Premium and Structural Breaks', *Journal of Finance*, 56: 1207–39.

Pedersen, A. W., Hatland, A., and Øverbye, E. (2001), 'Svarteperspill eller spleiselag?' Mimeo. Oslo: NOVA, Norsk institutt for forskning om oppvekst, velferd og aldring.

Pensioen-& Verzekeringskamer. (2002), *Pensioenmonitor: Niet-financiële gegevens pensioenfondsen* (Appeldorn: PVK).

Pestieau, P. E. (ed.) (1992), 'Public Finance in a World of Transition, Proceedings of the 47th Congress of the International Institute of Public Finance', *Public Finance*, 47 (Supp.): 334–56.

Petersen, C. (1988), 'De AOW in de toekomst', *Economisch Statistische Berichten*, 73: 264–6.

Peterson, P. (1996), *Will America Grow Up Before It Grows Old?*, New York: Random House.

Pierson, P. (1994), *Dismantling the Welfare State? Reagan, Thatcher, and the Politics of Retrenchment*, Cambridge: Cambridge University Press.

—— (1996), 'The New Politics of the Welfare State', *World Politics*, 48/2: 143–79.

—— (ed.) (2001), *The New Politics of the Welfare State*, Oxford: Oxford University Press.

Ploug, N. and Kvist, J. (1996), *Social Security in Europe, Development or Dismantlement?*, The Hague: Kluwer Law International.

Pochet, P. (2002), 'Pensions: avancées substantielles vers un objectif incertain', in C. Degryse and P. Pochet (eds.), *Bilan social de l'Union européenne 2001* (pp. 165–82). Brussels: Institut syndical européen and Observatoire social européen.

Ponds, E. H. M., Bosch, R., Breunesse, E. A., and Willemsen, B. J. (1999), 'Defined Contribution Versus Defined Benefit: pensioenfinanciering tussen keuzevrijheid en risicodeling', in J. B. Kuné (ed.), *Studies Naar Defined Benefit—en Defined Contribution Regelingen* (pp. 28–103). Den Haag: Stichting Pensioenwetenschap.

Premiepensionsmyndigheten (PPM). (2002), '14.1 % valde aktivt i årets premiepensionsval', Pressmeddelande No. 25 (Press release No. 25), 2002-04-23. Stockholm: Premiepensionsmyndigheten.

Radaelli, C. (2000), 'Whither Europeanisation? Concept Stretching and Substantive Change', *European Integration Online Papers (EioP)*, 4 (8) (available online at http://eiop.or.at/eiop/texte/2000-008a.htm).

—— (2002), 'The Code of Conduct Against Harmful Tax Competition: Open coordination method in disguise?', in R. Dehousse (ed.), *La méthode ouverte de coordination; convergence et politiques dans l'UE*, Paris: L'Harmattan, forthcoming.

Rapport au Premier Ministre. (1991), *Livre blanc sur les retraites, garantir l'équité des retraites de demain*, Paris: La Documentation Française.

Remery, C., Henkens, K., Schippers, J., Van Doorne-Huiskes, A., and Ekamper, P. (2001), *Organisaties, Veroudering en management: een onderzoek onder werkgevers*, NIDI-rapport 61. The Hague: Netherlands Interdisciplinary Research Institute (NIDI).

Renard, D. (1994), 'The Relations Between Assistance and Insurance in the Constitution of the French Welfare System' in MIRE Rencontres et. Recherches, *Comparing Social Welfare Systems in Europe, Volume I Oxford Conference* (pp. 93–115) Paris: MIRE.

Report of the Government Commission. (SOU) (1990), *Allmän Pension* (Universal Pension), SOU Report 1990: 76. Stockholm: Allmänna Förlaget.

—— (1994), *Reformerat Pensionssystem* (A Reformed Pension System), SOU Report 1994: 20. Stockholm: Fritzes.

Reynaud, E. (1994), *Les retraites complémentaires en France*, Paris: La Documentation Française.

—— (1996), 'La Banque Mondiale et les retraites: une synthèse de l'approche néolibérale', *Futuribles*, 210: 37–42.

—— (ed.) (1999), *Réforme des retraites et concertation sociale* (Genève: Bureau International du Travail).

—— (2000), 'Introduction and Summary', in E. Reynaud (ed.), *Social Dialogue and Pension Reform* (pp. 1–10). Geneva: International Labor Organisation.

—— and Tamburi, G. (1994), *Les Retraites en France: le rôle des régimes complèmentaires*, Paris: La Documentation Française.

Rhodes, G. (1965), *Public Sector Pensions*, London: Allen and Unwin.

Ritter, G.A. (1986), *Social Welfare in Britain and Germany*, Leamington Spa: Berg.

Rubery, J., Smith, M., and Fagan, C. (1999), *Women's Employment in Europe*, London: Routledge.

Ruellan, R. (1993), 'Retraites: l'impossible réforme est-elle achevée?', *Droit social*, 12: 911–29.

Sachverständigenrat zur Begutachtung der gesamtwirtschaftlichen Entwicklung. (2001), *Jahresgutachten 2001/02: Für Stetigkeit—Gegen Aktionismus* (Stuttgart: Metzger-Poeschel).

Salais, R. (1998), 'A la recherche du fondement conventionnel des institutions', in R. Salais, E. Chatel, and D. Rivaud-Danset (eds.), *Institutions Et Conventions: la Reflexivite de l'action economique* (pp. 255–91). Paris: Édition de l'École des Hautes Études en Sciences Sociales.

—— (2003), 'Work and Welfare: Towards a Capability Approach', in J. Zeitlin and D. Trubek (eds.), *Governing Work and Welfare in a New Economy*. Oxford: Oxford University Press.

Samwick, A. A. (1999), 'Social Security Reform in the United States', *National Tax Journal*, 52/4: 819–42.

Sapin, M. (2000), *Le droit des salariés et l'épargne salariale*, Report to the Socialist Party.

Sass, S. (1997), *The Promise of Private Pensions: The First Hundred Years*, Cambridge, MA: Harvard University Press.

Scharpf, F. W. (1997), *Games Real Actors Play*, Boulder, CO: Westview Press.

—— and Schmidt, V. (eds.) (2000), *Work and Welfare in Open Economies*, Oxford: Oxford University Press.

Schludi, M. (2001), 'Pension Reform in European Social Insurance Countries'. Paper presented at Biennial Meeting of the European Community Studies Association May 31–June 2, 2001, Madison, WI.

Schmähl, W. (1981), 'Über den Satz "Aller Sozialaufwand muß immer aus dem Volkseinkommen der laufenden Periode gedeckt werden" ', *Hamburger Jahrbuch für Wirtschafts- und Gesellschaftspolitik*, 26: 147–71.

—— (1989), 'Labour Force Participation and Social Pension Systems', in P. Johnson, C. Conrad, and D. Thomson (eds.), *Workers Versus Pensioners: Intergenerational Justice in an Ageing World* (pp. 137–61). Manchester: Manchester University Press.

Schmähl, W. (1990*a*), Demographic Change and Social Security—Some Elements of a Complex Relationship. *Journal of Population Economics*, 3: 159–77.

—— (1990*b*), 'Reformen der Rentenversicherung: Gründe, Strategien und Wirkungen—das Beispiel der "Rentenreform 1992" ', in B. Gahlen, H. Hesse, and H. J. Ramser (eds.), *Theorie und Politik der Sozialversicherung* (pp. 203–55). Tübingen: Mohr.

—— (1991*a*), 'Alterssicherung in der DDR und ihre Umgestaltung im Zuge des deutschen Einigungsprozesses: Einige verteilungspolitische Aspekte', in G. Kleinhenz (ed.), *Schriften des Vereins für Socialpolitik, Sozialpolitik im vereinten Deutschland I* (pp. 49–95). Berlin: Duncker & Humblot.

—— (1991*b*), 'On the Future Development of Retirement in Europe Especially of Supplementary Pension Schemes: An Introductory Overview', in W. Schmähl (ed.), *The Future of Basic and Supplementary Pension Schemes in the European Community: 1992 and Beyond* (pp. 31–70). Baden-Baden: Nomos Verlag.

—— (1992*a*), 'Changing the Retirement Age in Germany', *The Geneva Papers on Risk and Insurance* 17/62: 81–104.

—— (1992*b*), 'Transformation and Integration of Public Pension Schemes: Lessons from the Process of the German Unification', *Public Finance*, 47: 34–56.

—— (1993*a*), 'Proposals for Flat-rate Public Pensions in the German Debate', in J. Berghman and B. Cantillon (eds.), *The European Face of Social Security* (pp. 261–80). Aldershot: Avebury.

—— (1993*b*), 'The 1992 Reform of Public Pensions in Germany: Main Elements and Some Effects', *Journal of European Social Policy*, 3/1: 39–51.

—— (1995), 'Social Security and competitiveness', in International Social Security Association (ISSA) (ed.), *Social Security Tomorrow: Permanence and Change. Studies and Research No. 36* (pp. 19–28). Geneva: International Social Security Association.

—— (1997*a*), 'The Public–Private Mix in Pension Provision in Germany: The Role of Employer-based Pension Arrangements and the Influence of Public Activities', in M. Rein and E. Wadensjö (eds.), *Enterprise and the Welfare State* (pp. 99–148). Cheltenham: Edward Elgar.

—— (1997*b*), 'Avoiding Poverty in Old Age by an Obligatory Contribution-financed Minimum Insurance', in J. G. Backhaus (ed.), *Essays on Social Security and Taxation* (pp. 15–33). Marburg: Metropolis.

—— (1998), 'Insights from Social Security Reform Abroad', in R. D. Arnold, M. J. Graetz, and A. H. Munnell (eds.), *Framing the Social Security Debate: Values, Politics, and Economics*, 248–71 and 280–86. Washington, DC: Brookings Institution Press.

—— (1999), 'Pension Reforms in Germany: Major Topics, Decisions and Developments', in K. Müller, A. Ryll, and H. J. Wagener (eds.), *Transformation of Social Security: Pensions in Central-Eastern Europe* (pp. 91–120). Heidelberg: Physica Verlag.

—— (2000), 'Pay-as-You-Go versus Capital Funding: Towards a more balanced View in Pension Policy—Some concluding remarks', in G. Hughes and J. Stewart (eds.), *Pensions in the European Union: Adapting to Economic and Social Change* (pp. 195–208). Boston: Kluwer Academic Publishers.

—— (2001*a*), 'Finanzverflechtung der gesetzlichen Rentenversicherung', in K. D. Henke and W. Schmähl (eds.), *Finanzierungsverflechtung in der Sozialen Sicherung* (pp. 9–37). Baden-Baden: Nomos Verlag.

—— (2001*b*), 'Umlagefinanzierte Rentenversicherung in Deutschland, Optionen und Konzepte sowie politische Entscheidungen als Einstieg in einen grundlegenden Transformationsprozeß', in W. Schmähl and V. Ulrich (eds.), *Soziale Sicherungssysteme und demographische Herausforderungen* (pp. 123–04). Tübingen: Mohr Siebeck.

—— (2002), 'Die "offene Koordinierung" im Bereich Alterssicherung—aus wirtschaftswissenschaftlicher Sicht', in Verband Deutscher Rentenversicherungsträger (ed.), *Offene Koordinierung der Alterssicherung in der Europäischen Union,* Frankfurt: DRV-Schriften No. 34: 108–21.

—— (2003), 'A New Chapter in German Pension Policy: The "2001 Pension Reform" Based on a Paradigm Shift', in N. Takayama (ed.), *Taste of Pie: Searching for Better Pension Provisions in Developed Countries* (pp. 93–135). Tokyo: Maruzen Book Co. Ltd.

—— George, R., and Oswald, C. (1996), 'Gradual Retirement in Germany', in L. Delsen and G. Reday-Mulvey (eds.), *Gradual Retirement in the OECD Countries. Macro and Micro Issues and Policies* (pp. 69–93). Aldershot: Dartmouth Publishing Company.

—— and Jacobs, K. (1989), 'The Process of Retirement in Germany: Trends, Public Discussion and Options for its Redefinition', in W. Schmähl (ed.), *Redefining the Process of Retirement* (pp. 13–38). Berlin/Heidelberg: Springer Verlag.

—— and Michaelis, K. (eds.) (2000), *Alterssicherung von Frauen,* Wiesbaden: Westdeutscher Verlag.

—— and Rothgang, H. (1996), 'The Long-term Costs of Public Long-term Care Insurance in Germany. Some Guesstimates', in R. Eisen and F. A. Sloan (eds.), *Long-Term Care: Economic Issues and Policy Solutions* (pp. 181–222). Norwell, MA: Kluwer Academic Publishers.

—— and Viebrok, H. (2000), 'Adjusting Pay-As-You-Go Financed Pension Schemes to Increasing Life Expectancy', *Schmollers Jahrbuch, Zeitschrift für Wirtschafts- und Sozialwissenschaften,* 120/1: 41–61.

Schmid, G. (1997), 'The Dutch Employment Miracle? A Comparison of Employment Systems in the Netherlands and Germany', Discussion Paper FS 1 97-202. Berlin: Wissenschaftszentrum Berlin für Sozialforschung.

Schopflin, P. (1987), *Evaluation et sauvegarde de l'assurance vieillesse.* Ministère des affaires sociales et de l'emploi, Paris: La Documentation Française.

Schwartz, H. (2000), 'Internationalization and two welfare states: Australia and New Zealand', in F. Scharpf and V. Schmidt (eds.), *Welfare and Work in the Open Economy, Vol. II: Diverse Responses to Common Challenges* (pp. 69–130). Oxford: Oxford University Press.

Schwartz, F.W. (2001), 'The Viability of Advanced Welfare States in the International Economy', in S. Leibfried (ed.), *Welfare State Futures.* Cambridge: Cambridge University Press.

Seldon, A. (1960), *Pensions for Prosperity,* London: Institute for Economic Affairs.

Settergren, O. (2001), 'Two Thousand Five Hundred Words on the Swedish Pension Reform. Mimeo. Stockholm: National Social Insurance Board.

—— and Mikula, B. D. (2001), 'Financial Balance & Intergenerational Fairness in Pay-As-You-Go Pension Systems', Paper presented at the General Assembly of the International Social Security Association. Stockholm, 9–12 September 2001.

Sherraden, M. W. (1991), *Assets and the Poor: A New American Welfare Policy,* Armonk, NY: M. E. Sharpe.

Shiller, R. (2000), *Irrational Exuberance*, Princeton: Princeton University Press.

—— (2002*a*), 'Bubbles, Human Judgement, and Expert Opinion', *Financial Analysts Journal*, 58/3: 18–26.

—— (2002*b*), 'Current Estimates and Prospects for Change 1', in J. P. Williamson (ed.), *Equity Risk Forum* (pp. 51–9). Charlottesville, VA: Association for Investment Management and Research.

Shleifer, A. (2000), *Inefficient Markets: An Introduction to Behavioural Finance*, Oxford: Oxford University Press.

Shoven. J. (1999), 'Social Security Reform: Two Tiers are Better than One', in H. J. Aaron, J. B. Shoven, and B. M. Friedman (eds.), *Should the United States Privatize Social Security?* (ed.) (pp. 1–54). Cambridge, MA: The MIT Press.

Siebert, H. (1998), 'Pay-As-You-Go Versus Capital-funded Pension Systems: The Issues', in H. Siebert (ed.), *Redesigning Social Security* (pp. 3–33). Tübingen: Mohr.

Siegel, J. (2002), 'Historical Results 1', in J. P. Williamson (ed.), *Equity Risk Forum* (pp. 30–41). Charlottesville, VA: Association for Investment Management and Research.

Sociaal-Economische Raad (SER) (2000), *Pension Survey of the Netherlands*, SER Advisory Report 00/PK. The Hague: SER (Social and Economic Council the Netherlands).

—— (2001), *Nieuwe pensioenwet*, SER Advisory Report 01/06. The Hague: SER (Social and Economic Council the Netherlands).

—— (2002*a*), *Ageing Population and the EU*, Advisory Report 02/02 E. The Hague: SER (Social and Economic Council the Netherlands).

—— (2002*b*), *Rapport witte vlekken op pensioengebioed, quick scan 2001*, Rapport van de Pensioencommissie. The Hague: SER (Social and Economic Council the Netherlands).

Social Protection Committee (SPC). (2002), *Draft Progress Report of the Indicators Sub-group's Discussion on Pensions Indicators*, April, 2002. Brussels: EC.

—— and EPC. (2001), *Joint Report of the Social Protection Committee and the Economic Policy Committee on Objectives and Working Methods in the Area of Pensions: Applying the Open Method of Co-ordination.* No. 14098/01 SOC 469/ECOFIN 334, 23 November 2001. Brussels: EU.

Soros, G. (2002), *On Globalization*, Oxford: Public Affairs Ltd.

Sparling, R. P. (2002), 'Het externe vermogen van Nederland'. *Statistisch Bulletin*, Themanummer, Februari 2002. Amsterdam: De Nederlandsche Bank.

Statistisches Bundesamt. (2001), Einkommens-und Verbrauchsstichprobe 1998 (Stuttgart: Metzler-Poeschel).

Statistics Sweden and Finance Inspection (Finansinspektionen). 2000. FM17 SM 0002.

Stichting Van de Arbeid. (STAR). (1997), *Covenant inzake de Pensioenen.* The Hague: Stichting van de Arbeid (Dutch Labour Foundation).

—— (2001), *Conclusies getrokken door de stichting van de arbeid en het kabinet op grond van de evaluatie van het Covenant inzake arbeidspensioenen.* The Hague: Stichting van de Arbeid (Dutch Labour Foundation).

Stiglitz, J. (2002), *Globalization and Its Discontents*, New York: Norton.

Stone, D. (1999), 'Learning Lessons and Transferring Policy Across Time, Space and Disciplines', *Politics*, 19: 51–9.

Storper, M. and Salais, R. (1997), *Worlds of Production: The Action Frameworks of the Economy*, Cambridge, MA: Harvard University Press.

Strange, S. (1997), 'The Future of Global Capitalism: or Will Divergence Persist Forever?', in C. Crouch and W. Streeck (eds.), *Political Economy of Modern Capitalism* (pp. 182–91). London: Sage.

Supiot, A. (2001), *Beyond Employment: Changes in Work and the Future of Labour Law in Europe*, Oxford: Oxford University Press.

Sykes, R. S., Palier, B., and Prior, P. (2001), *Globalization and European Welfare States: Challenges and Changes*, Basingstoke: Palgrave.

Taddéi, D. (2000), *Retraites choisies et progressives*, Paris: La Documentation Française.

Teece, D. J. (2000), *Managing Intellectual Capital*, Oxford: Oxford University Press.

Teulade, R. (2000), *L' avenir des systèmes de retraite*, Paris: Conseil Économique et Social.

Thane, P. (2000), *Old Age in English History: Past Experiences, Present Issues*, Oxford: Oxford University Press.

Thompson, L. (1998), *Older and Wiser: The Economics of Public Pensions*, Washington, DC: The Urban Institute Press.

Titmuss, R. M. (1955), 'Pensions System and Population Change', *Political Quarterly*, 26: 152–66.

—— (1958), 'Pension Systems and Population Change', in R. M. Titmuss (ed.) *Essays on 'The Welfare State'* (pp. 56–74). London: Allen and Unwin.

Tsebelis, G. (1995), 'Decision Making in Political Systems: Veto Players in Presidentialism, Parliamentarism, Multicameralism and Multipartism', *British Journal of Political Science*, 25(3): 289–326.

United Nations Department of Economic and Social Affairs. (1996), *Demographic Yearbook 1996*, New York: United Nations.

US Government. (2001), *Private Pensions: Issues of Coverage and Increasing Contribution Limits for Defined Contribution Plans*, Report No. GAO-01-846. Washington DC: General Accounting Office.

—— (2002), 'Private Pension Plan Bulletin: Abstract of 1998 Form 5500 Annual Reports'. *Pension and Welfare Benefits Administration Bulletin* No. 11 (Winter 2001–2002). Washington DC: Department of Labor.

US Social Security Administration, Office of Policy and Office of Research Evaluation and Statistics. (1999), *Social Security Programs Throughout the World*. SSA Publication No. 13-11805 (August). Washington, DC: Department of Labor.

Van Ewijk, C. (2001), 'Beyond Maastricht', *De Economist*, 149/4: 509–22.

—— Kuipers, B., Van Der Ven, M., and Westerhout, E. (2000), *Ageing in the Netherlands*, The Hague: CPB Netherlands Bureau for Economic Policy Analysis.

Veillon, C. (1962), 'L'accord du 8 decembre 1961', *Droit Sociale*, 25/7–8: 415–8.

Viebrok, H. (2001), 'Die Bedeutung institutioneller Arrangements für den Übergang in den Ruhestand', in L. Leisering, R. Müller, and K. F. Schumann (eds.), *Institutionen und Lebensläufe im Wandel—Institutionelle Regulierungen von Lebensverläufen*, Weinheim: Juventa-Verlag.

Viossat, L.-C. (2000), *Les retraites, enjeux, crises, solutions*, Paris: Flammarion.

Visco, I. (2001), 'Paying for Pensions: How Important is Economic Growth?', *Banca Nazionale del Lavoro Quarterly Review*, 216: 73–102.

Visser, J. (2002), 'The First Part-time Economy in the World. A Model to be Followed?', *Journal of European Social Policy*, 12/1: 23–42.

—— and Hemerijk, A. C. (1997), *'A Dutch Miracle.' Job Growth, Welfare Reform, and Corporatism in the Netherlands*, Amsterdam: Amsterdam University Press.

Vording, H. and Goudswaard, K. (1997), 'Indexation of Public Pension Benefits on a Legal Basis: Some Experiences in European Countries', *International Social Security Review*, 50/3: 31–44.

Wagner, P. (1994), 'Dispute, Uncertainty and Institution in Recent French Debates', *Journal of Political Philosophy*, 2/3: 270–89.

Walker, A. (1991), 'Thatcherism and the New Politics of Old Age', in J. Myles and J. Quadagno (eds.), *States, Labour Markets and the Future of Old Age Policy* (pp. 19–36). Philadelphia: Temple University Press.

Weaver, R. K. (1998), 'The Politics of Pensions: Lessons from Abroad', in R. D. Arnold, M. J. Graetz, and A. H. Munnell (eds.), *Framing the Social Security Debate: Values, Politics and Economics* (pp. 183–229). Washington, DC: Brookings Institution Press for the National Academy of Social Insurance.

Wessels, W. (1997), 'Das politische System der Europäischen Union', in W. Ismayr (ed.), *Die politischen Systeme Westeuropas* (pp. 693–722). Opladen: Leske und Budrich.

Wetenschappelijke Raad Voor Het Regeringsbeleid (WRR). (1990), *Een werkend Perspectief: Arbeidsparticipatie in de Jaren '90*, The Hague: Wetenschappelijke Raad voor het Regeringsbeleid.

—— (1999), *Generatiebewust Beleid*, The Hague: Wetenschappelijke Raad voor het Regeringsbeleid.

Whiteside, N. (1997), 'Regulating markets', *Public Administration*, 75/3: 467–85.

—— (1999), 'Private Provision and Public Welfare', in D. Gladstone (ed.), *Before Beveridge: Welfare before the Welfare State*, London: IEA Health & Welfare Unit.

—— (2002), 'Security and the Working Life', in *Europe and the Politics of Capabilities: Report for the European Commission*, 325–43.

—— (2003), 'Searching for Security', History and Policy Available on line at http://www.historyandpolicy.org/main/policy-paper-//.html.

Williamson, O. (1985), *The Economic Institutions of Capitalism: Firms, Markets and Relational Contracting*, London: Collier Macmillan.

World Bank. (1994), *Averting the Old Age Crisis: Policies to Protect the Old and Promote Growth*, Oxford: Oxford University Press.

Zanden, J. L. V. and Van Riel, A. (2000), *Nederland 1780–1914: Staat, Instituties en Economische Ontwikkeling*, Amsterdam: Balans.

Zeitlin, J. (2003), 'Introduction', in J. Zeitlin and D. Trubek (eds.), *Governing Work and Welfare in a New Economy: European and American Experiments*, Oxford: Oxford University Press.

CITATION INDEX

SUBJECT INDEX

C000023044
SEASON
FIRST DIVISION
MAINE ROAD
MANCHESTER
ZINE 15p
TOMMY CATON
Saturday 10th September 1977
K.O. 3.00 pm.
OFFICIAL CLUB SPONSORS
brother
More than just features
LEAGUE DIVISION ONE
1997
brother
BARCLAYCARD PREMIERSHIP
FA Barclaycard Premiership
M.C.F.C v Manchester United
Kick-off Sunday 14th March 12:30pm
Name: Paper Ticket
Customer No: "BULK
Entrance: X
Aisle: 231
Row: F
Seat: B42
matchticket
MANCHESTER CITY
PETER BARNES
MANCHESTER CITY
A Cup Semi-Final
MANCHESTER C.
JOE CORRIGAN
MANCHESTER CITY
IPSWICH
In Celebration of The One-H
Football Association Challenge Cup
FINAL TIE
Manchester City
Tottenham Hots
1981
Saturday 9th May 1981
Kick-off 3.00
RICHARD DUNNE
Manchester City
Barclays Premiership
10th Feb 2008, KO 1.30pm
£39.00
Visitors
Stand Tier 1 Upper
BLOCK
E232
ROW
30
SEAT
18
E 30
FRANCIS LEE
VISITOR
PROGRAMM

THE POCKET BOOK OF MAN CITY

By Andy Buckley

To my late mother, Judy

Published by Vision Sports Publishing in 2010

Vision Sports Publishing
19-23 High Street
Kingston upon Thames
Surrey
KT1 1LL

www.visionsp.co.uk

ISBN: 978-1905326-96-9

Series editor: Jim Drewett
Series production: Martin Cloake
Design: Neal Cobourne
Illustrations: Bob Bond
Cover photography: Paul Downes, Objective Image
All pictures: Getty Images except where otherwise stated
Thanks to Tommy Muir and Rob Buckley

Printed and bound in China by Toppan Printing Co Ltd

A CIP catalogue record for this book is available from the British Library

THIS IS AN UNOFFICIAL PUBLICATION

All statistics in *The Pocket Book of Man City* are correct up until the end of the 2009/10 season.

CONTENTS

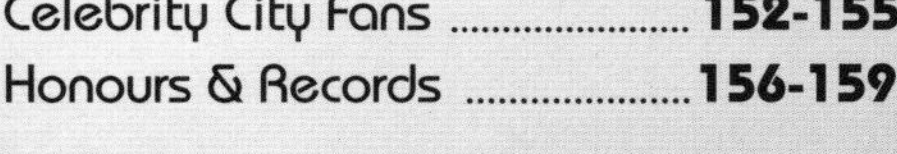

FOREWORD BY COLIN BELL

Manchester City will always have a special place in my heart after the wonderful times I have enjoyed at the club. The supporters have been so kind and generous to me since the day I signed from Bury in March 1966 for the princely sum of £45,000.

City were in the old Second Division at the time and I was just 20 years of age when the temptation to sign for Joe Mercer and Malcolm Allison was too much to resist. It seems so long ago since I first pulled on the famous sky blue shirt against Derby County at the Baseball Ground and I was lucky enough to score on my debut.

I can still recall the day we won the League Championship at Newcastle in 1968 and the cup glories that followed. To win the FA Cup, League Cup and European Cup-Winners' Cup in quick succession was quite special.

Under Joe and Malcolm, everything just clicked into place and I was fortunate enough to be part of that era. Importantly, I'd like to think we achieved our success with a certain style and I'm sure we won a lot of friends for the calibre of football we produced.

Those were the days and they certainly provided me with some terrific memories. I also know from speaking to supporters on a frequent basis that they remember that particular period with so much affection.

Hopefully, the good times are on the way back and, like everyone else, I have been following the developments on and off the field in the last couple of years with tremendous interest.

I am still a regular visitor to the City of Manchester Stadium and thoroughly enjoy my role as a matchday ambassador. A few of the old guard like Mike Summerbee, Tony Book, Tommy Booth and Joe Corrigan are still knocking about on match days and it gives us the chance to meet lots of old faces, as well as the new generation of supporters.

I must admit it is a huge honour to have a stand at the new stadium named after me. I was quite flattered, to be honest, and cannot express how much I appreciate the gesture.

Like many of the supporters, I was sad to see Maine Road demolished a few seasons ago because it held fantastic memories. Playing in front of the Kippax with the fans singing my name was a magical experience for me.

One thing I quickly learned after my arrival at City all those years ago was the bond that exists between the club and the supporters. It is widely recognised that the fans are the heart and soul of the club, helping create a spirit and tradition that makes City so unique.

...CLUB DIRECTORY...

Club address: Manchester City Football Club
City of Manchester Stadium
Sportcity, Rowsley Street,
Manchester, M11 3FF

General club enquiries: 0870 062 1894

Box Office/Ticket Info: 00870 062 1894 (option 1)

Online ticket sales: www.mcfc.co.uk

Stadium tours: 0870 062 1894 (option 8)

Match day hospitality: 0870 062 4141
sales@mcfc.co.uk

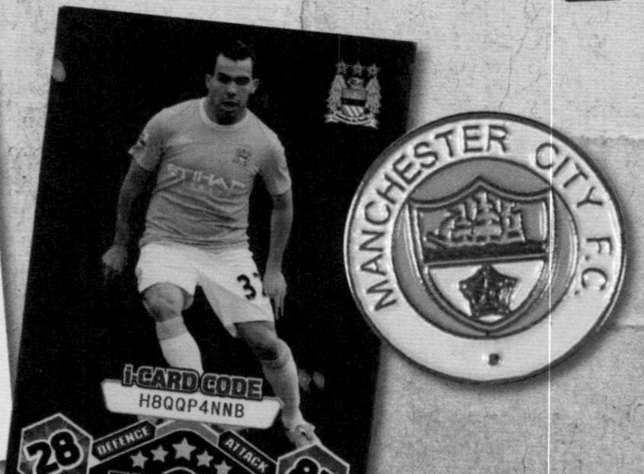

City in the Community:

0161 438 7711

citc@mcfc.co.uk

Conference and events:

www.cityofmanchesterstadium.co.uk

Club website: http://www.mcfc.co.uk/

Fan website: www.mcfc.co.uk/fans

Junior membership scheme: www.live4city.co.uk

Charity enquiries: charities@mcfc.co.uk

Platt Lane: complex 0161 224 3310

Platt Lane: gym 0161 224 0976

www.plattlane@mcfc.co.uk

adidas
11
AFA
AFA

THE CITY CHRONICLES
CITY PRIDE
1880-1965

A club for all Mancunians... that was the driving force behind the decision to choose the name Manchester City. Organisers wanted an identity which represented Manchester and all its citizens irrespective of their social status and background. And so, in 1894, the Manchester City all Blues fans know and love today evolved from Ardwick AFC.

MCFC had started life further back in 1880 as St Mark's (West Gorton), a church team set up as a means of curing some of the problems that affected the world's first industrial city.

An early postcard, printed in 1910

Several nationalities had come to east Manchester looking for work in the cotton mills, on the railways and in the engineering works. The population increased dramatically and so too did the tensions between the different communities. Living conditions were poor and gang warfare, poverty and domestic violence were all major concerns.

A woman called Anna Connell, the daughter of the rector of St Mark's Church, decided to take action and set up parish

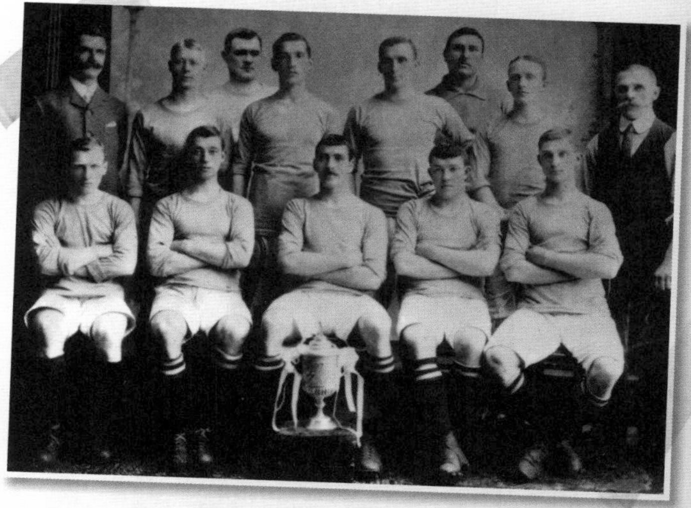

The FA Cup-winning team of 1904

meetings. Church wardens Thomas Goodbehere and William Beastow, both respected figures from the local ironworks, helped her set up a cricket team and, realising the men needed some activity in the winter, a football team was then created to further develop community spirit.

The first game was against another church side and the team progressed rapidly. Eventually, a more professional approach was adopted and the club was relaunched as Ardwick AFC in 1887 with the Hyde Road Hotel as headquarters.

Four years later Ardwick won the Manchester Cup for the first time and in 1892 they were admitted to the Football League.

The sport of Association Football was enjoying a surge in popularity and already a rivalry was developing with Newton Heath, later to change their name to Manchester United.

There was a feeling of enormous pride in Manchester when the Ship Canal opened in 1894 and Ardwick's secretary-manager Joshua Parlby recognised the need for the club to form a strong Mancunian identity developing that sense of unity.

Manchester City Football Club Limited became a registered company on Monday 16th April, and an application for re-election to the Second Division was successful. City won the Second Division title in the final year of the 19th century after a run of victories that included a 10-0 win over Darwen at Hyde Road. Fred Williams scored five goals and Billy Meredith claimed the third of four hat-tricks that season.

City, in the light shirts, in action against Arsenal at the London club's Plumstead ground in 1912

A photo opportunity for captain Jimmy McMullen in the run-up to the 1926 FA Cup final

Meredith was to score the winning goal in the FA Cup final in 1904 when Bolton were beaten at the Crystal Palace in London. The team arrived back in Manchester in a horse-drawn carriage driven by Albert Alexander Snr, who would later become the club's vice-chairman.

City twice went close to winning the league but an FA investigation found the club had been making additional payments to players. Manager Tom Maley and the chairman were suspended from football and a total of 17 players were suspended and fined. The punishment almost closed the club.

It was felt the southern-based FA had treated City unfairly, especially when the club was told to transfer players once their bans had expired. City somehow managed to battle on and, once war was over, re-established themselves as a dominant force.

An estimated crowd of 55,000 saw the match with eventual champions Burnley at Hyde Road in March 1921. However, the stadium was inadequate and the move to Maine Road in Moss Side was made two years later.

League form was inconsistent but City became the first Manchester side to play at the new Wembley Stadium when they lost to Bolton in 1926.

Bizarrely, in those days the position of manager and secretary was seen as one role and when Wilf Wild took charge in 1932 it meant he picked the team as well as paying the wages, plus getting involved in all other day-to-day operational tasks including management of the stadium.

His appointment was a masterstroke and he held the job until 1946, guiding the club to consecutive FA Cup finals. Malcolm Allison admitted his interest in the club stemmed from listening on the wireless to the 1933 final defeat by Everton!

In 1934 City captain Sam Cowan, hurt by losing a final seven years earlier, was determined to make it third time lucky and duly lifted the trophy with a 2-1 victory over Portsmouth.

The renowned cup fighters were also emerging as a force in the league to challenge the dominance of an Arsenal side that won the title four times in five seasons. In 1937, City claimed their first Championship with a side that contained the legendary Peter Doherty and stars like Frank Swift, Eric Brook, Sam Barkas, Ernie Toseland, Alec Herd and Fred Tilson.

City were unpredictable even in those days and the club were relegated the following season, before war took over. Indeed, the club flitted between divisions once football resumed, with Les McDowall assuming control in 1950.

The highlight of the decade was the 1956 FA Cup win over Birmingham City, 12 months after losing in the previous season's final. Skipper of the side was Roy Paul, who had been one of McDowall's first signings and had proved an inspiration.

The victory owed much to McDowall's great tactical brain and his introduction of the Revie Plan which involved Don Revie confusing the opposition defence by operating as a deep-lying centre forward.

McDowall spent the following seasons searching for a winning formula but relegation followed in 1963 and he left to be replaced by assistant George Poyser.

However, a period of decline followed and the match against Swindon Town in January 1965 was watched by an all-time low attendance of 8,015 – fewer than ten per cent of the club's record crowd of 84,569 who had turned up for the FA Cup tie against Stoke City some 30-odd years earlier.

City finished a disappointing 11th in the Second Division and there was a mood of gloom around Maine Road. Few could have imagined how dramatically things would change…

City and Birmingham take the pitch for the 1956 FA Cup final

BADGE OF HONOUR

Some might argue that supporting Manchester City has been an epic voyage of discovery down the years. Fans have grown accustomed to riding the waves of success and failure throughout the club's history. So it is perhaps appropriate that an image of a ship at sea in full sail has always formed part of the club crest.

The club badge has always featured a ship, taken from the City's coat of arms

The ship is taken from the Manchester coat of arms and is a symbol of trade and enterprise in a city that was the birthplace of the Industrial Revolution. Supporters take great pride in the football club's Manchester origins. So it is only right and proper that the Blues should have traces of the city's heritage woven into their famous strip as a reminder of that historic association.

For older supporters the round badge was an iconic image during a glorious chapter in the club's history, whereas younger fans will be more familiar with the present-day club crest adopted in 1997. Bizarrely, until that year merchandising rights were not under the direct control of the club, prompting then chairman Francis Lee to commission a new design consisting of a shield in front of a golden eagle.

Still there on the upper half of the shield reflecting

The modern club crest commissioned by Francis Lee in 1997

the city's trading links was the ship. Some assumed it represented the Manchester Ship Canal which opened in 1894, the same year the club was formed. But Manchester's coat of arms predates the canal. It certainly signified the part played by waterways like the Bridgewater Canal, the forerunner of the canal networks, as Manchester established itself as the workshop of the world.

The three diagonal stripes in the lower half recognise the city's three rivers – the Medlock, Irwell and the Irk. The lines were changed from the red and gold of the previous crest to blue and white to match the club's traditional colours. The eagle comes from the official badge of the City of Manchester, dating from 1957, while the three stars were added for decorative purposes.

The 1997 rebrand also saw a new club motto with the Latin phrase *Superbia In Proelio* meaning Pride in Battle. Boxer Ricky Hatton showed his devotion to his beloved Blues by

The original club crest was packed with symbolism

having a tattoo of the English translation inked on to his back before one of his world title fights.

The latest badge is just one of four crests used since Manchester City were formed in 1894.

The original emblem was the City Coat of Arms which, apart from the sailing references, had a globe symbolising Manchester's world trade covered by a swarm of bees to illustrate industry and activity.

The round 1970 badge featured three stripes symbolising the three rivers of the city…

Other features included a white heraldic antelope to represent engineering industries, and a lion with a castle as a crown, referring to the ancient Roman fort of Castlefield. The red roses on their shoulders are references to Lancashire, of which Manchester was once part.

The round badge brought in during the summer of 1970 incorporated a yellow ship over a red shield with three yellow stripes and was surrounded by two circles and the club name. It had been worn before on occasions but now it was permanent – but not

… which were replaced with a Lancastrian rose in the 1972 version

for long! It was replaced by another variation in 1972, with the shield making way for a red rose.

There was a tradition of reverting to the arms of the City of Manchester for cup finals as a symbol of pride in representing Manchester at a major event. However, this policy has not been strictly adhered to – one notable exception being the European Cup-Winners' Cup final of 1970 when no badge was worn.

Roberto Mancini and the current City crest

The badges have been altered at various times to celebrate particular milestones. One such occasion was the 50th anniversary of Maine Road in 1973 while 30 years later the Latin motto was substituted by 'Maine Road 1923-2003' to mark the closure of the ground.

Nowadays replica shirts are a valuable stream of income for clubs. At one stage controversial former owner Thaksin Shinawatra came up with the idea of an Oriental-style club crest to help market the club in the Far East. It was suggested an elephant symbolising his native Thailand might make its way into designs – but there will be many relieved he was not around long enough to see his plan through.

CASH MACHINE

Sheikh Mansour bin Zayeeed al-Nahyan – the man at the top

Manchester City fans could scarcely believe their luck when the Arab takeover in 2008 made them the wealthiest club in the world. In the blink of an eye the Blues went from Premier League financial also-rans to a mega-rich club whose owners had very deep pockets. Suddenly, they were major players in the world transfer market and life would never be the same again.

In the late summer of 2008, the staggering £220 million purchase of City by an investment company called the Abu Dhabi United Group catapulted the club's bank balance into the stratosphere. The stadium was immediately dubbed 'Middle-Eastlands' by disbelieving fans who turned up wearing tea-towels wrapped round their heads as makeshift Arab head-dress in a lighthearted tribute to their oil-rich new owners.

Rock star Noel Gallagher caught the mood of the moment by taunting Manchester United fans. "It'll be nice to know that every gallon of petrol a Manchester United fan buys is going into our kitty," bragged the Oasis frontman.

On the same crazy day, City snatched Real Madrid's Brazil ace Robinho from under Chelsea's noses for a British record £32.5 million. Cristiano Ronaldo was even mentioned as a possible target. A few months later they tabled an ill-fated world record bid of £100 million for AC Milan striker Kaka, offering him wages of £250,000 a week.

City fans were licking their lips at the prospect of huge stars playing for THEIR team. They had a seemingly unlimited transfer budget thanks to the Arab billions and suddenly were the talk of the football world.

However, attracting big names was not going to be as straightforward as it might have appeared with no Champions League football on offer to potential signings.

Still, the club's marketing men were rubbing their hands with glee and came up with a clever ploy that stirred up great controversy in Manchester.

In 2009, after Carlos Tevez left United to join City, a giant

The Arab investment is virtually a licence to print money

billboard featuring the Argentinian was put up in the middle of Manchester proclaiming: "Welcome to Manchester." It was a deliberate dig at the fact Old Trafford lies outside the city boundary and when Tevez proved a big hit in a City shirt it merely inflamed the rivalry.

The figures were mind boggling as manager Mark Hughes embarked on a lavish spending spree. In the first year alone he spent more than £200 million on the likes of Robinho, Carlos Tevez, Craig Bellamy, Emmanuel Adebayor, Gareth Barry, Wayne Bridge, Shay Given, Roque Santa Cruz, Jolean Lescott, Kolo Toure and Nigel de Jong.

Barely a decade after Francis Lee occupied the chairman's seat, a major Sheikh-up meant the club had a new owner whose name was more of a tongue-twister. Sheikh Mansour bin Zayed al-Nahyan has a personal wealth estimated at around £15 billion and his family have access to an oil fortune worth more than £500 billion.

Serious money for a man who made a tidy £1.4 billion profit after selling an 11 per cent stake in Barclays he had bought seven months earlier. The £12 million he sanctioned

A £12 million fee landed the services of Gareth Barry

for the purchase of Gareth Barry on the day he concluded that deal would have seemed just like loose change.

Sheikh Mansour has kept a low profile, leaving Emirati businessman Khaldoon al Mubarak to act as chairman, supervising chief executive Garry Cook who controls the day-to-day running of the football operation.

The fee for Carlos Tevez was rumoured to be as high as £47m

The Arabs saw the Blues as a way of establishing a significant presence in English football and raising their profile worldwide.

One of the Sheikh's first moves was to cancel loans of £305 million, including some debt inherited during the takeover from the previous owner, the former Thai Prime Minister Thaksin Shinawatra. Further shares were also bought for £90 million to meet the spiralling wage bill.

Sheikh Mansour is a member of the ruling family of Abu Dhabi and his 18 brothers include the president and crown prince of the Emirate. The Sheikh's own role is Minister for Presidential Affairs in the UAE cabinet and he has a hot-line to Barack Obama, the President of the United States.

Abu Dhabi was once a fishing nation but when oil was discovered in 1958 it created vast wealth, and the country eventually became the richest place in the world. In 2009, when Dubai felt the backlash of the global recession, it turned to its Gulf neighbour to bail it out.

How ironic that Manchester City, a club some might argue is cursed by a history of bad luck, should for once get so lucky? They are now playing fantasy football for real!

MAN CITY COMIC STRIP HISTORY 1

CITY DWELLINGS

There was hardly a dry eye in the house when Manchester City left their spiritual home of Maine Road. A million memories came tumbling down when the famous old stadium was bulldozed after 80 years of football in Moss Side. The final act was played out on Sunday, 11th May 2003, when the Blues lost 1-0 to Southampton. But the result was completely overshadowed by an occasion filled with nostalgia.

Fans who had once stood on the same spot on the Kippax every other week knew that life would never be the same again. Generations of supporters had grown up on one of the most famous terraces in the land. It ran the length of the pitch and would echo to the noise from the swaying masses cheering their idols.

Thankfully, a famous chant survived the move to the new stadium at Sports City. "We are City, we are City, super City from Maine Road," is still sung to this day. It seems some traditions will never die and a venue graced by legends like Bert Trautmann, Frank Swift and Colin Bell will forever remain in the hearts of the loyal supporters.

Maine Road had one of the best atmospheres in the country and was a popular choice as a neutral venue to host cup semi-finals and other sporting fixtures. But by the time it closed the layout had become disjointed and outdated after much of the more recent building work had been carried out piecemeal.

A significant moment in its history had come nine years earlier in April 1994 when the Kippax standing section was demolished to make way for a three-tier all-seater stand.

In contrast, the club's new home at the swish City of Manchester Stadium was perfectly configured and had made an easy transition from an athletics stadium for the 2002 Commonwealth Games to a venue suitable for Premier League football. The running track was ripped up and the pitch sunk several metres

Bert Trautmann claims a high ball in front of a packed house at Maine Road in 1951

to allow an extra tier of seating to be added.

Francis Lee had set the ball rolling for the ground move during his reign as chairman and, remembering his own days as a player, was adamant that City would not play inside a running track. He wanted the fans close to the action like at Maine Road.

Action from a Manchester derby in 1958, in the early days of the Kippax

It was in August 1923 that City had moved into Maine Road after their previous ground at Hyde Road, their home for 36 years, had come to be considered inadequate.

Wembley Stadium opened a few months before Maine Road. Both venues were constructed by the same builders, Sir Robert McAlpine, and after issues with crowd control at the first Wembley FA Cup final, between Bolton Wanderers and West Ham United, the capacity at Maine Road was set at just over 80,000.

Dubbed the Wembley of the North, Maine Road was the biggest ground in the country behind only Wembley itself. The crowd of 84,569 for the FA Cup tie with Stoke City in 1934 remains a record for an English club ground.

At the start of the 1936/37 season the Platt Lane Stand was extended, making the capacity 88,000. However, relegation from Division One in 1938 and the outbreak of war meant plans for further expansion were suspended.

Old Trafford was bombed during the Second World War so Manchester United shared the

EASTLANDS

BUILT: 2002
LOCATION: SPORTCITY, MANCHESTER
CAPACITY: 47,726

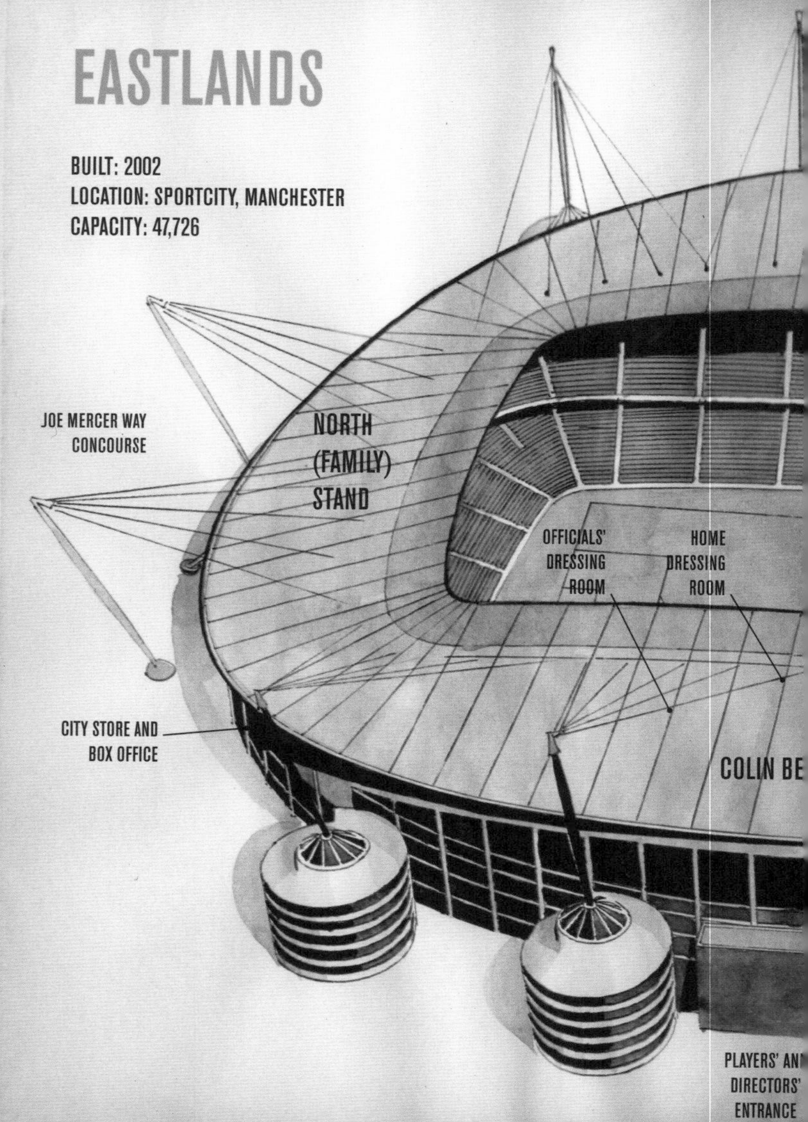

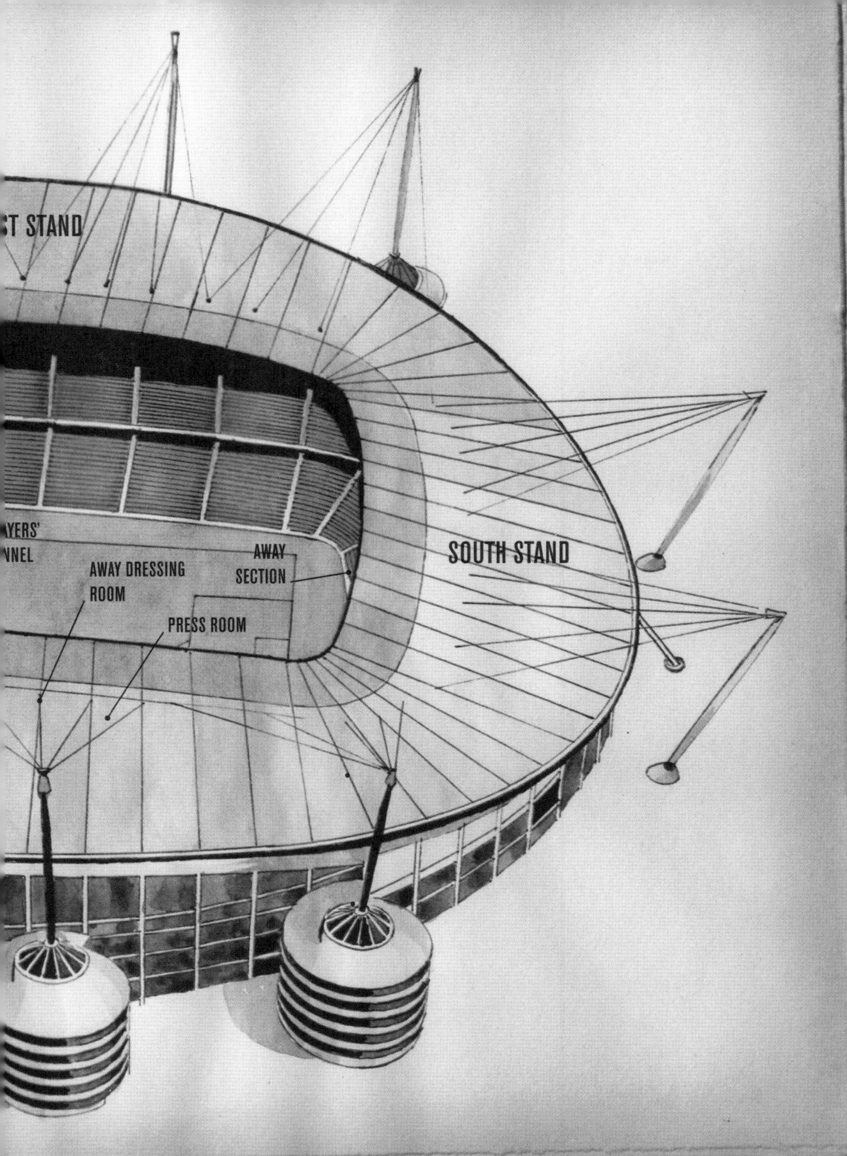

AWAY DRESSING ROOM
AWAY SECTION
PRESS ROOM
SOUTH STAND

ground for a time. It was during this period that the highest Football League attendance was recorded, with 83,260 fans watching Manchester United play Arsenal in January 1948.

City added floodlights in 1953 – they were replaced by more powerful lights 11 years later – and in 1957

By 1995, changes to Maine Road had created a disjointed ground with four stands of different heights and styles

the popular side was redeveloped and named the Kippax Stand after a nearby street. Unlike other clubs where the most vocal fans would gather behind the goal, City's most passionate support was on the full side of the pitch.

In 1963 wooden benches were added at the Platt Lane Stand which meant that City had more seats than any other club ground at the time.

A cantilevered North Stand was built at the start of the 1970s and a new roof went on to the Main Stand. A new Umbro Stand incorporating corporate boxes replaced the Platt Lane Stand in 1993 and a year later the Kippax closed amid great emotion when City played Chelsea. The stadium had to become all-seater to comply with the Taylor Report and a three-tier stand built in place of the Kippax became the tallest in the country.

All four sides of the ground were different heights and styles and by the time Maine Road closed the capacity was 35,150. For long periods the pitch was the widest in England and was also used as a venue

for Rugby League and music concerts – Oasis and Queen were among the many acts who performed there.

Nowadays, Maine Road is a housing estate as a new era of sky blue memories begins a few miles across town in east Manchester.

The first match staged at the City of Manchester Stadium – often referred to as Eastlands by the fans – was on Sunday 10th August, 2003, when the Blues defeated Barcelona 2-1 in a friendly. Nicolas Anelka scored the first goal at the stadium and the first competitive match was a 5-0 victory over Welsh side Total Network Solutions in the UEFA Cup.

It had taken a year to convert the ground from an athletics arena accommodating 35,000 spectators for the Commonwealth Games. Initially the stadium had two tiers at the east and west sides and one tier to the south. A temporary uncovered structure at the northern end was dismantled so a permanent stand could be built.

Extra tiers were added on the sides and the west stand re-named the Colin Bell Stand. The capacity

The rolling lines of the current City of Manchester stadium

moved to 48,000 and there are now plans by the club's owners to raise the limit to 60,000.

The stadium hosted the 2008 UEFA Cup final between Rangers and Zenit St Petersburg while England played Iceland and Japan there as a warm up to Euro 2004.

brother

GREAT GOALS

DENIS LAW 1974 DIVISION ONE V MAN UTD

As far as Manchester City fans were concerned there was no finer way for Denis Law to bring down the curtain on a glittering career.

His final act in League football was to score the winner against Manchester United at Old Trafford on the day the home side were relegated.

The 1-0 scoreline meant sheer unbridled joy for the blue half of Manchester – but a moment of sadness for the Law man who suspected he had back-heeled his old club into the Second Division a year after they had given him a free transfer.

Not for the first time the triumvirate of Mike Summerbee, Colin Bell and Francis Lee were all involved in the build-up to the goal with Law, a one-time Stretford End idol, left to apply the final blow with a clever flick of the boot.

Unsurprisingly, Law did not celebrate his late goal but it turned out United would have been relegated anyway even if the game had been drawn, though he was unaware of this at the time.

Law was substituted immediately and walked off the pitch with his head bowed. It was his last competitive appearance in a sky-blue shirt but he did wear the dark blue of his beloved Scotland later that summer in a swansong at the World Cup finals in Germany.

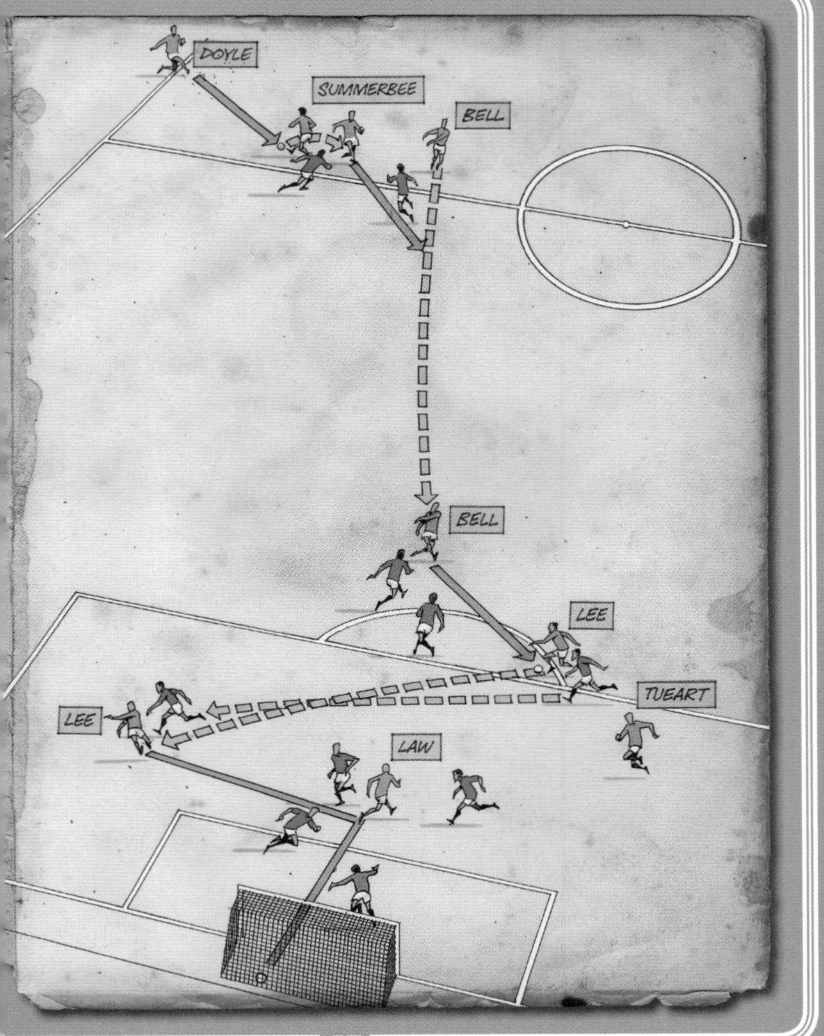
DOYLE
SUMMERBEE
BELL
BELL
LEE
TUEART
LEE
LAW

DENNIS TUEART 1976 LEAGUE CUP FINAL V NEWCASTLE

Wembley matchwinners do not come any better than Dennis Tueart's wonder goal. It is just a pity that, all these years on, there has not been one to follow it up. Even a goal of the scruffy variety would suffice for City fans starved of a major trophy since.

At least Tueart's brilliant overhead kick has gone down in League Cup history as the competition's finest moment. The accolade came in a fans' poll to mark the 50th final, an anniversary that brought back fond memories.

"For the supporters to vote my goal as the best League Cup moment makes me very proud," said Tueart, a former director of the club and still very much a fan.

Willie Donachie had sent a hopeful ball into the penalty area and Tommy Booth nodded it across towards a grateful Tueart. "Although I had my back to the net, I knew I only had to hit it right to score. I didn't actually see it go in but when I turned round I was mobbed."

Newcastle were the team he supported as a kid, making his strike extra special. Peter Barnes had opened the scoring before Alan Gowling equalised.

The last word, though, came from Tueart – to the delight of his manager Tony Book who had won the trophy six years earlier as a player.

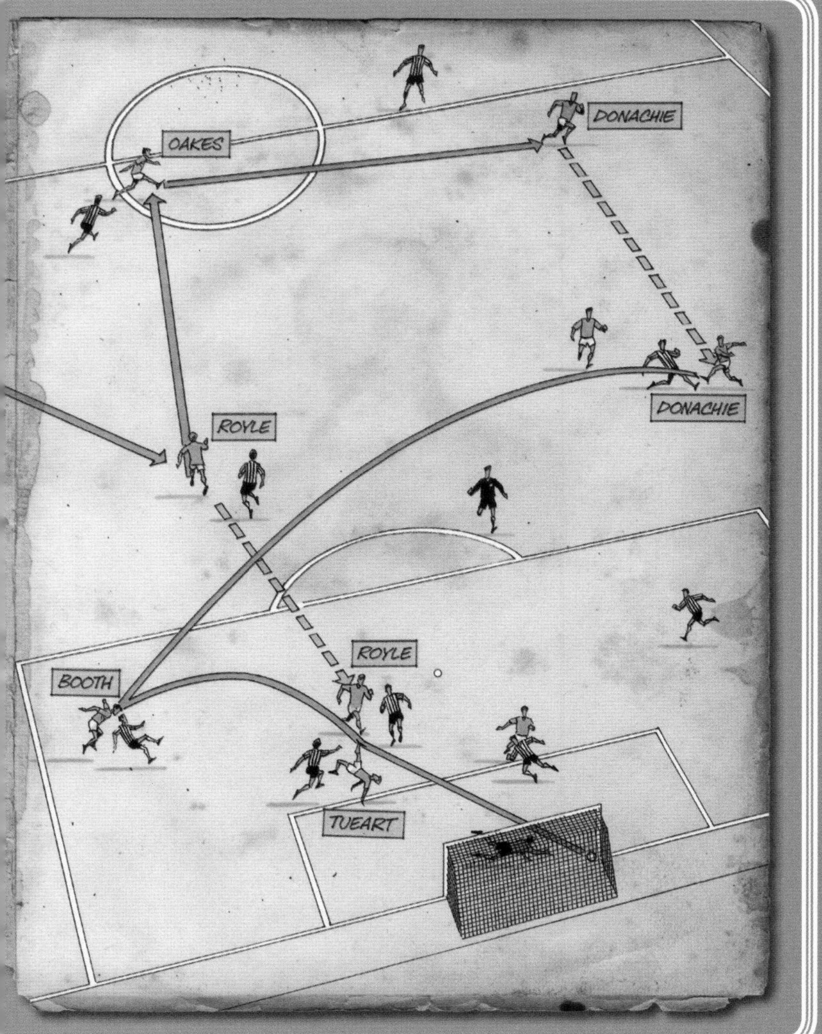
OAKES
DONACHIE
DONACHIE
ROYLE
ROYLE
BOOTH
TUEART

PETER BARNES
1977 DIVISION ONE V SPURS

These were heady times for one of the country's most entertaining wingers. Peter Barnes came from fine football stock, his father Ken having played for City with great distinction in the 1950s.

Peter had scored in the 1976 League Cup final and had become the first City player to be named PFA Young Player of the Year. Not bad for a player who was still just about in his teenage years when he took to the field against Tottenham in May 1977.

The Blues were pushing hard for the championship, though defeats at eventual champions Liverpool and Derby during the run-in were ultimately to prove decisive, leaving them to settle for the runners-up spot.

Nevertheless, City were determined to finish with a flourish and crushed struggling Spurs 5-0, helped by a virtuoso performance from Barnes.

He scored the third goal, latching on to a flick from his close friend Gary Owen before wriggling past a defender on the edge of the penalty area. Barnes still had the time and awareness to dummy goalkeeper Pat Jennings before casually chipping the ball over the Northern Ireland international.

It was not just the boyish good looks and blond hair that had got Peter noticed and later that year he went on to make his England debut, winning the first of 22 caps.

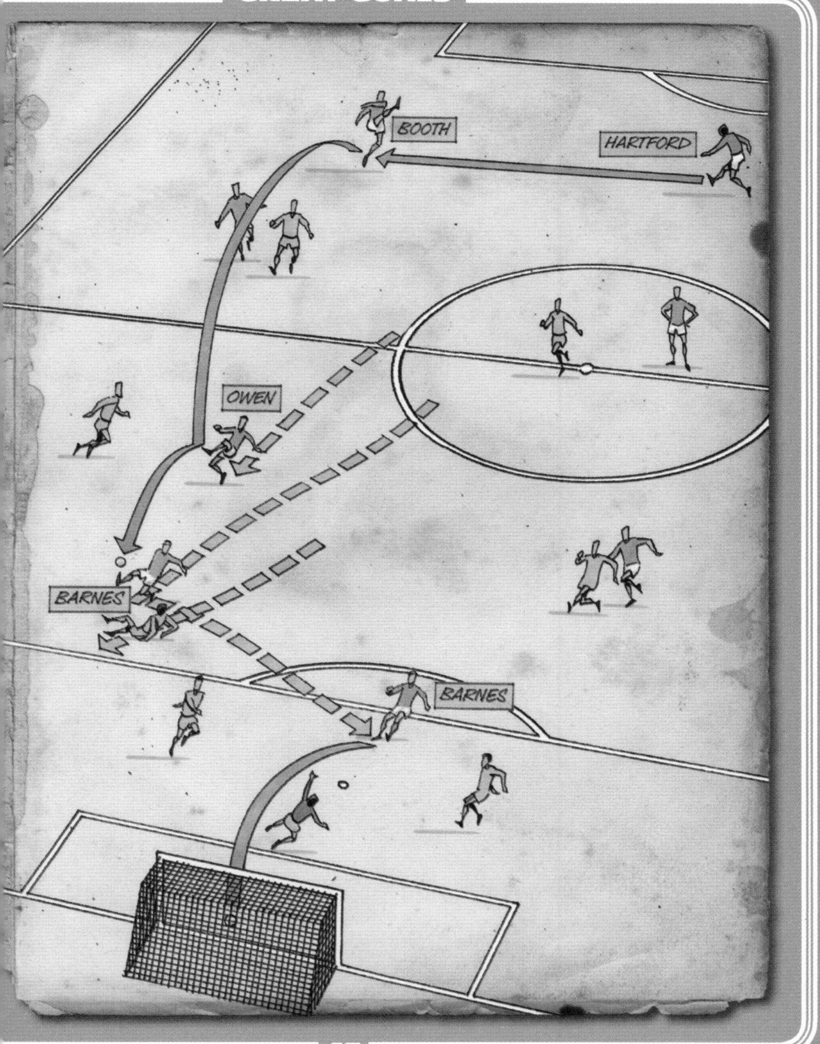
BOOTH
HARTFORD
OWEN
BARNES
BARNES

GEORGI KINKLADZE 1996 PREMIER LEAGUE V SOUTHAMPTON

Georgi Kinkladze became a cult figure in the three seasons he spent at Maine Road and lit up a gloomy period in the club's history.

He joined City in the summer of 1995 and was unveiled on the same day as Alan Ball arrived to take over as manager, two pivotal signings made by chairman Francis Lee.

It was to end in tears with Ball being sacked a year later following relegation and Kinkladze lasting two more troubled seasons. He did at least leave an abiding memory – a goal that must rank as one of best scored at Maine Road.

In a game against Southampton in March 1996, the Georgian genius weaved past four hapless defenders on a 40-yard run, invited Dave Beasant to commit himself and then delicately chipped the ball over the goalkeeper's body.

It typified his dazzling dribbling skills and sharp acceleration and underlined his reputation as one of the most exciting players in the country. Alan Ball compared it to Diego Maradona's second goal against England in the Azteca Stadium during the 1986 World Cup.

Kinkladze's solo effort also summed up the problem at the time – how best to accommodate such a supreme talent into a team pattern? "We just needed another two players on the same wavelength as him, and none of the managers could decide his best position," recalled Lee.

KINKLADZE
KINKLADZE
LOMAS

PAUL DICKOV
1999 DIVISION TWO PLAY-OFF FINAL V GILLINGHAM

Many Manchester City fans had to perform a sharp about-turn outside Wembley that grey May afternoon, not that they minded in the slightest.

They were drifting disconsolately out of the stadium with their side 2-0 down to Gillingham and were resigned to another season in the third tier of English football.

But when Kevin Horlock scored what seemed like a consolation goal with precisely 17 seconds left of normal time, the supporters hurried back through the exit doors and into the stands.

Moments later, an additional five minutes of stoppage time were signalled and City suddenly regained their self-belief as panic set in among the Gillingham players.

Four and a half minutes into injury time a loose ball dropped to Paul Dickov who struck a screaming shot into the top corner of the net to make it 2-2. Even now, City fans still pinch themselves when they reflect on the circumstances of that dramatic climax.

Neither side could break the deadlock in extra time but City won on penalties, thanks to Nicky Weaver's heroics in goal.

The consequences of defeat that day, and another season in the Nationwide League, do not bear thinking about. However, it was to prove the springboard for back-to-back promotions that saw Joe Royle's side elevated to the Premier League after a painful four-year absence.

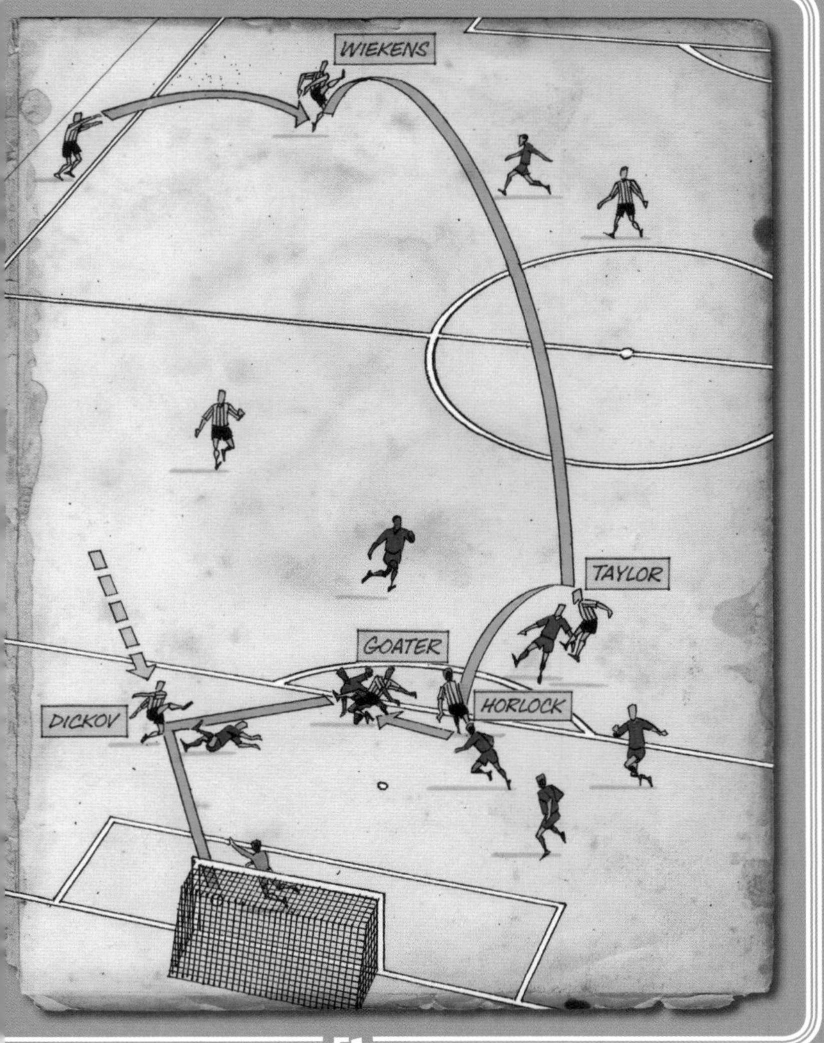
WIEKENS
TAYLOR
GOATER
DICKOV
HORLOCK

BENJANI 2008 PREMIER LEAGUE V MAN UTD

On the 50th anniversary of the Munich air crash, City faced United at Old Trafford.

Each of the City fans present at the game was given a retro-syle sky-blue-and-white scarf to commemorate the occasion and this has become a souvenir to be cherished as much as anything because of the result of the match and a sublime strike by Benjani in his first appearance in a City shirt.

Journalist Frank Swift, a former City goalkeeper, was among those killed in the Munich tragedy and before the match Sven Goran Eriksson joined counterpart Sir Alex Ferguson in laying wreaths either side of the centre circle.

The poignant tribute was observed impeccably by the 3,000-strong Blue contingent and Sven's men then proceeded to keep the United fans silent for the next 90 minutes by the way they conducted themselves out on the pitch.

Derby rivalry was all new to Benjani Mwaruwari, who was making his debut following his move from Portsmouth. But by the time the game was over his name was on the lips of every City fan.

Darius Vassell had put the visitors ahead and once the Zimbabwean had poached the second in first-half stoppage time, suddenly it dawned on the away supporters that a first victory at Old Trafford in 34 years was a possibility.

Benjani applied the faintest of flicks to Martin Petrov's superb inswinging delivery and the ball flew past Edwin Van der Sar into the far corner.

ONUOHA
DUNNE
RICHARDS
VASSELL
BENJANI
PETROV

ROBINHO 2008 PREMIER LEAGUE V ARSENAL

Only the best will do for the world's richest club, so Robinho appeared to fit the bill perfectly as a statement of the owners' intent.

The Brazilian trebled his wages by moving from Real Madrid in the summer of 2008 for a British record transfer fee of £32.5 million.

A gold-plated signing to complement the colour of the shirt he wears with pride for his country, Robson de Souza – to give him his full name – was a player to whet the appetite of the fans. The best from his collection of goals was arguably his wonder strike in the 3-0 triumph over Arsenal.

He had only got off the plane from South America the day before after playing for Brazil in a 6-2 friendly win over Portugal. But he had clearly brought some of the samba magic back with him as he raced on to a pass from Shaun Wright-Phillips before calmly chipping the ball over Gunners' goalkeeper Manuel Almunia.

The goal was so skilfully executed that it was almost a flashback to the days of the legendary Pele, the man who saw his protégé come through the ranks at Santos where he himself had achieved worldwide fame.

In truth, Robinho rarely scaled the heights in his 18 months at Eastlands but there were plenty of admirers among the crowds who appreciated the memory of this particular goal.

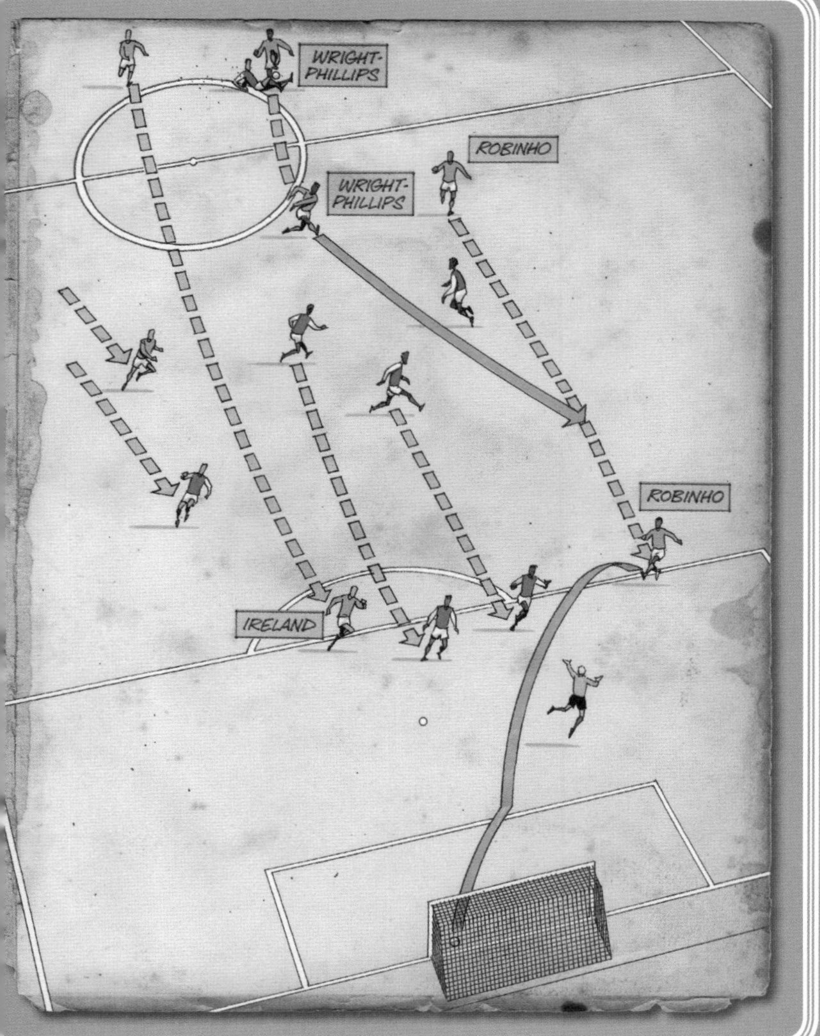
WRIGHT-
PHILLIPS
ROBINHO
WRIGHT-
PHILLIPS
ROBINHO
IRELAND

LET'S ALL GO BANANAS!

Manchester City fans were responsible for a football craze that blew up out of all proportion. Supporters went bananas as large inflatable pieces of the fruit turned up at matches and brought a smile to the game.

Credit for the idea is generally given to City fan Frank Newton who decided to take a five-foot banana to the first match of the season against Plymouth Argyle in August 1987.

He just did it for a laugh but could not have imagined it would lead to a craze that would sweep across the country.

The player who was unwittingly at the centre of it all was the much-travelled forward Imre Varadi who was scoring goals for fun for the Blues at the time. He was affectionately dubbed 'Imre Banana' – a nickname given to him during an away game at West Brom of all places.

The story goes that City fans started chanting for the appearance of "Imre Banana" when he was a substitute at the Hawthorns one night in November 1987. The moniker stuck and the rest, as they say, is history.

LET'S ALL GO BANANAS!

Wherever City went, the ripe yellow banana went with them. Even to this day Varadi, who works as a players' agent, is remembered fondly for the banana-rama.

"Two or three fans started waving bananas and shouting something about Imre Banana when I was jogging," he recalls. "Eventually there were thousands of them and then everyone wanted inflatables. English football was having a hard time after the Heysel tragedy and for a while it was good because it helped put fun back into the game.

"It was not as though Banana and Varadi rhymed but soon fans were dressing up the bananas in wigs, skirts and all sorts."

It was not until the following season that the inflatables craze really blew up. Bury had inflatable black puddings; Norwich City started selling inflatable canaries; West Ham United fans brought out the pumped up hammers and Grimsby Town supporters began waving puffed up giant fish.

It became a mass marketing exercise for the commercial managers of clubs up and down the country. The terraces looked more like huge market stalls, but imaginative City fans did not stop at fruit.

By this stage the creator Frank Newton had adopted a six-foot crocodile while other fans snapped into action with toy gorillas, sofas, panthers, sharks, penguins, golf clubs, a Spitfire, toucan, Frankenstein's monster… and even a paddling pool. Away matches in particular became an excuse to bring out the inflatables and there is one special game that sticks in the memory for the travelling Blue Army.

It was the trip to Stoke on Boxing Day 1988 when around 12,000 City fans turned the fixture at the Victoria Ground into a fancy dress party. The game ended in a 3-1 defeat for the Blues but that was overshadowed as the mass of bananas – dress code optional – made it a memorable day with away fans occupying two sides of the ground.

It is also worth remembering that the game of football had been scarred by the scourge of hooliganism at the time. The City fans – with their own 'banana republic' – had brought a touch of humour and frivolity at a time when it was much needed.

By this stage the nomadic Varadi had departed Maine Road to rejoin Sheffield Wednesday but he had left a lasting legacy. He even appeared on the BBC TV show *I Love the 80s* to talk about his contribution to a unique and fondly-remembered football phenomenon.

During that 1988/89 campaign the bananas remained at large and they were out in force again for the final game against Bradford City at Valley Parade.

The afternoon turned into one of those unforgettable occasions for the hordes of City fans and was capped by a late winner from Trevor Morley. His dramatic goal sent the Blues back into Division One and was scored at the end where the majority of City fans were gathered. David White supplied the cross which Morley prodded into the net and that was the cue for hundreds of bananas to be lifted into the air by jubilant fans.

It was a milestone for Manchester City. Not merely because the club had been promoted, but it also signalled the end of the bananas.

Not that the fans were deflated in any way, but by the time the team kicked off a new season against Liverpool at Anfield in August the inflatables were no longer a must-have fashion accessory.

One or two clubs were concerned they might block the spectators' view of the pitch and there was even a suggestion the bananas might have been a racist symbol, something which could not have been further from the truth.

It was purely a bit of fun and, like any gimmick, it was never going to last.

MAN CITY COMIC STRIP HISTORY 2

FULL BACK WAYNE BRIDGE REFUSED TO SHAKE THE HAND OF CHELSEA CAPTAIN JOHN TERRY BEFORE THE SIDES MET IN FEBRUARY 2010...

THE PAIR WERE ONCE FRIENDS AND TEAM-MATES AT STAMFORD BRIDGE, BUT FELL OUT AFTER TERRY'S ALLEGED AFFAIR WITH A FORMER GIRLFRIEND OF THE CITY MAN.

SO SUPPORTIVE WERE THE CITY PLAYERS OF THEIR COLLEAGUE IN THE WHOLE EPISODE THAT THEY RALLIED ROUND AND WON 4-2, CRAIG BELLAMY AND CARLOS TEVEZ EACH SCORING TWO GOALS.

THE CITY CHRONICLES
GLORY DAYS
1965–73

An ailing manager to help an ailing club – that would have been a harsh but accurate description of the circumstances that surrounded the appointment of Joe Mercer in July 1965.

The former Arsenal and Everton player took the brave decision to accept the Maine Road post barely a year after stepping down from his role as Aston Villa manager after suffering a stroke. His tracksuit days were over but within eight days he had brought in Malcolm Allison to act as his No 2. Like Mercer he was out of work, after being sacked by Plymouth Argyle.

Mike Summerbee, a new face for a new era under Mercer and Allison

One of their first moves was to sign Mike Summerbee, the player who had scored the winning goal for Swindon in front of just 8,015 fans at Maine Road seven months earlier.

One of Allison's other tasks was to remove an inferiority complex about Manchester United. It was a challenge he was more than happy to accept, issuing a warning to Sandy Busby, son of the United manager Matt Busby, at a celebration dinner to honour United's 1965 championship success. "You've had a 20-year start but we'll catch you in three," boasted Allison who also struck a £10 wager with Pat Crerand after the Scot had claimed City would never get 30,000 inside Maine Road again.

Francis Lee, who was to spark greater success for the Blues

After just two months of the season Allison had collected his tenner off Crerand after 34,000 saw a goalless draw with Norwich. His other prediction would also prove spot on.

First, City had to get back into the top flight which they duly achieved when Colin Bell scored the winner at Rotherham within a matter of weeks of signing from Bury.

England won the World Cup that summer and a few weeks later Tony Book joined City for what would become a season of consolidation in the First Division. The team was taking shape and left

Joe Mercer shows off the League Championship trophy at Maine Road in 1968

winger Tony Coleman added more balance to a side containing the likes of Mike Doyle, Neil Young, George Heslop, Glyn Pardoe and Alan Oakes. And goalkeeper Ken Mulhearn was brought in from Stockport County.

The most notable signing, though, was that of

Francis Lee from Bolton Wanderers and he provided the spark that was to launch the Blues on a terrific run that included one of the most famous games staged at Maine Road.

City destroyed Tottenham 4–1 in December 1967 in a game billed as 'Ballet on Ice' because of the snowy conditions. It was shown on the BBC's *Match of the Day* and underlined the formidable talents of a team on the verge of greatness.

Victory over United at Old Trafford the following March was a turning point before the First Division title was wrapped up with a thrilling 4–3 win over Newcastle at St James' Park.

The following season was something of an anti-climax with a mid-table finish in the league but there was ample compensation with a place in the FA Cup final. Tommy Booth scored the winner in the last minute of the semi-final against Everton.

The hero at Wembley was Neil Young whose goal gave City a 1-0 victory over Leicester City. It meant the club were back in Europe with a chance to make amends for a humiliating defeat by Fenerbahçe earlier that season in the first round of the European Cup.

Tony Coleman's biggest concerns before the cup final were the tattoos on his hand. He felt embarrassed shaking hands with royalty so a surgeon had the tattoos removed – an arrangement set up by Allison who gave the doctor two cup final tickets as a thank-you gesture.

Captain Tony Book and the FA Cup get the chair treatment after the 1969 final

Coleman, introduced to Princess Anne on the pitch before the game by skipper Tony Book, did not want to utter just the usual "Pleased to meet you ma'am" greeting so added the words "Give my regards to your mum and dad."

So the league title in 1968; the cup the next year… what lay in store the following season for fans revelling in the shift in power in Manchester derbies?

Mike Doyle celebrates his equaliser against West Brom in the 1970 League Cup final

The answer for 1970 was major domestic and European success via the League Cup and European Cup-Winners' Cup.

United were beaten 4-3 on aggregate in the semi-finals of the League Cup, making a final against West Brom an even sweeter occasion. Francis Lee played arguably his finest game in City colours as goals from Mike Doyle and Glyn Pardoe won the cup on a Wembley surface that had been left in a dreadful state after the Horse of the Year Show.

Conditions were also poor for the European final in Vienna the next month. That too ended in a 2-1 triumph for the Manchester side over Gornik Zabrze with Neil Young and Francis Lee the goalscorers.

The 1970/71 season ended trophyless and the defence of the Cup-Winners' Cup ended at the semi-final stage against FA Cup holders Chelsea.

The summer brought with it a host of changes,

including the widening of the Maine Road pitch; the opening of the new North Stand with its state-of-the-art electronic scoreboard; the signing of striker Wyn Davies and the appointment of new directors including a certain Peter Swales.

But trouble was brewing in the boardroom with Mercer and Allison placing their allegiances with different camps.

In October 1971, Mercer moved upstairs to become general manager and the following month City and United drew 3-3 in what is widely acknowledged as one of the greatest derby matches of all time.

By March, the Blues were four points clear at the top of the First Division and Rodney Marsh was signed from QPR for £200,000. Allison had wanted to show he could manage on his own but the gamble did not come off as the team lost impetus to miss out on the league by one point.

Francis Lee finished with 33 goals – a record 13 of them from the penalty spot earning him the nickname Lee Won Pen – and Mercer went to Coventry in June 1972, feeling he no longer had any influence.

The following year Allison joined Crystal Palace, claiming he could no longer motivate the players.

The glory days were well and truly over.

Rodney Marsh ties a Burnley defender in knots in 1970

11
2010

KIT PARADE

Bellamy or Bell... Tevez or Tueart...

the names on the field may change but the emotions are just the same. The sight of that famous sky-blue shirt racing towards goal is guaranteed to set the pulse racing. All City fans have their own favourite recollection of one of their heroes producing a moment of genius.

It might not necessarily have happened while wearing a blue shirt. Supporters of a certain vintage will never forget Neil Young smashing the winner in the 1969 FA Cup final against Leicester sporting red and black stripes.

An original classic, City started out wearing the famous cornflower blue

Paul Dickov even wore a shirt of fluorescent yellow with black stripes when he scored that unforgettable stoppage time equaliser in the Second Division play-off final against Gillingham some 30 years later.

But it is safe to assume that the picture framed in most minds will be painted in sky blue – for more than a century the first choice shirt of Manchester City FC and it was the chosen colour when the club were formed in 1894.

City were said to have links with the Masonic community in east Manchester and Cambridge light blue – a colour said to indicate friendship – was selected. The origins of the club's colours are unclear and before the days of MCFC it was thought the first proper kit was black with a white Maltese-style cross. A plain white shirt was also worn, although records are a little confused – as much as anything because the strip was washed so often the colours probably faded.

That could also have been the case with the shorts which were sometimes described as grey. In the days when the club were known as Ardwick AFC, a striped jersey featuring Oxford blue and white may also have been used.

What is known for certain is that the basic home colour scheme has remained relatively unchanged since 1894 with the shorts predominantly white.

There have been one or two exceptions to the shade of shirt down the years. The kit worn in the 1926 FA Cup final was described at the time as "cornflower blue" and the traditionalists were not too impressed to see a deeper "laser blue" emerge in the late 1990s.

Fashions have most certainly altered during the ages and so too have the combinations of shorts and

Don Revie and Johnny Hart in the 1956 cup final kit

The class of 69 in shirts chosen by Malcolm Allison to evoke the invincible AC Milan team of the time

socks. They have rotated between sky blue, dark blue and white in various combinations.

Maroon was also incorporated into the socks, most notably during the greatest period in the club's history in the late Sixties and early Seventies. Blue socks were trimmed with maroon and white hoops before the club indulged a brief flirtation with royal blue socks with red and white hoops.

Sky-blue shorts were introduced between 1976 and 1985 and were worn most famously during that era when City lost to Tottenham in the first FA Cup final that went to a Wembley replay. Tommy Hutchison scored at both ends in that 1981 final before Ricky

Villa stole the show in the replay. The blue shorts also made a brief reappearance in the 2006/07 season.

Inevitably, the sky-blue shirt has seen numerous changes in style to adapt to changing fashion trends. Collared necks, crew necks and V-necks have been worn at various intervals.

The main away colour has been maroon, worn most memorably in the cup finals of 1934 and 1956. The 1956 shirt had a stylish white stripe and it was while wearing stripes that City enjoyed their next Wembley success 33 years later.

They took to the field against Leicester City in red and black stripes, the away colours adopted by coach Malcolm Allison at that time to copy AC Milan. He felt it gave the side a look of invincibility and results during that period showed his assessment was right.

Indeed, there was a colour clash for that Leicester game but Big Mal volunteered to play in the alternative kit rather than toss a coin to decide which team should play in blue.

The continental look was also evident in a white shirt that had a red and blue diagonal strip and, most recently, a retro red and black sash on a white shirt.

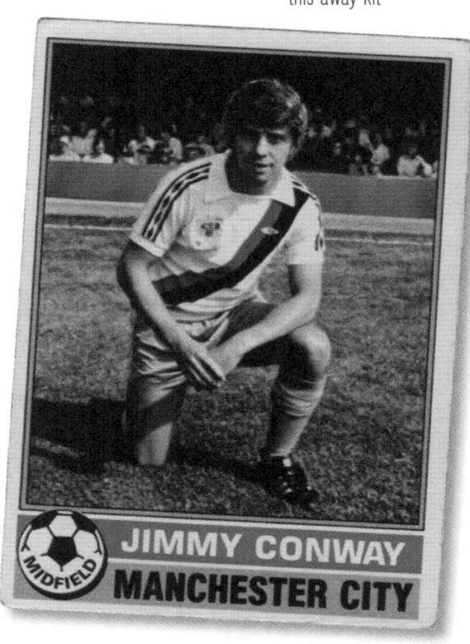

A continental influence was also evident in this away kit

Yellow has also been a popular alternative over the years and other colours, worn as either a second or third choice, include royal blue with diagonal stripes, black, silver, navy blue, white and even orange.

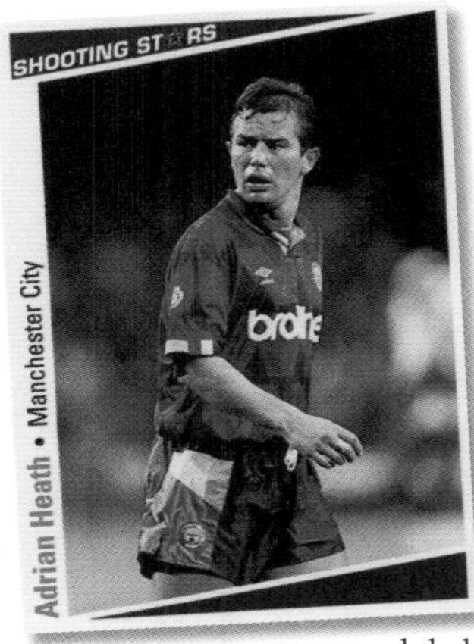

Maroon has been the main away colour, shown here in a typically busy design

For the cup final in 1933, City players made history by wearing numbers on their shirts for the first time. Opponents Everton were numbered 1-11 while City's shirts went from 12-22.

The advent of the Premier League in 1992 brought with it the practice of printing players' names on the back of shirts. As replica shirts became more and more popular, clubs seized on this marketing opportunity, especially with satellite television providing global exposure.

It was further good news for shirt sponsors who had arrived on the scene a decade earlier and, as one of the biggest clubs in the land, City became a prime target for companies wishing to use the national sport to advertise their business.

The Swedish car makers Saab became the first shirt sponsors in the early 1980s before the contract was handed over to the electronics giant Philips.

Another international company, Brother – makers of printers, fax machines and photocopiers – had links with Manchester through a base in Audenshaw and took over as official shirt sponsors between the late 1980s and early 1990s.

Computer game firm Eidos wanted City used as a vehicle to promote their Lara Croft brand, a relationship that lasted until 2002 when First Advice offered financial and legal help.

Then it was the turn of travel agents Thomas Cook before Etihad, the national airline of the United Arab Emirates, became an obvious partner for the club once they came under Arab ownership.

One number never to be seen on the back of a City shirt again is 23 – it was retired in 2003 as a mark of respect to midfielder Marc-Vivien Foe who died after collapsing on the pitch playing for Cameroon.

Carlos Tevez shows off City's 2009/10 shirt – knitted hairband optional

TERRACE LEGENDS

COLIN BELL

Colin Bell is widely regarded as the greatest player to wear the blue shirt of Manchester City.

His endless stamina led to him being called Nijinsky after the famous racehorse that won the Derby, a nickname given by World Cup team-mate Jeff Astle in 1970.

Bell was a real thoroughbred, a midfield genius in the glorious Manchester City team that lifted four major trophies. The names Bell-Lee-Summerbee still roll off the tongue today – a Holy Trinity that helped make City the best team in England in the late 1960s and early 1970s.

Colin Bell was signed from Bury in March 1966 for £45,000. He was spotted by assistant manager Malcolm Allison who deliberately misled the watching scouts who had come from other interested clubs by shouting from the directors' box at Gigg Lane: "He can't head and can't pass… he's hopeless."

The unusual tactic paid off and Bell blossomed at City, the perfect platform to display his all-round skill and supreme athleticism.

He was strong in the tackle and he could score goals too. Bell won 48 caps for his country, scoring nine goals, and was recognised as one of the finest midfield players England has produced.

"Colin Bell was the best player I ever worked with. His all-round ability was phenomenal"
Malcolm Allison

The 'King of the Kippax' made almost 500 appearances for his club, scoring more than 150 goals. It would have been a lot more but his career was cut short in its prime by a knee injury suffered in a Manchester derby in 1975. He was only 29.

He made a brave attempt at a comeback, receiving an emotional reception when he appeared as a substitute against Newcastle two years later. However, he could not recapture his earlier form and in 1979 this shy, modest man was forced to retire.

Bell's role in the club's history will never be forgotten and to reflect his cult status the west stand at the club's new stadium was named the Colin Bell Stand. He now works as an ambassador for the club and there could be no finer representative than this true hero.

Born: **Hesleden, County Durham; 26th February 1946**
Man City appearances: **498**
Man City goals: **153**
Honours won with Man City: **First Division Championship (1968), FA Cup (1969), European Cup-Winners' Cup (1970), League Cup (1970)**
Other clubs: **Bury (1963), San Jose Earthquakes (1980)**
International appearances: **England, 48**

COLIN BELL FACTFILE

TONY BOOK

Tony Book won more trophies than any other Manchester City captain – not bad for a man who spent most of his playing days working part-time as a bricklayer! Maybe he was laying the foundations for the twilight of his career when he would become one of the unlikely stars during the club's golden age?

Book made his debut for the Blues in August 1966, just two months short of his 31st birthday. He was bought from Plymouth Argyle for £17,000 and this slow starter had only made his League bow at the age of 29, having spent most of his career playing part-time for non-League Bath City while he worked in the building trade.

Joe Mercer feared he might be too old but was persuaded by Malcolm Allison, who was convinced Book had the fitness and qualities needed to take over at right back.

In the event, he missed just one match in the next two

seasons and was a natural choice as captain, earning the nickname 'Skip.'

He led City to the First Division title at Newcastle in 1968, the first of many highlights. The following year he was again hoisted aloft by team-mates after collecting the FA Cup; after League Cup and Cup-Winners' Cup successes it had become a well-rehearsed routine.

In 1969 he shared the Football Writers' player of the year award with Derby's Dave Mackay.

After his playing days, Book turned to coaching and became assistant to Ron Saunders in 1973, later taking over as manager. When City won the League Cup in 1976, Book made history as the first man to win the trophy as a player and a manager and with players of the calibre of Dennis Tueart, Asa Hartford and Peter Barnes in the ranks it was an exciting time.

City missed out on the First Division title by a point in 1977, finishing runners-up to Liverpool, and came joint fourth the following year. Malcolm Allison made an unsuccessful return as 'coaching overlord' in 1979, thereby weakening Book's influence.

Book later filled a variety of roles and was caretaker manager on numerous occasions.

"He did miracles for us and had great speed"
Joe Mercer

Born: **Bath, 4th September 1934**
Man City appearances: **312**
Man City goals: **5**
Honours won with Man City: **First Division Championship (1968), FA Cup (1969), European Cup-Winners' Cup (1970), League Cup (1970, 1976)**
Other clubs: **Frome Town, (1955), Bath City (1956), Toronto City (1964), Plymouth Argyle (1964)**
International appearances: **0**

TONY BOOK FACTFILE

ROY CLARKE

Wiry Welsh winger Roy Clarke completed an unusual hat-trick by a quirk of fate. He achieved the rare distinction of playing in three different divisions of the Football League in consecutive matches.

Clarke helped Cardiff gain promotion from the Third Division in 1946/47 and was then sold to Manchester City for £12,000, making his debut for the newly-crowned Second Division champions in the final match of the season.

His first goal for the Blues was against Wolves on the opening day of the following season in the First Division.

Clarke had worked in coal mines during the Second World War and was a natural all-round sportsman, excelling at swimming, rugby and even baseball as a schoolboy.

But it was as a footballer that he shone most of all, spending more than a decade dashing up and down the wing in a City shirt, refusing to be intimidated by giant defenders despite his slim frame.

Clarke suffered both delight and despair in the 1955 FA Cup semi-final, scoring the winning goal against Sunderland with a spectacular diving header only to suffer an injury late in the tie that kept him out of the final which City lost to Newcastle.

He was to make amends at Wembley the following year, setting up the opening goal in a 3-1 victory over Birmingham City. By now he had won the last of his 22 caps for Wales and had left an indelible mark for club and country.

His days at Maine Road were far from over, though, and in 1960 he founded the club's Development Association. Six years later he and wife Kath took over the management of the Blues' new social club which they ran for almcst 25 years, a haunt where players, management and fans could mix.

For good measure, he was a driving force behind the creation of the Former Players' Association and his affable nature meant he was a perfect ambassador for the club, a role he undertook by escorting fans on stadium tours. Roy passed away in March 2006.

"We put the FA Cup under our bed in 1956 after we were left with it at the end of the evening"
Roy's wife Kath

Born: **Newport, South Wales, 1st June 1925**
Man City appearances: **370**
Man City goals: **79**
Honours won with Man City: **FA Cup (1956)**
Other clubs: **Cardiff City (1942), Stockport County (1958)**
International appearances: **Wales, 22**

ROY CLARKE FACTFILE

RICHARD DUNNE

Richard Dunne might not sell shirts in Beijing but what he might have lacked in marketing appeal, he made up for as a model of consistency as the cornerstone of the City defence.

Such towering performances received deserved recognition when he was named the club's player of the year for an unprecedented four seasons in a row from the 2004/05 campaign.

The Republic of Ireland international was such a reformed character he became club captain – a far cry from the early days when he seemed intent on pressing the self-destruct button.

One of his biggest fans was former manager Joe Royle, who gave him his big break at Everton and then signed him for City for £3 million in October 2000. Dunne's team-mates on Merseyside nicknamed him the Honey Monster because of his hulky frame and lumbering style.

Accusations that he was an oversized and sluggish right back refused to go away during his early days in Manchester. To some he was more of a beer monster than a lovable character used to advertise breakfast cereal.

“I feared losing my job when the manager sent me home and told me not to come back for two weeks”
Richard Dunne

On one occasion a hungover Dunne was sent home from training by Kevin Keegan and suspended by the club after turning up in what was described as “a dishevelled state”. A club statement went on: “Richard Dunne has accepted the seriousness of his situation, having had similar disciplinary problems in the past.”

Eventually Dunne realised the error of his ways cleaned up his act. The resulting transformation to classy centre half was incredible. He became fitter physically and stronger mentally; his speed improved and so did his technical ability.

After nine years' service, he was sold to Aston Villa with the comments of City chief executive Garry Cook a year earlier probably still ringing in his ears. “China and India are gagging for football content to watch and we're going to tell them that City is their content. We need a superstar to get through that door. Richard Dunne doesn't roll off the tongue in Beijing.”

Born: **Tallaght, Dublin, 21st September 1979**
Man City appearances: **345**
Man City goals: **7**
Honours won with Man City: **Division One Championship (2002)**
Other clubs: **Everton (1994), Aston Villa (2009)**
International appearances: **Republic of Ireland, 54**

RICHARD DUNNE FACTFILE

SHAUN GOATER

The Manchester City fans certainly knew how to satisfy Shaun Goater's appetite for goals.

All they had to do was sing "Feed the Goat and he will score" and the Bermudan would start banging the goals in. And somehow the Goat always seemed hungry for more, inviting his adoring public to 'come dine with me'.

Goater was signed from Bristol City for £400,000 on transfer deadline day in March 1998. Joe Royle later described it as his shrewdest move as a manager.

It was, though, an unconvincing start for a player regarded as a journeyman striker. His gangling style was not easy on the eye; he was clumsy in front of goal and soon became a target for the boo boys.

His confidence was so low he even begged his manager to leave him out of the side as City headed for relegation to the Second Division.

But Goater never gave up and scored 21 goals the

following season to help the club to promotion. In the following campaign he topped the Division One scoring charts with 29 goals and was named the club's player of the season, final proof that he had won over the supporters.

Two years later he became the first City player since Francis Lee in 1972 to score more than 30 goals in a season.

> **"You'd have to go a long way to find such a well-liked and thorough professional as Shaun"**
> Joe Royle

He saw off the likes of George Weah and Paulo Wanchope in the fight for a place in the forward line. The arrival of two other big name strikers – Nicolas Anelka and Robbie Fowler – also failed to put Goater in the shade.

Opportunities were limited under Kevin Keegan but the Goat did finish with a flourish, scoring twice in a 3-1 win over Manchester United in the last derby game at Maine Road in November 2002. His first goal will be remembered for a mistake by Gary Neville – his second was his 100th for the Blues. In the return match he scored within nine seconds of coming on as a substitute.

Such was Goater's popularity that 400 City fans went to Southend in 2006 to see his final game in English football.

SHAUN GOATER FACTFILE

Born: **Bermuda, 25th February 1970**

Man City appearances: **212**

Man City goals: **103**

Honours won with Man City: **Division Two play-off winners (1999), Division One runners-up (2000), Division One Championship (2002)**

Other clubs: **Manchester United (1989), Rotherham (1989), Notts County (loan, 1993), Bristol City (1996), Reading (2003), Coventry (loan, 2005), Southend (2005)**

International appearances: **Bermuda, 36**

FRANCIS LEE

It is rare for a footballer to play for a club and then proceed to own it but that was precisely the path followed by Francis Lee.

Manager Joe Mercer described the club's record £60,000 signing from Bolton Wanderers as the final piece in the jigsaw. How prophetic his comments were. When Lee signed on the dotted line in October 1967 it was a defining moment with the Blues irrepressible from then on as they marched triumphantly to the League Championship.

Six years earlier Lee had made his Bolton debut against City as a 16-year-old, scoring past Bert Trautmann and setting up a winner for Nat Lofthouse.

At Maine Road, the barrel-chested forward was the ideal foil for his team-mates and he bagged 16 goals in 31 appearances in that 1967/68 season, the last of which came in the epic 4-3 title decider at Newcastle.

Lee's self-belief spread throughout the team and he

played his football with a style and a swagger which epitomised the side. He remained a prolific goalscorer season after season and in the 1971/72 campaign converted a record 15 penalties, earning the nickname Lee Won Pen.

He became the first City player to play for England in a World Cup finals in Mexico in 1970.

“One of my biggest regrets in management was that I couldn't take Francis Lee to Liverpool”
Bill Shankly

Four years later the new chairman, Peter Swales, sold him to Derby County, a move that would haunt the Blues as Lee returned to score the winner for his new club – who finished as League Champions. Lee had warned Swales he would regret selling him and, sure enough, that is how it transpired.

Lee was an entrepreneur and during his Bolton days had set up a waste paper business that was to make him a millionaire. He would later sell the company and concentrate his energies on training racehorses.

His wealthy position allowed him to return as chairman in 1994 following a bitter boardroom battle with Swales. However, within four years Lee had departed himself after failing to revive the glory days, although he was instrumental in sowing the seeds for the move to a new stadium.

Born: **Westhoughton, Bolton; 29th April 1944**
Man City appearances: **328**
Man City goals: **148**
Honours won with Man City: **First Division Championship (1968), FA Cup (1969), European Cup Winners' Cup (1970); League Cup (1970)**
Other clubs: **Bolton (1959), Derby County (1974)**
International appearances: **England, 27**

FRANCIS LEE FACTFILE

BILLY MEREDITH

Billy Meredith brought colour and controversy to football as one of the game's first genuine superstars.

As a household name he earned £4 a week, a fraction of the wages paid to contemporary music hall stars. Players had no insurance against injury and no guarantee of financial security once their careers were over.

Meredith set up the first players' union, the forerunner of today's PFA, and was the force behind the demand for higher wages. He had many disputes with his managers and was also firmly against women watching football.

His trademark was a toothpick he chewed while playing to help his concentration. It meant he could get his teeth into opponents with his tricky skills as a talented outside right. When play shifted to the other wing, he would entertain spectators with a touchline chat.

The Welsh international was a big star by the time he scored the only goal to give the Blues their first FA Cup final triumph in 1904. City also went close to winning the championship that year.

"A man who stood up for the rights of fellow professionals"
PFA Chief Executive Gordon Taylor

But 12 months later the club were in turmoil after they were found guilty by the Football Association of making additional payments to players.

Meredith was suspended for a year after he was accused of bribing an opposing player to lose a vital match. The club were forced to sell players and one of them was Meredith. To make matters worse, he was bought by Manchester United at auction for £500.

Having helped the blue half of Manchester claim their first major honour, he promptly did the same for the red half, leading United to two League titles and the FA Cup.

In 1921, he fell out with United and returned to Maine Road, ending with a career record of 146 League goals for the Blues.

He had remarkable longevity and played in an FA Cup semi-final at the age of 49!

Despite the bribery scandal, he was worshipped on the terraces and maintained his innocence until the day he died in 1958 at the age of 83.

BILLY MEREDITH FACTFILE

Born: **Chirk, North Wales, 30th July 1874**
Man City appearances: **393**
Man City goals: **152**
Honours won with Man City: **FA Cup (1904)**
Other clubs: **Manchester United (1906)**
International appearances: **Wales, 48**

MIKE SUMMERBEE

Mike Summerbee enjoyed the bachelor lifestyle to the full back in the Sixties and was a good friend of George Best.

They were men about town on the Manchester party scene, dating beauty queens and mixing in showbiz circles – after kicking lumps out of each other on the football field earlier in the afternoon.

The Manchester United player was even best man at Summerbee's wedding to Tina, whom he met on one of their nightclub visits.

It was a vintage era for Manchester football and Summerbee, known as Buzzer, was certainly savouring the good life at Maine Road. He was bought from Swindon Town for £35,000 in August 1965, the second signing made by manager Joe Mercer. "I was earning £35 a week at Preston and Joe said he could only afford to give me £40 a week because the club was skint," recalled Summerbee. "Malcolm Allison was the best coach this country has seen and he made me an international footballer."

Summerbee came from good footballing stock. His father George played for Preston in the same team as Bill Shankly and a third generation followed in dad's footsteps when Nicky left Swindon to join City in the 1990s.

"His switch to centre forward was one of the reasons for our championship success"
Malcolm Allison

Mike was a brilliant winger feared by full backs and was not frightened of a hard tackle. He was one of the game's colourful characters and enjoyed winding up defenders and opposing fans.

He possessed great pace, an ability to deliver a good cross and was equally at home in the role of centre forward, a position he filled for much of the championship-winning season.

It was Summerbee who set up Neil Young's winning goal in the 1969 FA Cup final, But injury prevented him from playing in the European Cup-Winners' Cup success the following year.

He captained City in the 1974 League Cup final against Wolves and a year later was transferred to Burnley.

He has plenty of amusing anecdotes about the old days and still works hard behind the scenes to ensure the club is the friendly, family club it was during his playing days.

MIKE SUMMERBEE FACTFILE

Born: **Preston, 15th December 1942**
Man City appearances: **449**
Man City goals: **68**
Honours won with Man City: **First Division Championship (1968), FA Cup (1969), European Cup-Winners' Cup (1970), League Cup (1970)**
Other clubs: **Swindon (1959), Burnley (1975), Blackpool (1976), Stockport County (1976)**
International appearances: **England, 8**

CARLOS TEVEZ

Carlos Tevez was bound to be an instant hit with the fans after scoring 29 goals in his first season at Manchester City.

But it was the Argentinian's words – as well as his actions – that further endeared him to the blue half of Manchester after his controversial move from Old Trafford.

"Fergie, Fergie sign him up," was the cry from fans after his every goal as they teased their fierce rivals over the United manager's apparent reluctance to get him to stay.

Tevez did not need asking twice about joining the revolution that was under way across town but he was a little slow out of the scoring blocks because of a lingering injury.

Once fully fit, the goals flowed as the stocky striker prospered in the free attacking role he claimed he had been denied by his previous employers. His fee was never disclosed, with £25 million the most quoted figure handed over to the management company who hold his registration as part of a complicated ownership arrangement. Whatever the amount, it was money well spent.

Tevez was at the centre of a spat between the clubs. The Blues put up a 'Welcome to Manchester' poster, featuring the player, in the city centre. Sir Alex Ferguson responded by describing City as "a small club with a small mentality" accusing them of acting like "noisy neighbours".

"I've learned a lot from Carlos – he's one of the best strikers in the world"

Argentina team-mate Lionel Messi

Tevez scored three goals against his old club in both legs of the Carling Cup semi-final in January 2010, doubtless motivated by a jibe from Gary Neville who was quoted as saying that United were right not to sign Tevez, indicating he was not worth £25 million.

In turn, Tevez called his former team-mate a "boot-licking moron" and relations soured still further when the pair exchanged insults and gestures during an explosive first meeting.

City eventually missed out on a place at Wembley but an appearance in a major cup semi-final had been long overdue. Furthermore, City were getting under the skin of their arch rivals just like during their halcyon days – and thanks largely to their talisman Tevez.

Born: **Buenos Aires, 5th February 1984**
Man City appearances: **38**
Man City goals: **29**
Honours won with Man City: **N/a**
Other clubs: **Boca Juniors (2001), Corinthians (2004) West Ham United (2006), Manchester United (2007)**
International appearances: **Argentina, 51**

CARLOS TEVEZ FACTFILE

SHAUN WRIGHT-PHILLIPS

Shaun Wright-Phillips was barely out of short pants when he watched his famous stepfather score twice in a Wembley final.

It was 1990 and proud Shaun, then just eight, peered over the heads in the stands as Ian Wright came on as a substitute for Crystal Palace against Manchester United.

Little did he imagine that 17 years later SWP, as he is known, was to play in an FA Cup final himself for Chelsea against United. Only this time, unlike his dad, Shaun would be on the winning team.

He probably did not grow that much between Wembley visits and at 5ft 5in it was his lack of height that threatened his career as a footballer. His family claim he was rejected by Nottingham Forest as a 15-year-old because he was too small, although their official line is that the travelling from his home in London had become too much.

But City manager Frank Clark saw potential and decided that size was not everything. He had recruited the highly-rated Jim Cassell to run the club's academy and Wright-Phillips was to become its most high profile product.

"I told his dad that Shaun is a very special player and will go right to the top"
Kevin Keegan

He made his League debut in October 1999 when there was already a glimpse of the speed, agility and balance that were to develop over subsequent seasons when he blossomed into an exciting wide player under Kevin Keegan.

He came to symbolise the club's revival and established himself as a fans' favourite with his willingness to sign autographs and present awards. Indeed, for a record four successive seasons he was voted the club's young player of the year by the fans.

Bradley Wright-Phillips was also on City's books but never emerged from the shadows of his older brother, who made his England debut as a goalscoring substitute against Ukraine in a game at St James' Park in 2004.

A year later he was bought by Chelsea for £21 million but after three seasons was back at Eastlands, entertaining the fans once again with his bravery and skill on the right wing.

Born: **London, 25th October 1981**
Man City appearances: **214**
Man City goals: **46**
Honours won with Man City: **Division One runners-up (2000); Division One champions (2002)**
Other clubs: **Nottingham Forest (1997), Chelsea (2005)**
International appearances: **England, 29 caps**

SHAUN WRIGHT-PHILLIPS FACTFILE

TO EUROPE!

Most City fans were robbed of witnessing one of the greatest nights in the club's history.

The 5,000 supporters who went to Vienna to watch the 1970 European Cup Winners' Cup final victory over Gornik Zabre were elated. They had seen their all-conquering heroes, a team made up entirely of English players, lift a major European prize on foreign soil.

But the occasion lost some of its prestige because, amazingly, it was not shown live on British television! A European final would have been shown in normal circumstances but the 1970 final clashed with the FA Cup final replay between Chelsea and Leeds United. That game was broadcast by the BBC and ITV were unable to screen the City match live, so featured only highlights later in the evening. Which meant City fans back home were deprived of sharing a proud moment with the sporting nation.

Unfortunately, those in Austria were not exactly looked

after either. The Prater Stadium was almost totally open and supporters had to stand in the pouring rain to watch a final that drew a crowd variously reported as between 7,968 and 12,000.

As Gornik were from behind the Iron Curtain, only 300 of the club's officials, players' wives and fans were allowed to travel to the final.

Colin Bell shoots on an atrocious pitch in Copenhagen in the 1971 ECWC play-off against Gornik

City won the game 2-1. Neil Young scored the first goal and was then fouled for a penalty converted by Francis Lee. Gornik replied midway through the second half but City thoroughly deserved their second piece of silverware of the season, having lifted the League Cup against West Bromwich Albion at Wembley a few weeks earlier.

It was a glorious climax to a campaign that had seen victories over Atletico Bilbao, SK Lierse, Academica Coimbra and Schalke 04 in the semi-final.

A sweet moment too for manager Joe Mercer and coach Malcolm Allison who, two years earlier, after winning the league had made his infamous remark: "We will terrify Europe." Big Mal had forgotten to say when but, in fact, was only a year late with his promise.

In 1968/69 City entered the European Cup for the first time, only to be given a rude awakening after

City's name is pulled in a European draw in 2003 for the first time in 24 years

underestimating Turkish side Fenerbahçe and losing 2-1 on aggregate in the first round.

As the holders of the Cup Winners' Cup, City began the 1970/71 campaign and their trophy defence with a win over Linfield on away goals. After overcoming Honved, the quarter-final draw again paired City with Gornik Zabre. Both clubs won their home leg 2-0 which meant a replay at a neutral venue was needed as drawn games were not decided on away goals then.

City ran out 3-1 winners in Copenhagen, putting them through to face Chelsea in the semi-final. But injuries caught up with Joe Mercer's boys and they lost both legs 1-0, ending hopes of becoming the first side to retain the trophy. Chelsea went on to beat Real Madrid in the final.

City's next foray into Europe was the UEFA Cup in 1972, courtesy of finishing fourth in the league. Joe Mercer had left and they went out at the first hurdle, losing 4-3 on aggregate to a Valencia side managed by the former Real Madrid great Alfredo Di Stefano.

Four years later Tony Book, by now the manager, guided City into the UEFA Cup but it proved short-lived, a 1-0 win over Juventus in the first leg – thanks to a Brian Kidd goal – wiped out by the Italians who won 2-0 in Turin.

The 1977/78 campaign was also fruitless, with a first round exit in the same competition against the Polish side Widzew Lodz. Losing a two-goal lead in the first leg proved costly as the Poles went through on the away goals rule.

Better times lay ahead in 1978/79 when City got to the quarter finals before losing to Borussia Mönchengladbach. In the previous round AC Milan were beaten 3-0 at Maine Road; the first meeting in the San Siro, which ended 2-2, was delayed by 24 hours because of fog.

It was another 24 years before City played in Europe again, results in the Fair Play League earning them a place in the UEFA Cup in 2003. Wins over TNS from Wales, and Belgium's Lokeren, were followed by defeat on away goals to Polish team Groclin.

In 2008/09, City got as far as the quarter-finals of the UEFA Cup before going out to Hamburg. They ended up playing 16 ties in Europe that season, having gone through three qualifying rounds to get to the group stage.

Nicolas Anelka in action against Groclin in 2003

Their season began as early as mid July when they played Streymur in the remote Faroe Islands. The hardest part was actually getting there and a group of intrepid fans even hired a fishing trawler, though rough seas meant they eventually had to travel by air.

Thomas
Cook

THE CITY CHRONICLES
CHANGING TIMES
1973-92

Peter Swales staked his reputation

on Ron Saunders as the man to revive the good old days. The Manchester businessman had taken over as chairman in October 1973 and had promised to make the Blues the top club in the country.

Saunders – a no-nonsense Sergeant Major-type figure – had taken Norwich City to the League Cup final and into the First Division for the first time in their history. Swales famously wrote in the match programme: "I thought he was the right man from all the interviews conducted. Having seen him at work I now know for sure he's the right one. If he goes down, I go with him – it's as blunt as that."

Dennis Tueart in action against Leeds in 1970

It was the first of many occasions the controversial City boss would pin his hopes on a manager and get it spectacularly wrong. Many times he would make outrageous statements that would return to haunt him.

Former captain Tony Book stepped up as manager in 1974

Before the season was over Saunders was sacked as Swales showed a ruthless streak that would cost several managers their jobs. The Blues had even reached the final of the League Cup against Wolves but that was not enough.

After the departure of Malcolm Allison, former player Johnny Hart had accepted the challenge rather reluctantly before stepping down on health grounds and it was another former old boy, Tony Book, who stepped into the breach in 1974. Two years later the club were back among the honours, again lifting the League Cup with a 2-1 triumph over Newcastle United.

The side included Dave Watson who was signed for £275,000 and went on to become one of the greatest defenders in the club's history. Another import from the Sunderland outfit that won the FA Cup in 1973 was Dennis Tueart, who scored with an overhead kick against Newcastle.

City had once again become one of the most attractive sides in the country with nine international players in their ranks. On their way to the final, they had beaten Manchester United 4-0 in a tie marred by a devastating injury to Colin Bell who was hurt in a

tackle by Martin Buchan. Bell attempted a comeback but sadly was never the same player again.

The 1976/77 season saw the Blues finish runners-up to Liverpool by one point and Book's team of entertainers followed that up the next year with a fourth-placed finish. City also did well on the

Peter Barnes scores City's first in the 2-1 League Cup final win over Newcastle in 1976

European stage and enjoyed a successful run to the quarter finals of the UEFA Cup, beating the mighty AC Milan along the way.

Then in January 1979 back came Malcolm Allison as 'coaching overlord' in a move designed to cement City's place at the forefront of the game.

Alas, it was a gamble that did not come off. Steve Daley was signed from Wolves for a massively inflated fee of almost £1.5 million pounds and players of the calibre of Peter Barnes, Gary Owen and Dave Watson were sold as part of the overhaul. League form suffered as a result.

The Book-Allison partnership was dismantled in October 1980 and in came John Bond, a flamboyant character who had done well at Norwich and was once a team-mate of Allison at West Ham.

He made an immediate impact, steering the club towards the semi-finals of the League Cup, where City were unlucky to lose to Liverpool, and into the final of the FA Cup. He brought in the experienced trio of Gerry Gow, Bobby McDonald and Tommy Hutchison, a move which galvanised a side which already had influential players like Paul Power, Tommy Caton and Joe Corrigan, a survivor from the 1970 side.

Hutchison scored at both ends in the Centenary cup final against Spurs, who went on to win the replay 3-2.

City had regained a spirit of adventure in their football and the signing of Trevor Francis for £1m

John Bond signed Trevor Francis for a cool £1m

was a clear signal of their intent. However, injury restricted his appearances and within a year he had left as the financial impact of Allison's excessive spending took its toll.

Bond walked out in 1983 and was succeeded by his assistant John Benson. One joke doing the rounds was that money was so tight the club could not afford to replace the 'JB' initials on the manager's tracksuit.

Defeat by Luton Town on the final day sent City down and in came Celtic legend Billy McNeill. Within two years he had restored the club to their rightful place in the top flight.

City won the FA Youth Cup in 1986, beating United with a side that included emerging young talent like Paul Lake, Ian Brightwell, David White and Andy Hinchcliffe. The club also reached the final of the inaugural Full Members' Cup, losing 5-4 to Chelsea in front of a crowd of 68,000 at Wembley.

McNeill walked out in September 1986 to join Aston Villa – a decision he later regretted – and assistant Jimmy Frizzell took over, eventually

David Phillips is delighted with his goal against Charlton in 1985

becoming general manager after the club were relegated at the end of that season.

Quiet man Mel Machin was next in the hot seat and after another two-year break the Blues were back in the First Division, courtesy of a Trevor Morley goal at Bradford. However, a memorable 5-1 derby win could not save Machin. What is less known about this period is that it was the first time strains of *Blue Moon* were heard, a song that became the club anthem over the next 20 years.

Niall Quinn gave City much-needed stability and firepower

Oldham boss Joe Royle was the next choice as manager but when he turned them down the board turned to Howard Kendall who managed to bring a degree of stability, helped by the signing of Niall Quinn from Arsenal.

Peter Swales must have been convinced he had finally made the right choice but it proved another false dawn with Kendall walking out to return to his first love, Everton.

Trusted lieutenant Peter Reid was put in charge and two fifth-placed finishes at the start of the 1990s suggested that happier times were just around the corner as the Premier League era began…

MAN CITY COMIC STRIP HISTORY 3

TACTICS

THE REVIE PLAN

An innovative tactical system paid handsome dividends for Manchester City as they lifted the FA Cup a year after suffering Wembley defeat.

The 3-1 triumph over Birmingham City will forever be remembered as the Trautmann final after the goalkeeper bravely soldiered on after breaking his neck diving at the feet of an opponent.

But this final also went down in the history books because it saw the Revie Plan work to perfection. There was, though, a danger it might not have been put into practice that day.

The system involved the traditional No 9 – in this case Don Revie – playing in a deep role behind two other forwards, making it difficult for the centre halves to pick him up. The tactic was based on the successful Hungarian national side but had been criticised the previous year when City used it and lost to Newcastle.

Revie had been out of favour with manager Les McDowall and would not have played had Billy Spurdle been fit. In the event, Revie was viewed by many as City's best player that day and his pivotal role coming into the centre of the field to receive the ball had the desired effect in upsetting the opposition's rhythm.

Indeed, Revie was at the heart of the move that saw Joe Hayes give City an early lead before Birmingham equalised. Two quick goals midway through the second half from Jack Dyson and Bobby Johnstone settled the contest.

The Revie Plan may have taken his name but it was not his idea. It was initially tried in the reserves with Johnny Williamson adopting the key role, while Ken Barnes was instrumental in its success on the bigger stage.

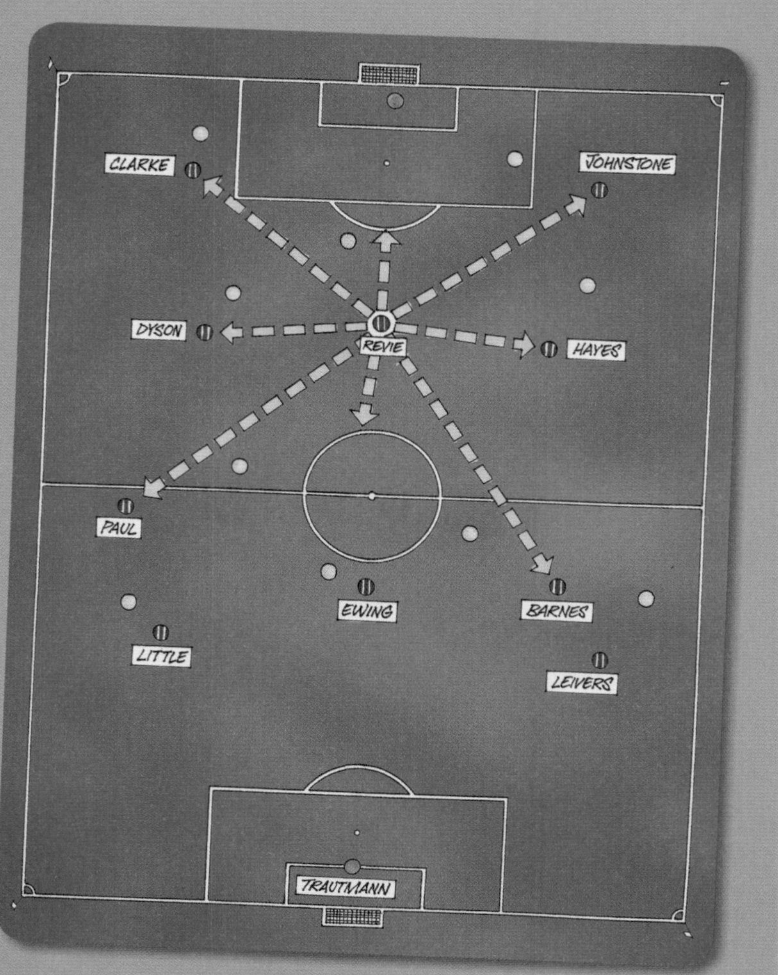
CLARKE
JOHNSTONE
DYSON
REVIE
HAYES
PAUL
EWING
BARNES
LITTLE
LEIVERS
TRAUTMANN

MARSH MAGIC

The Blues were four points clear at the top of the table when Rodney Marsh was bought from QPR for £200,000 in March 1972 and Malcolm Allison was convinced one of soccer's great entertainers was the man to take them over the finishing line.

In the event, an unfit Marsh disrupted the rhythm and City finished fourth, a point behind champions Derby. Two seasons later, the special talents of Marsh would feature in the most exciting attacking line-up in the country.

It was boosted by the homecoming of Denis Law who scored twice in a thrilling 3-1 victory over Birmingham in August 1973. With the marauding Marsh, the guile of an ageing Law and the irrepressible Bell, Lee and Summerbee it was a formidable front line.

For manager Johnny Hart it was something of a tactical nightmare. The established order of Bell, Lee and Summerbee knew the script and were well-drilled in their roles but Marsh was a law unto himself and would roam around the field playing his football off the cuff.

Law occupied his familiar role as leader of the attack and would be fed by Bell whose eye-catching runs from midfield would create havoc in the opposition defence. Marsh had come off the transfer list following Law's arrival for his final season.

The City all-stars were on parade later that season as City lost 2-1 to Wolves in the League Cup final.

Marsh blamed himself for the winning goal scored by John Richards and was so upset he refused to accept his runners-up tankard. As he walked off disconsolately, his team-mates applauded their opponents as they collected the trophy and Marsh later apologised for his actions.

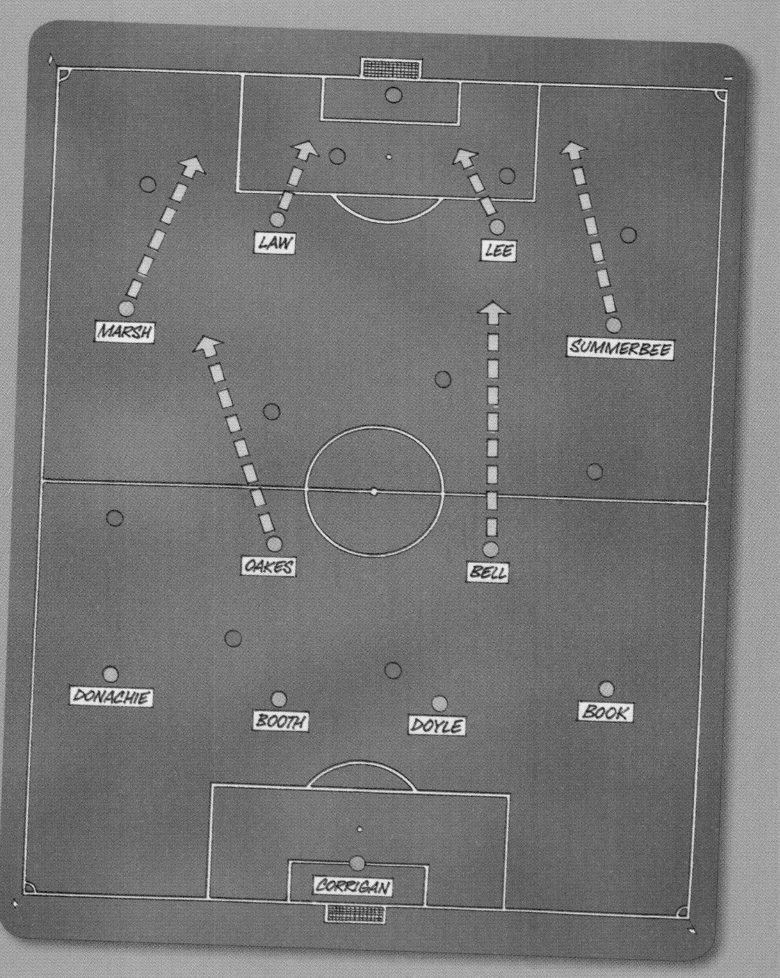
LAW
LEE
MARSH
SUMMERBEE
OAKES
BELL
DONACHIE
BOOTH
DOYLE
BOOK
CORRIGAN

HORTON'S FINEST HOUR

Manchester City and Spurs produced a vintage exhibition of football in October 1994 in a 5-2 City win that was a throwback to classic confrontations of yesteryear. It was described as one of City's finest matches of the decade and was undoubtedly Brian Horton's finest hour as manager.

"Their side was full of good footballers but so was mine," was the assessment by the popular boss whose adventurous style of play had endeared him to the long-suffering fans.

Paul Walsh scored twice against his former club and formed an impressive spearhead with Niall Quinn, scorer of one of the other goals along with midfield dynamoes Steve Lomas and Garry Flitcroft.

The Maine Road pitch had been widened giving Nicky Summerbee and Peter Beagrie scope to exploit extra space on the flanks, reviving the club's tradition of terrific wing play.

The Spurs manager Ossie Ardiles employed a bold five-pronged forward line of Teddy Sheringham, Darren Anderton, Nicky Barmby, the Rumanian Illie Dumitrescu and Jürgen Klinsmann whose arrival in English football had created quite a stir. However, the move backfired spectacularly as City served up some sumptious football that had the crowd purring with delight. It was just a shame a crowd of only 25,000 was there. A few months earlier the Kippax Stand had been knocked down and was in the process of being re-built.

Match of the Day cameras captured the action with John Motson observing: "It was the best match I've seen – in an attacking and entertainment context – in the English league for many years."

Two days later Ardiles was out of a job and, at the end of the season, Horton himself went through the exit door.

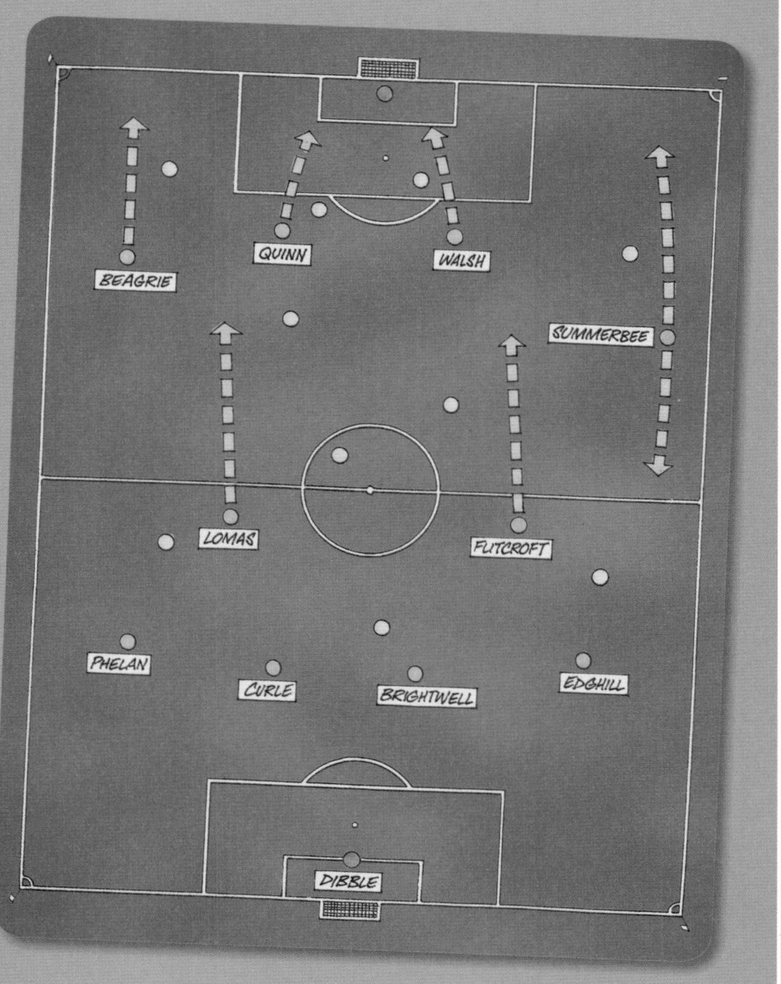

QUINN
WALSH
BEAGRIE
SUMMERBEE
LOMAS
FLITCROFT
PHELAN
CURLE
BRIGHTWELL
EDGHILL
DIBBLE

THE KEEGAN EFFECT

There was always a likelihood of fireworks when midfield maestros Ali Bernabia and Eyal Berkovic were on the pitch, especially at the same time.

Two of the game's most gifted players had plenty of tricks up their sleeve to entertain the fans but accommodating the creative playmakers in the same team was never an easy task.

Manager Kevin Keegan got the formula right more often than not in the 2001/02 season when the Blues stormed to the First Division title, finishing with an impressive 99 points. Midway through that season his team certainly hit the jackpot with a 5-1 win over a high-riding Burnley side.

While Bernabia and Berkovic supplied the ammunition, up front Shaun Goater would pull the trigger, amassing more than 30 goals that season, while Darren Huckerby helped himself to a tidy return of 26.

On this particular occasion it was strike partner Paulo Wanchope who stole the headlines with a first-half hat-trick, Berkovic also getting in on the act before the break. Substitute Darren Huckerby rounded off the scoring in front of a capacity crowd.

Keegan employed a flexible 3-5-2 formation that day with Richard Edghill and Danny Tiatto providing much-needed width in the wing back roles and Kevin Horlock occupying the anchor role in midfield.

Stuart Pearce missed the match through injury but he returned for a rousing finale to a glittering playing career, although his last game ended in slight embarrassment when he missed a penalty which would have given him a 100th career goal.

Psycho joined the coaching staff and later took over the manager's job when Keegan decided it was time to call it a day.

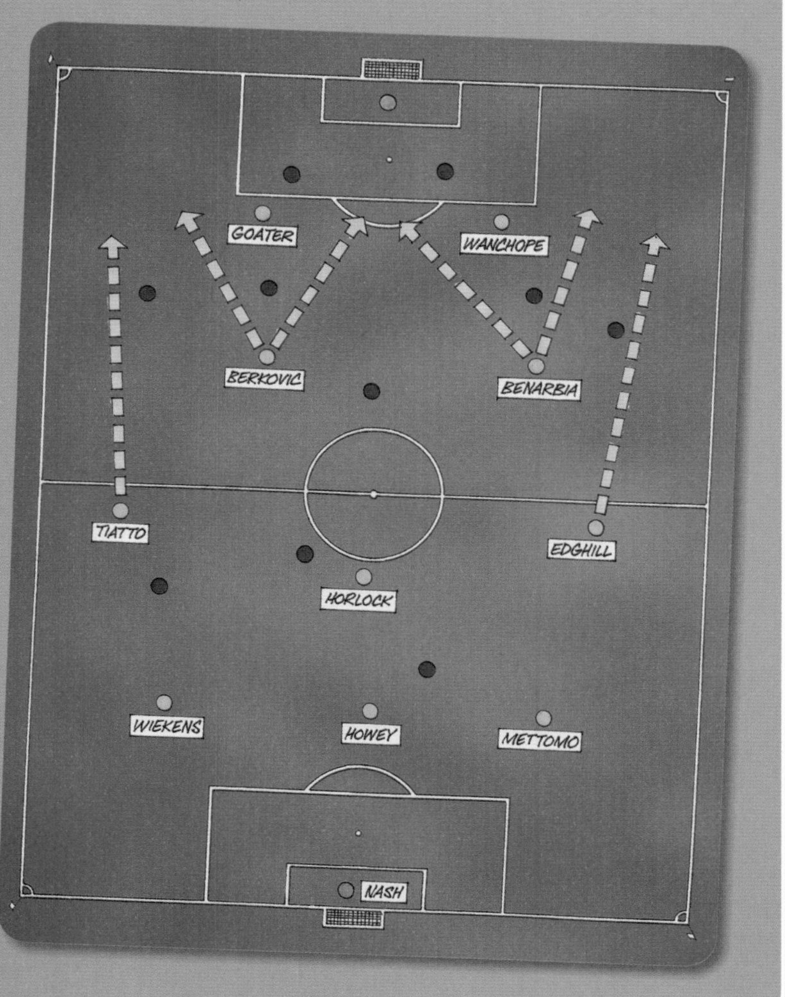

GOATER
WANCHOPE
BERKOVIC
BENARBIA
TIATTO
EDGHILL
HORLOCK
WIEKENS
HOWEY
METTOMO
NASH

MANCHESTER CITY F.C.

GREAT GAFFERS

Malcolm Allison, one of the game's most charismatic figures, puffed away contentedly on a big cigar, a glass of bubbly in one hand and his other arm wrapped around a beautiful model. Things could not get any better for one of football's most colourful coaches, who loved the lavish lifestyle and had every reason to party. In tandem with manager Joe Mercer, he had taken City from relative obscurity to League Champions within the space of three seasons.

Big Mal never usually needed an excuse to celebrate but here he was, in the summer of 1968, with a twinkle in his eye and toasting a job well done. He had formed an unlikely alliance with Genial Joe who, in the process, had just earned his place in folklore as the greatest manager in Manchester City's history.

As Mercer was later to remark: "We won the league, the FA Cup, the Cup-Winners' Cup and the League Cup — the only thing we didn't win was the Grand National."

Allison was his brash assistant, possessing one of the sharpest coaching brains in the country. Mercer was the far more conservative father figure. Together they provided the Maine Road faithful with what are readily accepted as 'the glory days', when City were top dogs in Manchester and the most entertaining side of the era.

One of the duo's first moves was to sign Mike Summerbee; Colin Bell and Francis Lee arrived in subsequent seasons.

Mercer had defied the odds, suffering a stroke at Aston Villa but ignoring medical advice to return to the game as manager at Maine Road in July 1965. He had noted Allison's attributes as a coach at Football Association gatherings and invited the former West Ham player to become his assistant.

Allison was an innovative number two, ahead of his time with his methods on the training field and with a suave image well suited to the vibrant Manchester scene. He loved the limelight and on one occasion walked up to the Stretford End and raised four fingers to indicate how many goals he expected his players to score against United that day. Allison ignored the

Allison and Mercer proved that unlikely coalitions can be successful

John Bond brought his own brand of charisma

abuse from the terraces and had the last laugh as City duly ran out 4-1 winners.

Sadly, the partnership would not last. Allison wanted to manage the team and Mercer was moved upstairs to become general manager. Both men supported opposite sides in a takeover battle, a rift that ended with Mercer moving to Coventry in 1972. Two years later he managed England on a caretaker basis.

Allison moved on in March 1973, heading south to become manager of Crystal Palace. He returned to Maine Road six years later but could not recapture the good old days despite investing heavily in the transfer market.

Allison's replacement in October 1980 was someone equally charismatic. John Bond arrived from Norwich City and brought in some seasoned campaigners to fashion an attractive side that reached the Centenary FA Cup final in 1981, only to lose to Tottenham in a replay. After a cup exit at Brighton in 1983, Bond resigned.

Assistant John Benson took over temporarily before Billy McNeill, a European Cup winner with Celtic in 1967, was appointed. But finances were tight and within three years he was on his way to Aston Villa.

Jimmy Frizzell and Mel Machin were tried out in the job before Howard Kendall accepted the now daunting challenge, a stay that lasted barely a year before he walked out and returned to Everton.

One of his players, Peter Reid, assumed control in 1990 and finished fifth in consecutive seasons but boardroom politics eventually saw him replaced by Brian Horton.

It was a taste of things to come as City strived for success amid a backdrop of mounting tensions among directors which eventually led to Francis Lee replacing the long-serving Peter Swales as club chairman.

City even had five managers in the 1996/97 season after the sacking of Alan Ball following relegation. The 1966 World Cup winner was followed by Asa Hartford, Steve Coppell, Phil Neal and Frank Clark —

Kevin Keegan established the club in the Premier League

a managerial soap opera that led to the Blues becoming the laughing stock of football.

No wonder broadcaster Stuart Hall dubbed Maine Road the 'theatre of comedy'.

Joe Royle was next on the managerial merry-go-round before Kevin Keegan took the reins in May 2001. Keegan lasted four years before resigning, although he had established the club in the Premier League and was the longest serving manager since Tony Book, the man who had led the club to their last trophy in 1976.

Stuart Pearce, another man with an England pedigree, was next in the hot-seat before former England manager Sven-Göran Eriksson accepted a lucrative contract. However, within a year he was gone and it was the turn of Mark Hughes as ownership changed from Far East influence (Thaksin Shinawatra) to Middle East control (Sheikh Mansour).

As ever, expectations were high and Hughes was ousted in December 2009 to make way

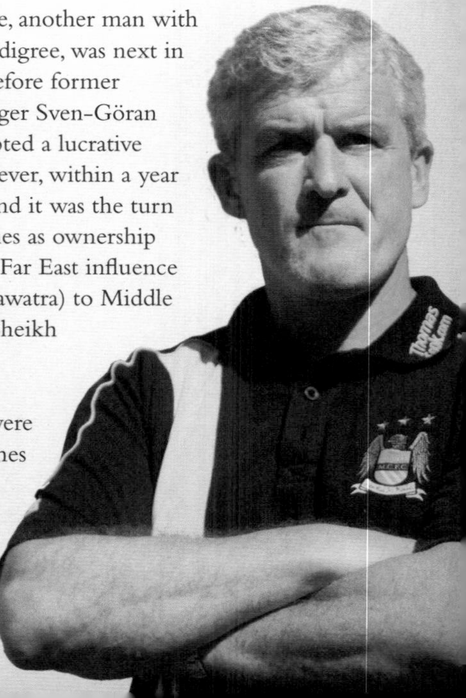

Mark Hughes used Middle East millions to shape a team...

for former Inter Milan coach Roberto Mancini. The Welshman had read about his dismissal in the tabloids on the morning of a league game against Sunderland and was told his fate officially after a 4-3 victory.

The Italian had already been lined up to take over and he immediately appointed former crowd favourite Brian Kidd as assistant.

Yet again the hot seat had claimed another casualty with the City post proving arguably the ultimate challenge in the game. Just ask Ron Saunders, who lasted less than six months in the post before his services were dispensed with in 1974.

...before being replaced by respected Italian Roberto Mancini

Going further back in time at least there had been a degree of stability before the Mercer era with Les McDowall in charge from 1950 until 1963, a spell which included an FA Cup success over Birmingham City in 1956.

City's longest serving manager Wilf Wild (1932-1946) took the club to the First Division title for the first time in 1937, while under Tom Maley the club registered their first FA Cup success in 1904.

Ireland

MEMORABLE MATCHES

BIRMINGHAM CITY 1 MANCHESTER CITY 3

FA Cup final, Wembley Stadium, 5th May 1956

Cup finals invariably produce heroes and in this one it was the turn of goalkeeper Bert Trautmann to earn Wembley immortality. The mere fact he was playing in England's showpiece sporting occasion was remarkable in itself for a man who had fought for Germany in the Second World War a decade earlier.

Trautmann was a paratrooper who managed to escape from the Russians and was then caught by the British, ending up at a prisoner of war camp near Wigan. He stayed in this country once hostilities were over and his talents as a footballer were noticed by Manchester City.

He was to become arguably the finest goalkeeper in the country and will forever be remembered for an act of incredible bravery.

With City leading 3-1 and a quarter of an hour left, he made a fearless save at the feet of the Birmingham striker Peter Murphy. Trautmann took a blow to the neck and, with no substitutes allowed, decided to play on despite suffering excruciating pain.

His head was leaning to one side as he collected

his winners' medal and three days later it was discovered he had actually broken his neck. A further knock in the closing moments of that final might even have cost him his life.

"The homecoming reception was in Albert Square and I remember Frank Swift slapping me with his enormous hands – it felt like I had been split right down the middle with an axe," said Trautmann.

Bert Trautmann is helped off the pitch after the game

The match entered Wembley folklore as the Trautmann final with skipper Roy Paul keeping his promise to avenge defeat by Newcastle at Wembley the previous year. Coincidentally, Sam Cowan had made the same promise after City had lost to Everton in the 1933 final and promptly returned to Wembley a year later to beat Portsmouth.

City wore their stylish maroon and white shirts in the 1956 final and adopted what later became known as the 'Revie plan', a formation in which the traditional centre forward plays in a deep role behind two other strikers, making it difficult for centre halves to pick him up.

Don Revie played the key role and executed the plan perfectly as City upset the hot favourites.

Man City:
Trautmann, Leivers, Little, Barnes, Ewing, Paul, Johnstone, Hayes, Revie, Dyson, Clarke

Scorer:
Hayes, Dyson, Johnstone

Attendance:
100,000

NEWCASTLE UNITED 3 MANCHESTER CITY 4

Division One, St James' Park, May 11th 1968

How ironic that on the afternoon Manchester City were crowned champions of England, the trophy should be locked away out of view at the home of their greatest rivals.

Mike Summerbee opened the scoring

It was stored in the Old Trafford vault after being hurriedly removed from the boardroom at Manchester United after the League Championship race had swung dramatically in the Blues' favour on the final day of the season.

Apparently, the football hierarchy had issued instructions to 'leave the trophy where it is' – in other words at United where it had remained since their title success just 12 months earlier.

Even the *Match of the Day* cameras were caught off guard and arrived at Old Trafford to cover the Sunderland match, with Matt Busby's side favourites to retain their crown.

City simply had to win to take the

title but they faced a tough visit to Newcastle and an estimated 17,000 away fans headed up the A1 to Tyneside for what skipper Tony Book described as his finest day in football.

Within two years of getting promotion, the managerial team of Malcolm Allison and Joe Mercer had created a fabulous team of entertainers whose style and skill was a credit to the game.

Earlier that season City had signed Francis Lee from Bolton, a move acknowledged by Mercer as the "last piece in the jigsaw".

Lee scored the final goal that day at Newcastle, a result that never looked in doubt once Neil Young had grabbed his second – and City's third – soon after half time. Mike Summerbee had opened the scoring before Newcastle recovered to make it 2-2 at the break.

A team of 11 Englishmen had secured the club's first League Championship for 31 years and Tony Book was carried shoulder high off the pitch at St James' Park.

The chaotic celebrations continued on the journey home when the team coach was caught up in a cavalcade of cars and coaches.

For the record, United lost 2-1 that afternoon and four days later, once the trophy had been 'found', it was paraded on a lap of honour before a friendly match with Bury.

Man City:
Mulhearn, Book, Pardoe, Doyle, Heslop, Oakes, Lee, Bell, Summerbee, Young, Coleman

Scorer:
Summerbee, Young (2), Lee

Attendance:
46,492

MANCHESTER CITY 10 HUDDERSFIELD 1

Division Two, Maine Road, 7th November 1987

Countless games lit up Maine Road over the years and what seemed like a run of the mill Second Division match ended up sticking in the memory for many supporters. It was just a pity there were fewer than 20,000 spectators inside the ground on a dreary November afternoon.

Paul Stewart was one of three hat-trick heroes

The match was notable for three hat-trick heroes, all presented with a signed ball as a souvenir of a memorable occasion.

The identity of those players has tricked many a football quiz enthusiast, as has the name of the player who scored the consolation for Huddersfield that day, especially as he once wore the sky blue of City.

David White, Paul Stewart and Tony Adcock finished the afternoon with beaming smiles and a place in the record books – Andy May was the glum-faced goalscorer for the away team, who were managed at the time by the former England striker Malcolm Macdonald.

May was warmly welcomed by the

Kippax when he ran out to face his former club and was cheered again when he converted a penalty in the final few minutes with the score at 9-0.

It became the highest scoring League game at Maine Road and Huddersfield had even missed three chances before Neil McNab opened the scoring in the 13th minute. City went on to lead 4-0 at the interval.

Midway through the second half Adcock became the first player to complete his treble to take the score to an extraordinary 7-0.

Stewart scored his third goal on 80 minutes and White ran riot with two further goals in the last five minutes past the hapless Brian Cox.

The Blues were managed by Mel Machin with Jimmy Frizzell acting in the role of general manager.

Supermac had only been in charge of Huddersfield for a month and survived in the job until his team were relegated, though he did have the satisfaction of beating City 1-0 in the return match.

Tony Adcock was swapped for Trevor Morley shortly afterwards; Paul Stewart was sold to Spurs for £1.7 million at the end of the season and David White was a regular in the City side for seven seasons before moving to Leeds.

Man City:
Nixon, Gidman, Hinchcliffe, Clements, Lake, Redmond, White, Stewart, Adcock, McNab, Simpson

Scorer:
McNab, Adcock (3), Stewart (3), White (3)

Attendance:
19,583

TOTTENHAM 3 MANCHESTER CITY 4

FA Cup fourth round replay, White Hart Lane, 4th February 2004

The Manchester City fans are well known for their sense of humour but being three goals down at half time and reduced to ten men was no laughing matter.

"We're gonna win the cup," was the defiant cry from the travelling support, a chant that amused the ranks of smug Spurs fans who were now expecting to win by a landslide.

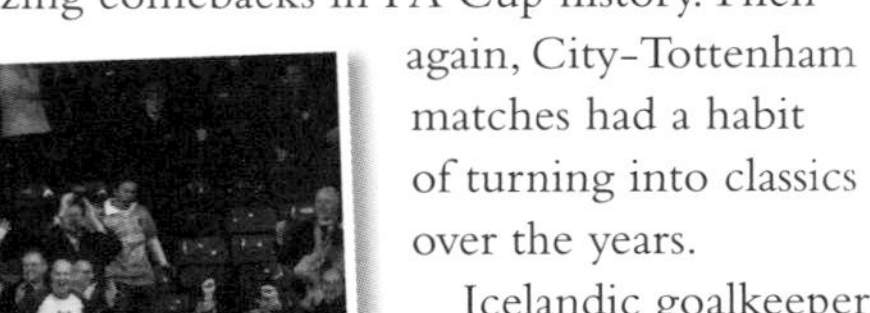

How wrong they were as City produced one of the most amazing comebacks in FA Cup history. Then again, City-Tottenham matches had a habit of turning into classics over the years.

Sheer delight at a once-in-a-Blue-Moon comeback

Icelandic goalkeeper Arni Arason made his debut in goal that night for the cup-tied David James and must have wondered what he had let himself in for as the home side rattled in goals from

Ledley King, Robbie Keane and a Christian Ziege free kick.

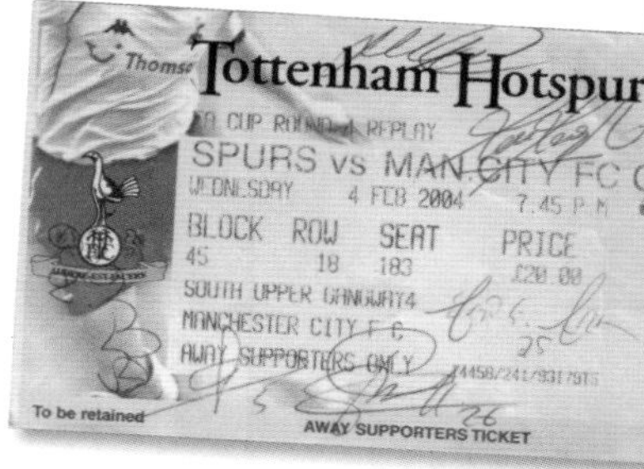

Joey Barton was booked for the challenge that led to the third goal and carried on arguing his case with referee Rob Styles after the whistle blew for half time, resulting in a red card. To make matters worse, Nicolas Anelka had limped off injured. And Kevin Keegan's side had won only one of their previous 18 fixtures.

"We're 3-0 down and a man down," said the manager to coach Derek Fazackerley as they came out for the second half. "Where's the nearest job centre?"

Three minutes into the second half Sylvain Distin made it 3-1 with a header and on the hour mark Paul Bosvelt gave City hope with a deflected shot.

With ten minutes remaining they were level through Shaun Wright Phillips and, with extra time looming, Michael Tarnat sent over a cross allowing Jon Macken to plant a glorious header past a startled Kasey Keller in the Spurs goal.

"The fans were our 11th man," agreed Keegan as he tried to come to terms with the scale of what had been achieved.

The true Blues who made their way to White Hart Lane that night had been rewarded for their loyal support, although even they knew a miracle was needed at half time.

Man City:
Arason, Jihai, Dunne, Distin, Tarnat, Wright Phillips, Barton, Bosvelt (Sibierski), Sinclair (McManaman), Fowler, Anelka (Macken)

Scorer:
Distin, Bosvelt, Wright-Phillips, Macken

Sent Off:
Barton

Attendance:
30,400

MAN CITY COMIC STRIP HISTORY 4

THE CITY CHRONICLES
AMAZING JOURNEY
1992-2010

The Premier League revolution has changed football beyond recognition and there has been no finer example than Manchester City. The game has reached all corners of the globe with virtually every kick of the ball shown live on television. Money has flooded into the sport thanks to lucrative TV deals and the worldwide exposure means that football is now as popular in Asia as in Ardwick.

The rivalry is anything but friendly as Keith Curle squares up to Eric Cantona in 1994

Certain clubs, like City, have struck gold with huge levels of investment from wealthy owners. Today, the Blues enjoy the support of oil-rich Arabs. When the Premier League era dawned they were not so lucky.

Money was tight when their former hero Francis

Lee took control of the club early in 1994. He had been involved in a bitter boardroom battle with former chairman Peter Swales, whose obsession with outdoing Manchester United had impaired his judgement during much of a 20-year reign which had brought just one trophy – the League Cup triumph in 1976.

Uwe Rosler, a legend in light blue

Lee had to find money to rebuild the ground as well as the team. The Kippax Stand came down as part of the move to an all-seater stadium and Brian Horton, who had replaced Peter Reid as manager, brought in the likes of Uwe Rosler and Paul Walsh as he moulded an exciting team.

However, Lee wanted his own man in charge. The subsequent arrival of Alan Ball did little to fire the imagination of the supporters or the dressing room. "I'm a winner," Ball told the players at training on his first day in charge. "They all go on about winning this and winning that but I'm a World Cup winner… I've done it all."

Wild celebrations after the extraordinary Second Division play-off victory at Wembley in 1999…

As far as City fans were concerned he was a loser as the side suffered relegation despite the presence of the gifted Georgi Kinkladze.

Ball resigned at the start of the 1996/97 season and the managerial saga became a fiasco with no fewer than five people holding the position in as many months. Asa Hartford, who had served the club with distinction as a player, acted as caretaker before Steve Coppell arrived to much fanfare.

He walked out after less than a month so assistant Phil Neal was promoted, before Frank Clark arrived. The team continued to struggle and Joe Royle's appointment in February 1998 came too late to stop the club sliding into the third tier of English football for the first time in their history.

By this time Francis Lee had admitted defeat in his battle to restore the club's fortunes. David Bernstein became chairman and, thankfully, City achieved promotion in dramatic fashion with an astonishing comeback in the play-off final against Gillingham at Wembley.

The momentum carried forward to the following year when the Blues regained their Premier League status. It was, though, a short-lived stay in the top flight. Royle made way for Kevin Keegan whose brief was to re-establish the club in the Premier

. . . and more on the pitch at Ewood Park after securing promotion again in 2000

League before the move to the City of Manchester Stadium in 2003.

He did just that with a record-breaking season that saw City crowned as First Division champions. The side finished on 99 points and scored 108 goals in the process, equalling the number of goals scored in the 1926/27 season.

The highlight of the final season at Maine Road was a 3-1 win over Manchester United and emotions ran high on the last day of the campaign when the famous old stadium was consigned to the scrapheap after 80 years.

It was regarded as one of the best grounds in the country for atmosphere and had witnessed countless moments of joy and sadness for generations of City supporters so it was perfectly understandable that many tears were shed on 11th May 2003.

The last player to score for City at Maine Road was Marc-Vivien Foe, who passed away during an international match for Cameroon that summer.

City had qualified for the UEFA Cup via the Fair Play League but their European adventure did not last long and the league form was patchy despite a 4-1 win over United in the first derby at Eastlands.

Kevin Keegan resigned in March 2005 and was replaced by former player Stuart Pearce, whose tasks included selling Shaun Wright-

Phillips to Chelsea for £21 million.

Sven Goran-Eriksson became the club's first overseas manager in 2007 and a year later was sacked to make way for Mark Hughes. Hughes led the club into Europe, once again through the Fair Play League, and City got as far as the quarter finals of the UEFA Cup before bowing out to Hamburg.

By this time City had again won the FA Youth

Kevin Keegan with new signings Michael Tarnat and David Seaman in 2003

With a new stadium and new owners, City's future looks bright

Cup, more than 20 years after their last success in the competition. And once again the club were making headlines for their activities in the boardroom with former Thai Prime Minister Thaksin Shinawatra having bought the club from reluctant chairman John Wardle.

Shinawatra did not hang around for long and, conveniently for City, new owners with deep pockets were waiting in the wings. The Abu Dhabi United Group paid a staggering £220 million for control and overnight City were the richest club in the world. A fortune was spent on new players, including a record £32.5 million on Brazilian star Robinho from Real Madrid.

By now Garry Cook, who had made his name with Nike, had been installed as chief executive with Khaldoon al Mubarak appointed chairman by Sheikh Mansour, a member of the ruling family of Abu Dhabi.

The demand for success was so great that Hughes was cast aside at the end of 2009 and Roberto Mancini, who had won Serie A titles with Inter Milan, was told Champions League football was the priority.

He was to fall short in his ambitions although fifth place represented the club's highest finishing position in the Premier League, enough to guarantee a place in the Europa League in 2010/11. The Argentinian striker Carlos Tevez was a deserved winner of the player of the year award after scoring 29 goals.

CELEBRITY CITY FANS

Noel, Liam and Frank – those Gallaghers certainly know how to throw a party but, then again, they are all Manchester City fans. The Oasis brothers do not need telling how to rock 'n' roll and as die-hard Blues who have experienced more lows than highs are entitled to sing *Don't Look Back in Anger*. The third Gallagher is *Shameless*'s Frank, a deadbeat dad down on his luck who might well have been driven to drink by the frustration of following his favourite team over the years.

Actor David Threlfall, who portrays the loveable

Noel and Liam rebelled against United-supporting family members…

layabout in the Channel 4 drama series set in Manchester, is a devoted Blue and proud of his Manc roots, having grown up in Blackley and then Burnage.

...while actor David Threlfall was introduced to the Blues by his grandad

His family owned a corner shop which had to be knocked down to make way for the club car park at the City of Manchester Stadium. He was flattered to make a top ten list of great City fans in the match programme and was privileged to be asked to present the half-time lottery draw on the pitch. As a youngster, Threlfall was first introduced to the Maine Road experience by his grandad during the Sixties. It is a little known fact that the young Threlfall was part of the same youth team as former club captain Paul Power.

Noel and Liam Gallagher would have loved nothing better than to have kicked a ball wearing a blue shirt on the hallowed turf, but they have at least appeared on stage in front of big crowds at Maine Road and the City of Manchester Stadium.

As their rock-star status was earning them worldwide acclaim and attention, they were always keen to declare their passion for the Blues, a love affair that began when the brothers were growing up in Burnage. Most other members of their family were United fans but, typically, Liam and Noel rebelled and were taken by their father to watch City at Maine Road.

When Noel went to the last game there in 2003 he had mixed emotions. He had enjoyed some memorable nights there, both as a musician and a football fan watching the likes of Colin Bell in action. But, as he pointed out, the stadium had hardly been a lucky ground for City over the years.

The closest Ricky Hatton has ever come to singing professionally is probably on a karaoke machine at his local pub after one of his world title fights. But it would be a brave man who dares to tell the Hyde boxer that his voice lacks the same power as his fists.

The Hitman and them – a constellation of City-supporting stars

Hatton would emerge into the boxing arena to the strains of the City anthem *Blue Moon*, wearing sky blue shorts and bearing a City tattoo. He has his own private box at Eastlands and a good number of the City team would turn up to watch his fights. He even risked the wrath of his fellow supporters in Las Vegas on one occasion when his good friend Wayne Rooney carried one of his belts into the ring.

Hatton's links with City run in the family – his father Ray was once a reserve team player at Maine Road.

Indeed, there can be no other team like City with such a mix of celebrity support. After the actor, boxer and the musicians comes… the rogue trader!

Back in 1995, Nick Leeson was splashed across front

pages and television screens all over the world, earning notoriety as the man who broke the bank. He single-handedly caused the collapse of the UK's oldest investment bank Barings – personal bankers to The Queen – by gambling on the Far East trading markets. He ran up debts of more than £800 million and fled Singapore before he was eventually caught – wearing a City shirt!

Rogue trader Nick Leeson was arrested wearing his City shirt back in 1995

Leeson, who later served a six-year jail sentence, explained that although he was from Watford he had supported City since the age of five, probably influenced by Dennis Tueart's overhead kick in the 1976 League Cup final.

After his release, Leeson was invited to various City supporters club functions around Manchester and a much sought-after souvenir was a blank cheque signed by him. His incredible story was immortalised in the film *Rogue Trader* starring Ewan McGregor.

Well known supporters also include comedians Jason Manford, Eddie Large and the late Bernard Manning; and from the world of music, Damon Gough (Badly Drawn Boy); guitarist Johnny Marr (The Smiths); Mike Pickering (M People) and Rick Wakeman (Yes).

Former England cricket captain Bob Willis is a City fan as are England Rugby Union World Cup winner Will Greenwood and former Arsenal full back Lee Dixon.

Add to that list broadcasters John Stapleton and Mark Radcliffe and actor John Henshaw, who played landlord Ken in *Early Doors* and stars in the adverts for the Post Office, and the artist LS Lowry.

HONOURS AND RECORDS

MAJOR HONOURS

WINNERS

Football League Champions 1937, 1968

FA Cup 1904, 1934, 1956, 1969

League Cup 1970, 1976

European Cup-Winners' Cup 1970

RUNNERS-UP

Football League 1904, 1921, 1977

FA Cup 1926, 1933, 1955, 1981

League Cup 1974

MINOR HONOURS

WINNERS

Football League Second Division/First Division (second tier) 1899, 1903, 1910, 1928, 1947, 1966, 2002

Football League Second Division play-off winners (third tier) 1999

Charity Shield 1937, 1968, 1972

FA Youth Cup 1986, 2008

WINNERS

Football League Second Division/ First Division (second tier) 1896, 1951, 1937, 2000

Charity Shield 1934, 1956, 1969, 1973

Full Members' Cup 1986

FA Youth Cup 1979, 1908, 1989, 2006

RECORDS

Most points in a league season: 62, 1946/47 (2 points for a win); 99, 2001/02 (3 points for a win)

Most league wins in a season: 31, 2001/02

Most consecutive league wins: 9, 8th April 1912 – 28th Sept 1912

Most consecutive home league wins: 16, 13th Nov 1920 – 27th Aug 1921

Most league goals in a season: 108, 1926/27, 2001/02

Most home league goals in a season: 70, 1927/28

Most away league goals in a season: 51, 1936/37

Record win: Manchester City 11 Lincoln City 3, 23rd Mar 1895

Record defeat: Small Heath 10 Manchester City 2, 17th Mar 1893

Biggest winning league margin: 11–3 v Lincoln City, 23rd Mar 1895

Record Cup victory: 12–0 v Liverpool Stanley, 4 Oct 1890

INDIVIDUAL RECORDS

Most appearances: Alan Oakes, 676

Most League appearances: Alan Oakes, 561

Most FA Cup appearances: Mike Doyle, 44

Most League Cup appearances: Mike Doyle, 52

Most European appearances: Joe Corrigan, 27

Youngest player: Glyn Pardoe, 15 years 314 days, 11 April 1962 v Birmingham

Oldest player: Billy Meredith, 49 years 8 months, 29 March 1924 v Newcastle

Most goals scored: 198, Horace Barnes (inc war time)

Most League goals: 158, Eric Brook and Tommy Johnson

Most League goals in a season: 38, Tommy Johnson, First Division, 1928/29

Most goals scored in European competition: 10, Francis Lee

Most goals in the FA Cup: 22, Fred Tilson

Most goals in the League Cup: 18, Colin Bell, Dennis Tueart

Highest transfer fee paid: £32.5m, Robinho from Real Madrid, Sept 2008

Highest transfer fee received: £21m, Shaun Wright-Phillips (pictured right) to Chelsea, July 2005

MAINE ROAD RECORDS

Highest attendance: 84,569, Manchester City v Stoke, FA Cup, 3rd March 1934

Highest league attendance: 83,260, Manchester United v Arsenal, First Division, 17th Jan 1948

Last debut at Maine Road: Robbie Fowler, 1st Feb 2003 v WBA

ATTENDANCE RECORDS AT CITY OF MANCHESTER STADIUM

Highest league attendance: 47, 348 City v Chelsea, Premier League, 9th Dec 2009

Highest average league attendance: 46,384, 2003/04

First debut at City of Manchester Stadium: David Seaman, Michael Tarnat, Paul Bosvelt, Trevor Sinclair, 14th Aug 2003 v Total Network Solutions, UEFA Cup

MISCELLANEOUS

- Tony Book and Dave Mackay of Derby County were jointly named Footballer of the Year in 1969, the only time the honour has been shared. Bert Trautmann and Don Revie had won the accolade in successive seasons in the 1950s
- **City secured European qualification via their league results in 2009/10 for the first time since Tony Book's team finished fourth in 1977/78**
- Eric Nixon played in all four divisions of the Football League in the 1986/87 season while on loan from Manchester City. He played for Wolves, Southampton, Bradford City and Carlisle United
- **When Ronald Waterreus played in goal for Manchester City in the 7-1 League Cup win over Barnsley, the opposing goalkeeper was Nick Colgan. In the same 2004/05 season, Waterreus kept goal for Rangers in a 7-1 victory over Dundee United in the semi final of the Scottish League Cup – the Dundee keeper on that occasion was one Nick Colgan**
- Tommy Hutchison is one of only three players to have scored for both sides in an FA Cup Final. His feat came in 1981 against Spurs and six years later Gary Mabbutt, of Tottenham, did the same against Coventry. The precedent was set by Charlton's Bert Turner

in the 1946 final against Derby County. All three men finished with runners-up medals

- **Denis Law scored six goals for Manchester City in an FA Cup tie against Luton Town in 1960/61 but the goals were wiped from the record books when the match was abandoned with just 20 minutes remaining. To make matters worse, Luton won the replay**
- City had to play their Full Members' Cup final against Chelsea at Wembley just 24 hours after drawing 2-2 in a Manchester derby. A crowd of 68,000 saw the Blues lose 5-4 to the Londoners
- **When Francis Lee appointed Alan Ball as manager in 1995, it meant a re-union for two men who had played in the same England team in the 1970 World Cup. Many years earlier they had played in the same Bolton Boys under-14 team and even appeared in the same cricket league, Lee for Westhoughton and Ball turning out for Farnworth**
- Peter Schmeichel was the last goalkeeper to appear in a first team game at Maine Road. He retired having never lost in a derby, a record City fans were delighted he kept intact earlier that season by appearing in a victory over his old club United

CUP COMPETITI
FINA
Leicester City
v
Manchester City
SATURDAY 26th A
Kick-Off 3p.m.
EMPIRE STADIUM WE
CRAIG BELLAMY
FORWARD
14
71
FORWARD
83
28
MANCHESTER
City
SAAB
TER CITY
L CLUB
5p.
MANCHESTER CITY
GOALKEEPER
82
4
rsday 14th May 1981 Kick
One-Hundredth Football Association Challenge Cup
FINAL
Manchester City Footb
Supporting our supporte
www.mcfc.co.uk
F.A. BARCLAYCARD PREMIERSHI
M.C.F.C V SOUTHAMPTON
Sun 11th MAY 2003 KICK U
MAIN STAND
AREA J
ROW 24
SEAT 0002
COMPLIMENTA
£0.00
GMR
RETAIN THIS PORTION OF THE TICK
DENNIS TUEART
MANCHESTER CITY
FORWARD
IAN BISHOP
MANCHESTER
PRICE
15pence
MANCHESTER CITY F.C.